BUSINESS ETHICS
MISTAKES AND
SUCCESSES

Robert F. Hartley
Cleveland State University

JOHN WILEY & SONS, INC.

www.wiley.com/college/hartley

Senior Aquisitions Manager	Jayme Heffler
Associate Publisher	Judith Joseph
Marketing Manager	Heather King
Editorial Assistant	Jessica Bartelt
Associate Production Manager	Kelly Tavares
Production Editor	Sarah Wolfman-Robichaud
Managing Editor	Kevin Dodds
Illustration Editor	Wendy Stokes Hodge

This book was set in 10/12 New Caledonia by Leyh Publishing LLC, and printed and bound by Courier Westford. The cover was printed by Phoenix Color.

This book is printed on acid-free paper. ∞

ISBN 0-471-66373-5

Printed in the United States of America

10 9 8 7 6 5 4 3 2

PREFACE

Thank you for choosing this casebook on ethical mistakes of business firms. If ever there was a time when we could ignore ethical behavior in business, that time has long passed. The firm that disregards an ethical stance does so at its peril in today's environment of investigative reporters, a media quick to sensationalize, scrutiny by various governmental agencies and attorneys general, and lawsuits by eager trial lawyers.

Business Ethics Mistakes confronts critical issues head-on, presenting cases—lessons from the past—from which we can learn. These are real scenarios and dilemmas faced by real companies. In them, we are privy to the major factors behind ill-advised actions and to their sorry consequences. The book starkly reveals both causes and effects, dissecting some of the most noteworthy violations of the public trust in recent history. Therein, we should find deeper learning experiences both from the firm's perspective and that of society. Analyzing such mistakes may help us avoid similar mistakes in the future, as well as learn to better cope should an ethical dilemma arise in our own business experiences.

The cases range from those of great culpability to others where naiveté or carelessness led to trouble; from those whose consequences were monumental in terms of human suffering, to those of less drastic consequences but that were still abusive, unethical, and illegal. Some of the cases involve substantial controversy, and we will examine whether the criticisms against the company's actions were truly justified.

This book is a line extension of the enduring *Marketing Mistakes* and *Management Mistakes* books. The format has been well received with the first book now in its 9th edition, a life of more than twenty-five years, while *Management Mistakes* is in the 8th edition and has been around for almost as long.

For those of you who are new to the *Mistakes* (with also some *Successes*) format, you will find this considerably different from other casebooks. You and your students will find it very readable, very hands-on with its various discussion questions, role-playing exercises, debate possibilities, and devil's advocate invitations. Some cases even bring to life major characters in the scenario. We have been told many times that these books transform dry and rather remote concepts into a challenging reality, and give our students good experiences in both creative thinking and critical thinking.

Each chapter is a complete case unto itself. Each chapter contains one or more Issue or Information Boxes linked to related text material. Here and at the end of each chapter students are challenged with both defending and attacking various issues and behavior, and exploring how things could have been handled better than they actually were handled. We invite students to place themselves in the shoes of those principally involved and ponder how they themselves might have reacted. For example, would they have become whistleblowers and publicized the company's misdeeds at the risk of job and career? The Learning Insights at the end of each chapter and summarized in the final chapter are guides for future executives.

For those of you who are already users of one or more *Mistakes* books, and are pleased, you will find this format comfortingly similar, even though most, though not all the cases, will be different. Still, ethical issues are often present in marketing and management mistakes and successes. I have found that some of the most vigorous class discussions involve situations with ethical undertones.

We have designed the book into four parts. First we look at present-day cases of firms in various dimensions of ethical misconduct. Part II presents classic misdeeds, from the celebrated Nader confrontation with GM's Corvair back in the 1960s, to some cases with legal consequences still not entirely resolved by 2004, such as the *Exxon Valdez* Alaskan oil spill of 1989. Part III investigates three well-known and successful firms whose ethical conduct faces critical scrutiny today. In Part IV we look at two paragons of good ethical conduct.

TARGETED COURSES

The book can be used in a great variety of courses, both undergraduate and graduate, ranging from management and marketing courses, to business and society, retailing, finance, as well as any number of other courses where the issue of ethics is a topic to be discussed. For those schools with ethics courses, this should be a welcome tool for teaching a rather difficult subject.

An *Instructor's Manual* written by the author accompanies the text to provide additional ideas for stimulating class discussion and role plays, as well as possible answers for the pedagogical material within and at the ends of chapters.

ACKNOWLEDGMENTS

I wish to thank, in particular, Cindy Claycomb, associate professor at Wichita State University, for researching and writing up the WorldCom case.

A number of other persons have provided encouragement, information, advice, and constructive criticism through the years. I appreciate the help and support of my colleagues at Cleveland State University, particularly Ram Rao, John Gardner, Margaret Bahniuk, Sanford Jacobs, and Benoy Joseph. I also thank the following reviewers who have given me their valuable suggestions and insights: John Bunch, Kansas State University; Al Gini, Loyola University, Chicago; Howard Smith, University of New Mexico.

At John Wiley & Sons, my thanks to Judy Joseph and Jessica Bartelt for your enthusiasm about this idea of an ethics mistakes book, and your nice support for all the *Mistakes* books.

Robert F. Hartley
Professor Emeritus
Cleveland State University
Cleveland, Ohio
RFHartley@aol.com

ABOUT THE AUTHOR

Bob Hartley is Professor Emeritus at Cleveland State University's College of Business. There he taught a variety of undergraduate and graduate courses in management, marketing, and ethics. Prior to that he was at the University of Minnesota and George Washington University. His MBA and Ph.D. are from the University of Minnesota, with a BBA from Drake University.

Before coming into academia, he spent thirteen years in retailing with the predecessor of Kmart (S. S. Kresge), J.C.Penney, and Dayton-Hudson and Target. Positions held included store management, central buying, and merchandise management.

His first textbook, *Marketing; Management and Social Change,* was published in 1972. It was ahead of its time in introducing social and environmental issues to the study of marketing. Other books, *Retailing, Sales Management, and Marketing Research,* followed.

In 1976, the first Marketing Mistakes supplemental book was published, and brought a new approach to case studies: student-friendly books, and ones more relevant to career enhancement than existing books. In 1983, *Management Mistakes* was published. These books are now in the 9th and 8th editions respectively, and have been widely translated. In 1992, Professor Hartley wrote *Business Ethics: Violations of the Public Trust,* which was the predecessor to this *Business Ethics Mistakes and Successes.* He is listed in Who's Who in America, and Who's Who in the World.

CONTENTS

CHAPTER ONE

Introduction and Perspective

GENERAL PERSPECTIVE

The American philosopher George Santayana noted, "Those who cannot remember the past are doomed to repeat it."

We are not on a witch hunt. We are not seeking to sensationalize corporate misdeeds and blacken the image of business. Rather, we want to find lessons from the past that would help avoid similar mistakes today and in the future. We seek insights into the factors leading to misconduct, and how the dire consequences both for the firm and for society might be avoided or at least be better handled than they were. In some cases the misconduct is open to question, is controversial, and as such deserves our objective appraisal. We will be wearing two hats: that of concerned citizens and that of should-be-concerned executives. The book offers this thesis:

> The interests of a firm are best served by giving careful attention to the public interest and by seeking a *trusting relationship* with the various publics with which it is involved. In the process society is also best served.

These various publics, or *stakeholders*, are a firm's customers, suppliers, employees, stockholders, financial institutions, communities in which it dwells, and the various governments—local, state, and federal. To these groups must be added the press, which cannot be relied upon to deliver objective and unbiased reporting but is influenced by the firm's reputation and its relations with the other publics.

Any course of action that does not consider the public interest is vulnerable in today's business climate. Compared to earlier decades, firms today face more critical public and governmental scrutiny in an environment with constant threats of regulatory and litigious actions. A measure of how far we have come toward a more enlightened business climate is this: A firm that violates the public trust today is vulnerable to competitors more eager to develop good relationships.

The overwhelming majority of business dealings are noncontroversial, but abuses receive publicity. Whenever corporate misdeeds are publicized, blame often falls on

1

business schools; allegations resound that the schools have given short shrift to ethical topics in their zeal for stressing coldly analytical tools and processes.

Admittedly, ethics is not easy to teach, and even being well taught does not assure acceptable behavior. Perhaps the best we can do is to expose you, our students, to examples of unethical behavior. We can alert you to various ethical dilemmas and temptations you may face, and show you the consequences of bad practices in the hope that you will take the moral high road.

In this book, we seek what can be learned from the mistakes of well-known firms. Such mistakes can lead to insights regarding both *avoidance and response* decisions.

A firm should learn from its own mistakes, as well as from those of other firms, to be wary—to use care to *avoid* situations and actions that might harm its trusting relationships. For example, the A. H. Robins Company (discussed in Chapter 14) blundered into an aggressive promotional strategy with its Dalkon Shield: the product was inadequately tested for safety, and harmed thousands of women. Robins also blundered badly with its *response* to the situation: first, denial, and then a vain effort to cover up.

Sometimes a firm faces a catastrophe, suddenly and without warning. This happened to Union Carbide in 1984 (discussed in Chapter 12) when its chemical plant in Bhopal, India, leaked forty tons of toxic chemicals. Although the company quickly rushed aid to almost 300,000 victims, it was bitterly condemned for the carelessness and loose controls that permitted the accident to happen in the first place. The company CEO was even arrested by Indian officials when he visited the site.

By no means do all the cases in this book involve physical injury and death. For example, our first case examines deceptive selling practices—no loss of life here. MetLife, a huge insurance firm, permitted an agent to deceive customers on a grand scale, in the process enriching himself and the company. Attorneys general of several states condemned these practices, and fines and lawsuits totaled almost $2 billion.

Many learning experiences can be found in these *lessons from the past*. Again, they address how to avoid the worst scenarios, and how best to respond should they happen.

ETHICS

Ethics refers to standards of right conduct. Unfortunately, there is not always complete agreement as to what constitutes ethical conduct. At the extremes, of course, there is little dispute. But some practices fall into a gray area with opinions differing as to what is ethical and what is unacceptable. Some examples from this gray area include the following:

- Using high-pressure tactics to persuade naive customers to buy
- Misleading customers into thinking they are getting a bargain
- Cheating on expense accounts
- Exaggerating advertising claims
- Giving expensive "gifts" to clients or potential clients

Where do you draw the line? As another example, would you be in favor of more pollution if it would bring more employment to your community? These issues are complicated and very controversial.

Other actions clearly violate the socially accepted norms of behavior. Examples include competitive espionage; bribery; falsifying costs for defense contractors; deceptive and outright falsehoods regarding product claims; callous disregard for the health and welfare of customers, employees, and the general public; environmental pollution on a grand scale; and looting a firm by top executives for their own personal gain.

Ethics and the Law

The relationship between ethical conduct and the law is sometimes confusing. Some would rationalize that lawful actions are therefore ethical and perfectly justifiable. But an "if it's legal, it's ethical" attitude disregards the fact that the law "codifies only that part of conduct that society feels so strongly about that it is willing to support it with physical force."[1] Many practices are within the law, such as firing an employee just before retirement benefits become vested, or charging a naive customer more than a fair price. However, many people would see these as unethical practices. Or how about an executive brought in to turn around a company who quickly decimates the labor force to cut costs, as described in Chapter 5 in the savaging of Sunbeam and Scott Paper by Al Dunlap?

Can actions be ethical but illegal? Violating fair trade laws, which at one time prohibited retailers from selling certain brands below designated prices, is a case in point: If a firm engaged in illegal price cutting, was this unethical? Or if a community had blue laws that prohibited doing business on Sunday, were violators unethical? Most people saw such actions as ethical, even though they were against the law at the time. The law is not infallible.

Quasi-Legal Practices

Certain practices can be condemned at the extreme but may be tolerated in moderation. Ethical as well as legal considerations may be involved, especially in matters such as gift giving, which at the extreme becomes commercial bribery. The attempt to influence by a gift of some sort can be considered an unfair method of competition under the Federal Trade Commission Act. Various state and federal laws specifically prohibit bribing government employees. And the Foreign Corrupt Practices Act of 1977 makes it a criminal offense to bribe a foreign official to obtain a contract (this law does not prohibit small payoffs to low-level officials to "grease" the transaction process). No other industrialized nation has imposed such restrictions on its business executives, and the law has been criticized as putting U.S. firms at a competitive disadvantage in those countries where payoffs are a way of life.

---

1. John H. Westing, "Some Thoughts on the Nature of Ethics in Marketing," in *Changing Marketing Systems,* Reed Mayer, ed., 1967 Winter Conference Proceedings , Chicago: American Marketing Association, 1968, p. 162.

What constitutes *commercial bribery?* The free lunch? Free football tickets? The bottle of scotch or the fruit basket at Christmas time? Probably not. These are traditional gifts and commonly accepted industry practices. But where does one draw the line? It is just one more next step from the Christmas present to the cash gift, the paid "business" vacation at an expensive resort, or where a big sale might be influenced, an entertainment center, a fur coat, or a car. Because modest hospitality or gifts can escalate into a semblance of bribery and can affect objective business judgment, some firms, including the Defense Department, have a policy that purchasing agents and other executives may not accept even token gifts or free meals.

Ethics and Profits

Many businesspeople assume that the more strictly one interprets ethical behavior, the more profits suffer. Certainly the constrained sales efforts that may result from toning down product claims or resisting customer hints and even demands (especially in some foreign countries) for bribes or kickbacks could hurt profits. Yet, a strong argument can also be made that scrupulously honest and ethical behavior is better for business and for profits. A reputation for honest dealings can be a powerful competitive advantage, and can even lead to a healthier business environment for an entire industry. (This follows our thesis of the desirability of developing trusting relationships, not only with customers but also employees, suppliers, and the other publics of a firm.)

Ethical conduct is compatible with maximizing profits in the long run, although in the very short run disregard of high moral principles may temporarily yield more profits.

Incentives for Questionable Practices

Certain conditions tend to motivate shady practices, especially given the belief that such practices yield more sales and profits. These conditions include the following, among others:

1. Overemphasis on performance
2. Intensity of competition
3. Expediency, indifference, and carelessness
4. Custom
5. Groupthink, or going along with the consensus developed in the group
6. Personal gain or looting, a truly selfish motive that often is accompanied by fraudulent accounting which can hide losses in the billions of dollars

Overemphasis on Performance

In most firms, higher pay and promotion depend on achieving greater sales and profits. This is true not only for individuals but also for departments, divisions, and the entire firm. The value that investors, creditors, and suppliers place on a firm depends to a large extent on growth in sales and profits. The better the growth rate, the more money available for further expansion from investors and creditors at attractive rates.

Suppliers and customers are more eager to do business. Top-notch personnel are also more easily attracted. This emphasis on quantitative measures of performance, however, has some potential negative consequences:

> Men are not measured on the basis of their moral contribution to the
> business enterprise. Hence they become caught up in a system which is
> characterized by an ethic foreign to and often lower than the ethics of
> man. There is always the temptation for the individual to push harder
> even though there are infractions of the 'rules' of the game. [2]

An ambitious manager, or perhaps an employee interested in substantially increasing his or her immediate income, can be tempted to cross the line of scrupulously honest behavior, as we see in the first case. Should top management be blamed for such deviant actions? Some argue that it should: Management sets the tone. If it also sets heavy demands for performance goals, management can hardly escape responsibility for subordinate misdeeds.

Intensity of Competition

An intensely competitive environment, especially if coupled with a firm's inability to differentiate its products substantially from those of competitors, can motivate unethical behavior. Actions of one or a few firms in a fiercely competitive industry may generate a follow-the-leader situation, pressuring the more ethical competitors to choose lower profits or lower ethics.

Expedience, Indifference, and Carelessness

An attitude of expedience and indifference to customers' best interests accounts for some questionable practices. These attitudes, whether permeating an entire firm or affecting only a few individuals, are hardly conducive to repeat business and customer loyalty—the trusting relationship we advocated. They are more prevalent in firms with many small customers and in those firms where repeat business is not important, such as used cars, home repairs, and recreational land. Here deceptive practices and even fraud are not uncommon. Similarly, indifference to the environment encourages pollution, as well as disregard for employees' and community's best interests.

Carelessness is such a human tendency, it hardly seems deserving of much disciplinary action unless habitual. We all make mistakes, and they usually are not serious. But what about the surgeon, or the pharmacist filling prescriptions, or the nurse administering them? Sometimes terrible things happen through simple carelessness. We can hardly forget Union Carbide's Bhopal, India, plant. And then there was the Exxon Valdez oil spill, which did horrendous damage to the environment.

Custom

The adage *caveat emptor*, "Let the buyer beware," applied to many business dealings until the last few decades. Now customers are more knowledgeable and demanding,

---

2. Robert J. Holloway and Robert S. Hancock, *Marketing in a Changing Environment* (New York: Wiley, 1968), p. 212.

competitors are more eager to develop good relationships, and government and the legal system are constraining. Yet, the tradition of the marketplace still may be perceived as an arena of psychological conflict between buyer and seller.

The Groupthink Mentality

As we will examine in Chapters 3 and 10, the phenomenon of groupthink may lead committees of executives to approve actions (including even a lack of concern for safety or environmental dangers) that no executive acting alone would possibly condone. This mindset is not unrelated to the lynch-mob mentality of ages past. It reflects the decision-by-committee syndrome in which the lowest-common-denominator action can be agreed upon in an atmosphere where no one person can be held responsible.

Looting and Personal Gain

Top executives through fraudulent accounting have looted their organizations and hidden their excesses. With a compliant board of directors some have received exorbitant compensation, lavish expense accounts and retirement packages, even planes and yachts. Especially is this a travesty when a firm has to retrench with massive layoffs and shareholder losses, while top management keeps its perks.

ORGANIZATION OF BOOK

The cases in this book are well known, and are widely publicized examples of corporate misdeeds that have come to light. Despite the press coverage, we need more objective and less sensationalized treatment if we are to gain a better perspective of the parameters leading to the abuses and how they were handled.

Some cases involve great culpability, callousness, and blame. Other firms had the problem thrust upon them unexpectedly: they may have been careless or exercised poor judgment, but the intent was hardly damning. In some cases the social consequences were drastic and deadly, such as again in the Bhopal disaster and the *Exxon Valdez*. In other cases, consequences were far less severe and anything negative was arguably blown out of proportion by activists, as in the targeting of Nike for abusive labor practices in underdeveloped countries, when Nike was only one of many U.S. firms shifting manufacturing to cheaper labor overseas.

Similarly, Wal-Mart has been depicted as a big bully, and criticized for destroying small-town merchants, toy merchandisers, and supermarket competitors with its lowest prices, as well as suppliers with its coercive dictates. And, oh yes, with encouraging illegal immigrants and placing unreasonable demands on low-paid employees.

We will also examine two paragons of enlightened ethical and social responsible conduct.

Figure 1.1 presents a matrix based on culpability and, consequences of the misdeeds. Representative cases are plotted on this matrix.

Contemporary Ethical Misconduct (Part I)

In this first part we examine more recent cases of corporate malpractice. Such violations of the public trust start with the previously described deceptive sales practices of a MetLife representative that briefly brought him acclaim as the company's top producer.

Figure 1.1   Positioning of cases by culpability and by severity of consequences.

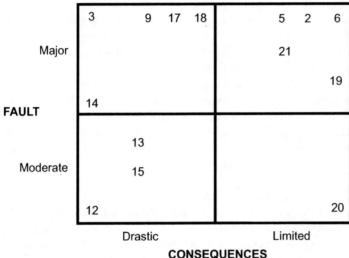

Representative Cases:

2. MetLife
3. Firestone/Ford
5. Al Dunlap's savaging
6. United Way
9. WorldCom/MCI
12. Union Carbide's Bhopal
13. Nestlé's infant formula
14. Dalkon Shield
15. Exxon's Alaskan oil spill
17. Lockheed's overseas bribery
18. General Dynamic's fleecing
19. Wal-Mart
20. Nike
21. DaimlerChrysler

Do you agree with these placements?

Product safety lapses that result in injuries and even loss of life are among the worst ethical abuses. Even worse is when such risks are allowed to continue for years. Ford Explorers equipped with Firestone tires were associated with more than 200 deaths from tire failures and vehicle rollovers. As the media brought worldwide attention, Ford and Firestone each blamed the other. Eventually, a host of lawsuits led to massive recalls and billions in damages.

ADM presents a paradox. It was a highly successful firm, but its success was tarnished by unethical practices and even illegal price fixing. A dictatorial CEO also fostered political cronyism. A whistleblower brought jail sentences to several company executives, and himself as well.

Albert Dunlap fostered a reputation as a turnaround wizard who fired enough people to send a company on the road to prosperity again. Doing so earned him the nickname of "Chainsaw Al." Over time, however, he was revealed as the premier hatchet man who would come into a sick organization and fire enough people to make it *temporarily* profitable. Somehow, with Sunbeam this seemingly proven downsizing did not work, and Dunlap himself was fired by the board of directors. Later investigations found fraudulent accounting.

United Way of America is a not-for-profit organization. The man who led it to prominence as the nation's largest charity came to perceive himself as virtually beyond authority. Exorbitant spending, favoritism, conflicts of interest—these were uncontrolled and uncriticized until investigative reporters from the *Washington Post* brought to light the scandalous conduct. Amid the hue and cry, contributions plummeted as the organization desperately sought to rectify the situation and cope with image destruction.

The tobacco industry was guilty for decades of callousness to public health, both in the United States and abroad. With its formidable political influence, it pursued a profit-maximizing strategy despite abundant research evidence on the dangers of smoking. Finally, increasing lawsuits led to a November 1998 deal with state attorneys general in which the industry would pay some $200 billion over twenty-five years and thus gain some relief from the lawsuits.

An entire industry came under scrutiny in the savings and loan debacle of the late 1980s. Here was the ultimate repudiation by management of its responsibility to stockholders and depositors. Admittedly, management was not alone in culpability; state and federal regulators and a naive Congress also shared the blame. The final bailout was in the hundreds of billions of dollars.

WorldCom is an example of the well-publicized business scandals of this new century in which major corporations were looted by top executives through fraudulent accounting that allowed their abuses to go unrecognized for years.

Classic Ethical Violations (Part II)

Some of these cases go back to the 1960s. Chapter 10 describes the confrontation between Ralph Nader and General Motors over its "killer" car, the Corvair, a confrontation that led to widespread consumer repudiation of business practices that ignored public safety and the environment, known as *consumerism.*

The next case shows the consumer movement continuing to grow in strength and effectiveness against a chemical manufacturer's pollution abuses. Union Carbide, in the 1960s and early 1970s, finally capitulated to public hostility and the marshalling of media and governmental pressure. The tradeoff between jobs and the environment was decided in favor of the environment in this instance.

Hardly a decade later, Union Carbide was guilty of the worst industrial disaster in history up to that time, with its Bhopal, India, plant. (Less than two years later, however, the Chernobyl nuclear plant in Russia spewed radioactive material over thousands of square miles.)

In the Nestlé case, we see that good and evil can exist simultaneously. Nestlé's infant formula, aggressively marketed in underdeveloped Third World countries, was both a blessing and a curse in countries that did not always have the sanitation necessary to make the product safe. Worldwide criticism of Nestlé in the 1970s and into the 1980s eventually led to boycotts and overwhelming public pressure for reforms.

As previously mentioned, the Dalkon Shield, an intrauterine contraceptive, was introduced by A. H. Robins company without adequate and unbiased testing.

Just after midnight, on March 24, 1989, the worst maritime environmental disaster in U.S. history began as a huge oil tanker, the *Exxon Valdez*, ran aground. The resulting Alaskan oil spill thrust on the world the issue of how much responsibility corporations have for environmental protection. Although Exxon eventually spent $2.5 billion in cleanup efforts, these payments did not allay the criticisms.

ITT was a multinational corporation that attempted to protect its holdings in Chile in the early 1970s, even to the point of overthrowing the Chilean government—in particular, its president, Salvador Allende. The CEO of ITT, Harold Geneen, apparently believed the end (preserving ITT property in a small, Third-World country) justified the means (whatever it took to save the firm's holdings). ITT's abuse of power and its interference in a foreign government brought critical scrutiny of all multinationals and how they needed to be constrained.

In the mid-1970s, revelations surfaced that Lockheed, a major defense contractor, had given millions of dollars in bribes to foreign officials, even to a prince and a prime minister. Chapter 17 discusses major facets of the controversy concerning overseas payoffs.

Defense contractors have a sordid history of trying to fleece the government. One of the worst violators of Defense Department trust was General Dynamics. Massive cost overruns, fraud, bill padding, bribery—these were some of the allegations against General Dynamics during the 1970s and 1980s. Sadly, other defense contractors were also culpable. And who paid the bills? We the people.

Controversial Ethical Behavior (Part III)

Sometimes a firm engages in practices that vocal critics condemn as intolerable and unethical, while others condone as simply increasing efficiency and lowering prices. We examine in Part III three well-known and successful firms that faced severe criticisms from generally a minority of vocal critics.

Wal-Mart is the biggest retailer in the world, and the champion of lowest prices. Size can bring coercive power, especially of smaller suppliers. It can also drive out of business smaller competitors, and even change the social structure of small towns. Wal-Mart has also been criticized for its dictatorial employee relations, and even for using illegal aliens for some of its contracted services.

Nike, with perhaps the best-known brand in the world alongside Coca-Cola, has been targeted for its "sweat-shop" conditions of low-paid foreign production workers, as mentioned earlier in this chapter.

The merger of Chrysler with the huge German firm, Daimler, maker of Mercedes, was supposed to be a merger of equals—so the Germans assured Chrysler. But Chrysler management soon found they were lied to, as top Chrysler executives were replaced by Stuttgart, Germany, bosses. Unethical, or just hard-nosed business? In any case, problems of assimilation and coordination plagued the merger for years.

Paragons of Good Ethical Practices (Part IV)

For contrast, we have included two examples of enlightened corporate ethical behavior.

Johnson & Johnson exemplified a superb example of responsible reaction under the most severe circumstances: loss of life directly connected with its flagship product, Tylenol. J&J became a role model on how to "keep the faith" with its customers, putting their best interests ahead of the firm's and in the process enhancing a public image as a responsive and caring firm.

Herman Miller, maker of top-of-the-line office furniture, had long been extolled in management books and classrooms for successfully melding good business operations and altruistic employee and environmental relations. In recent years these policies were seriously tested as demand for its high-price products declined and harsh realities pitted altruism against viability.

CONCLUSIONS

In our concluding chapter we summarize and categorize the many insights that can be drawn from these cases. Again, the great value of these cases is the learning that can be gained and transferred to other firms, other industries, other times—learning that can guide executives in avoiding ethics-related mistakes and coping better and more responsibly with crisis situations.

Where possible, we have depicted the major personalities involved in these cases. We invite you to imagine yourself in their positions, facing the temptations, the problems, and the decisions they faced. What would you have done differently, and why? We invite you to participate in the discussion questions and role-playing episodes that appear within and at the end of each chapter. We urge you to consider the pros and cons of alternative actions and to be objective in your analyses and proposals. May you be motivated to seek the high road of ethical behavior!

QUESTIONS

1. Why does the groupthink of committees sometimes dilute the ethical stance of an organization?

2. "A nice gift to a customer is not bribery if it is given after the sale—then it is merely a token of appreciation and should be both ethical and legal." Discuss this statement.

3. What is the relationship between unethical behavior and profitability?

PART ONE

CONTEMPORARY VIOLATIONS OF THE PUBLIC TRUST

CHAPTER TWO

MetLife: Deceptive Sales Tactics

*I*n August 1993, the state of Florida cracked down on the sales practices of giant Metropolitan Life, a company dating back to 1868, and the country's second largest insurance firm. MetLife agents based in Tampa, Florida, were alleged to have duped customers out of some $11 million. Thousands of these customers were nurses, lured by the sales pitch to learn more about "something new, one of the most widely discussed retirement plans in the investment world today."[1] In reality, this was a life-insurance policy in disguise, and what clients were led to think were savings deposits were actually insurance premiums.

The growing scandal rocked MetLife, eventually costing it several billion dollars in fines and restitutions. What was not clear for certain was the full culpability of the company: Was it guilty only of not monitoring agent performance sufficiently to detect unethical and illegal activities, or was it the great encourager of such practices? Regardless, MetLife did not react well to the legal and public relations stigma that enveloped it.

RICK URSO: THE VILLAIN?

The first premonitory rumble that something bad was about to happen came to Rick Urso on Christmas Eve 1993.

At home with his family, he received an unexpected call from his boss, the regional sales manager. In disbelief, he heard there was a rumor going around the executive suites that he was about to be fired. Now, Urso had known that the State of Florida had been investigating, and that company auditors had also been looking into sales practices. On September 17, two corporate vice-presidents had even shown up to conduct the fourth audit that year, but on leaving they had given him the impression that he was complying with company guidelines.

---

1. Suzanne Woolley and Gail DeGeorge, "Policies of Deception?" *Business Week* (January 17, 1994), p. 24.

Urso often reveled in his good fortune and attributed it to his sheer dedication to his work and the company. He had grown up in a working-class neighborhood, the son of an electrician. He had started college, but dropped out before graduating.

His sales career started at a John Hancock agency in Tampa, in 1978. Four years later, he was promoted to manager. He was credited with building up the agency to number two in the whole company.

Urso left John Hancock in 1983 for MetLife's Tampa agency. His first job was as trainer. Only three months later he was promoted to branch manager. Now his long hours and overwhelming commitment were beginning to pay off. In a truly inspiring success story, his dedication and his talent as a motivator of people swept the branch from a one-rep office to one of MetLife's largest and most profitable. By 1993, the agency employed 120 reps, seven sales managers, and thirty administrative employees. And he was the head. In 1990 and 1991, Urso's office won the company's Sales Office of the Year award. With such a performance history, the stuff of legends, he became the company's star, a person to look up to and to inspire trainees and other employees.

Urso's was the passion of a TV evangelist: "Most people go through life being told why they can't accomplish something. If they would just believe, then they would be halfway there. That's the way I dream and that's what I expect from my people."[2] He soon became known as the "Master Motivator," and increasingly was the guest speaker at MetLife conferences.

On the Monday after that Christmas, the dire prediction came to pass. He was summoned to the office of William Groggans, the head of MetLife's Southeast territory, and there was handed a letter by the sober-faced Groggans. With trembling hands he opened it and read that he was fired. The reason: improper conduct.

The Route to Stardom

Unfortunately, the growth of his Tampa office could not be credited to simple motivation of employees. Urso found his vehicle for great growth to be the whole-life insurance policy. This was part life insurance and part savings. As such, it required high premiums, but only part earned interest and compounded on a tax-deferred basis; the rest went to pay for the life insurance policy. What made this so attractive to company sales reps was the commission: A Met whole-life policy paid a 55 percent first-year commission. In contrast, an annuity paid only a 2 percent first-year commission.

Urso found the nurses' market to be particularly attractive. Perhaps because of their constant exposure to death, nurses were easily convinced of the need for economic security. He had his salespeople call themselves "nursing representatives," and his Tampa salespeople carried their fake retirement plan beyond Florida, eventually reaching thirty-seven states. A New York client, for example, thought she had bought a retirement annuity. But it turned out to be insurance even though as a single woman, she didn't need such coverage.[3]

---

2. Weld F. Royal, "Scapegoat or Scoundrel," *Sales & Marketing Management* (January 1995), p. 64.

3. Jane Bryant Quinn, "Yes, They're Out to Get You," *Newsweek* (January 24, 1994) p. 51.

As the growth of the Tampa agency became phenomenal, his budget for mailing brochures was upped to nearly $1 million in 1992, ten times that of any other MetLife office. This gave him national reach.

Urso's own finances increased proportionately as he earned a commission on each policy his reps sold. In 1989, he was paid $270,000. In 1993, as compensation exceeded $1 million, he moved his family to Bay Shore Boulevard, the most expensive area of Tampa.

Early Warnings

A few complaints began surfacing. In 1990, the Texas insurance commissioner warned MetLife to stop its nursing ploy. The company made a token compliance by sending out two rounds of admonitory letters. But apparently nothing changed. See the following Information Box about the great deficiency of token compliance without follow-up.

An internal MetLife audit in 1991 raised some questions about Urso's pre-approach letters. The term *nursing representative* was called a "made-up" title. The auditors also questioned the term *retirement savings policy* as not appropriate for the product. However, the report concluded by congratulating the Tampa office for its contribution to the company. Not surprisingly, such mixed signals did not end the use of misleading language at that time.

INFORMATION BOX

THE VULNERABILITY OF COMPLIANCE THAT IS ONLY TOKEN

A token effort at compliance to a regulatory complaint or charge tends to have two consequences, neither good in the long run for the company involved:

1. Such tokenism gives a clear message to the organization: "Despite what outsiders say, this is acceptable conduct in this firm." Thus is set the climate for less than desirable practices.
2. Vulnerability to future harsher measures. As malpractice continues, regulators who are convinced that the company is stalling and refusing to cooperate, will eventually take more drastic action. Penalties will move beyond warnings to become punitive.

The firm may not have intended to stall, but that is the impression conveyed. If the cause of the seemingly token effort is really faulty controls, one wonders how many other aspects of the operation are also ineptly controlled so that company policies are ignored.

INVITATION TO DISCUSS

Discuss what kinds of controls MetLife could have imposed in 1990 that would have made compliance actual and not token.

Allegations Intensify

In the summer of 1993, Florida state regulators began a more in-depth examination of the sales practices of the Urso agency. The crux of the investigations concerned promotional material Urso's office was sending to nurses nationwide. From 1989 to 1993, millions of direct-mail pieces had been sent out. Charges finally were leveled that this material disguised the product agents were selling. For example, one brochure coming from Urso's office depicted the Peanuts character Lucy in a nurse's uniform. The headline described the product as "retirement savings and security for the future a nurse deserves." Nowhere was insurance even mentioned, and allegations were that nurses across the country unknowingly purchased life insurance when they thought they were buying retirement savings plans.

As the investigation deepened, a former Urso agent, turned whistleblower, claimed he had been instructed to place his hands over the words "life insurance" on applications during presentations.

As a result of this investigation, Florida Insurance Commissioner Tom Gallagher charged MetLife with serious violations.

METLIFE CORRECTIVE ACTIONS, FINALLY

Under investigation by Florida regulators, the company's attitudes changed. At first, MetLife denied wrongdoing. But eventually it acknowledged problems. Under mounting public pressure, it agreed to pay $20 million in fines to more than forty states as a result of unethical sales practices of its agents. It further agreed to refund premiums to nearly 92,000 policyholders who bought insurance based on misleading sales information between 1989 and 1993. These refunds were expected to reach $76 million.

MetLife fired or demoted five high-level executives as a result of the scandal. Urso's office was closed, and all seven of his managers and several reps were also discharged. Life insurance sales to individuals were down 25 percent through September 1994 over the same nine-month period in 1993. Standard & Poor's downgraded Met's bond rating based on these alleged improprieties.

Shortly after the fines were announced, the Florida Department of Insurance filed charges against Urso and eighty-six other MetLife insurance agents, accusing them of fraudulent sales practices. The insurance commissioner said, "This was not a situation where a few agents decided to take advantage of their customers, but a concerted effort by many individuals to dupe customers into buying a life insurance policy disguised as a retirement savings plan."[4]

Now MetLife attempted to improve its public image by instituting a broad overhaul of its compliance procedures. It established a corporate ethics and compliance department to monitor behavior throughout the company and audit personal insurance sales offices. The department was also charged to report any compliance deficiencies to senior management and to follow up to ensure the implementation of corrective actions.

In MetLife's *1994 Annual Report*, Harry Kamen, CEO, and Ted Athanassiades, president, commented on their corrective actions regarding the scandal:

4. Sean Armstrong, "The Good, The Bad and the Industry," *Best's Review, P/C* (June 1994), p. 36.

We created what we think is the most effective compliance system in the industry. Not just for personal insurance, but for all components of the company. We installed systems to coordinate and track the quality and integrity of our sales activities, and we created a new system of sales office auditing.

Also, there were organizational changes. And, for the first time in twenty-two years, we assembled all of our agency and district managers—about a thousand people—to discuss what we have done and need to do about the problems and where we were going.[5]

Meantime, Rick Urso started a suit against MetLife for defamation of character and for reneging on a $1 million severance agreement. He alleged that MetLife made him the fall guy in the nationwide sales scandal.

The personal consequences on Urso's life were not inconsequential. More than a year later he was still unemployed. He had looked for another insurance job, but no one would even see him. "There are nights he can't sleep. He lies awake worrying about the impact this will have on his two teenagers." And he laments that his wife cannot go out without people gossiping.[6]

WHERE DOES THE BLAME LIE?

Is Urso really the unscrupulous monster who rose to a million-dollar-a-year man on the foundations of deceit? Or is MetLife mainly to blame for encouraging, and then ignoring for too long, practices aimed at misleading and even deceiving?

The Case Against MetLife

Undeniably Urso did things that smacked of the illegal and unethical. But did the corporation knowingly provide the climate? Was his training such as to promote deceptive practices? Was MetLife completely unaware of his distortions and deceptions in promotional material and sales pitches? There seems to be substantial evidence that the company played a part; it was no innocent and unsuspecting bystander.

At best, MetLife top executives may not have been aware of the full extent of the hard selling efforts emanating at first from Tampa and then spreading further in the organization. Perhaps they chose to ignore any inkling that things were not completely on the up and up, in the quest for exceptional bottom-line performance. "Don't argue with success" might have become the corporate mindset.

At the worst, the company encouraged and even demanded hard selling and tried to pretend that such could still be accomplished with ethical standards of performance. If such ethical standards were not met, then, company top executives could argue, they were not aware of such wrongdoings.

There is evidence of company culpability. Take the training program for new agents. Much of it was designed to help new employees overcome the difficulties of selling life insurance. In so doing, they were taught to downplay the life insurance

5. *MetLife 1994 Annual Report*, p. 16.

6. Royal, p. 65.

aspects of the product. Rather, the savings and tax-deferred growth benefits were to be stressed.

In training new agents to sell insurance over the phone, they were told that people prefer dealing with specialists. It seemed only a small temptation to use the title *nursing representative* rather than *insurance agent*.

After the scandal, MetLife admitted that the training might be faulty. Training had been decentralized into five regional centers, and the company believed that this may have led to a less standardized and less controlled curricula. MetLife has since reorganized so that many functions, including training and legal matters, are now done at one central location.[7]

The company's control or monitoring was certainly deficient and uncoordinated during the years of misconduct. For example, the marketing department promoted deceptive sales practices while the legal department warned of possible illegality but took no further action to eliminate.

AN INDUSTRY PROBLEM?

The MetLife revelations focused public and regulatory attention on the entire insurance industry. The Insurance Commissioner of Florida also turned attention to the sales and marketing practices of New York Life and Prudential. The industry itself seemed vulnerable to questionable practices. Millions of transactions, intense competition, and a widespread and rather autonomous sales force—all these afforded opportunity for misrepresentation and other unethical dealings.

For example, just a few months after the Tampa office publicity, MetLife settled an unrelated scandal. Regulators in Pennsylvania fined the company $1.5 million for "churning." This is a practice of agents replacing old policies with new ones, in which additional commissions are charged and policyholders are disadvantaged. Class-action suits alleging churning have also been filed in Pennsylvania against Prudential, New York Life, and John Hancock.

But problems go beyond sales practices. Claims adjusters may attempt to withhold or reduce payments. General agents may place business with bogus or insolvent companies. Even actuaries may create unrealistic policy structures.

With a deteriorating public image, the industry faced further governmental regulation from both state and federal offices. But cynics, both within and outside the industry, wonder whether deception and fraud are so much a part of the business that nothing can be done about them.[8]

ANALYSIS

Here we have an apparent lapse in complete feedback to top executives. But maybe they did not want to know. After all, nothing was life-threatening here, no product safety features were being ignored or disguised, nobody was in physical danger.

---

7. "Trained to Mislead," *Sales & Marketing Management* (January 1995), p. 66.

8. Armstrong, p. 35.

This raises a key management issue. Can top executives hide from less than ethical practices—and even illegal ones—under the guise that they did not know? The answer should be *No!* See the Information Box, "The Ultimate Responsibility," for a discussion of management accountability.

So, we are left with top management of MetLife grappling with the temptation to tacitly approve the aggressive selling practices of a sales executive so successful as to be the model for the whole organization, even though faint cries from the legal staff suggested that such might be subject to regulatory scrutiny and disapproval.

The harsh appraisal of this situation is that top management cannot be exonerated for the deficiencies of subordinates. If controls and monitoring processes are defective, top management is still accountable. The pious platitudes of MetLife management that they have now corrected the situation hardly excuse them for permitting this to have developed in the first place.

Ah, but embracing the temptation is so easy to rationalize. Management can always maintain that there was no good, solid proof of misdeeds. After all, where do aggressive sales efforts cross the line? Where do they become more than simply puffing, and become outright deceptive? See the Information Box on the following page regarding puffing, and this admittedly gray area of the acceptable. Lacking indisputable evidence of misdeeds, why should these executives suspect the worst—especially since their legal departments, not centralized as they were to be later, were timid in their denunciations?

Turning to controls, a major caveat should be posed for all firms: In the presence of strong management demands for performance—with sometimes imagined

INFORMATION BOX

THE ULTIMATE RESPONSIBILITY

With MetLife the problem was gradually eroding ethical practices. Top management still had ultimate responsibility and cannot escape blame for whatever goes wrong in an organization. Decades ago, President Truman coined the phrase, "The buck stops here," meaning that in this highest position rests the ultimate seat of responsibility.

Any manager who delegates to someone else the authority to do something will undoubtedly hold them responsible to do the job properly. Still, the manager must be aware that his or her own responsibility to higher management or to stockholders cannot be delegated away. If the subordinate does the job improperly, the manager is still responsible.

Going back to MetLife, or to any corporation involved with unethical and illegal practices, top executives can try to escape blame by denying that they knew anything about the misdeeds. This should not exonerate them. Even if they knew nothing directly, they still set the climate.

INVITATION TO DISCUSS

In Japan, the chief executive of an organization involved in a public scandal usually resigns in disgrace. In the United States, top executives often escape full retribution by blaming their subordinates and maintaining that they themselves knew nothing of the misdeed. Is it truly fair to hold a top executive culpable for the shortcomings of some unknown subordinate?

INFORMATION BOX

WHERE DO WE DRAW THE LINE ON PUFFING?

Puffing is generally thought of as mild exaggeration in selling or advertising. It is generally accepted as simple exuberance toward what is being promoted. As such, it is acceptable business conduct. Most people have come to regard promotional communications with some skepticism—"It's New! The Greatest! A Super Value! Gives Whiter Teeth! Whiter Laundry!..." and so on. We have become conditioned to viewing such blandishments with suspicion. But dishonest, or deceptive? Probably not. As long as the exaggeration stays mild.

But it can be a short step from mild exaggeration to outright falsehoods and deceptive claims. Did MetLife's "nursing representatives," "retirement plans," and hiding the reality of life insurance cross the line? Enough people thought so, including state insurance commissioners and the victims themselves.

INVITATION TO DISCUSS

Do you think all exaggerated claims, even the mild and vague ones known as puffing, should be banned? Why or why not?

pressure to produce at all costs, or else—the ground is laid for less than desirable practices by subordinates. After all, their career paths and even job longevity depend on meeting these demands.

In a climate of decentralization and laissez faire, such abuses are more likely to occur. Such a results-oriented structure suggests that it's not how you achieve the desired results, but that you meet them. So, while decentralization on balance is usually desirable, in an environment of top management laxity of good moral standards, it can lead to undesirable practices.

At the least, it leads to opportunistic temptation by lower- and middle-level executives. Perhaps this is the final indictment of MetLife and Rick Urso. The climate was conducive to his ambitious opportunism. For a while it was wonderful. But the abuses of accepted behavior could not be disguised indefinitely.

And wherever possible, top management will repudiate its accountability.

The Handling of the Crisis

MetLife responded slowly to the allegations of misconduct. A classic mode for firms confronted with unethical and/or product liability charges is to deny everything, until evidence becomes overwhelming. Then they are forced to acknowledge problems under mounting public pressure—from regulatory bodies, attorneys, and the media—and have to scramble with damage control to try to undo the threats to public image and finances. In MetLife's case, fines and refunds approached $100 million early on. They would eventually reach almost $2 billion.

Being slow to act, to accept any responsibility, and, for top executives exhibiting aloofness until late in the game, are actions tantamount to inflaming public opinion and regulatory zeal. How much better for all involved, victims as well as the organization itself, if initial complaints are promptly followed up? And, if complaints are serious, they should be given top management attention in a climate of cooperation with any agencies involved as well as the always-interested media.

LATER DEVELOPMENTS

On August 18, 1999, MetLife agreed to pay out at least $1.7 billion to settle final lawsuits over its allegedly improper sales practices. In the agreement (in which MetLife admitted no wrongdoing), about six million life insurance policyholders and a million annuity contract holders were involved. Essentially, these customers were expected to get one to five years of free term-life insurance coverage.

MetLife argued for years that it had done nothing wrong. It had previously dispensed with most of its litigation problems by settling rather than going to trial. The incentive for settling these final class-action suits even at the cost of a massive charge, was to clear the way for MetLife's planned conversion to a stockholder-owned company from its current status as a policyholder-owned mutual company. "Clearly it's something they needed to put behind them before they demutualized," or went public.[9]

Harry Kamen, CEO of MetLife, brought Robert Benmosche, age fifty-seven, an ex-Wall Streeter, on board in 1995 to turn things around. Benmosche solved many of MetLife's problems and became chairman when Kamen retired in 1998. In April 2000, he took the company public and the stock offering raised $5.2 billion.

In his relentless restructuring, Benmosche axed poor performers, some 1,300 including 154 assistant vice presidents and higher in 2001—and demanded better results and ethical standards. He required agents to work full time, instead of part time, as many had previously done: "I knew this was needed after I met someone who complimented one of my agents for his plumbing skills," explained Benmosche. He also compelled all agents to get securities licenses so they could sell investments like variable annuities. Bonuses were now tied into performance reviews and a division's financial results, and officer's bonuses were partly paid in stock that they were discouraged from selling: "If the top people ... don't do what they have to do to make sure the company strongly survives, we should lose our shirts." MetLife's revenues in 2001 were $32 billion, up 18 percent since Benmosche became chairman.[10]

WHAT CAN BE LEARNED?

Beware the head-in-the-sand approach to looming problems or public complaints. Ignoring or giving only token attention to suspected problems and regulatory complaints sets a firm up for a possible massive crisis. Covering one's eyes to malpractices and danger situations does not make them go away; they tend to fester and become more serious. Prompt attention, investigation, and action is needed to prevent these

9. Deborah Lohse, "MetLife Agrees to Pay Out $1.7 Billion or More to Settle Policyholder Lawsuits," *Wall Street Journal* (August 19, 1999), p. B14.

10. Carrie Coolidge, "Snoopy's New Tricks," *Forbes* (April 15, 2002), pp. 100–102.

problem areas from getting out of hand. MetLife could have saved itself several billion dollars if it had acted on the early complaints of misrepresentation and misleading customers.

Unethical and illegal actions do not go undetected forever. It may take months, it may take years, but a firm's dark side will eventually be uncovered. Its reputation may then be besmirched, it may face loss of customers and competitive position, and it may face heavy fines and increased regulation.

The eventual disclosure may come from a disgruntled employee (a whistleblower). It may originate from a regulatory body or an investigative reporter. Or it may come from revelations emanating from a lawsuit. Eventually, the deviation is uncovered, and retribution follows. Such a scenario should be—but is not always—enough to constrain those individuals tempted to commit unethical and illegal actions.

What made the MetLife deceptive practices particularly troubling is that they were so visible, and yet were so long tolerated. Much of the sales organization seemed to lack a clear definition of what was acceptable and what was not. Something was clearly amiss both in the training and in the controlling of agent personnel.

The control function is best centralized in any organization. Where the department or entity that monitors performance is decentralized, tolerance of bad practices is more likely than when centralized. The reason is rather simple. Where legal or accounting controls are decentralized the persons conducting them are more easily influenced and are likely to be neither as objective nor as critical as when they are further from the situation. So, reviewers and evaluators should not be close to the people they are examining. And they should report only to the top management.

A strong sales incentive program invites bad practices. The lucrative commission incentive for the whole-life policies—55 percent first-year commission—was almost bound to stimulate abusive sales practices, especially when the rewards for this type of policy were so much greater than for any other. Firms often use various incentive programs and contests to motivate their employees to seek greater efforts. But if some are tempted to cross the line, the end result in public scrutiny and condemnation may not be worth whatever increases in sales might be gained.

Large corporations are particularly vulnerable to public scrutiny. Large firms, especially ones dealing with consumer products, are very visible. This visibility makes them attractive targets for critical scrutiny by activists, politicians, the media, regulatory bodies, and the legal establishment. Such firms ought to be particularly careful in any dealings that might be questioned, even if short-term profits have to be restrained. In MetLife's case, the fines and refunds eventually approached $2 billion. Although the firm in its *1994 Annual Report* maintained that all the bad publicity was behind it, that there were no ill effects, some analysts wondered how quickly a besmirched reputation could truly be restored, especially with competitors eager to grab the opportunity presented.

Sometimes a tarnished reputation can be rather quickly restored. Contrary to some experts, there is compelling evidence that customers tend to quickly forget misdeeds, as they apparently did with MetLife under the new management of

Benmosche. We will see a similar restoration of reputation with the unsafe tires of Firestone in Ford Explorers in Chapter 3. Perhaps these experiences should be comforting to a firm that incurs image damage, perhaps through its own fault, or maybe because of factors not directly under its control. It does help, however, if there is a change in top management. Still, in cases of unethical conduct, fines and perhaps a plethora of lawsuits are more immediate consequences of culpability.

CONSIDER

What additional learning insights do you see?

QUESTIONS

1. Do you think Rick Urso should have been fired? Why or why not?
2. Do you think the MetLife CEO and president should have been fired? Why or why not?
3. Why was the term, "life insurance," seemingly so desirable to avoid? What is wrong with life insurance?
4. Given the widespread publicity about the MetLife scandal, do you think the firm could regain consumer trust in a short time?
5. "This whole critical publicity has been blown way out of proportion. After all, nobody was injured. Not even in their pocketbook. They were sold something they really needed. For their own good." Evaluate.
6. "You have to admire that guy, Urso. He was a real genius. No one else could motivate a sales organization as he did. They should have made him president of the company. Or else he should become an evangelist." Evaluate.
7. Do you think the arguments are compelling that the control function should be centralized rather than decentralized? Why or why not?

HANDS-ON EXERCISES

Before

1. It is early 1990. You are the assistant to the CEO of MetLife. Rumors have been surfacing that life insurance sales efforts are becoming not only too high pressure but also misleading. The CEO has ordered you to investigate. You find that the legal department in the Southeast Territory has some concerns about the efforts coming out of the highly successful Tampa office of Urso. Be as specific as you can about how you would investigate these unproven allegations, and explain how you would report this to your boss, assuming that some questionable practices seem apparent.
2. It is 1992. Internal investigations have confirmed that Urso and his "magnificent" Tampa office are using deceptive selling techniques in disguising

the life insurance aspects of the policies they are selling. As the executive in charge in the Southeast, describe your actions and rationale at this point. (You have to assume that the later consequences are completely unknown at this point.)

After

3. The ____ has hit the fan. The scandal has become well publicized, especially with such TV programs as *Dateline* and *20/20*. What would you do as top executive of MetLife at this point? How would you attempt to save the public image of the company?

TEAM DEBATE EXERCISE

The publicity is widespread about the "misdeeds" of MetLife. Debate how you would react. One position is to defend your company and rationalize what happened and downplay any ill effects. The other position is to meekly bow to the allegations and admit wrongdoing and be as contrite as possible.

INVITATION TO RESEARCH

Is MetLife still prospering under Benmosche? Can you find any information that contradicts that the situation has virtually been forgotten by the general public? Can you find out whether Rick Urso has found another job? Could you develop the pros and cons of a mutual (policyholder owned) firm and a public firm owned by stockholders?

CHAPTER THREE

Ford Explorers with Firestone Tires— A Killer Scenario

A product defect that leads to customer injuries and deaths through manufacturer carelessness constitutes the most serious crises that any firm should face. In addition to destroying brand reputation, ethical and social responsibility abuses are involved, and then with legal and regulatory consequences. Managing such a crisis becomes far worse, however, when the manufacturer knew about the problems and concealed them, or denied them.

This case is unique in that two manufacturers were culpable, but each blamed the other. As a result, Firestone and Ford were savaged by the press, public opinion, the government, and a host of salivating lawyers. Massive tire recalls destroyed the bottom line and even endangered the viability of Bridgestone/Firestone, while sales of the Ford Explorer, the world's best-selling sport-utility vehicle (SUV), plummeted 22 percent in April 2001 from the year before, while domestic sales of SUVs overall climbed 9 percent.

A HORROR SCENARIO

Firestone tires mounted on Ford Explorers were linked to more than 200 deaths from rollovers in the United States, as well as more than sixty in Venezuela and a reported fourteen in Saudi Arabia and neighboring countries. A widely publicized lawsuit took place in Texas in the summer of 2001. It had been expected that the jury would determine who was most to blame for the deaths and injuries from Explorers outfitted with Firestone tires.

Ford settled its portion of the suit for $6 million one month before the trial began. While Firestone now became the sole defendant, jurors were also asked to assess Ford's responsibility for the accident.

The lawsuit was brought by the family of Marisa Rodriguez, a mother of three who was left brain-damaged and paralyzed after the steel belt and tread of a Firestone tire tore apart during a trip to Mexico in March 2000. As a result, the Explorer rolled over three times, crushing the roof above Mrs. Rodriguez in the rear seat, her husband, Joel, who was asleep in the front passenger seat was also injured. The live pictures of Mrs. Rodriguez in a wheelchair received wide TV coverage.

After the federal court jury in the Texas border town of McAllen had been dead-locked for four days, a settlement was reached with Bridgestone/Firestone for $7.85 million. (The plaintiffs originally had asked for $1 billion.)

The out-of-court settlements with both Ford and Firestone did not resolve the issue of who was most to blame for this and the hundreds of other injuries and deaths. But a lawyer for the Rodriguez family predicted that sooner or later a verdict would emerge: "There's going to be trials and there's going to be verdicts. We've got Marisa Rodriguezes all over the country."[1]

ANATOMY OF THE PROBLEM

The Ford/Firestone Relationship

Ford and Firestone have had a long, intimate history. In 1895, Harvey Firestone sold tires to Henry Ford for his first automobile. In 1906, the Firestone Tire & Rubber Company won its first contract for Ford Motor Company's mass-produced vehicles, a commitment that continued through the decades.

Henry Ford and Harvey Firestone became business confederates and best friends who went on annual summer camping trips, riding around in Model T's along with Thomas Edison and naturalist John Burroughs. Further cementing the relationship, in 1947 Firestone's granddaughter, Martha, married Ford's grandson, William Clay Ford, in a dazzling ceremony in Akron, Ohio, that attracted a Who's Who of dignitaries and celebrities. Their son, William Clay Ford, Jr., was to become Ford's chairman.

In 1988, Tokyo-based Bridgestone Corporation bought Firestone, twenty years after the Japanese company sold its first tires in the United States under the Bridgestone name. In 1990, Ford introduced the Explorer sport-utility vehicle to replace the Bronco II in the 1991 model year. It became the nation's top-selling SUV, and the Explorer generated huge profits for more than a decade. Bridgestone/Firestone was the sole supplier of the Explorer's tires.

The Relationship Worsens

The first intimation of trouble came in 1999 when, after fourteen fatalities occurred, Ford began replacing tires of Explorers in Saudi Arabia and nearby countries. The tire failures were blamed on hot weather and underinflated tires. At the time, overseas fatalities did not have to be reported to U.S. regulators, so the accidents received scant attention in the media.

---

1. "Firestone Agrees to Pay $7.5 Million in Tire Suit," *Cleveland Plain Dealer* (August 25, 2001), pp. A1, A13; Milo Geyelin and Timothy Aeppel, "For Firestone, Tire Trial Is Mixed Victory," *Wall Street Journal* (August 27, 2001), pp. A3, A4.

The media caught the scent in early 2000 when television reports in Houston revealed instances of tread separation on Firestone's ATX tires, and the National Highway Traffic Safety Administration (NHTSA) started an investigation. By May, four U.S. fatalities had been reported, and NHTSA expanded the investigation to 47 million ATX, ATXII, and Wilderness tires.

In August 2000, as deaths began mounting leading to increasing pressure from consumers and multiple lawsuits, Firestone voluntarily recalled 14.4 million 15-inch radial tires because of tread separation. The plant in Decatur, Illinois, was implicated in most of these accidents. Ford and Firestone agreed to replace the tires, but estimated that 6.5 million were still on the road. Consumer groups sought a still wider recall, charging that Explorers with other Firestone tire models were also prone to separation leading to rollovers.

In December 2000, Firestone issued a report blaming Ford for the problems, claiming that the Explorer's design caused rollovers with any tread separations. On April 20, 2001, Ford gave NHTSA a report blaming Firestone for flawed manufacturing.

In May 2001, Ford announced that it was replacing all remaining 13 million Firestone Wilderness AT tires on its vehicles, saying that the move was necessary because Ford had no confidence in the tires' safety. "We feel it's our responsibility to act immediately," Ford CEO Jacques Nasser said. Ford said the move would cost the automaker $2.1 billion, although it hoped to get this back from Firestone.

Firestone Chairman and CEO John Lampe defended his tires, saying, "no one cares more about the safety of the people who travel on our tires than we do. When we have a problem, we admit it and we fix it."[2]

The Last Days

It is lamentable when a long-lasting close relationship is severed. But on May 21, 2001, Lampe abruptly ended the ninety-five-year association, accusing Ford of refusing to acknowledge safety problems with its vehicles and thus putting all the blame on Firestone.

The crisis had been brewing for months. Many Firestone executives did not trust Ford and even exchanging documents was done with rancor, with major disagreements in interpreting the data. Firestone argued that tread-separation claims occurred ten times more frequently on Ford Explorers than on Ranger pickups with the same tires, thus supporting their contention that the Explorer was mostly at fault. Ford rejected Firestone's charges about the Explorer, saying that for ten years the model "has ranked at or near the top in terms of safety among the twelve SUVs in its class." It stated that 2.9 million Goodyear tires mounted on more than 500,000 Explorers had "performed with industry-leading safety."[3]

The climax came in a May 21 meeting of Lampe and a contingent of Ford officials, during which with both sides maintaining that the other was to blame. Discussions

---

2. Ed Garsten, Associated Press, as reported in "Ford Tire Tab $2.1 Billion," *Cleveland Plain Dealer* (May 23, 2001), pp. 1C, 4C.

3. Timothy Aeppel, Joseph B. White, and Stephen Power, "Firestone Quits as Tire Supplier to Ford," *Wall Street Journal* (May 22, 2001), pp. A3, A12.

broke down regarding any working together to examine the Explorer's role in the accidents. At that point, Lampe ended their relationship. Each party then was left to defend itself before Congress and the court of public opinion, and ultimately a siege of lawsuits. See the Information Box, "How Emotion Influences Company Reputation," for a discussion of how emotion drives consumers in their perception, good and bad, of companies.

Advantage to Competitors

Major competitors Goodyear and Michelin as well as smaller competitors and private-label tire makers predictably raised tire prices 3 to 5 percent. Goodyear then tried to increase production robustly to replace the millions of Firestone tires recalled or soon to be, but it was trying to avoid overtime pay to bolster profits. In a written statement, Goodyear said, "We are working very closely with Ford to jointly develop an aggressive plan to address consumers' needs as quickly as possible."[4]

INFORMATION BOX

HOW EMOTION INFLUENCES COMPANY REPUTATION

The second annual corporate-reputation survey conducted by the Harris market-research firm and the Reputation Institute involving 26,011 respondents found that Emotional Appeal—trust, admiration and respect, and generally good feelings toward—was the driving force in how people rated companies. The survey found that advertising did not necessarily change opinions. For example, despite a $100 million advertising campaign about what a good citizen Philip Morris Company was in feeding the hungry and helping victims of domestic violence, the company still received low marks on trust, respect, and admiration. But the most recent poll showed that Philip Morris no longer had the worst reputation in America. This distinction went to Bridgestone/Firestone, with Ford receiving the lowest reputation rating among auto companies.

Once lost, a company's reputation or public image is usually difficult to regain. For example, ExxonMobil's reputation for environmental responsibility was still given low grades more than a decade after the destructive Alaskan oil spill involving the oil tanker *Exxon Valdez*.

INVITATION TO DISCUSS

Do you think Firestone's quest to improve its reputation should face the same problems as those occurring from the *Exxon Valdez*? Why or why not?

Source: Ronald Alsop, "Survey: Emotion Drives Public Perception of Companies," *Wall Street Journal*, February 11, 2001, p. 5H.

---

4. Thomas W. Gerdel, "Goodyear, Michelin Raising Consumer Tire Prices," *Cleveland Plain Dealer* (May 23, 2001), pp. 1C, 4C.

The decrease in auto sales in the slowing economy that began in 2000 had led Goodyear to production cutbacks, including cutting 7,200 workers worldwide as it posted an 83 percent decline in profits in 2000. Now it was challenged to gear up to handle the windfall of the ending of the Ford/Firestone relationship.

WHEREIN LIES THE BLAME?

In years to come, courts and lawyers will sort out the culpability controversy. The final outcome is in doubt, and the finger of blame points to a number of sources, though the weighting is uncertain. While Ford and Firestone should share major responsibility, the NHTSA and the motoring public were hardly blameless.

Ford

The question of whether the design of Ford's Explorer made it more prone to roll over than other SUVs will be decided in the courtroom. One thing seems clear: Ford recommended a low inflation level for its tires, and this would subject them to more flex in the sidewall and greater heat buildup. With high-speed driving in hot weather, such a high-profile vehicle would be more prone to roll over with any tire trouble, especially with inexperienced drivers. For example, Ford's recommended tire pressure was 26 pounds and this would bring the car's center of gravity lower to the ground. This would seem good, but only at first look. Required by the government, the Uniform Tire Quality Grade (UTQG) provides comparative manufacturer information. Tires are subjected to a series of government-mandated tests that measure performance in treadwear, traction, and temperature resistance. All testing is done by the tire manufacturer. Ford was alone among SUV makers in equipping the Explorer with "c" tires rather than the more heat-resistant "b" tires that were the near-universal standard on most sport utility vehicles. To make the "c" grade, tires had to withstand only two hours at 50 mph when properly inflated and loaded, plus another 90 minutes at speeds up to 85 mph. This standard dated back to 1968 when sustained highway speeds were much lower than today. Now, people drive hour after hour at speeds well above 70 mph.

The c-rated Firestones were used on millions of Ford pickup trucks without problems. However, in contrast with SUVs, most pickup trucks are not taken on long-haul, high-speed road trips filled with family and luggage.

Ford CEO Jacques Nasser justified replacing 13 million tires by claiming the Firestones were failing at a rate higher than Goodyears mounted on two million Explorers in the mid-1990s. But the Goodyears carried the "b" rating. The dangerous effect of heat buildup was shown by most Explorers' accidents taking place in hot Southern states and other hot-climate countries with high speed limits.

Ford engineers should have been aware of these dangers, if not immediately, certainly after a few years, and adapted the Explorer to customers who drive fast, pay little attention to tire maintenance, and are prone to panic with a blowout and flip the car. Unfortunately, the American legal environment, the tort system, makes the manufacturer vulnerable to lawsuits and massive damage claims should it acknowledge in retrospect that it had made a bad mistake in its tire selection and pressure recommendation. So the temptation was to blame the tiremaker, and spend millions to create it as a media monster.

Bridgestone/Firestone

Firestone tires were far from blameless. Early on, investigations of deadly vehicle accidents linked the causes to tire failure, notably due to shoddy manufacturing practices at the Firestone Decatur, Illinois, plant; the 6.5 million tire recall by Firestone was of the 15-inch radial ATX and ATX11 tires and Wilderness AT tires made in this plant. In June 27, 2001, the company announced the plant would be closed. But Firestone's poorly controlled manufacturing process proved not to be limited to this single operation. See the Information Box, "A Whistleblower 'Hero,'" about the whistleblower who exposed another plant's careless disregard of safe tire production.

INFORMATION BOX

A WHISTLEBLOWER "HERO"

Alan Hogan was honored in June 2001 by the Civil Justice Foundation for exposing how employees at a Bridgestone/Firestone plant in North Carolina routinely made defective tires. This consumer advocacy group, founded by the Association of Trial Lawyers of America, bestowed similar "community champion" awards on tobacco whistleblower Jeffrey Wigand, and on Erin Brockovich, who exposed hazardous-waste dangers and was the subject of a popular movie.

With his insider's knowledge of shoddy tire-building practices, Hogan was widely credited with bringing about the first recall. He testified at a wrongful-death lawsuit in 1999 that he witnessed the crafting of countless bad tires built with dried-out rubber and wood bits, cigarette butts, screws, and other foreign materials mixed in. Hogan, who had quit the company and opened an auto-body shop in his home town, became a pariah among many people for his revelations about the community's major employer, and company attorneys looked into his work and family life for anything they could use to discredit him. They tried to portray him as a disgruntled former employee. An anonymous fax accused him of spreading "vicious, malicious allegations" about the company. Employees were warned not to do business with car dealerships that dealt with his body shop.

But he persevered, and eventually won recognition and accolades. "I'm surprised it took this long," he said. "Maybe now people will see this is the way it's been since 1994, 1995, when they started covering this up." His whistle-blowing credentials were now in high demand as an expert witness in other lawsuits.

INVITATION TO DISCUSS

Do you see any reasons why Hogan may not have been completely objective in his whistle-blowing efforts?

Source: Dan Chapman, Cox News, as reported in "Firestone Ex-Worker Called Hero in Recall," *Cleveland Plain Dealer* (May 29, 2001), p. 1C.

Still, there were contrary indications that the fault was not all Bridgestone/Firestone's, that Ford shared the blame. General Motors had detected no problems with Firestones it used as standard equipment in fourteen of its models. In fact, in July 2001 GM named Firestone as its supplier of the year for the sixth consecutive time. Honda of America was also loyal to Firestones, which it used on its best-selling Civics and Odysseys.[5]

On September 14, 2001, months after all Firestones had been recalled from Ford Explorers, an apparently skilled driver, a deputy bailiff driving home from court, was killed when he lost control of his Explorer and it flipped over a guardrail, slid down an embankment, and rolled over several times.[6]

Government

Public Citizen and other consumer groups were critical of the government, maintaining that it was too slow in completing its initial Firestone investigation and had dragged its feet in any investigation of the Explorer. A Public Citizen study saw the use of the specific Firestone tires as coming from cost- and weight-saving miscalculations and gambles by Ford, "making what was already a bad problem into a lethal one." Not just the companies were at fault, but federal regulators were lax in not toughening standards on SUVs to prevent roofs from collapsing in rollover crashes. "The human damage caused is barbaric and unnecessary," the study concluded.[7]

The Driver

There is no doubt that drivers contributed to accidents. They did so by neglecting tire pressure so that it was often below even the low recommendations of Ford, by heavily loading vehicles, and by driving too fast over long periods so that tires could heat up to dangerous levels. Added to this, a lack of driving expertise to handle emergency blowouts was often the fatal blow. Yet could a carmaker, tiremaker, or government really expect the average consumer to act with strict prudence? Precautions, be they car standards or tire standards, needed to be imposed with worst scenarios in mind as to consumer behavior.

CONSEQUENCES

Each company maneuvered primarily to cast blame on the other. Ford announced in May 2001 it would triple the size of the Firestone recall, a $2.8 billion prospect, a cost Ford wanted to shift to the tiremaker. Firestone, at that point, severed its long relationship with Ford by refusing to supply the company with more tires. Firestone

5. Ed Garsten, Associated Press, as reported in "Ford Tire Tab, $2.1 Billion," *Cleveland Plain Dealer* (May 23, 2001), pp, 1C and 4C; and Alison Grant, "Bridgestone/Firestone Faces Struggle to Survive," *Cleveland Plain Dealer* (August 5, 2001), pp. H1, H5.

6. "SUV Flips, Killing Deputy Bailiff, 24," *Cleveland Plain Dealer* (September 15, 2001), p. B5.

7. Alison Grant, "Government, Goodyear Still Navigating a Bumpy Road," *Cleveland Plain Dealer* (August 5, 2001), p. H5.

CEO Lampe maintained Ford was trying to divert scrutiny of the rollover-prone Explorer by casting doubt on the safety of Firestone tires.

Both parties suffered in this name-calling and buck-passing. By fall 2001, sales of Explorers were off sharply, as consumers wondered whether the hundreds of Explorer crashes were due to the SUV's design, or Firestone tires, or both. Ford lost market share to Toyota and other foreign rivals in the SUV market. In July 2001, it reported its first loss from operations since 1992. It also faced 200 product-liability lawsuits involving Explorer rollovers. Still, Ford was big enough to absorb problems with one of its models.

Smaller Bridgestone/Firestone faced a more serious situation. In 2000, its earnings dropped 80 percent, reflecting the costs of recalling millions of tires as well as a special charge to cover legal expenses. The Firestone unit, which accounted for 40 percent of the parent company's revenue, posted a net loss of $510 million after it took a $750 million charge for legal expenses. Sales were forecast to plunge 20 percent in 2001, and costs of lawsuits could eventually reach billions of dollars, to the point where some analysts doubted Firestone as a brand could survive.[8]

Options Firestone Faced

This esteemed brand, launched more than a century ago, had been the exclusive tire supplier to the Indy 500. Now its future was in doubt, despite decades of brand loyalty. The brand faced three options:

Option #1: Some thought the company should try to de-emphasize Firestone, and push business to the Bridgestone label. This would likely result in some loss of market segmentation and the flexibility of having distinct low-end, mid-level, and premium tires. Others thought, however, that such a half-hearted approach would simply prolong the agony of hanging on to a besmirched brand.

Option #2: Obliterate the Firestone name, it being irretrievable. "Firestone should just give up," said one public relations analyst. "They've damaged themselves so severely." A University of Michigan Business School professor called the brand dead: "Can you imagine any jury claiming that somebody who's suspected of building bad tires is innocent?"[9]

Option #3: Try to salvage the brand. Some questioned the wisdom of abandoning the century-old Firestone name, with its rich tradition and millions of cumulative advertising dollars. They thought that with money, time, and creative advertising, Bridgestone/Firestone should be able to restore its image. But to do so, Roger Blackwell of Ohio State University thought the company needed to make an admission of regret: "The lawyers will tell them not to admit blame... But they need to do what Johnson & Johnson did when someone was killed by their product [cyanide-tainted Tylenol]. A credible spokesman got on TV and had tears

---

8. Akiko Kashiwagi, "Recalls Cost Bridgestone Dearly; Firestone's Parent's Profit Drops 80%," *Washington Post* (Feb. 23, 2001), p. E3.

9. Grant, "Bridgestone/Firestone Faces Struggle to Survive," p. H5.

in his eyes when he spoke." (See Chapter 22 for this Johnson & Johnson classic case.) An independent tire dealer who lost $100,000 in sales in 2000 but was confident of a rebound supported this option: "The American public is quick to forget," he said.[10]

POSTMORTEM

For years, buyers of Ford Explorers equipped with Firestone tires faced far higher risks of deaths and injuries, both in the United States and abroad, than they would have from other models. The *New York Times* reported that the tire defects, and their contribution to accidents, were known in 1996.[11] Not until August 1999 did Ford begin replacing tires on Explorers in Saudi Arabia, calling the step a "customer notification enhancement program." Fourteen fatalities had already been reported. Not until March 2000, after television reports of problems, did federal regulators and the two manufacturers take all this seriously.

Ford, in its concern with the bottom line, stubbornly refused to admit that anything was wrong with its SUV, while Firestone couldn't seem to clean up its act in the Decatur, Illinois, plant, and even some other plants, where carelessness and lack of customer concern prevailed. Minor ethical abuses became major when lives were lost, but the foot-dragging continued until lawyers came on the scene. Then these two tried to cover their mistakes with finger pointing, while a vulnerable public continued to be in jeopardy. Throughout this whole time, saving lives did not apparently have a very high priority. Eventually the consequences came back to haunt the companies, with hundreds of lawsuits, millions of tire recalls, and the denigration of their public image.

How could this have been permitted to happen? After all, top management were not deliberately vicious men. They were well intentioned, albeit badly misguided. Perhaps their worst sin was to at first ignore, and then refuse to admit and to try to cover up increasingly apparent serious risk factors.

Part of the problem was the stubborn mindset of top executives that nothing was wrong: A few accidents reflected driver carelessness, not a defective product. Neither company would assume the worst scenario: that this was a dangerous product used on a dangerous product that was killing people, and neither Ford nor Firestone could escape blame.

Forty years ago a somewhat similar situation occurred with the GM Corvair, a rear-engine car that exhibited instability under extreme cornering conditions causing it to flip over. Ralph Nader gained his reputation as a consumer advocate in his condemnation of this "unsafe" car with a best-selling book, *Unsafe At Any Speed.* But GM executives refused to admit there was any problem, until eventually the evidence was overwhelming and lawsuits flourished, and the federal government stepped in with the National Traffic and Motor Vehicle Safety Act of 1966, which among other things required manufacturers to notify customers of any defects or flaws later discovered in their vehicles. (See Chapter 10 for more details.)

10. *Ibid.*

11. Keith Bradsher, "SUV Tire Defects Were Known in '96 but Not Reported; 190 Died in Next 4 Years," *New York Times* (June 24, 2001), p. 1N.

GM executives, like those of Ford and Firestone forty years later, were honorable men. Yet, something seems to happen to the conscience and the moral sensitivity of top executives. They commission actions in their corporate personas that they would hardly dream of doing in their private lives. John DeLorean, former GM executive, was one of the first to note this dichotomy:

> "These were not immoral men who were bringing out this car [the Corvair]. These were warm, breathing men with families and children who as private individuals would never have approved [this project] for a minute if they were told, 'You are going to kill and injure people with this car.' But these same men, in a business atmosphere, where everything is reduced to terms of costs, corporate goals, and production deadlines, were able to approve a product most of them wouldn't have considered approving as individuals."[12]

We have to raise the question: Why this lockstep obsession with sales and profits at all costs? See the accompanying Information Box, "The 'Groupthink' Influence," for a discussion of this issue.

UPDATE

On October 30, 2001, Ford Motor Company announced that Jacques Nasser would be replaced as CEO by William Clay Ford, Jr., age forty-four—the first Ford family member to be in charge since 1979. Ford is the son of William Clay Ford Sr., who is the grandson of founder Henry Ford and brother of Henry Ford II. Nasser had been under pressure for months for Ford's loss of market share and tumbling profitability and the adverse publicity of the Explorer.

In December 2001, the newly designed 2002 Ford Explorer received a top score in a crash test from the Insurance Institute for Highway Safety. Changes in the 2002 Explorer to improve passenger protection were part of the automaker's "commitment to continuous improvements," a Ford spokesperson said.[13]

Firestone also bounced back, despite dire predictions of the brand's demise as U.S. operations suffered a $1.7 billion loss in 2001 on top of a $510 million loss in 2000.

Some called this "the most unlikely brand resurrection in marketing history." Much of the credit for the survival was credited to Firestone CEO John Lampe, who crisscrossed the country giving pep talks to hundreds of Firestone's 10,000 dealers. These dealers became fiercely loyal at a time when 75 percent of tire buyers were influenced by dealers' recommendations, according to industry estimates. Several splashy new tires were brought out, including the Firehawk Indy 500, which became a hit with racing fans. "We are selling as many Firestone tires as we've ever sold," one large dealer noted.

---

12. J. Patrick Wright, *On a Clear Day You Can See General Motors* (Grosse Point, Mich.: Wright Enterprises, 1979), pp. 5–6.

13. Christopher Jensen, *Cleveland Plain Dealer* (December 12, 2001), pp. C1, C4.

INFORMATION BOX

THE "GROUPTHINK" INFLUENCE

The callousness about "killer" cars would, as John DeLorean theorized, probably never have prevailed if an individual was making the decision outside the corporate environment. But bring in groupthink, which is decision-by-committee, and add to this a high degree of organizational loyalty (versus loyalty to the public interest), and such callousness can manifest itself. Why can the moral standards of groupthink be so much lower than individual moral standards?

Perhaps the answer lies in the "pack mentality" that characterizes certain committees or groups highly committed to organizational goals. All else then becomes subordinated to these goals, being a single-minded perspective. Within any committee, individual responsibility for decision is diluted since this is a committee decision. Furthermore, without the contrary arguments of a strong "devil's advocate" (i.e., one who argues the opposing viewpoint, sometimes simply to be sure that all sides of an issue are considered), a follow-the-leader syndrome can take place, with no one willing to oppose the majority views.

But there is more to it than that. Chester Barnard, a business executive, scholar, and philosopher, noted the paradox: People have a number of private moral codes that affect behavior in different situations, and these codes are not always compatible. Codes for private life, regarding family and religion, may be far different from codes for business life. Throughout the history of business, it has not been unusual to find that the scrupulous and God-fearing churchgoer is far different when he or she conducts business during the week: A far lower ethical standard prevails during the week than on the Sabbath. Nor has it been unusual to find that a person can be a paragon of love, understanding, and empathy with his or her family but be totally lacking in such qualities with employees or customers.[14] We might add that even tyrants guilty of the most extreme atrocities, such as Hitler and Saddam Hussein, have been known to exude great tenderness and consideration for their intimates.

INVITATION TO DISCUSS

What does it take for a person to resist and not accept the majority viewpoint? What do you think would be the characteristics of such a person? Do you see yourself as such a rebel?

With communication improving between the two companies, Lampe could see signs that the rift with Ford was ending, and William Clay Ford even mentioned his great-grandfather Harvey Firestone in a Ford commercial. "It was a very honest thing to do. He didn't have to do that," Lampe observed.[15]

14. Chester I. Barnard, *The Functions of the Executive* (Cambridge, Mass.: Harvard University Press, 1938), p. 263.

15. Todd Zaun, "Defying Expectations, Bridgestone Embarks on a Turnaround," *Wall Street Journal* (March 12, 2002), p. A21; Jonathan Fahey, "Flats Fixed," *Forbes* (May 27, 2002), pp. 40–41.

WHAT CAN BE LEARNED?

A firm today must zealously guard against product liability suits. Any responsible executive needs to recognize that product liability suits, in today's litigious environment, can even bankrupt a firm. The business arena has become more risky, more fraught with peril for the unwary or the naively unconcerned. Consequently, any firm needs careful and objective testing of any product that can affect customer health and safety. Sometimes such testing may require that production be delayed, even if competition gains some advantage from this delay. The risks of putting an unsafe product on the market outweigh competitive concerns.

Suspicions and complaints about product safety must be thoroughly investigated. We should learn from this case that immediate and thorough investigation of any suspicions or complaints must be undertaken, regardless of the confidence management may have in the product or of the glowing recommendations of persons whose objectivity could be suspect. To procrastinate or ignore complaints poses what should be unacceptable risks.

Sometimes the root of the problem is not obvious, or is more complex than first thought. In this Ford/Firestone case, objective research should have focused on both the Explorer and the Firestone tires, and how the situation could be remedied to minimize rollovers and save lives.

The health and safety of customers is entirely compatible with the well-being of the firm. It is a lose/lose situation if this is ignored: The customer is jeopardized, but eventually the firm is, too, as lawsuits grow and damages increase. Why, then, the corporate mindset of "us versus them"? There should be no conflicting goals. Both win when customer welfare is maximized.

In the worst scenario, go for a conciliatory salvage strategy. Ford and Firestone faced a crossroads by late 1999 and early 2000. Reports of fatalities linked to Ford Explorers and Firestone tires were trickling in, the first occurring in the hot climate of Saudi Arabia, and these were in a matter of months to become a flood. How should a company react?

A salvage strategy can be attempted by toughing it out, trying to combat the bad press, denying culpability, blaming someone else, and resorting to the strongest possible legal defense. This essentially is what Ford opted to do, as it blamed Firestone for everything and spent millions advertising to promote this contention.

Firestone was more vulnerable since its shredded tires could hardly be denied, and it was forced to recall millions of tires, although it stoutly maintained that the cause of the shredding was underinflation and the wrong quality of tire, as well as the Explorer itself. At stake were company reputations, economic positions, and even viability for Firestone, and, most importantly, also the lives of hundreds of users.

Conciliation usually is the better salvage strategy. This involves recognition and full admission of the problem and removal of the risk, even if this entails a full-market withdrawal until the source of the problem can be identified and correction made. Expensive, yes, but far less risky for the viability of the company and certainly for the health of those customers involved.

Neither strategy is without substantial costs. But the first course of action puts major cost consequences in the future, where they may turn out to be vastly greater as legal expenses and damage awards skyrocket. The second course of action poses an immediate impact on profitability, and will not avoid legal expenses, but may save the company and its reputation and return it to profitability in the near future.

Where blame is most likely shared, the solution of the problem lies not in confrontation but in cooperation. This is the most grievous component of the violations of the public trust by Ford and Firestone: denial and confrontation, rather than cooperation to solve the problem of product safety.

CONSIDER

Can you think of additional learning insights?

QUESTIONS

1. Can a firm guarantee complete product safety? Discuss.

2. Based on the information presented, which company do you think is more to blame for the deaths and injuries? What led you to your conclusion?

3. "If an Explorer driver never checks the tire pressure and drives well above the speed limit, he has no one to blame but himself in an accident—not the vehicle and not the tires." Discuss.

4. Do you think the government should be blamed in the Explorer deaths and injuries? Why or why not?

5. Would you give credence to the "community champion" awards bestowed by a consumer advocacy group founded by the Association of Trial Lawyers, and given to Alan Hogan in June 2001 for exposing careless tire production? Why or why not?

6. "Admittedly the groupthink mindset may be responsible for a few unethical and bad decisions, but this mindset is more likely to consider the consequences to the company of delivering unsafe products and to support aggressive corrective action." Evaluate this argument.

7. Have you had any experience with a Ford Explorer? If so, what is your perception of its performance and safety?

8. Have you had any experience with Firestone tires? What is your perception of their performance and safety?

HANDS-ON EXERCISES

1. Place yourself in the position of John Lampe, CEO of Firestone, as the crisis worsens and accusations mount. Discuss how you would try to change the climate with Jacques Nasser of Ford from confrontational to cooperative. Be as specific as you can. Do you think you would be successful?

2. Firestone is on its knees after massive tire recalls and monstrous damage suits. You are a consultant brought in to help the firm recover. Be as specific as you can in recommendations, and in the priority of things to do. Make any assumptions you need to, but keep them reasonable. Defend your recommendations. (Do not be swayed by what actually happened. Maybe things could have been done better.)

3. You are a trusted aide of Nasser. Support his confrontational stance with Firestone before the Ford board of directors.

4. Be a devil's advocate. In a staff meeting the topic comes up that your SUVs have been involved in a number of deaths. The group passes this off as due to reckless drivers. Argue persuasively a contrary position.

TEAM DEBATE EXERCISE

Debate the issue of dropping or keeping the Firestone name. Defend your position and attack the other side.

INVITATION TO RESEARCH

Can you find statistics as to how competing tire companies, particularly Goodyear and Michelin, fared during and after the Firestone recall? Are Ford and Firestone friends again? Is the Ford Explorer still the top SUV?

CHAPTER FOUR

ADM: Price Fixing, Political Cronyism, and a Whistleblower

*I*n June 1995, a whistleblower informed federal agents of the scheme of a giant multi-national conglomerate, Archer-Daniels-Midland, to control sales of a widely demanded food additive and thus keep prices high worldwide. For three years, he had been secretly recording meetings of the firm's senior executives with Asian and European competitors. The whistleblower, Mark E. Whitacre, was revealed to ADM by an attorney who was supposedly conferring with him as a possible client.

Repercussions quickly followed. The company charged him with stealing from the firm and fired him. The plot became more complicated. But overhanging all was the role of the corporation and its seventy-seven-year-old top executive: Did they truly act unethically and illegally, or were the allegations ballooned out of all proportions? What kind of a person was this whistleblower, a hero or a villain?

THE WHISTLEBLOWER, MARK E. WHITACRE

Mark Whitacre joined Archer-Daniels in 1989, and spent about half his career there helping antitrust investigators. He was a rising star, recruited to head the fledgling BioProducts division, where he rose to become a corporate vice president and a leading candidate to become the company's next president while still in his thirties.

He had been recruited from Degussa AG, a German chemical company where he was manager in organic chemicals and feed additives. However, his resume inflated his credentials with the title executive vice-president; he was only a vice-president.

While at ADM, he earned a business degree from a home-study school in California. Later ADM issued biographical material crediting him with an MBA from Northwestern University and the prestigious J.L. Kellogg School of Management. In an interview, Whitacre admitted the claims about his MBA were inflated to impress Wall Street analysts, but he blamed ADM: "I feel bad about it. I, along with other executives that speak at analysts meetings, cooperated ... it's a common practice."[1]

---

1. "ADM Informant Faces Widening Allegations; He Attempts Suicide," *Wall Street Journal* (August 14, 1995), p. A4.

His ambition was to become president of ADM, which he claimed was promised him repeatedly.[2] How becoming a governmental informer would help him with this ambition seems murky.

Over three years he secretly helped investigators obtain videotapes revealing two senior executives meeting with Asian and European competitors in various places around the world. The executives were vice-chairman Michael D. Andreas, son and heir apparent of the seventy-seven-year-old Dwayne Andreas, chairman and chief executive; and vice president Terrance Wilson, head of the corn-processing division. Sometimes Whitacre would wear a hidden microphone to obtain the incriminating evidence of price-fixing. We will follow the later travails of Whitacre, but let us examine whistleblowing in general in the following Information Box.

INFORMATION BOX

WHISTLEBLOWING

A whistleblower is an insider in an organization who publicizes alleged corporate misconduct. Such misconduct may involve unethical practices of all kinds, such as fraud, restraint of trade, price-fixing, bribes, coercion, unsafe products and facilities, and violations of other laws and regulations. Presumably, the whistleblower has exhausted the possibilities for changing the questionable practices within the normal organizational channels and, as a last resort, has taken the matter to government officials and/or the press.

Since whistleblowing may result in contract cancellations, corporate fines, and lost jobs, those who become whistleblowers may be vilified by their fellow workers and fired and even framed by their firms. This makes whistleblowing a course of action only for the truly courageous, whose concern for societal best interest outweighs their concern for themselves.

However, there is sometimes a thin line between an employee who truly believes the public interest is jeopardized and the individual who has a gripe or is a fanatic. There are some who believe management is condoning misconduct when in fact such misconduct is isolated and without management awareness or acceptance. And some see whistleblowing as a means of furthering their own interests, such as gaining fame or even advancing their careers.

Ralph Nader, in a 1972 book on whistleblowing, suggested that corporate employees have a primary duty to protect society that exists over and above secondary obligations to the corporation. He give examples of whistleblowing heroes, as well as courses of action for other would-be whistleblowers.[3]

INVITATION TO DISCUSS

Do you think you could ever be a whistleblower? Under what circumstances?

---

2. *Ibid.*

3. Ralph Nader, Peter Petkas, and Nate Blackwell, *Whistleblowing* (New York: Bantam Books), 1972.

FBI agents on the night of June 27 entered the headquarters of the huge grain-processing company in Decatur, Illinois. They carted off files and delivered grand jury subpoenas seeking evidence of price collusion of ADM and competitors. Whitacre was one of the executives subpoenaed, and met with an attorney recommended by the company's general counsel's office, a common practice when companies face governmental inquiries.

Shortly after this meeting, the attorney disclosed to ADM that Whitacre was the federal informant in their midst, thus imperiling Whitacre's position in the company. This seemed a clear ethical violation of the confidentiality of lawyer/client relations. But the attorney, John M. Dowd of a prominent law firm doing business with ADM, claimed that Whitacre authorized him to do so. Whitacre and his new attorney angrily denied any such authorization.

In any case, now the company had the knowledge to retaliate. They fired him, accused him of stealing $2.5 million, and reported these findings to the Justice Department. Later the company increased the amount it claimed Whitacre had stolen to $9 million. They charged that he had been embezzling money by submitting phony invoices for capital expenditures, then channeling the payments into off-shore bank accounts.

The Justice Department saw the credibility of their key witness being weakened by such allegations, especially since Whitacre acknowledged that he had indeed participated in the bogus invoice schemes, although he said the payments were made with the full knowledge and encouragement of company higher-ups. Nevertheless, he and as many as twelve other ADM executives came under criminal investigation for evading taxes. The Justice Department's criminal fraud section further examined allegations that the off-the-books payments were approved by top management.[4]

A few days later, Whitacre tried to kill himself. At dawn, he drove his car into the garage of his home, closed the door, and left the engine running. On this morning he was supposed to fly to Washington to meet with federal authorities. He had arranged for the gardener to come to work late that morning, but the gardener arrived shortly after seven and found Whitacre unconscious in his car.

Shortly before the suicide attempt, Whitacre had written a letter to the *Wall Street Journal*, acknowledging that he had received money from ADM through unusual means: "Regarding overseas accounts and kick-backs; and overseas payments to some employees. Dig Deep. It's there! They give it; then use it against you when you are their enemy."[5]

On September 13, F. Ross Johnson, an ADM board member, in a talk at Emory University's Goizueta Business School commented on Whitacre's suicide attempt: "You know, he tried to commit suicide. But he did it in a six-car garage, which, I think, if you're going to do it, that's the place to do it. [The audience laughed.] And the gardener just happened to come by. So now he is bouncing around."[6]

---

4. Ronald Henkoff, "Checks, Lies and Videotape," *Fortune* (October 30, 1995), p. 110.
5. "ADM Informant Faces..." *Ibid.*, p. A 1.
6. "ADM and the FBI 'Scumbags'," *Fortune* (October 30, 1995), p. 116.

Whether the suicide attempt was genuine or contrived, Whitacre apparently faced a traumatic period in his life. He wound up in a suburban Chicago hospital with no job and no place to live. He had money problems, being unable to touch any of the funds in his overseas accounts. He and his wife had moved out of their $1.25 million estate near Decatur, Illinois, after contracting to buy a house near Nashville for $925,000. After the suicide attempt, they attempted to back out of the deal, only to be sued for breach of contract.

With all this, somehow Whitacre seemed to have landed on his feet by early October. True, he and his family were living in a rented house in the Chicago area, but he had become chief executive of Future Health Technologies, a startup biotechnology firm, at a six-figure salary comparable to what he earned legally at ADM.

THE ALLEGATIONS AGAINST THE COMPANY

By fall 1995, three grand juries were investigating whether ADM and some of its competitors conspired to fix prices. Three major product lines of ADM were allegedly involved: lysine, high-fructose corn syrup, and citric acid. Lysine is an amino-acid mixed with feed for hogs and chickens to hasten the growth of lean muscles in the animals. High-fructose corn syrup is a caloric sweetener used in soft drinks. Citric acid, like lysine, is a corn-derived product used in the detergent, food and beverage industries.

The importance of these products in the total product mix of ADM is indisputable. For example, while lysine is virtually unknown to the public, it is a key ingredient in the feed industry. About 500 million pounds are produced annually. Prices since 1961 have been averaging more than $1 a pound. So millions of dollars are at stake to manufacturers. With modern facilities at its sprawling complex in Decatur, Illinois, ADM can produce about half the world's purchases of lysine annually. And this is one of the company's highest profit products.

The sweetener, high-fructose corn syrup, is a major product for ADM, with a $3 billion-a-year market worldwide. Soft drinks account for more than 75 percent of annual production.

ADM entered the citric-acid business in 1991 when it acquired a unit of Pfizer. Today it is the primary U.S. maker of this additive. One of the largest customers is Procter & Gamble, which uses it for detergents.

As one example of the seemingly incriminating evidence of price fixing uncovered in videotapes, Michael Andreas is shown during a meeting he attended with lysine competitors at the Hyatt Regency Hotel at Los Angeles International Airport. There the participants discussed sales targets for each company as a means of limiting supply. This would destroy the free supply/demand machinations of the market and would permit prices to be kept artificially high, thus increasing the profits of the participants.[7] Although the evidence seemed to be substantial, still success at beating the

---

price-fixing charges might well depend on how well ADM could convince that Whitacre, the government's star witness, was a liar and a thief.

With the charges and countercharges of Whitacre and the company, investigations went beyond price-fixing to tax-evasion for high-level executives sanctioned by top management. Whitacre may have been the tip of the iceberg. The criminal-fraud division of the Justice Department began investigating whether the company illegally paid millions of dollars in off-the-books compensation to an array of company executives through foreign bank accounts. If so, then the culpability of Whitacre would be muted, and his value as a witness greatly enhanced.

It is worth noting the severity of the penalties if suits successfully come to pass. Fines for price fixing can range into the hundreds of millions of dollars, and some executives could even be given jail sentences. Furthermore, class-action suits by shareholders and customers can result in heavy damage awards. See the following Information Box for a discussion of the famous price-fixing conspiracy of 1959 that set the precedence for jail sentences for executives involved.

INFORMATION BOX

THE FAMOUS PRICE-FIXING CONSPIRACY OF 1959

In 1959, the biggest conspiracy of its kind in U.S. business history impacted the nation's thinking regarding business ethics.

Twenty-nine companies, including such giants as General Electric, Westinghouse, and Allis-Chalmers, were found guilty of conspiring to fix prices in deals involving about $7 billion of electrical equipment. The products involved in the conspiracy included power transformers, power switchgear assemblies, turbine generators, industrial control equipment, and circuit breakers. The companies were fined $1,924,500. Of particular note in this case, fifty-two executives (none of these top executives) were prosecuted and fined about $140,000. Even more startling, seven of the defendants received jail sentences. This was a first under federal antitrust laws.

On top of all that, almost 2,000 private-action, treble-damage cases were brought as a result of the court findings. In one of these alone, damages of $28,800,000 were awarded.

Incentives for the illegal actions stemmed from several sources. Without doubt, top management was exerting strong pressure on lower executives to improve their performance. Collusion with executives in other firms seemed to be a practical way to do this, especially in an environment rather blasé toward antitrust collusion. This attitude changed with the harsh penalties imposed by Judge J. Cullen Ganey.

INVITATION TO DISCUSS

Those executives who lost their jobs and went to jail were readily offered equivalent jobs in other corporations. The business community accepted them with open arms. Do you think they deserved such acceptance?

ADM AND DWAYNE ANDREAS

The story of Archer-Daniels-Midland Co. is really the story of its chairman, Dwayne O. Andreas. In 1947, ADM chairman, Shreve Archer, died after choking on a chicken bone. Dwayne Andreas was a vice-president at Cargill, a rival firm. For the next eighteen years he advanced steadily in the industry and became wealthy, while Archer-Daniels showed little growth. In 1966, at age forty-seven, Andreas was asked to become a director at ADM. The founding families sold him a sizable amount of stock and proposed to groom him for the top spot. Four years later, he was named chief executive officer.

In 1995, Andreas was still firmly in command and running the publicly traded company almost as a personal dynasty. In twenty-five years he had built up the firm into the nation's biggest farm-commodity processor, with $12.7 billion in annual revenue. Table 4.1 shows the steady growth of revenues since 1986, while Table 4.2 shows the growth of earnings, not quite as steady but still almost two and a half times greater than in 1986.

POLITICAL MANEUVERING

Although company headquarters were at Decatur, Illinois, Andreas's influence in Washington was probably unparalleled by any other business leader. ADM led corporate America in political contributions; it contributed hundreds of thousands of dollars to both parties. Furthermore, Andreas supported Jimmy Carter's campaign—ADM even bought his struggling peanut farm in 1981. But Andreas also contributed generously to Ronald Reagan and George Bush. During the Reagan years, when U.S. firms were entering the Soviet market, ADM was in the vanguard. Andreas became

TABLE 4.1   ADM Revenues, 1986–1995

Year ending June 30	Sales (millions)	Year-to-Year Percent Increase
1986	$5,336	
1987	5,775	10.8
1988	6,798	11.8
1989	7,929	11.6
1990	7,751	(2.2)
1991	8,468	9.3
1992	9,232	9.0
1993	9,811	6.5
1994	11,374	15.9
1995	12,672	11.4
1986–1995		137.5%

Source: Adapted from 1995 *ADM Annual Report.*

TABLE 4.2   ADM Net Earnings, 1986–1995

Year ending June 30	Earnings (millions)	Year-to-Year Percent Increase
1986	$230	
1987	265	15.2
1988	353	33.2
1989	425	20.3
1990	484	13.9
1991	467	(3.5)
1992	504	7.9
1993	568	12.7
1994	484	(14.8)
1995	796	64.5
1986–1995		246.1%

Source: Adapted from 1995 *ADM Annual Report.*

close to then-Soviet president, Mikhail Gorbachev. But as a hedge, he also courted Boris Yeltsin, Gorbachev's emerging rival.

Perhaps his greatest political supporter became Senator Robert Dole, who is from the farm state of Kansas. When Dole's wife, Elizabeth Dole, took over administration of the American Red Cross, Andreas donated $1 million to the cause. Dole also was given use of an ADM corporate plane, for which he paid the equivalent of a first-class ticket. An added factor in the friendship and rapport was the proximity of their vacation homes: Dole and his wife owned a unit in Sea View, Florida, as did David Brinkley, a renowned TV newsman, and Robert Strauss, an ADM board member, and, of course, Dwayne Andreas.[8] Interestingly, President Clinton also regarded Andreas as an ally.

Such political presence has brought great rewards to the company. ADM is a major beneficiary of federal price supports for sugar. Because such supports have kept sugar prices artificially high, ADM's sweetener, high-fructose corn syrup, has been attractive for giant companies such as CocaCola. Estimates are that fructose generates about 40 percent of ADM's earnings.[9]

Archer-Daniels also benefits from the 54-cent-a-gallon excise-tax break on ethanol, being the major producer of this corn-based fuel additive. Indeed, it is doubtful if the ethanol industry would exist without this tax break, and Bob Dole has been its most ardent congressional supporter.

Despite all the campaign contributions and personal rapport with the seats of power in Washington, Andreas and ADM have done little direct lobbying. Rather,

8. Reported in "How Dwayne Andreas Rules Archer-Daniels By Hedging His Bets," *Wall Street Journal* (October 27, 1995), p. A8.
9. *Ibid.*

such efforts have been done indirectly through various commodity and trade associations. For example, the American Peanut Shellers Association, with ADM support, handles the lobbying on peanut price supports.[10]

The Board of Directors

The investigations and the charges and countercharges drew fire from some of the major institutional holders of ADM stock. For example, the California Public Employees Retirement System—Calpers, as it is known, and owner of 3.6 million shares of Archer-Daniels—complained, charging that the board was too closely tied to Chairman and CEO Dwayne Andreas. "The ADM board is dominated by insiders, many of whom happen to be related to the CEO," Calpers complained. Calpers also criticized the ADM board for approving a 14 percent pay raise for Andreas, "rather than demand the CEO's resignation."[11] Other institutional investors also joined the criticisms: for example, the United Brotherhood of Carpenters, the Teamsters Union, and New York's major pension funds.

Shareholders had several other major criticisms of the board. It was supposed to authorize all capital expenditures above $250,000. The alleged claims for offshore pay were disguised as requests for spending on plant and equipment, and these the board passed with no hesitation. As to the charges of price-fixing and the allegations against major executives, the board was conspicuously uncritical, and finally made some token efforts to look further into the charges.

Brian Mulroney, former prime minister of Canada, co-chaired the special committee charged with coordinating the company's response to the federal investigations. One would think that part of his job was to safeguard the interests of shareholders. But major institutional shareholders doubted his objectivity, and noted his very close relations to Dwayne Andreas. Critics contended that what was needed was not a rubber-stamp special committee but "a team of experts to lead a full-blown, independent investigation."[12]

Regarding the composition of the board, critics seemed to have a case: the board was hardly objective and unbiased toward company top management; rather, it was highly supportive and dominated by insiders, many of whom were related to the CEO. For example, four of Archer-Daniels seventeen directors were members of the Andreas family. An additional six directors were retired executives or relatives of senior managers. The outside directors also had close connections to Andreas, such as Robert S. Strauss, the Washington lawyer whose firm represented ADM, and Mulroney, who was also with a law firm used by the firm. Even Harvard University Professor Ray Goldberg, a member of the board, had strong ties with Andreas, dating back to his dissertation.

---

10. *Ibid.*

11. Joann S. Lublin, "Archer-Daniels-Midland Is Drawing Fire from Some Institutional Holders," *Wall Street Journal* (October 11, 1995), p. A8.

12. Henkoff, p. 110.

While close bonds of boards with management are not unusual with many companies, such cozy relations can be detrimental to shareholders' best interests.

ANALYSIS

ADM's Conduct

Was ADM guilty of unethical conduct, and even illegalities? At the time this first was written, three grand juries were investigating the price fixing. The Department of Justice was looking into the tax-evasion charges. But nothing had been decided or proven. Perhaps ADM was guilty of price fixing, and perhaps not. Maybe the firm was guilty of nefarious practices to enable its high-level executives to avoid some income taxes through off-the-books compensation. If proven, such practices would not only be unethical, but also illegal and subject to harsh penalties.

Certain other activities of this giant company posed some ethical controversies even if they were not illegal—for example, packing the board with cronies dedicated to preserving the establishment at the expense of stockholders; the great quest for preferential treatment in the highest corridors of power; and just perhaps, the setting up of Whitacre. Let us examine these ethical issues.

Packing the board so that it is exceptionally supportive of the entrenched management may be condemned as not truly representing the rights of stockholders. But in its twenty-five years with Andreas at the helm, ADM's stock value rose at an annual average rate of 17 percent over the last decade. Few stockholders could dispute Andreas's contribution to the firm, even though they might fume at his riding roughshod over his critics—especially institutions holding large amounts of stock. Of course, if grand juries do return indictments, the autocratic tactics of Andreas will bring him down if it is proven that he knew of any such illegal activities.

Some would maintain that the courting of favoritism and special treatment from high-level Washington politicians may have gone too far. But should not any organization have the right to do its best to push for beneficial legislation and regulation? Of course, some will be more effective than others in doing so. Is this so much different from competition in the marketplace?

Whitacre's Role

Why did Whitacre choose to be a government mole? Still in his thirties, Whitacre had advanced to a high position in the company, with corresponding substantial compensation (enough to afford an estate valued at more than a million dollars), and who was at least one of the top candidates for the presidency of the firm. And yet he had been secretly taping supposedly illegal discussions. Why? What did he have to gain? There was so much to lose.

Added to this, he must have been a very capable executive, yet he was naive enough to leave himself vulnerable by accepting, and maybe even initiating, illegal scams through false invoices and overseas bank accounts. And he apparently naively confessed to a company lawyer his involvement as an informant for the FBI, not just recently but for three years. It doesn't make much sense, does it?

UPDATE

In October 1996, ADM pleaded guilty to criminal price-fixing charges and paid a record $100 million fine and nearly that amount again to settle lawsuits by customers and investors. But ADM's troubles were not ended.

Early in December 1996, a federal grand jury charged Michael Andreas, earning $1.3 million annually as the number-two executive at ADM and heir apparent to his father to run the company, and Terrance Wilson, former head of ADM's corn-processing division, with conspiring with Asian makers of lysine to rig the price of the livestock feed additive. Andreas took a leave of absence with full pay, and Wilson retired. It was thought that any conviction or guilty plea by Michael Andreas would destroy his chances of continuing his family's three-decade-long reign over ADM. However, Dwayne Andreas could yet preserve the patrimony: His nephew, G. Allen Andreas, a fifty-three-year-old lawyer, was one of three executives named to share Dwayne Andreas's responsibility in a newly formed office of chief executive.

In a surprising twist to the case, Mark Whitacre, the whistleblower, was also indicted.

The Verdict

The verdicts came in late 1998. After a week of deliberation in a two-month trial, the jury found Andreas, Wilson, and Whitacre guilty in a landmark price-fixing case, thereby giving the Justice Department its biggest convictions in a push against illegal global cartels. The federal prosecutors had been thwarted in how to rebuild the case after their mole, Whitacre, had been convicted of embezzle-ment and was already serving a nine-year prison sentence. The problem was solved by wringing confessions from Asian executives who were also involved in the conspiracy.

The bizarre behavior of Whitacre, after initially providing documentation of the birth of a price-fixing scheme, was unexpected and almost disastrous, and hard to explain even given that he was a big spender who openly pined to become president of ADM.

The End of the Andreas Dynasty

On August 13, 2001, ADM announced that Dwayne Andreas, eighty-three years old, was leaving its board and that his imprisoned son would not have a job there waiting for him. Five directors who had been handpicked by Andreas for their seats in the boardroom also were being ousted. His son, Michael Andreas, fifty-two, still serving a three-year sentence, agreed to repay $8 million of the legal expenses ADM accumulated defending him as the most prominent U.S. business executive ever sent to prison on price-fixing charges. "This closes a chapter on six difficult years," the company said.[13]

---

13. Scott Kilman, "ADM Says Ex-Chief Dwayne Andreas Will Leave Board," *Wall Street Journal* (August 13, 2001), p. A6.

WHAT CAN BE LEARNED?

Price fixing is one of the easiest cases to prosecute. Conspiracies to fix prices are direct violations of the Sherman Act. The government does not need to prove that competition was injured or that trade was restrained. All that needs to be proven is that a meeting took place with agreements to fix prices, bids, or allocate market share.

The penalties for price conspiracies have greatly increased since the celebrated electrical equipment industry conspiracy of 1959. Given the ease of prosecution, one would think that no prudent executive would ever take such a risk. Yet, there have been sporadic instances of price-fixing since then, and maybe we have it here with Michael Andreas, the son of Dwayne. Is there no learning experience?

Is political patronage necessary? We know that ADM sought political patronage and preferential treatment to an extraordinary degree—perhaps more than any other firm. Is this so bad?

Purists argue that this distorts the objectivity of our governmental institutions. Others say it is part of the democratic process in a pluralistic society. It might be so vital to our type of government that it cannot be eliminated—at best, can only be curbed.

On the other hand, it simply adds one more dimension to the competitive environment. Other firms can be invited to flex their muscles in the halls of government.

But when it comes to violations of the law, which supposedly reflects the wishes of society, then no firm is immune from the consequences. Even if its political patronage has been assiduously cultivated, it cannot escape the consequences of its illegal actions. The press, and the legal establishment, see to that.

Beware the "shareholder be damned" attitude. Some shareholders of ADM suspect that ADM had this attitude. As a consequence, the company faced at least two dozen shareholder lawsuits. As it approached the 1995 October annual meeting, nine big institutional investors announced plans to vote against reelecting ADM directors. But the move was largely symbolic, since their combined shares represented only 4.9 percent of the 505 million outstanding shares.[14] And their views received little attention in the meeting. Nor, apparently did those of other shareholders. The *Wall Street Journal* reported that at the meeting Andreas squelched criticisms of the issue of the antitrust probe and other allegations as he "summarily cut off a critic by turning off his microphone: 'I'm chairman. I'll make the rules as I go along,' Mr. Andreas said."[15]

A cozy relationship with the board encourages such attitudes. And when operating performance is continually improving, such shareholder criticisms may be seen as merely gnats striving for attention, and thus worthy of being ignored. If the top executive is inclined to be autocratic, then the environment is supportive.

14. "Probe Tears Veil of Secrecy at Archer Daniels Midland," *Cleveland Plain Dealer* (October 18, 1995), p. 3-C.
15. "How Dwayne Andreas Rules..." p. A1.

But is this wise? I think not. Should adversity set in, sometime in the future, then such attitudes toward investors can be self-destructive, even with a supportive board. If performance deteriorates, no board can maintain its sheeplike support for incumbent management, not in the face of vehement shareholders (especially large institutional investors) or major creditors.

But does adversity have to come? Only the profoundest optimist can think that success is forever. In ADM's case, adversity may be on the threshold, if Justice Department investigations result in grand jury indictments.

An organization's ethical tone is set by top management. If top management is unconcerned about ethical conduct, or if it is an active participant in less than desirable practices, this sets the tone throughout the organization. It promotes erosion of acceptable moral conduct in many areas of the operation. It becomes contagious as even those inclined to be more morally scrupulous join their colleagues. Then we have the "follow-the-leader" mindset.

In such an unhealthy environment, a few whistleblowers may arise and attempt to right the situation, often unsuccessfully and at great personal risk. Others who cannot tolerate the decline in moral standards, but don't have the courage to be whistleblowers, will leave the company. Almost inevitably, the misconduct will come to light, and repercussions of the severest kind result. Perhaps top management can escape the blame, though lower-level executives will be sacrificed. Occasionally, top management also comes under fire, and is forced to resign. Unfortunately, too often with healthy retirement benefits.

CONSIDER

Can you think of other learning insights?

QUESTIONS

1. What is your position regarding top management's culpability for the misdeeds of their subordinates?

2. Do you think ADM's efforts at gaining political favoritism went too far? Why or why not?

3. "If Dwayne's son is found guilty of price-fixing, there's no way that the big man himself cannot be found guilty." Evaluate this statement.

4. "With all the false invoices and persons involved in these millions of dollars of payouts off-the-books, there's no way the company could not have known what was going on." Evaluate.

5. Speculate on what would lead Whitacre to "betray" his company. If a number of possibilities are mentioned, which do you think is most compelling?

6. With the severe penalties and ease of prosecution of price-fixing cases, why would any firm or any executive attempt it today?

7. Why do you suppose, with all its efforts to gain preferential treatment through courting the mighty in government, ADM has not resorted to direct lobbying? Has it missed a golden opportunity to further its causes?

HANDS-ON EXERCISES

Before

1. Assume that Dwayne Andreas wants to maintain high ethical standards in his organization. Describe how he should go about this.

After

2. Assume that several key executives have indeed been found guilty of price-fixing; assume further that there are also indictments of illegal payments to certain executives. Further, the Senate ethics committee is investigating whether there have been improprieties in dealings with some members of Congress. How would you as CEO attempt damage control?

TEAM DEBATE EXERCISE

Debate the ethics of aggressively courting prominent politicians and government administrators. The two extreme positions would be: (1) going as far as you can short of being charged with outright bribery; (2) limiting relationship building to a few token contributions to trade association lobbying efforts.

INVITATION TO RESEARCH

Has ADM's public image been badly tarnished by all this publicity, or can you determine this? Has the firm continued to grow and prosper?

CHAPTER FIVE

Al Dunlap Savages Scott Paper and Sunbeam

$\mathbf{A}$l Dunlap was hired in July 1996 by two large Sunbeam investors to turn Sunbeam around. He had gained a reputation as a turnaround artist extraordinaire, most recently from his efforts at Scott Paper. His philosophy was to cut to the bone, and the press frequently called him "Chainsaw Al." But he met his comeuppance with Sunbeam. In the process, his philosophy came under bitter attack, as well as his character. How far do you cut into an organization, and to the living, breathing people involved, before you cross the line? Opinions may differ on this, but the telling blow was "cooking the books" to make his performance look far better than it really was.

ALBERT J. DUNLAP

Dunlap wrote an autobiography, *Mean Business: How I Save Bad Companies and Make Good Companies*, describing his business philosophy and how it had evolved. The book became a best seller. Dunlap grew up in the slums of Hoboken, New Jersey, the son of a shipyard worker, and was imbued with the desire to make something of himself. He played football in high school and graduated from West Point. A former army paratrooper, he was known as a quick hitter, a ruthless cost cutter, and a tough boss. But he got results, at least in the short term.

In 1983, Dunlap became chief executive of Lily Tulip Co., a maker of disposable cups that was heavily in debt after a buyout. Dunlap quickly exhibited the management philosophy that was to make him famous. He slashed costs, decimating the headquarters staff, closing plants, and selling the corporate jet. When he left in the mid-1980s, the company was healthy. In the latter 1980s, Dunlap became the number-one operations man for Sir James Goldsmith, a notorious raider of corporations. Dunlap was involved in restructuring Goldsmith's acquisitions of Crown-Zellerbach and International Diamond. In 1991, he worked on a heavily debt-laden Australian conglomerate, Consolidated Press Holdings. Two years later, after his "chainsaw approach," Consolidated Press was 100 divisions lighter and virtually free of debt.

By now Dunlap was a wealthy man, having made close to $100 million on his various restructurings. Still, at fifty-six, he was hardly ready to retire. When the board of Scott Paper heard that he was available, they wooed him, even purchasing his $3.2 million house in Florida from him.

SCOTT PAPER—A SICK COMPANY— AND DUNLAP'S RESULTS

An aged Scott Paper was reeling in the early 1990s. Per share earnings had dropped 61 percent since 1989 on flat sales growth. In 1993, the company had a $277 million loss.

Part of the problem stemmed from Scott's commercial paper division, S. D. Warren. In 1990, the company spent to increase capacity at Warren. Unfortunately, the timing could not have been worse. One of the worst industry slumps since the Great Depression was just beginning. Three subsequent "restructurings" had little positive effect.

Table 5.1 shows the decline in sales from 1990 through 1993. Table 5.2 shows the net income and loss during these four years. Of even more concern was Scott's performance relative to the major competitors Procter & Gamble and Kimberly-Clark during these four years. Table 5.3 shows the comparisons of profits as a percent of sales, with Scott again showing up most poorly. Undoubtedly this was a company needing fixing.

TABLE 5.1   Sales of Scott, 1990–1993 (billions)

1990	$3.9
1991	3.8
1992	3.9
1993	3.6
Total change, 1990–1993	(7.7%)

Source: Company annual reports.

Commentary: The company's deteriorating sales come at a time of great economic growth and advancing revenues for most firms.

TABLE 5.2   Net Income of Scott and Percent of Sales, 1990–1993

	(millions)	% of sales
1990	$148	3.8%
1991	(70)	(1.8)
1992	167	4.3
1993	(277)	(7.7)

Source: Company annual reports.

Commentary: The company's erratic profit picture, culminating in the serious loss of 1993, deserved deep concern, which it received.

TABLE 5.3   **Profit as a Percentage of Sales: Scott, Kimberly-Clark, and Procter & Gamble, 1990–1993**

	1990	1991	1992	1993
Scott	3.8%	(1.8%)	4.3%	(7.7%)
P&G	6.6	6.6	6.4	(2.1)°
Kimberly-Clark	6.8	7.5	1.9	7.3

Source: Company annual reports.

° Extraordinary charges reflecting accounting changes.

Commentary: Scott again shows up badly against its major competitors, both in the low percentage of earnings to sales and their severe fluctuations into earnings losses.

In characteristic fashion, Dunlap acted quickly once he took over as chief executive officer on April 19, 1994. That same day, to show his confidence and commitment, he invested $2 million of his own money in Scott. A few months later, after the stock had appreciated 30 percent, he invested another $2 million.

Only hours on the job, Dunlap offered three of his former associates top positions in the company. On the second day, he disbanded the powerful management committee. On the third day, he fired nine of the eleven highest ranking executives. To complete his blitzkrieg, on the fourth day he destroyed four bookshelves crammed with strategic plans of previous administrations.

Can such drastic and abrupt changes be overdone? Should change be introduced more slowly and with more reflection? See the Issue Box "How Soon to Introduce Drastic Changes" on the following page for a discussion of these questions.

At the annual meeting in June 1994, barely two months after assuming command, Dunlap announced four major goals for the first year. First, he vowed to divest the company of nonstrategic assets, most notably S. D. Warren, the printing and publishing papers subsidiary that had received major expansion funding only a few years before. Second, he would develop a core team of accomplished senior managers. Third, Scott was to be brought to "fighting trim" through a one-time-only global restructuring. Last, he promised to develop new strategies for marketing Scott products around the world.

In one of the largest relative restructurings in corporate America, more than 11,000 positions out of a total of 25,900 worldwide were eliminated. This included 71 percent of the headquarters staff, 50 percent of the salaried employees, and 20 percent of the production workers. Such draconian measures certainly cut costs. But were they overdone? Might such cuts potentially have detrimental long-term consequences? Please see the Issue Box "How Deep to Cut?" for a discussion of these topics.

In addition to cutting staff, Dunlap sought to reduce other costs, including outsourcing some operations and services. If these could be provided cheaper by other firms, then they should be farmed out. Dunlap announced that with the restructuring completed by year-end, pre-tax savings of $340 million were expected.[1]

1. *The New Scott 1994 Annual Report*, p. 5.

ISSUE BOX

HOW SOON TO INTRODUCE DRASTIC CHANGES?

Some new administrators believe in instituting major changes as quickly as possible. They reason that an organization is expecting this and is better prepared to make the adjustments needed than it ever will be again. Such managers are often referred to as gunslingers who "shoot from the hip." Other managers believe in moving more slowly, gathering more information, and taking action only when all the pros and cons can be weighed. But sometimes such delays can lull an organization into a sense of false calm, and make for even more trauma when the changes eventually come.

Relevant to the issue of moving swiftly or slowly is the health of the entity. If a firm is sick, in drastic need of help, we would expect a new manager to move more quickly and decisively. A firm doing well, although perhaps not as well as desired, reasonably should not require such drastic and abrupt disruption.

It has always baffled me how a fast-acting executive can acquire sufficient information to make the crucial decisions of who to fire and who to retain and what operations need to be pruned and which supported—all within a few days. Of course, operating statistics can be studied before formally taking charge. But the causes of the problems or successes—the whys—can hardly be understood so soon.

Boards, investors, and creditors want a fast turnaround. Waiting months before taking action to fix a sick company is not acceptable. However, not all companies are easily fixable; some can defy the best efforts of past and new managers.

INVITATION TO DISCUSS

Do you think Dunlap acted too hastily in his initial sweeping changes? Playing the devil's advocate (one who takes an opposing view for the sake of debate), support a position that he did indeed act far too hastily.

By late fall of 1994, Dunlap's plans to divest the company of nonstrategic assets bore fruit. S. D. Warren was sold for $1.6 billion to an international investment group. Other asset sales generated more than $2 billion. Dunlap was able to lower debt by $1.5 billion and repurchase $300 million of Scott stock. This led to the credit rating being upgraded.

The results of Dunlap's efforts were impressive indeed. Second-quarter earnings rose 71 percent; third-quarter earnings increased 73 percent, the best quarterly performance for Scott in four years. Fourth-quarter earnings were 159 percent higher than in 1993, establishing an all-time record. For the whole year, net income increased 82 percent over the previous year, and the stock price performance since Dunlap took over stood at the top one percent of major companies traded on the New York Stock Exchange.[2]

Still, the cost-slashing was not helping market share. In the fiscal year ended April 2, 1995, Scott's bath-tissue sales in key U.S. markets slipped 1 percent, while in paper towels, Scott lost 5.2 percent.[3]

2. *Ibid.*, p. 6.

3. Joseph Weber and Paula Dwyer, "Scott Rolls Out a Risky Strategy," *Business Week* (May 22, 1995), p. 45.

ISSUE BOX

HOW DEEP TO CUT?

Bloated bureaucratic organizations are the epitome of inefficiency and waste, whether in business corporations or in governmental bodies, including school systems. Administrative overhead might even exceed actual operating costs. But remedies can be overdone, they can go too far. In Scott's case, was the axing of 11,000 of 25,900 employees overdone?

Although we are not privy to the needed cost/productivity records, we can raise some concerns. Did the massive layoffs go well beyond fat and bloat into bone and muscle? If so, future operations might be jeopardized. Another concern ought to be: Does an organization owe anything to its loyal and long-standing employees, or should they simply be considered pawns in the pursuit of maximizing profits? Where do we draw the line between efficiency and responsibility to faithful employees? And even to the community itself?

INVITATION TO DISCUSS

You may want to consider some of these questions and issues. They are current in today's downsizing mindset.

On July 17, 1995, Dunlap's efforts to make Scott an attractive acquisition candidate were capped by Kimberly-Clark's $7.38 billion offer for the firm. In the process, Dunlap himself would be suitably rewarded, leaving far richer than after any of his seven previous restructuring efforts. But Dunlap insisted, "I am still the best bargain in corporate America."[4]

THE SUNBEAM CHALLENGE

Sunbeam was a maker of blenders, electric blankets, and gas grills. These old-line products had shown little growth, and revenues and profits languished. After Dunlap's well-publicized turnaround success at Scott, it was not surprising he was courted for the top job at Sunbeam, and he entered the fray with gusto.

The day he was hired, Sunbeam stock rose 50 percent, "on faith." It eventually rose 300 percent. With his customary modus operandi Dunlap terminated half of Sunbeam's 12,000 employees and cut back its product offerings. Gone were such items as furniture and bed linens, and efforts were concentrated on things like grills, humidifiers, and kitchen appliances. In 1996, he took massive write-offs amounting to $338 million, of which almost $100 million was inventory.

In 1997, it looked like Dunlap was accomplishing another of his patented "miracles." Sales were up 22 percent to $1.168 billion, while income had risen from a loss of $196 million the previous year to a gain of $123 million in 1997. For stockholders this translated into earnings per share of $1.41 from a $2.37 loss in 1996. Table 5.4 shows the trend in revenues and income of Sunbeam through 1997.

4. Joann S. Lublin and Steven Lipin, "Scott Paper's 'Rambo in Pin Stripes' Is on the Prowl for Another Company to Fix," *Wall Street Journal* (July 18, 1995), p. B1.

Table 5.4   **Trend of Sunbeam Revenues and Income 1991–1997 (in millions)**

	1991	1992	1993	1994	1995	1996	1997
Revenues	886	967	1,066	1,198	1,203	964	1,168
Net Income	47.4	65.6	88.8	107.0	50.5	−196.0	123.0

Sources: Company annual reports.

Commentary: Dunlap came on the scene in July 1996, the year that Sunbeam incurred $196 million in losses. The $123 million profit for 1997 showed a remarkable and awesome recovery, and would seemingly make Dunlap a hero with his slash-and-burn strategy. Unfortunately, a reaudit did not confirm these figures. The inaccurate figures were blamed on questionable accounting, including prebooking sales and incorrectly assigning costs to the restructuring. The auditors said the company overstated its loss for 1996, and overstated profits for 1997. The revised figures showed a loss of $6.4 million for 1997, instead of the $123 million profit. (*Sources:* Martha Brannigan, "Sunbeam Audit to Repudiate '97 Turnaround," *Wall Street Journal* (October 20, 1998), p. A3; "Audit Shows Sunbeam's Turnaround Really a Bust," *Cleveland Plain Dealer* (October 21, 1998), pp. 1C, 2C.)

In October 1997, barely a year on the job, Dunlap announced that the turn-around was complete and that he was seeking a buyer for Sunbeam. Stockholders had much to be pleased about. From a low of $12 a share in 1996, the price had risen to $50. Unfortunately, there was a serious downside to this, as Dunlap was soon to find: The high price for Sunbeam stock took it out of the range for any potential buyer; $50 gave a market capitalization of $4.6 billion, or four times revenues, a multiple reserved for only a few of the premier companies. So for the time being, the stock-holders were stuck with Dunlap.

Since he was not successful in selling the company, Dunlap went on a buying spree. He began talking about his "vision," with such words as "We have moved from constraining categories to expanding categories. Small kitchen appliances become kitchen appliances. We'll move from grills to outdoor cooking. Healthcare moves from just a few products to a broad range of products."[5]

So, Dunlap bought Coleman Company, Signature Brands and its Mr. Coffee, and First Alert for an aggregate of approximately $2.4 billion in cash and stock. Part of this was financed with $750 million of convertible debentures, as well as $60 million of accounts receivable that were sold to raise cash. Critics maintained he had paid too much for these, especially the $2.2 billion for money-losing Coleman. The effect of these acquisitions on Sunbeam's balance sheet was sobering if any stockholders looked closely.

When Dunlap took over Sunbeam, though it was performing poorly, it had only $200 million in debt. By 1998, Sunbeam was over $2 billion in debt, and its net worth had dropped from $500 million to a negative $600 million.[6]

---

5. As quoted in Holman W. Jenkins, Jr., "Untalented Al? The Sorrows of a One-Trick Pony," *Wall Street Journal* (June 24, 1998), p. A19.

6. Matthew Schifrin, "The Unkindest Cuts," *Forbes* (May 4, 1998), p. 45.

THE DEBACLE OF 1998, AND THE DEMISE OF DUNLAP

The first quarter of 1998 showed a complete reversal of fortunes. Revenues were down and a first-quarter loss was posted of $44.6 million—all this far below expectations. Sunbeam's stock price plunged 50 percent, from $53 to $25. By midsummer it was to reach a low of $4.62.

Dunlap conceded that he and top executives had concentrated their attention too much on "sealing" the acquisitions of Coleman and the two smaller companies, allowing underlings to offer "stupid, low-margin deals" on outdoor cooking grills. He pointed to glitches with new products, a costly recall, and even El Niño. "People don't think about buying outdoor grills during a storm," he said. "Faced with sluggish sales, a marketing executive offered excessive discounts," he further said. More job cuts were promised, through eliminating one-third of the jobs at the newly acquired companies.[7]

On Monday, June 15, 1998, after deliberating over the weekend, Sunbeam's board abruptly fired Al Dunlap, having "lost confidence in his ability to carry out the long-term growth potential of the company."[8] Now a legal fight ensued as to what kind of severance package, if any, Dunlap deserved as a consequence of his firing. A severance package for Dunlap would be "obscene—an obscenity on top of an obscenity, capitalism gone crazy," said union leader Michael Cavanaugh.[9] Other comments were reported in the media; a sampling is in the following Information Box.

Allegations of Fraud

At the end of a three-month audit after Dunlap's departure, auditors discovered accounting irregularities that struck down the amazingly high reported profits for 1997, the first full year of Dunlap's leadership. Rather than a turnaround, the good results came from improper accounting moves that adversely affected 1996 and 1998 results. The restated numbers showed that Sunbeam actually had a small operating loss in 1997, while 1996 showed a modest profit.

On May 15, 200l, the Securities and Exchange Commission (SEC) formally charged that Dunlap and some of his executives broke security laws to make Sunbeam look healthier and more attractive for a buyer. This was done by fraudulently shifting revenue to inflate losses under the old management and boosting income to create the false impression of the rapid turnaround in financial performance for 1997. Furthermore, revenue was increased in 1997 at the expense of future results by inducing retail customers to sell merchandise more quickly than normal, a practice known as channel stuffing. By the next year, the company was getting desperate to hide its mounting financial problems and misrepresented its performance and prospects in quarterly reports, bond offerings material, press releases, and statements

---

7. James R. Hagerty and Martha Brannigan, "Sunbeam Plans to Cut 5,100 Jobs as CEO Promises Rebound from Dismal Quarter," *Wall Street Journal* (May 12, 1998), pp. A3, A4.

8. Martha Brannigan and James Hagerty, "Sunbeam, Its Prospects Looking Ever Worse, Fires CEO Dunlap," *Wall Street Journal* (June 15, 1998), pp. A1, A14.

9. Martha Brannigan and Joann S. Lublin, "Dunlap Faces a Fight Over His Severance Pay," *Wall Street Journal* (June 16, 1998), p. B3.

INFORMATION BOX

THE POPULARITY OF "CHAINSAW" AL DUNLAP

Not surprising, the slashing policy of Dunlap did not bring him a lot of friends, even though he may have been admired in some circles. The following are some comments reported in the press immediately after his firing:

He finally got what he's been doing to a lot of people. It was a taste of his own medicine. (union representative)

I'm happy the son-of-a-bitch is fired. (former supervisor)

Somebody at that company finally got some sense. (small-town mayor)

I couldn't think of a better person to deserve it. It tickled me to death. We may need to have a rejoicing ceremony. (small-town mayor)

I guess the house of cards came tumbling down ... when you reduce your workforce by 50 percent, you lose your ability to manage. (former plant manager)

Is there a lesson to be learned from such comments as these? Perhaps it is that the human element in organizations and communities needs to be considered.

INVITATION TO DISCUSS

Taking a devil's advocate position (one who takes an opposing viewpoint for the sake of argument and full discussion), defend the philosophy of Dunlap.

Sources: Thomas W. Gerdel, "Workers at Glenwillow Plant Cheer Firing of 'Chainsaw' Al," *Cleveland Plain Dealer* (June 16, 1998), 2C; "No Tears for a Chainsaw," *Wall Street Journal* (June 16, 1998), p. B1.

---

to stock analysts. Dunlap denied any involvement or knowledge of such matters and that any accounting changes by the auditors were "judgment calls" on matters subject to interpretation.[10]

The company was forced to restate financial results for eighteen months, and it filed for bankruptcy protection in February 2001.

In early September 2002, Dunlap agreed to settle the suit by the SEC by paying $500,000 and agreeing never to be an officer or director of another public company. He neither admitted nor denied the SEC's claim that he masterminded the accounting fraud. A month earlier, Dunlap also paid $15 million in a settlement of a class-action suit filed by shareholders for their losses due to Sunbeam's fraudulent business practices.[11] All thoughts of a severance package for Dunlap after his firing were long forgotten.

---

10. Martha Brannigan, "Sunbeam Slashes Its 1997 Earnings in Restatement," *Wall Street Journal* (October 21, 1998), p. B23.

11. Jill Barton, Associated Press, as reported in "Sunbeam's 'Chain Saw Al' to Pay $500,000 Judgment," *Cleveland Plain Dealer* (September 5, 2002), p. C1.

The SEC came to believe there was funny accounting also at Scott Paper when Dunlap was running it. But this suspicion came at the height of the Enron furor, and the SEC had bigger game to pursue.[12]

ANALYSIS

Was Dunlap's Management Style of "Slash and Burn" Appropriate?

We see conflicting evidence in the Scott and Sunbeam cases. Without doubt, Dunlap achieved his goal to make Scott an attractive acquisition candidate, and thus reward shareholders and himself (although suspicions later arose that the sterling results may have been tainted). That he did this so quickly seemed at the time a strong endorsement of his strategy for turning around sick companies—simply decimate the organization, sell off all ancillary units, cut costs to the bone, and virtually force the company into increased profitability.

The flaw with this reasoning is that it tends to boost short-term performance at the expense of the longer term. Morale and dedication of surviving employees are destroyed. Vision and innovative thinking may be impaired since the depleted organization lacks time and commitment to deal effectively with more than day-to-day basic operations.

Dunlap's strategy backfired with Sunbeam. When he couldn't sell the company after manipulating the performance statistics for 1997, he was left with a longer-term management challenge that he was by no means equal to. It is ironic that the reputation for turning around sick companies acted against him with Sunbeam. Investors were so confident of his ability to quickly turn around the company that they bid the price up so high no other firm would buy it. And they were stuck with Dunlap.

Did the Adversity Require Such Drastic Changes?

Sales of both Scott and Sunbeam were flat, with profit performance deteriorating. Stock prices were falling counter to a bull market and investors were disillusioned. Did such situations call for draconian measures?

Neither company was in danger of going belly-up. True, they both were off the growth path, but their brands continued to be well regarded by consumers. On the other hand, many firms become too bureaucratic, burdened with high overhead and chained to established policies and procedures. Such organizations desperately need paring down, eliminating bloated staff and executive levels, and, not the least, curbing the red tape that destroys flexibility and creativity.

The best answer lies in moderation, cutting the deadwood, but not bone and muscle. The worst scenario is to cut with little investigation and reflection. This cost-cutting climate may degenerate to the extent that worthy operations and individuals are cut regardless of their merit and future promise. We would expect better long-term performance in an organization that is not decimated with shattered morale.

---

12. Floyd Norris, *New York Times,* as reported in "Fraud Surrounded 'Chainsaw Al', Yet Little Was Done," *Cleveland Plain Dealer* (September 8, 2002), p. G3.

Dunlap quickly sold off the S. D. Warren unit of Scott, and this added $1.6 billion to Scott coffers. Previous Scott management had invested heavily in what seemed a reasonable diversification into commercial paper, only to encounter an unexpected industry downturn. How could this have been predicted? Was Warren worth keeping? Research and investigation might have found that it was.

Creeping Bureaucracy

Bureaucratic excesses often come about after years of reasonable success and viability. Bureaucracy seemed to have been rampant at Scott. After all, Dunlap eliminated 71 percent of the headquarters staff and four bookshelves crammed with strategic plans of previous administrations. Too many administrators and staff people bring higher overhead costs than leaner competitors, thus placing the firm at a competitive disadvantage. Some pruning needed to be done.

Was the same thing true with Sunbeam? Perhaps not to the same extent, although without more specific information we cannot know for sure. We can suspect, however, that Dunlap, caught up in his success at Scott, simply transferred his strategy to Sunbeam with no consideration of their differences. We might call this "slashing by formula," and it suggests a rigid mindset devoid of flexibility or compassion.

Paying Too Much for Acquisitions

With Sunbeam, Dunlap made three questionable acquisitions, and burdened the firm with several billions of dollars of debt. In particular, the $2.2 billion paid for money-losing Coleman seemed another of Dunlap's "shooting from the hip" decisions. Such questionable research in acquisitions decisions followed the pattern of his personnel-slashing decisions and the quick sale of S. D. Warren. Furthermore, the reckless accumulation of debt for these acquisitions almost suggests a masochistic mindset. Or did Dunlap think that if the share price now dropped drastically, Sunbeam would become an attractive acquisition candidate?

Detection of Fraud Destroys Any Perception of Management Competence

Dunlap apparently had a long history of manipulating records to make himself look better, as we will further see in the following section. This fraud pales in comparison with the massive misdeeds of Enron, Tyco, WorldCom, and others, simply because Dunlap's were much smaller firms, but it can no more be condoned than those of the bigger firms. Dunlap could yet face jail time, should the SEC decide to turn its attention to less publicized cases.

LATER DEVELOPMENTS

Dunlap's exploits brought turmoil to the executive-search industry. It seems major search firms checking his employment history prior to being hired by Sunbeam failed to uncover that he had been fired from two previous positions. He was terminated at Max Phillips & Sons in 1973 after only seven weeks. Three years later, in 1976, he was fired as president of Nitec Paper Corp. under circumstances of alleged fraud involving misstated profits, a situation not unlike his departure from Sunbeam.

While these episodes took place twenty years before the recruiting for Scott Paper and Sunbeam and were apparently overlooked because of his supposedly strong track record in recent years, still significant and pertinent omissions in Dunlap's job history were not caught by search firms supposedly conducting thorough background checks. Along the way, Dunlap erased both jobs from his employment history, and no one who checked his background discovered the omissions.[13]

WHAT CAN BE LEARNED?

How to jumpstart a languid organization. Can we find any keys to stimulating an organization not performing up to potential? Or maybe even to inspire it to perform beyond its potential? The challenge is not unlike that of motivating a discouraged and downtrodden athletic team to rise up and have faith in itself and recommit itself to quality of performance.

In both athletics and business, the common notion is that personnel changes have to be made. Dunlap introduced the idea of severe downsizing. But this is controversial, and in view of Dunlap's problems with Sunbeam, now almost discredited. So how much should be cut, how quickly should changes be made and how sweeping should they be, and what kind of information is most vital in making such decisions? Furthermore, there is the question of morale and its importance in any restoration.

We find more art than science in this mighty challenge of restoration. In particular, the right blend or degree of change is crucial. Let us look at some considerations:

- How much do we trim? In most revival situations, some pruning of personnel and operations is necessary. But how much is too much, and how much is not enough? Is an ax always required for a successful turnaround? One would hope not. Certainly those personnel who are not willing to accept change may have to be let go. And weak persons and operations that show little probability of improvement need to be pruned, just as the athlete who can't seem to perform up to expectations may have to be let go. Still, it is often better to wait for sufficient information as to the "why" of poor performance, before assigning blame for the consequences.

- How long do we wait? Mistakes can be made both in taking action before all the facts are known and in waiting too long. If the changemaker procrastinates for weeks, an organization that at first was psychologically geared to major change might find it more traumatic and disruptive.

---

13. Joann S. Lublin, "Search Firms Have Red Faces in Dunlap Flop," *Wall Street Journal* (July 17, 2001), pp. B1, B4; Floyd Norris, "Uncovering Lost Years of Sunbeam's Fired Chief," *New York Times*, reported in *Cleveland Plain Dealer* (July 17, 2001), pp. C1, C4.

- What should be the role of strategic planning? Major actions should hardly be taken without some research and planning, but strategic plans too often delay change implementation. They tend to be the products of a fumbling bureaucracy and of some abdication of responsibility. (Despite the popularity of strategic planning, it often is a vehicle for procrastination and blame-dilution: e.g., "I simply followed the strategy recommendations of the consultants.") Dunlap had an aversion to strategic planning, seeing this as indicative of a top-heavy bureaucratic organization. Perhaps he was right on this, when it is carried to an extreme. But going into an organization and heedlessly slashing positions without due regard for the individuals involved and the potential is akin to "shooting from the hip," with little regard for careful aiming. Then there is the matter of morale.

- Morale considerations. Major restructuring usually is demoralizing to the organizations involved. The usual result is massive layoffs and forced retirements, complete reassignment of people, traumatic personnel and policy changes, and destruction of accustomed lines of communication and authority. This is hardly conducive to preserving stability and morale and any faint spark of teamwork.

Moderation is usually best. Much can be said for moderation, for choosing the middle position, for example, between heavy cost-cutting and little cost-cutting. Of course, the condition of the firm is a major consideration. One on the verge of bankruptcy, unable to meet its bills, needs drastic measures promptly. But the problems both of Scott and Sunbeam were by means so serious. More moderate action could have been taken.

It is better to view the restoration challenge as a *time for building rather than tearing down.* This focuses attention more on the longer view than on short-term results that may come back to haunt the firm, as well as the changemaker, like Dunlap.

Periodic housecleaning produces competitive health. In order to minimize the buildup of dead wood, all aspects of an organization periodically ought to be objectively appraised. Weak products and operations should be pruned, unless solid justification exists for keeping them. Such justification might include good growth prospects or complementing other products and operations or even providing a desired customer service. In particular, staff and headquarters personnel and functions should be scrutinized, perhaps every five years, with the objective of weeding out the redundant and superfluous. Most important, these "axing" evaluations should be done objectively, with decisive actions taken where needed. While some layoffs may result, they might not be necessary if suitable transfers are possible.

Ethical considerations should be involved in downsizing. The impact severe downsizing has on people and communities is usually overlooked in these decisions. They are considered subordinate to the best interests of the firm (and it's investors). Still we intuitively wonder if at the extremes of downsizing some ethical issues do not arise. Perhaps such issues should pertain not alone to the severity of the job cuts, but to how they are handled: For examples, Is the decision made with due research and reflection, or is it made quickly and ruthlessly, and perhaps by formula, such as cut 20 percent or 30 percent, or as was done, 50 percent of Sunbeam's employees? Is any attempt made to help fired employees find alternate employment or retraining? How fair is the severance package and/or notice of termination.

In Dunlap's handling of Scott Paper and Sunbeam, we see an absence of any humanity. This doesn't necessarily make his actions unethical in the eyes of many people, provided that the greater good of the business is fostered. Later developments, however, even denied that business benefit, as fraudulent accounting led to reported profitability during the Dunlap years, when there was none.

CONSIDER

Can you add any other learning insights?

QUESTIONS

1. "Periodic evaluations of personnel and departments aimed at pruning cause far too much harm to the organization. Such 'axing' evaluations should themselves be pruned." Argue this position as persuasively as you can.

2. Now marshal the most persuasive arguments for such "axing" evaluations.

3. Describe a person's various stages of morale and dedication to the company as it goes through a restructuring, with massive layoffs expected and realized, but with the person finding himself or herself one of the survivors. How, in your opinion, would this affect productivity and loyalty?

4. Is it likely that any decades-old organization will be bloated with excessive bureaucracy and overhead? Why or why not?

5. What decision guides should be used to determine which divisions and subsidiaries are to be divested or sold?

6. What arguments would you make in a time of restructuring for keeping your particular business unit? Which are likely to be most persuasive to an administration committed to a program of heavy pruning?

7. Do you see any ethical problems in heavy downsizing of a sick company? How about one not so sick?

HANDS-ON EXERCISES

1. You are one of the nine high-ranking executives fired by Dunlap his third day on the job. Describe your feelings and your action plan at this point. (If you want to make some assumptions, state them specifically.)

2. You are one of the two high-level executives kept by Dunlap as he sweeps into office. Describe your feelings and your likely performance on the job.

3. You are one of the three outsiders brought into Scott vice-presidential jobs by Dunlap. You have worked for him before and must have impressed him. Describe your feelings and your likely performance on the job. What specific problems, if any, do you foresee?

4. *Devil's advocate position.* Several board members are concerned about the ethical aspects of Dunlap's downsizing plans. Argue as persuasively as you can that they essentially are, at best, of questionable ethics.

TEAM DEBATE EXERCISE

1. It is early 1996. The board of Sunbeam is considering bringing in a turn-around team. One is the team of Dunlap, which argues for major and rapid change. Another team under consideration is Clarence Ripley's, who advocates more modest immediate changes. Array your arguments and present your positions as persuasively as possible. Attack the recommendations of the other side as aggressively as possible. We are talking about millions of dollars in fees and compensation at stake for the winning team.

2. Debate the issue of the ethics of Dunlap in his severe downsizing. (For the purpose of this debate, disregard the subsequent fraud charges from deceptive accounting.)

INVITATION TO RESEARCH

What is Dunlap up to after being fired by the Sunbeam board in mid-1998? Has he gracefully retired or is he running scared pending legal charges? Is he still fighting for severance pay? Who replaced Dunlap, and how well is he doing? Are his policies much different from Dunlap's?

CHAPTER SIX

United Way: A CEO Batters a Giant Nonprofit

*T*he United Way, the preeminent charitable organization in the United States, celebrated its 100-year anniversary in 1987. It had evolved from local community chests, and its strategy for fund-raising had proven highly effective: funding local charities through payroll deductions. The good it did seemed unassailable.

Abruptly in 1992, the image that United Way had created was jolted by revelations from investigative reporters of free-spending practices and other questionable deeds of its greatest builder and president, William Aramony. A major point of public concern was Aramony's salary and uncontrolled perks in a lifestyle that seemed inappropriate for the head of a charitable organization that depended mostly on contributions from working people.

We are left to question the callousness and lack of concern with the ethical impact on the public image of such a major charitable and not-for-profit entity. After all, unlike business firms that offer products or services to potential customers, charitable organizations depend on contributions that people give freely out of a desire to help society, with no tangible personal benefits. An image of high integrity and honest dealings without any semblance of corruption or privilege would seem essential for such organizations.

THE STATURE AND ACCOMPLISHMENTS OF THE UNITED WAY

For its 100th anniversary, then-President Ronald Reagan summed up what the United Way stood for in the letter on the following page.

Organizing the United Way as the umbrella charity to fund other local charities through payroll deductions established an effective means of fund-raising. As a not-for-profit entity, the United Way became the recipient of 90 percent of all charitable donations. It gained strong employer support by involving them as leaders of annual campaigns, amid widespread publicity. This would consequently cause such an executive acute loss of face if his or her own organization did not go "over the top" in meeting

December 10, 1986

United Way Centennial, 1887–1987
By The President Of The United States Of America
A Proclamation

Since earliest times, we Americans have joined together to help each other and to strengthen our communities. Our deep-roots spirit of caring, of neighbor helping neighbor, has become an American trademark—and an American way of life. Over the years, our generous and inventive people have created an ingenious network of voluntary organizations to help give help where help is needed.

United Way gives that help very well indeed, and truly exemplifies our spirit of voluntarism. United Way has been a helping force in America right from the first community-wide fund raising campaign in Denver, Colorado, in 1887. Today, more than 2,200 local United Ways across the land raise funds for more than 37,000 voluntary groups that assist millions of people.

The United Way of caring allows volunteers from all walks of life to effectively meet critical needs and solve community problems. At the centennial of the founding of this indispensable voluntary group, it is most fitting that we Americans recognize and commend all the good United Way has done and continues to do.

The Congress, by Public Law 99–612, has expressed gratitude to United Way, congratulated it, and applauded and encouraged its fine work and its goals.

NOW, THEREFORE, I RONALD REAGAN, President of the United States of America, by virtue of the authority vested in me by the Constitution and laws of the United States, do hereby proclaim heartfelt thanks to a century of Americans who have shaped and supported United Way, and encourage the continuation of its efforts.

IN WITNESS WHEREOF, I have hereunto set my hand this tenth day of December, in the year of our Lord nineteen hundred and eighty-six, and of the Independence of the United States of America the two hundred and eleventh.

Ronald Reagan

campaign goals. As a result, employers sometimes used extreme pressure to achieve 100 percent participation of employees. A local United Way executive admitted that "if participation is 100 percent, it means someone has been coerced."[1]

For many years, outside of some tight-lipped gripes of corporate employees, the organization moved smoothly along, with local contributions generally increasing every year, although the needs for charitable contributions invariably increased all the more.

1. Susan Garland, "Keeping a Sharper Eye on Those Who Pass the Hat," *Business Week* (March 16, 1992), p. 39.

The national organization, United Way of America (UWA), is a separate corporation and has no direct control over the approximately 2,200 local United Way offices. Most of the locals voluntarily contributed one cent on the dollar of all funds they collected. In return, the national organization provided training and promoted local United Way agencies through advertising and other marketing efforts.

Much of the success of the United Way movement in becoming the largest and most respected charity in the United States was due to the twenty-two years of William Aramony's leadership of the national organization. When he first took over, the United Ways were not operating under a common name. He built a nationwide network of agencies, all operating under the same name and using the same logo of outstretched hands, which became nationally recognized as the symbol of charitable giving. Unfortunately in 1992, an exposé of Aramony's lavish lifestyle as well as other questionable dealings led to his downfall and burdened local United Ways with serious difficulties in fund-raising.

WILLIAM ARAMONY

During Aramony's tenure, United Way contributions increased from $787 million in 1970 to $3 billion in 1990. He increased his headquarters budget from less than $3 million to $29 million in 1991. Of this, $24 million came from the local United Ways, with the rest coming from corporate grants, investment income, and consulting. He built up the headquarters staff to 275 employees.[2]

Aramony moved comfortably among the most influential people in our society. He attracted a prestigious board of governors, including many top executives from America's largest corporations, but only three of the thirty-seven came from not-for-profit organizations. The board was chaired by John Akers, chairman and CEO of IBM. Other board members included Edward A. Brennan, CEO of Sears; James D. Robinson III, CEO of American Express; and Paul J. Tagliabue, commissioner of the National Football League. The presence of such top executives brought prestige to United Way and spurred contributions from some of the largest and most visible organizations in the United States.

Aramony was the highest paid executive in the charity field. In 1992, his compensation package was $463,000, nearly double that of the next highest paid executive in the industry, Dudley H. Hafner of the American Heart Association. The board fully supported Aramony, regularly giving him 6 percent annual raises.[3]

Investigative Disclosures

The *Washington Post* began investigating Aramony's tenure as president of United Way of America in 1991, raising questions about his high salary, travel habits, possible cronyism, and dubious relations with five spin-off companies. In February 1992, it released the following information on Aramony's expense charges:[4]

2. Charles E. Shepard, "Perks, Privileges and Power in a Nonprofit World," *Washington Post* (February 16, 1992), p. A38.

3. Joseph Finder, "Charity Case," *New Republic* (May 4, 1992), p. 11.

4. Shepard, "Perks, Privileges, and Power"; Kathleen Telstch, "United Way Awaits Inquiry on its President's Practices," *New York Times* (February 24, 1992), p. A12 (L).

- Aramony had charged $92,265 in limousine expenses to the charity during the previous five years.

- He had charged $40,762 on airfare for the supersonic Concorde.

- He had charged more than $72,000 on international airfare that included first-class flights for himself, his wife, and others.

- He had charged thousands more for personal trips, gifts, and luxuries.

- He had made twenty-nine trips to Las Vegas, Nevada, between 1988 and 1991.

- He had expensed forty-nine journeys to Gainesville, Florida, the home of his daughter and a woman with whom he had had a relationship.

- He had allegedly approved a $2 million loan to a firm run by his chief financial officer.

- He had approved the diversion of donors' money to questionable spin-off organizations run by long-time aides and provided benefits to family members as well.

- He had passed tens of thousands of dollars in consulting contracts from the UWA to friends and associates.

United Way of America's corporate policy prohibited the hiring of family members within the actual organization, but Aramony skirted the direct violation by hiring friends and relatives as consultants and within the spin-off companies. He paid hundreds of thousands of dollars in consulting fees, for example, to two aides in vaguely documented and even undocumented business transactions.

The use of spin-off companies provided flexible maneuvering. One of the spin-off companies Aramony created to provide travel and bulk purchasing for United Way chapters purchased a $430,000 condominium in Manhattan and a $125,000 apartment in Coral Gables, Florida, for Aramony's use. Another of the spin-off companies hired Aramony's son, Robert Aramony, as its president. Loans and money transfers between the spin-off companies and the national organization raised questions. No records showed that the board of directors had been given the opportunity to approve such loans and transfers.[5]

CONSEQUENCES

When the information about Aramony's salary and expenses became public, reaction was severe. Stanley C. Gault, chairman of Goodyear Tire & Rubber Co., asked, "Where was the board? The outside auditors?" Robert O. Bothwell, executive director of the National Committee for Responsive Philanthropy, said, "I think it is obscene that he is making that kind of salary and asking people who are making $10,000 a year to give 5 percent of their income."[6] At this point let us examine the issue of executive

5. Shepard, "Perks, Privileges, and Power," p. A38.

6. Susan Garland, p. 39; Felicity Barringer, "United Way Head Is Forced Out in a Furor Over His Lavish Style," *New York Times* (February 28, 1992), p. A1.

compensation. Are many executives overpaid? See the Issue Box, "Executive Compensation: Is It Too Much?"

As a major consequence of the scandal, some United Way locals withheld their funds, at least pending a thorough investigation of the allegations. John Akers, chairman of the board, noted that by March 7, 1992, dues payments were running 20 percent behind the previous year, saying "I don't think this process that the United Way of America is going through, or Mr. Aramony is going through, is a process that's bestowing a lot of honor."[7]

In addition to the decrease in dues payments, UWA was in danger of having its not-for-profit status revoked by the Internal Revenue Service due to the relationship of loans made to the spin-off companies. For example, it loaned $2 million to a spin-off

---

ISSUE BOX

EXECUTIVE COMPENSATION: IS IT TOO MUCH?

At the time of criticisms of United Way's Aramony, controversy began mounting over multi-million-dollar annual compensations of corporate executives. For example, in 1992, the average annual pay of CEOs was $3,842,247; the twenty highest salaries ranged from over $11 million to a mind-boggling $127 million (for Thomas F. Frist, Jr., of Hospital Corporation of America).[8] Pay of corporate executives has continued to climb robustly since 1992.

Activist shareholders, including some large mutual and pension funds, began protesting the high compensations, especially for top executives of firms that were not even doing well. New disclosure rules imposed in 1993 by the Securities and Exchange Commission (SEC) spotlighted questionable executive pay practices. In the past—and still not uncommon today—complacent boards, themselves well paid and often closely aligned with the top executives of the organization, condoned liberal compensations. The major argument supporting high executive compensations is that compared with salaries of some entertainers and athletes, they are modest. And are their responsibilities not far greater than those of any entertainer or athlete?

In light of the for-profit executive compensations, Aramony's salary was modest. And results were on his side: He made $369,000 in basic salary while raising $3 billion; Lee Iacocca, on the other hand, made $3 million while Chrysler lost $795 million. Where is the justice?

Undoubtedly Aramony, as head of a large for-profit corporation, could have earned several zeros more in compensation and perks, with no raised eyebrows. But is the situation different for a not-for-profit organization, especially when revenues are derived from donations of millions of people of modest means? This is a real controversy. On one side, shouldn't a charity be willing to pay for the professional competence to run the organization as effectively as possible? But how do revelations of high compensation affect the public image and fund-raising ability of such not-for-profit organizations?

INVITATION TO DISCUSS

What is your position regarding Aramony's compensation and perks, relative to the many times greater compensation of for-profit executives?

---

7. Felicity Barringer, "United Way Head Tries to Restore Trust," *New York Times* (March 7, 1992), p. 8L.

8. John A. Byrne, "Executive Pay: The Party Ain't Over Yet," *Business Week* (April 26, 1993), pp. 56–64.

corporation of which the chief financial officer of UWA was also a director, this being a violation of not-for-profit corporate law. UWA also guaranteed a bank loan taken out by one of the spin-offs, also a violation of not-for-profit corporate law.[9]

The adverse publicity benefited competing charities, such as Earth Share, an environmental group. United Way, at one time the only major organization to receive contributions through payroll deductions, now found itself losing donations to other charities able to garner contributions in the same manner. All the building that William Aramony had done for the United Way as the primary player in the American charitable industry was now in danger of disintegration because of his uncontrolled excesses.

On February 28, amid mounting pressure from local chapters threatening to withhold their annual dues, Aramony resigned. In August 1992, the United Way board of directors hired Elaine Chao, the Peace Corps director, to replace Aramony.

Elaine Chao

Chao's story was one of great achievement for one only thirty-nine years old. She was the eldest of six daughters in a family that came from Taiwan to California when Elaine was eight years old. She did not know a word of English. Through hard work, the family prospered. "Despite the difficulties ... we had tremendous optimism in the basic goodness of this country, that people are decent here, that we would be given a fair opportunity to demonstrate our abilities," she told an interviewer.[10] Chao's parents instilled in their six daughters the conviction that they could do anything they set their minds to, and all the daughters went to prestigious universities.

Elaine Chao earned an economics degree from Mount Holyoke College in 1975, then went on for a Harvard MBA. She was a White House fellow, an international banker, chair of the Federal Maritime Commission, deputy secretary of the U.S. Transportation Department, and director of the Peace Corps before accepting the presidency of the United Way of America.

Her salary was $195,000, less than one-half of Aramony's. She cut budgets and staffs: no transatlantic flights on the Concorde, no limousine service, no plush condominiums. The board of governors was expanded to include more local representatives and she established committees on ethics and finance. Still, Chao had no illusions about her job: "Trust and confidence once damaged will take a great deal of effort and time to heal."[11] The Information Box, "Public Image," discusses the particular importance of the public image for not-for-profit agencies.

Local United Way's Concerns

In April 1993, for the second time in a year, United Way of Greater Lorain County (Ohio) withdrew from the United Way of America. The board of the local chapter was still concerned about the financial stability and accountability of the national agency. In particular, it was concerned about the retirement settlement for Aramony. A significant "golden parachute"

9. Shepard, "Perks, Privileges, and Power"; Charles E. Shepard, "United Way Chief Says He Will Retire," *Washington Post* (February 28, 1992), p. A38.
10. "United Way Chief Dedicated," *Cleveland Plain Dealer* (March 28, 1993), p. 24A.
11. *Ibid.*

INFORMATION BOX

PUBLIC IMAGE FOR NOT-FOR-PROFIT ORGANIZATIONS

Product-oriented firms ought to be concerned and protective of their public image; even more so not-for-profit organizations such as schools, police departments, hospitals, politicians, and most of all, charitable organizations should be concerned. Let us consider the importance of public image for representative not-for-profits.

Large city police departments often have a poor image among important segments of the population. The need to improve this image is hardly less important than for a manufacturer faced with a deteriorating brand image. A police department can develop a campaign to win friends; examples of possible activities aimed at creating a better image are promoting tours and open houses of police stations, crime laboratories, police lineup, and cells; speaking at schools; and sponsoring recreation projects, such as a day at the ballpark for youngsters.

Public school systems, faced with taxpayers' revolts against mounting costs and image damage owing to teacher strikes, need conscious effort to improve their image in order to obtain more public support and funds.

Many nonbusiness organizations and institutions, such as hospitals, governmental bodies, even labor unions, have grown self-serving, dominated by a bureaucratic mentality so that perfunctory and callous treatment is the rule and the image is in the pits. Improvement of the image can only come through greater emphasis on satisfying the public's needs.

Not-for-profits are particularly vulnerable to public image problems because they depend solely on voluntary support. The need to be untainted by any scandal becomes crucial. In particular, great care should be exerted that contributions are being spent wisely and equitably, that overhead costs are kept reasonable, and that no opportunities exist for fraud and other misdeeds. The threat of investigative reporting must be feared and guarded against.

INVITATION TO DISCUSS

How can a not-for-profit organization be absolutely assured that moneys are not being misspent, and that there are no ripoffs?

retirement package was being negotiated by the national board and Aramony; it was in the neighborhood of $4 million. Learning of this triggered the Lorain County board's decision to again withdraw from UWA.

There were other reasons as well for this decision. The national agency was falling far short of its projected budget because only 890 of the 1,400 affiliates that had paid membership dues two years before were still paying. Roy Church, president of the Lorain agency, explained the board's decision: "Since February ... it has become clear that United Way of America's financial stability and ability to assist locals has been put in question. The benefit of being a United Way of America member isn't there at this time for Lorain's United Way."[12]

Elaine Chao's task of resurrecting United Way of America would not be easy.

12. Karen Henderson, "Lorain Agency Cuts Ties with National United Way," *Cleveland Plain Dealer* (April 16, 1993), p. 7C.

ANALYSIS

The lack of accountability to the donating public was a major contributor to the UWA's problems. Such a loosely run operation, with no one to approve or halt administrators' actions, encouraged questionable practices. It also opened the way for great shock and criticism, come the revelation. The fact that voluntary donations were the principal source of revenues made the lack of accountability all the more crucial. In a for-profit organization, lack of accountability affects primarily stockholders; for a major charitable organization, it affects million of contributors, who see their money and/or commitment being squandered.

Where full disclosure and a system of checks and balances is lacking, the organization invites vulnerability on two fronts. The worst-case scenario is outright "white-collar theft," when unscrupulous people find it an opportunity for personal gain. The absence of sufficient controls and accountability can make even normally honest persons succumb to some temptation. Second, insufficient controls tend to promote a mindset of arrogance and allow people to play fast-and-loose with the system. Aramony seemed to fall into this category with his spending extravagances, cronyism, and other conflict-of-interest activities.

The UWA theoretically had an overseer: the boards, similar to the board of directors of business corporations. But when such boards act as rubber stamps, where they are closely in the camp of the chief executives, they are not really exercising control. This appeared to be the case with United Way of America during the "reign" of Aramony.

Certainly a board's failure to fulfill its responsibility is not unique to not-for-profits. Corporate boards have often been notorious for promoting the interests of the incumbent executives. Although this situation of compliant boards has received some publicity and criticism of late, and is changing in some organizations, it still prevails in others. See the Issue Box, "Role of the Board of Directors," for a discussion.

UPDATE

William Aramony was convicted of defrauding the United Way out of $1 million. He was sentenced to seven years in prison for using the charity's money to finance a lavish lifestyle.

Despite this, a federal judge ruled in late 1998 that the charity must pay its former president more than $2 million in retirement benefits. "A felon, no matter how despised, does not lose his right to enforce a contract," U.S. District Judge Shira Scheindlin in New York ruled.[13]

WHAT CAN BE LEARNED?

Beware the arrogant mindset. A leader's mindset that he or she is superior to subordinates and even to concerned outsiders—that other opinions are not acceptable—

13. Reported in *Cleveland Plain Dealer* (October 25, 1998), p. 24A.

ISSUE BOX

WHAT SHOULD BE THE ROLE OF
THE BOARD OF DIRECTORS?

In the past, most boards of directors have tended to be closely allied with top executives and even composed mostly of corporate officials. In some organizations today this is changing, mostly in response to critics concerned about board tendencies to support the status quo and perpetuate the "establishment."

More and more, opinion is shifting to the idea that boards must assume an active role:

> The board can no longer play a passive role in corporate governance. Today, more than ever, the board must assume an activist role—a role that is protective of shareholder rights, sensitive to communities in which the company operates, responsive to the needs of company vendors and customers, and fair to its employees.[14]

Incentives for more active boards have been the increasing risks of liability for board decisions as well as liability insurance costs. Although the board of directors has long been seen as responsible for establishing corporate objectives, developing broad policies, and selecting top executives, these duties are no longer viewed as sufficient. Boards must also review management's performance—acting as a control mechanism—to ensure that the company is well run and that stockholders' interests are furthered. And, today, they must ensure that society's best interests are not disregarded. All of this translates into an active concern for the organization's public image or reputation—its ethical conduct.

But the issue remains: To whom should the board owe its greatest allegiance—the entrenched bureaucracy or the external publics? Without having board members representative of the many special interests affected by the organization, the inclination is to support the interests of the establishment.

INVITATION TO DISCUSS

Do you think a more representative and activist board will prevent a similar scenario from damaging United Way in the future? Why or why not?

---

is a formula for disaster, both for an organization and for a society. It promotes dictatorship, intolerance of contrary opinions, and an attitude that "we need answer to no one." The consequences are such as we have seen with William Aramony: moving over the edge of what is deemed by most as acceptable and ethical conduct, assuming the role of the final authority who brooks no questions or criticisms. The absence of real or imagined controls or reviews seems to bring out the worst in humans. We seem to need periodic scrutiny to avoid falling into the trap of arrogant decision-making devoid of responsiveness to other concerns.

Checks and balances—controls—are even more important in not-for-profit and governmental bodies than in corporate entities. For-profit organizations have

14. Lester B. Korn and Richard M. Ferry, *Board of Directors Thirteenth Annual Study* (New York: Korn/Ferry International, February 1986), pp. 1–2.

"bottom-line" performance (i.e., profit and loss performance) as the ultimate control and standard. Not-for-profit and governmental organizations do not have this control, so they have no ultimate measure of their effectiveness.

Consequently, not-for-profit organizations should be subject to the utmost scrutiny of objective outsiders. Otherwise, abuses seem to be encouraged and perpetuated. Often these not-for-profit organizations are sheltered from competition, which usually also demands greater efficiency. Thus without objective and energetic controls, not-for-profit organizations have a tendency to be out of hand, to be run as little dynasties unencumbered by the constraints that face most businesses. Fortunately, investigative reporting and increasing litigation by allegedly abused parties today act as the needed controls for such organizations. In view of the revelations of investigative reporters, we are left to wonder how many other abusive and reprehensible activities have not as yet been detected.

Marketing of not-for-profits depends on trust and is particularly vulnerable to bad press. Not-for-profits depend on donations for the bulk of their revenues. They depend on people to give without receiving anything tangible in return (unlike businesses). And the givers must have trust in the particular organization, trust that the contributions will be well spent, that the beneficiaries will receive maximum benefit, and that administration costs will be low. Consequently, when publicity surfaces that causes such trust to be questioned, the impact can be devastating. Contributions can quickly dry up or be shunted to other charities.

With governmental bodies, of course, their perpetuation is hardly at stake with bad publicity. However, officials can be recalled, impeached, or not reelected.

CONSIDER

Can you add to these learning insights?

QUESTIONS

1. How do you feel, as a potential or actual giver to United Way campaigns, about the "high living" of Aramony? Would these allegations affect your gift giving? Why or why not?

2. What prescriptions do you have for thwarting arrogance in nonprofit and/or governmental organizations? Be as specific as you can, and support your recommendations.

3. How do you personally feel about the coercion that some organizations exert for their employees to contribute substantially to the United Way? What implications, if any, do you see as emerging from your attitudes about this?

4. "Since there is no bottom-line evaluation for performance, nonprofits have no incentives to control costs and prudently evaluate expenditures." Discuss.

5. How would you feel, as a large contributor to a charity, about its spending $10 million for advertising? Discuss your rationale for this attitude.

6. Do you think the action taken by UWA after Aramony was the best way to salvage the public image? Why or why not? What else might have been done?

INVITATION TO ROLE PLAY

1. You are an advisor to Elaine Chao, who has taken over the scandal-ridden United Way. What advice would you give her for as quickly as possible restoring the confidence of the American public in the integrity and worthiness of this preeminent national charity organization?

2. You are a member of the board of governors of United Way. Allegations have surfaced about the lavish life style of the highly regarded Aramony. Most of the board, being corporate executives, see nothing at all wrong with his perks and privileges. You, however, feel otherwise. How would you convince the other members of the board of the error of condoning Aramony's activities? Be as persuasive as you can in supporting your position.

TEAM DEBATE EXERCISE

Debate this issue: No not-for-profit organization can ever attain the efficiency of a business firm that always has the bottom line to be concerned about.

INVITATION TO RESEARCH

What is the situation with United Way today? Are local agencies contributing to the national? Have donations matched or exceeded previous levels? Has Elaine Chao restored confidence? What is Elaine Chao doing now?

CHAPTER SEVEN

Tobacco: Long Callousness to Public Health

Cigarettes are among the world's most profitable consumer products. A cigarette "costs a penny to make, sell it for a dollar, it's addictive, and there's fantastic brand loyalty." So said master investor Warren Buffett as he unsuccessfully sought to take over RJR Nabisco, the tobacco conglomerate.[1] Perhaps because of its profitability, the morality of the business has long been suspect.

Criticisms have accelerated in recent years and bans widely imposed. Still, the tobacco industry remained stubbornly focused on its own best interests. That most critics saw tobacco's best interests as diametrically opposed to society's best interests mattered little to the industry as it aggressively struck back at critics.

Near the end of the old millennium, lawsuits began to show some fruit and their potential increased. Finally, in November 1998, a tobacco deal was agreed upon between the industry and forty-six states to settle state lawsuits filed to recover Medicaid money spent treating diseases related to smoking. Some said the industry got off far too easy, as this seemingly ended the largest-ever legal and financial threat to the industry. But other threats were on the horizon.

Philip Morris has been the dominant player in this industry, the one most obdurate in self interest. Now its position seems to be changing as the environment has changed.

PAST CONTROVERSIAL STRATEGIES IN A SHRINKING MARKET

Targeting Minorities

Uptown

This new cigarette was packaged in a showy black-and-gold box and was the first cigarette aimed specifically at African American smokers. It followed the new strategy of tobacco companies to introduce new brands directed to specific groups, such as women. Now, using careful research and design, everything about Uptown was tailored to black consumers. The results were a surprise.

1. "The Tobacco Trade: The Search for El Dorado," *Economist* (May 16, 1992), p. 21.

79

A storm of protests quickly ensued. Critics maintained that the marketing of Uptown represented a cold-blooded targeting of blacks, who already suffered a lung cancer rate 58 percent higher than whites. The protests even reached the office of Louis Sullivan, the Secretary of Health and Human Services. He quickly sided with the critics: "Uptown's message is more disease, more suffering, and more death for a group already bearing more than its share of smoking-related illness and mortality." He condemned "the attempts of tobacco merchants to earn profits at the expense of the health and well-being of our poor and minority citizens."[2]

Given the virulence of the protests, R. J. Reynolds abandoned the brand, bitterly decrying the negative attention being focused on it "by a few zealots." The critics had won, this time.

Dakota

Another new cigarette, also targeted to a specific group, was beset with controversy. Dakota was aimed at "virile females," non-college-educated women age 18–24 with blue-collar jobs. Critics of tobacco's relationship with lung cancer and heart disease were quick to attack this as a nefarious appeal to women.[3]

Another group was especially upset. In some Native American languages, *dakota* means "friend." Yet, to a group that already had high rates of smoking addiction, such a brand name seemed a betrayal.

Controversies over Tobacco Company Sponsorships

Following the 1971 federal ban on cigarette advertising on TV and radio, tobacco companies desperately sought other media to place their hundreds of millions of advertising dollars. By the early 1990s, serious questions were raised about their use of certain media, such as billboards, promoting smoking and alcohol in African American neighborhoods.

Advertising support of black publications by tobacco companies also came under fire, even though few other major firms were advertising in black media. Many small minority publications would have folded without the advertising dollars of tobacco companies.

Tobacco company support for minority organizations also began to be questioned. The National Association of Black Journalists turned down a Philip Morris donation: "We couldn't take money from an organization deliberately targeting minority populations with a substance that clearly causes cancer," said the group's president.[4]

The tobacco industry also liberally provided money to women's sports at a time when other money sources were virtually nonexistent. For example, Virginia Slims' funding brought women's tennis into prominence. The controversy concerning this is discussed in the following Issue Box.

---

2. Ben Wildavsky, "Tilting at Billboards," *New Republic* (August 20, 1990), p. 19.

3. Paul Cotton, "Tobacco Foes Attack Ads That Target Women, Minorities, Teens and the Poor," *Journal of the American Medical Association* (September 26, 1990), p. 1505.

4. *Ibid.*, p. 1506.

ISSUE BOX

TOBACCO COMPANY SPONSORSHIP OF ATHLETIC EVENTS

Is it right to allow tobacco companies to sponsor certain athletic events? What seems like a simple question becomes far more complex when we consider tennis tournaments such as Virginia Slims. There is no longer any doubt that smoking causes serious damage to heart and lungs, yet tennis requires top physical fitness and aerobic capacity.

Such sponsorship had particular advantages from the industry's perspective. It created the false association of smoking with vitality and good health, and it directly targeted women. Philip Morris essentially was taking advantage of the inadequate funding of women's sports by making itself a strong presence in this sector.

So we have an unhealthy product sponsoring a prestigious athletic event for women, an event that at least in the early days, would probably not have been able to get started without such funding. Do we refuse this funding? Do we ban all cigarette promotions that appear to have some tie-in with health and fitness? Does the evil outweigh the good?

INVITATION TO DISCUSS

You are a feminist leader with convictions that women's athletic events should be promoted more strongly. The major funding for tennis and golf tournaments has been the tobacco industry, with no alternative major sponsors likely in the near future. Discuss your position regarding accepting such tobacco company sponsorships. Present your rationale as persuasively as you can.

The Old Joe Camel Controversy

In 1988, R. J. Reynolds stumbled upon a promotional theme for its slumping Camel brand. Using a sunglasses-clad, bulbous-nosed cartoon camel that it called Joe, the company instituted a $75 million-a-year advertising campaign. It featured Joe in an array of macho gear and targeted the campaign to appeal to younger male smokers who had been deserting the Camel brand in droves.

The campaign was an outstanding success. In only three years, Camel's share of sales among the eighteen to twenty-four age group almost doubled, from 4.4 percent to 7.9 percent.

But the appeal of Old Joe went far beyond the target age group. It was found to be highly effective in reaching children under thirteen, who were enamored with the character. Six-year-olds in the United States recognized Joe Camel at a rate nearly equal to their recognition of Mickey Mouse. Children as young as three could even identify the cartoon character with cigarettes. Of even more concern to critics, Camel's share of the market of underage children who smoke was nearly 33 percent, up from less than 1 percent before the Old Joe campaign. See Table 7.1 for other results of the survey.

TABLE 7.1 Survey Results of Knowledge and Attitudes Regarding Camel's Old Joe Advertisements

	Students	Adults
Have seen Old Joe	97.7%	72.2%
Know the product	97.5	67.0
Think ad looks cool	58.0	39.9
Like Joe as a friend	35.0	14.4
Smokers who identify Camel as a favorite brand	33.0	8.7

Source: Data from the *Journal of the American Medical Association*, as presented in Walecia Konrad, " I'd Toddle a Mile for a Camel," *Business Week* (December 23, 1991), 34. The results are based on a survey of 1,055 students, ages twelve to nineteen years, and 345 adults, aged twenty-one to eighty-seven years.

Controversies over Billboard Advertising

Critics of Uptown initially focused on its billboard advertising in African American neighborhoods. They soon expanded their protests to cigarettes in general and to alcohol, and began whitewashing offending billboards. Their only recourse, they argued, was to use civil disobedience to attract attention to their cause.

Reverend Calvin O. Butts, III, fiery pastor of Harlem's Abyssinian Baptist Church, led his flock to paint signs with black paint to denote their Afrocentric perspective. Agitation against billboards spread beyond Harlem. In Dallas, County Commissioner John Wiley Price led a group that whitewashed twenty-five billboards and were arrested on misdemeanor charges. And Chicago priest Michael Pfleger was also arrested for painting billboards. Antismoking and antibillboard activists were having a field day.

Business began heeding the mounting pressure. In June 1990, the Outdoor Advertising Association of America, representing 80 percent of billboard companies, recommended voluntary limits on the number of billboards advertising cigarettes and alcohol near schools, places of worship, and minority neighborhoods.

Targeting Foreign Markets

With increasing restraints on cigarette advertising in the United States and diminishing per capita consumption of cigarettes, the industry turned to foreign markets. But criticisms and restraints surfaced there also.

At least as early as 1984, the Royal College of Physicians in the United Kingdom harshly denounced tobacco usage, stating that smoking killed 100,000 people a year in the U.K. alone. But the Royal College particularly condemned the lack of availability of low-tar cigarettes, "which are practically unknown in the Third World. Developed countries bear a heavy responsibility for the worldwide epidemic of smoking."[5] Most of Europe imposed some bans on advertising by 1991.

With Western Europe's mounting inhospitality to the industry, U.S. tobacco firms eagerly pushed into Asia, Africa, Eastern Europe, and the former Soviet Union.

5. "Developing Countries: Governments Should Take Action Against Cigarettes before Too Many People Acquire the Potentially Lethal Habit," *New Scientist* (December 1, 1983), p. 42.

These were big markets and local cigarette makers were thought vulnerable to the aggressive efforts of U.S. firms.

Countries in the expanding sales area had few marketing or health labeling controls. In Hungary, for example, Marlboro cigarettes were even handed out to young fans at pop music concerts.[6]

ASSESSING THE CONTROVERSIES

Minority Targeting

Was R. J. Reynolds with its new Uptown brand an ogre, as critics claimed? Without question, inner-city African Americans had higher usage rates of tobacco and alcohol than their suburban counterparts. There was little doubt that the tobacco firms thought they had developed an effective targeting strategy with brands like Uptown. The dispute hinged on this: Are certain minority groups so susceptible to advertising that they need to be protected from potentially unsafe products?

Although proponents of controls argued that certain groups, such as young blacks, needed such protection, others saw that protection as paternalism. Even some black leaders decried the billboard whitewashing and the contentious preaching of certain ministers. Certainly, tempting people was hardly the same as oppressing them. After all, no one was forced to buy cigarettes and alcohol.

Regardless of the pro and con arguments concerning the susceptibility of inner-city youth to advertisements for unhealthy products, there was more validity to the claims of susceptibility when we consider the vulnerability of children to the attractive models found in most of these commercials and advertisements.

Finally, if legislation should be enacted to ban certain products from billboards, as was done with radio and TV advertising decades ago, where should the line be drawn? Should promotions in minority neighborhoods be banned for products that are economically extravagant, such as expensive athletic shoes? Or should promotions be banned for high-cholesterol foods that might cause high blood pressure, or for "muscle" cars that tempt reckless driving?

Assessing Joe Camel

Not surprisingly, criticism abounded after the American Medical Association's disclosure of the study that found Joe Camel so appealing to children. The basis for the concern, of course, was that the popular ads would encourage children to start smoking.

RJR would not yield. It denied that the ads were effective with children: "Just because children can identify our logo doesn't mean they will use the product."[7] It stoutly maintained its right to freedom of speech.

Some advertising people believed RJR's stubbornness was misguided: "By placing Old Joe as a freedom-of-speech issue instead of an unintentional marketing overshoot, [it] risks goading Congress into bans and restrictions on all tobacco advertising...

---

6. "The Tobacco Trade: The Search for El Dorado," *Economist* (May 16, 1992), p. 23.

7. "Old Joe Must Go," *Advertising Age* (January 13, 1992).

which would shift responsibility for tobacco products to the Food and Drug Administration [which] could regulate the tobacco industry into oblivion."[8] In 1997, without fanfare, RJR quit using the character.

See the following Issue Box for identification of more cigarette issues.

Assessment of Tobacco's Push Overseas

A firm seems entitled to make all the profit it can. If certain markets are being severely constrained, should the firm not have the right to aggressively develop other markets? This is what the tobacco firms were doing.

The issue is clouded because while smoking is generally conceded to be hazardous to health, the consequences are a long time in coming. As long as many people are willing to take the risk, should the industry be so negatively judged?

When sophisticated and aggressive promotional efforts are directed to countries where consumers are more easily swayed and far more vulnerable to promotional blandishments, does our perception of what is ethical and what is undesirable change? *Should* it change?

THE SIEGE INTENSIFIES

Allegations of Rigging Nicotine Levels

A new threat arose to severely test the complacency of the tobacco industry: charges of long-time rigging of nicotine levels to ensure that smokers stay hooked. Adding fuel

---

ISSUE BOX

CONTROVERSIES ABOUT SMOKING

The controversies concerning cigarettes go beyond those detailed in this chapter. For example:

- Should smoking be restricted in the workplace? In restaurants? On airplanes?
- What about some firms not allowing employees to smoke even when they are not at work?
- Should the tobacco industry pay for employee suits concerning their "right to smoke"?
- Should nonsmokers be protected from passive smoke?
- In general, are the rights of smokers being violated?

INVITATION TO DISCUSS

Discuss, and even debate, these questions and any other smoking issues you come up with.

---

8. Craig Stoltz, "RJR Appears Intent on Sticking with Old Joe to the Bitter End," *Adweek* Eastern Edition (March 23, 1992), p. 18.

to such allegations were Brown & Williamson Tobacco Corp. internal documents, including a fifty-four-page handbook, obtained by the *Wall Street Journal,* that indicated the tobacco companies had been adding ammonia-based compounds to their cigarettes. Such compounds essentially increase the potency of the nicotine a smoker actually inhales. The B & W documents asserted that Philip Morris's Marlboro, the top brand with a 30 percent share of the U.S. market at the time, may have been the first to use such ammonia technology. Regardless of who was the trailblazer, the practice seemingly had been widely emulated within the tobacco industry.[9]

Nicotine was viewed by most scientists as the active ingredient that caused cigarettes to be addictive. Anything that enhanced the delivery of this into the bloodstream, then, would increase the addictive potential. The industry would not admit this. It maintained that the ammonia compounds simply provided better flavor: "The primary purpose for using DAP [an ammonia additive] is to increase taste and flavor, reduce irritation, and to improve body." While admitting that this also increased nicotine delivery, a B & W spokesperson called this "an incidental effect."[10] And tobacco companies at that time still doggedly denied any links between cigarette smoking and heart disease, cancer, or other ailments.

But in 1996, newly disclosed documents suggested that Philip Morris, the nation's foremost tobacco company, had in place as far back as the 1970s, a system to hide and destroy potentially damaging data about smoking and health because of liability suits: "These documents appear to be further evidence of the industry's extraordinary effort to keep information secret. These are just the tip of the iceberg of evidence of document destruction."[11]

Repercussions

The industry was already under heavy fire before the latest revelations regarding the ammonia component. The increasing pressure, spearheaded by David Kessler, commissioner of the Food and Drug Administration (FDA), was a sharp contrast to the situation when he assumed office in 1990. Then, a few health coalitions were complaining about smoking, but that had been going on for decades. Few people in government paid any attention, mostly because the tobacco industry seemed invulnerable: it had the support of powerful tobacco-state congressmen, and it also had great monetary resources to provide for the finest legal arsenal and lobbying efforts.

Though perhaps not obvious to tobacco executives, the climate was subtly changing. In 1985, the Colorado ski resorts of Aspen and Vail banned smoking in restaurants. Other scattered bans followed. The slow trend abruptly accelerated in 1993 when the Environmental Protection Agency declared smoke a carcinogen. By the end of that year, 436 cities had smoking restrictions. Smoking came to be banned from all domestic air flights regardless of length.

9. Alix M. Freedman, "Tobacco Firm Shows How Ammonia Spurs Delivery of Nicotine," *Wall Street Journal* (October 18, 1995), pp. A1 and A6.

10. *Ibid.*, p.A6.

11. Alix M. Freedman and Milo Geyelin, "Philip Morris Allegedly Hid Tobacco Data," *Wall Street Journal* (September 18, 1996), p. B11.

Even the courts were now joining the act. In addition to criminal investigations by the Justice Department in New York and Washington, thirteen other states were seeking reimbursement from the industry for the costs of treating smoking-related illnesses. More, the industry was facing eight class-action suits, filed by smokers claiming they became hooked while the industry concealed the addictive nature of its product. Dr. Kessler added the resources of the FDA to the struggle against cigarettes.

Previous defense strategies of the industry had always been that it was a smoker's free choice to smoke despite an "unproven" risk of lung cancer, so how dare the government interfere. Now Dr. Kessler, given the newest revelations about the ability of the industry to control nicotine with its powerful addictive hold, had a new strategy to present to Capitol Hill. Former Surgeon General C. Everett Koop exhorted him, "Do anything you can" to regulate tobacco. "The country is going to be behind you."[12]

On August 10, 1995, in the White House, President Clinton, with Dr. Kessler standing nearby, unveiled tough proposed regulations on cigarette marketing and sales. This marked the new FDA role against tobacco and one of the most aggressive federal moves ever against the industry.

Even the seemingly fertile overseas markets were rising against tobacco. An aggressive European ad campaign by Philip Morris backfired and had to be abandoned amid a barrage of lawsuits, complaints to regulators, and government criticism. The campaign had cited scientific studies to claim that second-hand smoke was not a meaningful health risk to nonsmokers. It even suggested that inhaling secondary smoke was less dangerous than eating cookies or drinking milk.[13]

The stakes were high, with Philip Morris's $11.4 billion in European tobacco sales in 1995. But resentment against the tobacco industry was rising by governments struggling to contain burgeoning healthcare costs.

Joe Camel was doing somewhat better in Argentina, despite intense criticism by antismoking activists. The first such advertising campaign in Latin America saw sales of the formerly marginal Camel brand shooting up 50 percent, a gain perhaps reflecting that Argentina had no national cigarette age limit.[14]

THE INDUSTRY FIGHTS BACK

The fight was on. Tobacco firms as well as the advertising industry attacked with lawsuits against the FDA, while tobacco-state legislators desperately worked to replace the proposed regulations with friendlier laws. In the first half of 1996, more than $15 million was spent for lobbying. More millions went to campaign donations to influence lawmakers, and additional millions to defend against lawsuits.[15]

12. Laurie McGinley and Timothy Noah, "Long FDA Campaign And Bit of Serendipity Led to Tobacco Move," *Wall Street Journal* (August 22, 1995), p. A4.

13. Martin Du Bois and Tara Parker-Pope, "Philip Morris Campaign Stirs Uproar in Europe," *Wall Street Journal* (July 1, 1996), p. B1.

14. Jonathan Friedland, "Under Siege in the U.S., Joe Camel Pops Up Alive, Well in Argentina," *Wall Street Journal* (September 10, 1996), p. B1.

15. "Tobacco Lobbyists Spend Millions," *Cleveland Plain Dealer* (September 9, 1996), p. 8A.

The tobacco industry had been notorious for defending its position aggressively and being confrontational. For example, the professor in Georgia whose study found that Joe Camel was almost as recognizable as Disney characters, thereby calling into question the tobacco industry's claims that their ads were not targeting children, became a target himself. The industry pressured the school administration to fire him. "The only protection he really had was tenure."[16] This saved his job.

Philip Morris had been the most aggressive player in attacking critics. In 1994, it sued the city of San Francisco, trying to overturn one of the nation's toughest anti-smoking ordinances. The ordinance had banned smoking in offices and would shortly also ban it in restaurants. Philip Morris sought to have the court declare the ordinance invalid and unenforceable.

Geoffrey Bible, chairman of Philip Morris, declared an all-out war on tobacco's enemies, with legal attacks and newspaper ads. "We are not going to be anybody's punching bag," he said. "When you are right and you fight, you win."[17] Bible had spent his career pushing Philip Morris around the world, and he practiced what he preached: smoking cigarettes and attacking all critics.

Those struggling to preserve the tobacco industry and its efforts to avoid regulation were by no means limited to cigarette producers. Tobacco was so ingrained in many sectors of our economy that many would suffer were it curbed—for example, local distributors, truckers, people who own and/or replenish vending machines, those involved with billboard ads for cigarettes, and the hundreds of thousands of vendors who saw cigarette sales as a major part of their total business, not to mention those tobacco growers in the southern states who could not countenance switching their crops to lower-yielding alternatives. Against the arguments that alternative employment would replace cigarette dependence, many looked back over decades of such dependence and cringed at the thought of losing it.

Results

Hopes that campaigns against smoking were becoming more effective were dispelled by a study published in the November 1998 *Journal of the American Medical Association*. The research, carried out at 116 four-year colleges, found 28 percent of college students smoking in 1997, up from 23 percent in 1994. The report concluded that this is a cause for national concern.[18]

In 1998, Philip Morris's share of the U.S. cigarette market passed 50 percent for the first time ever. In addition to its aggressive use of the Marlboro Man on billboards and magazine ads, it had a sales-incentive program called Retail Masters that rewarded retailers with payouts based on sales and display of Philip Morris cigarettes. This program was particularly effective with the rapidly expanding cigarette outlet stores, numbering some 5,800 by 1998, that sold nothing but cigarettes at 10 to 15 percent less

16. Example cited in Maureen Smith, "Tenure," *University of Minnesota Update* (November 1995), p. 4.

17. Suein L. Hwang, "Philip Morris's Passion to Market Cigarettes Helps It Outsell RJR," *Wall Street Journal* (October 30, 1995), p. A1.

18. H. Wechsler et al, "Increased Levels of Cigarette Use Among College Students: A Cause for National Concern," *Journal of the American Medical Association*, Vol. 280, No. 19 (November 18, 1998), pp. 1673–78.

than convenience stores because of generous manufacturer rebates and display fees. Other tobacco firms also had incentive programs but they were outmuscled by Philip Morris.

Overseas, Philip Morris captured nearly a quarter of the cigarette market in Turkey. It did this by enlisting help of influential people and lobbying heavily to eliminate the government's control of tobacco prices and distribution. Its prime bargaining chip was the promise that it would invest millions of dollars in the country. True to its word, Philip Morris opened a factory there in 1993, and expanded it into a $230 million facility. Now it could engineer cigarettes to appeal to Turkish tastes but with a stronger kick than local brands. Its salesmen, dressed as cowboys, spread across the country to 130,000 stores with a lavish in-store promotional and incentive plan. Of course, it advertised the Marlboro Man heavily, with cowboy scenes and panoramic vistas. In late 1996, pressured by antitobacco groups, Turkey's Parliament passed one of the strictest cigarette advertising bans in the world. Philip Morris got around this by omitting the word "Marlboro" in its ads and displays, but leaving the easily identifiable red chevron. The company also shrewdly noted that the ban did not cover all nontobacco products and events, and so its Marlboro jeans and other paraphernalia became best sellers and potent promoters of the brand.

Tobacco companies found a new target market for future smokers in women in developing countries. To woo these potential users, they sponsored sporting and entertainment events geared to female audiences; they offered cigarettes with free crystal, designer scarves, and silk camisoles; they sent sample cigarettes as congratulatory gifts to new female college graduates. In the Philippines, a devoutly Catholic nation, calendars were even distributed featuring the Virgin Mary and other women saints praying over cigarette packs.[19]

THE TOBACCO DEAL

In spring 1997, new developments portended monumental changes for the tobacco industry in the United States. In late March, the solidarity of the industry was shaken as Liggett Group settled a lawsuit with twenty-two states, and in the process, finally admitted that smoking was addictive and caused cancer. Further information from Liggett showed that children were targeted for tobacco sales.

In April 1997, Philip Morris and RJR Nabisco began talks with attorneys general for twenty-five states suing to recover billions of dollars in public healthcare costs for sick smokers. The industry sought protection from all current and future litigation and was willing to contribute an amazing $300 billion over a twenty-five-year period to a settlement fund as well as making certain other concessions. When Congress took up ratifying the agreement in early 1998, it raised the price to $516 billion and cigarette makers were denied the legal immunity they sought in return. Not surprisingly, the industry did not accept this.

19. Information for this section has been compiled from a number of sources including Yumiko Ono, "For Philip Morris, Every Store Is a Battlefield," *Wall Street Journal* (June 29, 1998), B1, B4; Suein L. Hwang, "How Philip Morris Got Turkey Hooked On American Tobacco," *Wall Street Journal* (September 11, 1998), pp. A1, A8; and Stephanie Stapleton, "Tobacco Targeting Third-World Women," *Cleveland Plain Dealer* (November 10, 1998), p. 3F.

In November 1998, a milder deal was negotiated, amounting to $206 billion spread over twenty-five years. Undoubtedly tobacco's position was bolstered by a major victory that Reynolds scored in a Florida state court on May 5, 1997, where a jury found that the firm was not responsible for the death of a three-pack-a-day smoker who died of lung cancer at age forty-nine. The trial had been closely watched as a bellwether for future litigation against the industry.

Forty-six states accepted the new deal. Four other states had already settled their individual suits for a total of $40 billion. The deal seemingly put an end to antismoking groups' hopes for a broader agreement that would combat teenage smoking and bring the industry under federal regulation.

THE BATTLE CONTINUED

As of August 1999, despite a stack of lawsuits and other actions filed against it, Philip Morris was still a very profitable company, bullying its competitors and outselling its nearest one, RJR, two to one. Despite a 70-cents-a-pack price hike to pay off forty-six states and their lawyers, demand was almost as big as ever. Not even a partial injunction granted in a lawsuit filed against Philip Morris by its competitors, alleging antitrust violations in its Retail Masters sales-incentive program, could phase Philip Morris. It confidently planned to appeal the injunction. Meantime, with tens of millions of smokers on its computers, its "relationship marketing programs" were geared to keeping these dedicated smokers in the Philip Morris camp.

The situation was not as good for U.S. tobacco companies in international markets as the millennium neared. Not even in Asia, home to half of the billion smokers in the world, was the situation encouraging. In China, for example, the state-owned China National Tobacco Corp. had a virtual monopoly with a 200 percent import duty on cigarettes to go along with major distribution restrictions. Elsewhere in Asia, import duties and restraints brought slumping market shares to foreign firms, with their tobacco products not only hard to find and difficult to advertise and promote, but priced out of reach of most consumers. For Philip Morris, international tobacco sales were expected to decline 4 percent in 1999.

In the United States, suddenly the industry found that the legal battle was not over. On September 22, 1999, the Justice Department reopened the battle by filing a massive lawsuit claiming that forty-five years of industry deception about the dangers of cigarettes had contributed to the federal government's spending more than $20 billion a year to treat ill smokers.

On October 13, 1999, Philip Morris announced that it would spend about $100 million a year, or about 5 percent of its total ad budget, on a new TV campaign aimed at presenting a "friendlier public face." Antitobacco groups promptly criticized this as an attempt "to win court cases and stave off political change."[20]

---

20. Compiled from these sources: Gordon Fairclough, "Philip Morris TV Ad Campaign Seeks to Repair Cigarette Maker's Image," *Wall Street Journal* (October 13, 1999), p. B16; David S. Cloud and Gordon Fairclough, "U.S. Sues Tobacco Makers in Massive Case," *Wall Street Journal* (September 23, 1999), pp. A3, A8; Seth Lubove, "Brand Power," *Forbes* (August 9, 1999), pp. 98–104; and Andrew Tanzer, "Where There's Smoke …," *Forbes* (March 22, 1999), pp. 84–86.

ON THE ROPES

Louis Camilleri, forty-eight, took over as CEO from Geoffrey Bible in April 2002. He was a chain smoker, just like his predecessor (one wonders if being a chain smoker was one of the criteria for high executive positions). Things looked rosy now after the multibillion-dollar November 1998 settlement with states' attorneys general. Profit was growing and the threat of lawsuits had diminished. With Philip Morris's acquisition of Kraft Foods, it was decided to rename the company Altria Group, and play down the tobacco role.

By 2003, the situation had worsened for Philip Morris and for the other major players in the industry. Indicative of the hostile climate, now Camilleri could no longer even light up in his office because of a new ban on workplace smoking enacted by New York City; such bans seemed to be sweeping the country. Profit was being savaged due to a price war with upstart makers of deep-discount cigarettes. They had rushed into the market with names like Bronco, Ranger, Rave, and Hi-Val, as Philip Morris and its kind had kept raising prices to pay for the tobacco settlements and still make good profits to pay good dividends, while states were also raising excise taxes on cigarettes. By the end of 2002, the cut-rate smokes had already captured 10 percent of the market, versus 3 percent in 1998, and were growing fast.

On top of all this, an Illinois court had just awarded $10.1 billion in a class-action suit against Philip Morris. Despite the 1998 settlement, the risks of litigation were far from over. In an attempt to get the court to reconsider the immense award, Camilleri threatened to take the company into bankruptcy, which would stop its continuing payments to the states under the 1998 settlement.

Faced with these real and potential threats, Philip Morris decided on a massive strategy switch, one undreamed of ever before. It would try to make friends with the FDA in an effort to get the tobacco industry under government regulation. In doing so, this would make an alliance of longstanding bitter enemies, and bring together tobacco executives and anti-smoking advocates, northeastern and tobacco-state legislators, farmers, and urban liberals.

Philip Morris had always been in the vanguard opposed to government restrictions on the tobacco industry, for example, on cigarette advertising. But after the sweeping 1998 settlement of state lawsuits, it found that these restrictions resulted in protecting Marlboro's already well-established market share. FDA regulation would force the upstart firms to adhere to new standards for product manufacturing, thereby reducing their price advantage. The FDA could create new marketing rules, such as better disclosure of harmful ingredients, and even require nicotine levels to be reduced. Furthermore, government regulation ought to improve the image problems of the industry.

As of the end of 2003, this marriage with the FDA was no done deal. But Philip Morris had just about won over its tobacco farmers whose support was crucial in influencing their legislators.

It seemed that Philip Morris's self interest had become melded with that of the FDA. What a wonder!

In October 2003, RJR and British American Tobacco (BAT), the second- and third-largest tobacco companies in the United States, agreed to merge into a new company to be called Reynolds American. It would have a 32 percent share of the market compared to Philip Morris's 49.6 percent. The deal was felt necessary to counter the increasingly perilous environment of multibillion-dollar lawsuits and competition from cheaper brands of cigarettes.[21]

WHAT CAN BE LEARNED?

Is it ethical to promote a product seen by many as unsafe and even deadly? This issue gets to the heart of the whole matter of tobacco production and marketing. Considered by practically all health experts as dangerous and, in the long run, life threatening, tobacco had long been protected by powerful governmental interests, but now such support is eroding.

Even though the industry stubbornly admitted some health charges, it refused to soften its aggressiveness in promoting its products until very recently. Worse was its vigorous invasion of third-world countries, even though these efforts were now facing major obstacles in many countries.

The industry is huge with stakeholders: tobacco growers, processors, retailers, tax collectors, influential people in the halls of government, even the lowly paster of billboard ads. Not the least of the supporters of the industry have been the users themselves—though this now declines a little from year to year. Loyal users tended to discount health dangers as being both far in the future and affecting only a minority of users. "And never me!"

What about morality? It is easy for stakeholders to rationalize that any bad consequences are uncertain at best, that the good outweighs any bad possibilities. Still we wonder if the profit motive is not the overriding consideration, far ahead of societal health risks.

Does a militant minority represent acceptable behavior in promoting its own self interest? In a pluralistic society, minorities are encouraged to trumpet their positions. the issue becomes one of degree. What level of critical behavior—no matter how justified many might see such criticisms—is acceptable? Is white-washing billboards acceptable behavior? What about destroying offending bill-boards or firebombing the stores of opportunistic shopowners? Where do we draw the line? Furthermore, who is to be the judge of what is acceptable and unacceptable: a firebrand preacher, a government agency, the police department, or the courts?

---

21. Compiled from Associated Press, as reported in "Struggling Tobacco Titans Plan to Merge," *Cleveland Plain Dealer* (October 28, 2003), p. D3; George Fairclough, "Cheap Smokes Are Squeezing Big Tobacco," *Wall Street Journal* (November 14, 2002), pp. C1, C3; Vanessa O'Connell, "Why Philip Morris Decided to Make Friends with FDA," *Wall Street Journal* (September 25, 2003), pp. A1, A12; and Gordon Fairclough and Vanessa O'Connell, "Altria's CEO Faces a Pack of Problems," *Wall Street Journal* (April 14, 2003), pp. B1, B9.

Is it not perfectly right for any firm or industry, to pursue its own best interests, as long as it stays within the present law? Ah, this is the rationale that supports tobacco efforts, whether Joe Camel, targeting naive consumers, foreign markets, or nicotine enhancement in pursuit of addiction. The actions formerly were considered entirely legal. Do not laws reflect the majority views on what is moral and ethical? Many would say that they do not reflect prevailing majority views, that they rather reflect the positions of powerful special interests. Many would see tobacco regulations—or lack therein—as such.

Perhaps the real issue is whether a firm's best interests should take precedence over those of its customers and of society. Either position can be argued. On the one hand, should not a firm seek to foster a better corporate image and benefit both society and itself? On the other, should not a firm seek to to maximize profitability to the benefit of stockholders, creditors, suppliers, employees and the like, regardless of outside critics?

Is a firm's public image of little consequence as long as it has a loyal body of customers who support it? This was the position of the tobacco industry: defiant of critics, secure in the loyalty of a sizable group of addicted customers, aided and abetted by powerful political interests whose constituents had an economic stake in the viability of the industry. For decades this mindset of disregard for the public image had successfully prevailed, despite the critics, including most of the medical profession.

Now, finally, the cigarette makers—and Philip Morris, the industry's most ardent defender—have come to realize that they were wrong to assume that the past can dictate the future and that attitudes and power positions would remain unchanged.

Perhaps it is high time they seek to develop a more healthy cigarette, even if this lessens the addiction and alienates diehards who demand their nicotine cocktail. The late-breaking news that Philip Morris is starting image-building advertising and even making overtures to the FDA for regulation suggests an about-face in recognizing the importance of public relations—if nothing else, to tone down jury awards. At the same time, these overtures to the FDA suggest a shrewd strategy to keep low-priced cigarette makers at bay.

In today's litigious environment, callousness regarding society's growing concerns may be courting disaster. The tobacco industry proudly boasted that it had never lost a lawsuit accusing it of responsibility for lung cancer and other physical ills and deaths. The industry had always successfully defended itself on the grounds of unproven charges of cigarette smoking contributing to such health hazards, and also on the grounds of individual choice and individual freedom. Now this defense has crumbled. Some at least would see that the industry capitulated in accepting the $206 billion tobacco deal. Others would say that it was the state attorneys general who capitulated in accepting a deal far milder than the 1997 one. Still, our litigious environment is doing what lawmakers in a pluralistic society with diverse agendas have been unable to do: bring the tobacco industry to heel.

In these learning insights we have raised more questions than answers or caveats. But the questions raised ought to be of concern to tobacco executives—

and executives of other firms whose products and ways of doing business may not be in the best interests of the general public. A reckoning may be lurking in the wings.

CONSIDER

Can you propose other learning insights or ethical issues?

QUESTIONS

1. Do you actually think Joe Camel led youngsters to become smokers when they got older? Why or why not?

2. Do you have any problems with the idea of militant ministers leading their followers to whitewash offensive billboards? If not, is tearing down such billboards acceptable? Please discuss as objectively as possible.

3. Do you consider the proof adequate that cigarettes pose a substantial health threat and should be banned or tightly constrained? If you accept this position, should tobacco growers be allowed to continue growing such "unsafe" harvests without restraints?

4. Playing the devil's advocate (one who argues an opposing position for the sake of examining all sides), what arguments would you offer that cigarette manufacturers should be permitted complete freedom in targeting developing countries?

5. How do you weigh the relative merits of the tangible financial contributions the tobacco industry has made to various minority groups and media, against the negative health consequences of smoking?

6. What is the ethical difference between promoting cigarettes and promoting fatty, cholesterol-laden foods?

7. Do you agree with banning cigarettes from public buildings, workplaces, restaurants, airplanes, and so on? Why or why not?

8. Are the rights of nonsmokers being too highly emphasized? Do smokers have any rights?

HANDS-ON EXERCISES

1. You are the public relations spokesperson for Philip Morris. You have been ordered by Geoffrey Bible to plan a public relations campaign to overturn some of the banning of cigarettes. Be as specific and creative as you can. How successful do you think such efforts would be?

2. You are an articulate young African American woman who uses Uptown cigarettes and likes them. At a church outing, your minister denounces Uptowns

and the company that makes them. Describe how you might respond to such a tirade against your favorite brand.

3. You have been asked by the executive committee of a major tobacco firm to draw up plans for changing the negative public image of the tobacco industry. the hope thereby is to defuse the probability of upcoming federal legislation that would be detrimental, as well as curb the vulnerability to lawsuits. What do you propose? Be as specific as possible.

TEAM DEBATE EXERCISES

1. A great controversy is brewing in the executive offices of Philip Morris. One group led by CEO Bible is strongly in favor of aggressively attacking all critics and defending cigarettes with no holds barred. Still, there is another group supported by some prominent board members who believe the company and the industry should soften its stance. Debate the two sides of this issue.

2. Debate the issue: The rights of nonsmokers are being emphasized too much. Smokers have rights, too.

3. Debate the great $206 billion deal of the tobacco industry. Who won? Should the attorneys general have held stronger against the industry? (You may need to research the provisions of the final agreement with what might have been.)

INVITATION TO RESEARCH

1. What is the current situation regarding overseas incursions by U.S. tobacco companies?

2. Has the tobacco industry encountered any new criticisms?

3. Has the tobacco deal been advantageous to the industry?

4. Has smoking by college students changed since the JAMA report of 1998?

5. Is Geoffrey Bible still alive, or has he died of lung cancer?

6. Has Philip Morris succeeded in bringing regulation to the tobacco industry? If so, has this lessened the inroads of the discount smokes?

CHAPTER EIGHT

The Savings and Loan Disaster: Management's Repudiation of Responsibility

*I*n the 1980s, a monumental financial disaster suddenly intruded on the public consciousness. It involved the savings of ordinary people, and the long-term consequences would be borne by all taxpayers. Wild excesses of spending and lending brought huge losses, and violated depositor, shareholder, and community trust.

The savings and loan (S & L) industry, the source of home ownership for millions of Americans, was on the verge of total collapse; indeed, hundreds of institutions would go bankrupt. Thankfully, the savings of the depositors were protected by the federal government, though the government bailout would be the costliest in history.

How could these ethical mistakes have happened? What can we learn from them? And what were the keys to the success of the S & Ls that survived and prospered during this time?

A SAMPLING OF FIASCOS

Sunbelt Savings

Edwin T. McBirney III was twenty-nine years old when he began his run to a vast fortune in the savings and loan business. The year was 1981. While still in college, he had shown unusual business acumen, starting his own business of leasing refrigerators to college students. Upon graduating, he turned to real estate, becoming a broker and investor in the booming Dallas market.

In December 1981, he formed an investment group that began buying small S & Ls. One of these was Sunbelt Savings, an obscure S & L in Stephenville, Texas. McBirney was to merge these holdings into one large S & L, which he named Sunbelt Savings Association. In less than four years, Sunbelt became the nucleus of a $3.2 billion financial empire. Its growth came mostly from commercial real-estate loans that were so risky that Sunbelt gained the nickname *Gunbelt* for its shoot-from-the-hip lending policies. As one example, Sunbelt lent $125 million (secured only by raw land) to an inexperienced Dallas developer in his twenties, who went on to lose $80 million.[1] In its heyday, Sunbelt owned mortgage and development-service companies, had a

---

1. Howard Rudnitsky and John R. Hayes, "Gunbelt S & L," *Forbes* (September 19, 1988), p. 120.

commercial-banking division, and made real estate loans to developers from California to Florida.

McBirney and his executives soon were covering Texas in the company's fleet of seven aircraft. McBirney liked to throw sumptuous parties. He would serve lion and antelope to hundreds of guests at his palatial Dallas home. In 1984 and 1985, Sunbelt footed $1.3 million for Halloween and Christmas galas, including a $32,000 fee to his wife for organizing the parties. It seemed that no end was in sight for these Texas big spenders. But it was there, just around the corner.

In 1984, the Empire Savings and Loan of Mesquite, Texas, collapsed after funding massive high-risk investments. Its demise raised troubling questions about the entire industry. Edwin Gray, chairman of the Federal Home Loan Bank Board, a regulator of S & Ls, became fearful of a disaster and slammed on the brakes. He forced reappraisals based on current market values, he increased capital requirements, he limited direct appraisals, and he hired hundreds of new examiners and supervisory agents. Appraisers found that the collateral backing billions of dollars of loans had been overvalued by up to 30 percent. Many thrift organizations had to lower the book value of their loans, thereby reducing their already weak capital positions. And then real estate values plummeted as Texas's economy began collapsing, led by declining oil prices. The domino effect took over as a rash of loan delinquencies led to one foreclosure after another.

Now the excesses of McBirney's heyday came home to roost. Hundreds of examiners descended on the Dallas home-loan office in the spring of 1986, and most of the Sunbelt S & Ls were declared insolvent. Although Sunbelt was spared temporarily, McBirney was forced to resign as chairman by June. Of the foreclosed real estate on Sunbelt's books, only a few million out of its $6 billion portfolio of troubled assets could be sold off. By late 1988, the Federal Home Loan Bank Board estimated that it would cost as much as $5.5 billion just to keep Sunbelt alive over the next ten years.[2]

To add to the insult, a lawsuit filed against McBirney and other insider shareholders charged that nearly $13 million in common and preferred dividends had been taken out in 1985 and 1986—this at a time when Sunbelt's capital was rapidly evaporating because of wild expenditures and devaluation of assets.

Shamrock Federal Savings Bank

In Shamrock, Texas, the little savings and loan on the corner went belly-up. The collapse of the Shamrock Federal Savings Bank left a bitter pill for this town of 3,000 in the Texas Panhandle. It was a common story for many Texas communities: a small-town thrift taken over by an outsider; fast growth followed by sudden insolvency; a trail of incompetent management and soured high-risk ventures in places far beyond the town limits. "We made a mistake selling it. We should have kept it under local control, making loans in our community," declared one of the original directors of the town's only savings and loan.

Back in 1977, Phil Cates, a state representative and head of the local Chamber of Commerce, had a vision of a financial institution that would serve Shamrock and

2. For more detail, see "Why Our S & Ls Are in Trouble," *Reader's Digest* (July 1989), pp. 70-74.

other small towns near the Oklahoma line. He started pushing townsfolk to start their own savings and loan association in view of the oil and gas boom that was bringing hundreds of people into the town. Shamrock's two family-owned banks shunned long-term home mortgages and refused to pay competitive interest rates. Cates sold the idea of a local S & L to hundreds of local residents. When the Red River Savings and Loan Association opened in 1979, it had more than 350 stockholders in a town of 2,834. Community pride ran high.

These were the days of S & L deregulation, and small-town thrifts like Red River were hot properties, targets for promoters and speculators. One such was Jerry D. Lane. He offered $21 a share, more than double the original price, and the townspeople jumped at the opportunity. The name was changed to Shamrock Savings Association, and in three years deposits rocketed from $11.6 million to $111.3 million. This was mainly accomplished by shifting the thrift's focus far beyond the small town of Shamrock, with offices opened as far away as Amarillo, Texas, and Colorado Springs, Colorado. Lane also began buying other thrifts' outstanding loans.

Disaster struck in 1987 when the Federal Savings and Loan Insurance Corporation filed a $150 million racketeering suit against Lane and others after the 1985 failure of State Savings of Lubbock, Texas, where Lane had been chief executive officer. Federal regulators had found a pattern common to the S & L industry, and they would soon find it at Shamrock: making fraudulent loans to developers, concentrating an "unsafe" amount of credit with one client, basing loans on inflated property appraisals, and making them without proper credit documentation. "Loans were made over lunch with a handshake."

Shamrock was closed by federal regulators in November 1987; it owed $16.6 million more than it was worth. But its betrayal of the local communities occurred before that. It had been conceived to make loans locally for homes and other projects that could help the community. But with its buyout and the shift of emphasis far beyond the local community, it had little interest in providing less lucrative but less risky local loans.

Shamrock was characteristic of a large segment of S & Ls, especially in the heady days of the oil boom when Texas and other southwestern states thought there was no stopping the runaway building boom built on the belief that oil prices could only go up. But prices dropped to $14 a barrel in the early 1980s, knocking the cash supports out from under commercial real estate projects all across the Southwest.[3]

Lincoln Savings and Loan: Political Scandal

Charles Keating is the former owner of California's Lincoln Savings and Loan. He purchased Lincoln in 1984 and switched it from investing in safe single-family mortgages to speculating in raw land, junk bonds, and huge development projects like the $900-a-night Phoenician Resort in Scottsdale, Arizona.

Keating was a heavy campaign contributor, giving to five prominent U.S. senators: Glenn, Cranston, McCain, Riegle, and De Concini. In total, these influential politicians received $1.3 million. When his failing S & L came under the scrutiny of the Federal Home Loan Bank Board, which found enough bad loans and shaky business practices

3. Adapted from "Small Town's Dreams Vanish," *Cleveland Plain Dealer* (August 13, 1989), p.3C.

to shut it down, he sought help from these senators. Action was delayed for two years because of their intervention. During this time, the federally guaranteed cost of paying back Lincoln's depositors increased by $1.3 billion to $2.5 billion, making this one of the costliest thrift failures.[4]

Eventually, Keating was convicted of racketeering, fraud, and conspiracy in using the institution's funds and sent to prison. The senators were reprimanded for their complicity. So we see in this sampling of S & L blunders a repudiation of any concern for shareholders and employees, with megabuck deals made on the spur of the moment, without investigation, heedless of risks and probable consequences. In other words, a wild gambling mentality prevailed with many S & L top executives. But do not the managers have responsibility and accountability that cannot be repudiated? The next Information Box explores the responsibilities of managers.

THE FULL FLAVOR OF THE S & L DEBACLE

By 1988, of the nation's 3,178 so-called thrift institutions, 503 were insolvent. Another 629 had less capital on their books than regulators usually require. In 1987, 630 thrifts had lost an estimated $7.5 billion, half as much as the earnings of all the rest combined.[5] Most of the "terminal" S & Ls got into trouble making risky loans. But fraud also contributed to the failures of nearly fifty.[6] More than half the troubled thrifts were to be found in Texas. But other thrifts were also crashing. Beverly Hills Savings & Loan in California, which had much of its $2.9 billion in assets invested in dicey real estate ventures and junk bonds, closed in 1985. Sunrise Savings & Loan of Florida, with $1.5 billion in assets, was liquidated in 1986. In Arkansas, First South Federal Savings & Loan was closed in 1986 after 64 percent of its $1.4 billion in loans were found to be speculative. (See Table 8.1 for a sampling of Sunbelt S & Ls on the "deathwatch" as of September 30, 1988.) Still, the worst excesses occurred in Texas. And there were suspicions that some of the insolvent Texas S & Ls were shuffling bum loans from one to another to stay a step ahead of the bank examiners.

Undeniably, part of the motivation for taking wild risks with deposits was that individual accounts were insured up to $100,000 by the Federal Savings and Loan Insurance Corporation (FSLIC). But even the resources of this government agency would have been insufficient to cope with the problem without congressional appropriations in the billions of dollars.

The lurking danger, of course, was that depositor panic would create a devastating run on the nation's $932 billion in thrift deposits, bringing down scores of S & Ls, threatening the $14 billion of capital in the twelve regional Federal Home Loan Banks (which would have to supply emergency funds to the thrifts) and potentially swamping the FSLIC. The simplest solution would be to write off the insolvent thrifts and payoff their depositors. But this would exceed the FSLIC's original resources and could cost more than $100 billion. Taxpayers would eventually have to foot the bill.

---

4. Margaret Carlson, "$1 Billion Worth of Influence," *Time* (November 6, 1989), pp 27–28.

5. John Paul Newport Jr., "Why We Should Save the S & Ls," *Fortune* (April 11, 1988), p. 81.

6. Robert E. Norton, "Deep In the Hole in Texas," *Fortune* (May 11, 1987), p. 61.

Table 8.1 S & Ls on the "Deathwatch" as of September 30, 1988.°

State	Thrift	Negative Net Worth (millions)
Texas	Gill Savings, Hondo	($542.7)
	Meridian Savings, Arlington	($387.7)
New Mexico	Sandia Federal, Albuquerque	($482.6)
Arizona	Security S & L, Scottsdale	($351.6)
Arkansas	Savers Federal, Little Rock	($286.5)
California	Westwood S & L, Los Angeles	($222.7)
	Pacific Savings, Costa Mesa	($206.6)
Florida	Freedom S & L, Tampa	($231.6)

Sources: SNL Securities, Inc., and *Fortune* (January 30, 1989), p. 9.

°This is only a sampling.

INFORMATION BOX

WHAT IS THE RESPONSIBILITY OF MANAGERS?

Managers are well paid. Isn't responsibility for protecting assets a condition of management, even if these assets are somewhat protected by the government? Is there not also a responsibility to the enterprise, that it continue and not be destroyed by gross negligence or reckless abandon or illegal activities? Are not managers custodians of shareholders' trust?

Does a high-roller gambler in pin stripes fit this responsibility mode? The stakeholders of a typical savings and loan are far different from those of many corporations. They typically are people of moderate means and unsophisticated financial acumen; many are retirees. The preservation of customers' savings, and employees' jobs, are particularly important. Can we really accept the repudiation of such managers' responsibilities in their heedless quest for extravagance and high-risk endeavors? Should such managers guilty of gross misconduct face stiffer penalties than simply ouster from a well-paying job with most of their assets intact?

These are some of the troubling questions that arise when management has been completely oblivious to the greater good of the corporation and its shareholders (and depositors). *USA Today* opened a hot line for the public's response to the S & L mess.[7] Here is a sampling of responses:

> I don't see how they could have squandered this money and not get prosecuted.

> When I mishandle my money, I have nobody to go bail me out. If (S & Ls) are incapable of handling the trust that was placed in them, maybe they should go belly up.

> The guilty parties to this fraud should be paying off these banks, If a guy owns a $2 million home, it should be auctioned off, and he should be put in jail. They've got to take responsibility for their actions.

INVITATION TO DISCUSS

As the manager of a failed S & L, your defense is that you acted in the best interest of your investors. How could you have foreseen that your high-risk real estate ventures would have defaulted? Discuss the acceptability of this defense.

---

7. Denise Kalette, "Callers Want S&L Cheats Punished," *USA Today* (February 15, 1989), p. 13.

HISTORY OF THE SAVINGS AND LOAN INDUSTRY

At first they were called building and loans, and they filled a real need. Before the Great Depression, many commercial banks would not lend on middle-class residential property. Working-class people were eventually forced to band together to form cooperative associations to take their deposits and lend those funds out as home mortgages. The Depression saw the failure of thousands of banks and building and loans, and the Roosevelt administration created the two deposit-insurance funds we know today, the FSLIC for S & Ls, and the Federal Deposit Insurance Corporation (FDIC), which insures commercial bank deposits.

In the late 1960s, the S & Ls began experiencing some troubles. By law, the federally regulated S & Ls were required to lend long with home mortgages, but they borrowed short, with most of their lendable funds coming from passbook savings accounts. This situation of long-term loans and short-term lendable resources posed no problem at first, until inflation started rising. When this happened, the value of the S & L portfolios fell, like that of all fixed-rate long-term debt. In 1971, the S & L industry had a negative net worth of $17 billion. But the inflation rate in the 1970s worsened, and the industry faced ever larger losses on its loan portfolios.

The environment was changing in other ways as well. In particular, money-market mutual funds came on the scene, aided by computer technology. These money-market funds accumulated high-yielding financial instruments, such as jumbo certificates of deposit (CDs), commercial paper, and government notes, and then allowed the small investor to own a piece of the high-yielding package. Technology enabled customers to write checks on these money funds, while still receiving high interest. Computers made possible the extremely complex bookkeeping for such transactions.

The effect on banks and S & Ls was, of course, substantial. Money flowed out of them and into money-market funds by the hundreds of billions of dollars. This, combined with the double-digit inflation of the late 1970s, brought the S & L industry, with its long-term loans at low interest rates, seemingly to the point of disaster. By 1981, 80 percent of the thrifts were losing money and 20 percent were below the minimum capital requirements set by regulators.[8] (See Table 8.2 for a summary of the worsening S & L situation during the 1980s.)

In order to save the thrift industry from a potentially devastating outflow of funds, Congress passed the Depository Institutions Deregulation and Monetary Control Act in 1980, which gradually phased out interest-rate ceilings on deposits and allowed S & Ls to make various kinds of consumer loans. The FSLIC's insurance coverage was also raised from $40,000 to $100,000—essentially, the government deregulated the industry. But then a rate war developed among the thrifts, with some paying depositors double-digit interest rates.

Congress acted again to "remedy" the situation, only the remedy led to worse abuses. In 1982, the Garn–St. Germain Act was passed. This further loosened the restraints on S & Ls, now giving them lending powers to make acquisition, development, and construction loans, form development subsidiaries, and make direct investments. If properly handled, the new freedom should have enabled S&Ls to better match assets

---

8. John J. Curran, "Does Deregulation Make Sense?" *Fortune* (June 5, 1989), pp.184, 188, and 194.

Table 8.2 Summary of the Worsening S & L Situation During the 1980s

1980–1982: Congress begins phasing out interest-rate limits. Banks and S & Ls are allowed to offer new savings accounts that compete with market interest rates. Federal deposit insurance is boosted from $40,000 to $100,000 per account. Money that flowed out of S & Ls in 1980, when deposit rates were capped at 5.5 percent, begins flowing back. But the new deposits cost more than S & Ls can earn on the old fixed-rate mortgages made in the 1960s and 1970s at rates as low as 6 percent and even lower. Now, S & Ls are losing billions of dollars, and hundreds fail. The Garn–St. Germain bill is passed in 1982, allowing S & Ls new lending and investment freedom.

Mid–1980s: A lending spree develops, with billions of dollars loaned for apartments, office buildings, and other projects, especially in the booming Southwest. Many S & Ls are seeking high-profit investments to make up for the low rates on old mortgages. In a climate of drastically loosened controls, wild speculation and outright fraud characterize the operations of hundreds of thrifts.

1986: Oil prices plunge, the Texas economy collapses, and the overbuilding comes home to roost as developer loans are defaulted and the properties foreclosed are worth only fractions of building costs. More S & Ls are brought to insolvency. The Federal Savings and Loan Insurance Corporation finds its capital depleted by earlier S & L failures and needs massive infusions of capital. Prospective acquirers are attracted to take over the dead and dying thrifts under most favorable terms.

1988–1989: A massive government bailout is prepared and enacted.

and liabilities and find a sounder footing. They could begin lessening their dependence on mortgage lending and instead seek higher yielding investments. Figure 8.1 shows the decline in mortgage lending by S & Ls over the last eighteen years.

By now, with the constraints of regulation mostly unraveled and a new business environment in place, S & Ls needed to give careful attention to their strategic planning. Most important, they needed to reevaluate their company mission. (See the Information Box on *company mission.*)

The deregulatory solution to S & L problems did not reckon with the unbridled greed that was soon to accompany this greater freedom. It was particularly inviting

Figure 8.1 Decline in mortgage lending by S & Ls over eighteen years.
Source: Federal Reserve.

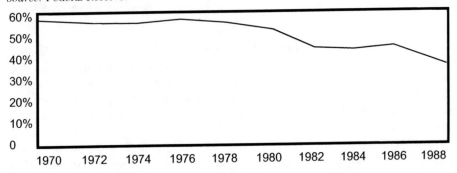

Percent of mortgage debt for one to four family homes held by savings and loans, excluding mortgage securities.

INFORMATION BOX

WHAT SHOULD OUR MISSION BE?

A company's mission involves a decision: "What business should we seek to be in?" Such a determination should involve the following factors:

1. Assessing the environment and how it is changing or is expected to change.

2. Appraising competitive factors and how these may be changing.

3. Weighing the particular strengths and weaknesses of the company—what it does best and where it has been deficient.

Mission statements can be too broad—for example, "to make a profit"—or too narrow, focusing on a particular product or service that may become obsolete as technology and customer requirements change. Narrow definitions restrict perspectives and the grasping of different opportunities, just as too broad a definition is useless as a guide for definitive action. An example of a definitive and useful mission statement of a manufacturer is the following:

> The mission is to serve the industry and government with quality instruments used for the primary measurement, analysis, and local control of fluid flow, level, pressure, temperature, and fluid properties. Markets served include instrumentation for oil and gas production, gas transportation, chemical and petrochemical processing, cryogenics, power generation, aerospace, government and marine, as well as other instrument and equipment manufacturers.[9]

A company's mission, whether formally stated or merely held in the top executive's mind, can be distorted to a reckless abandonment of former successful and durable practices. It can repudiate community best interest and trust, as we saw with Shamrock and with Sunbelt. Government deregulation in the early 1980s provided S & Ls with a vastly expanded arena for doing business. Far too many managers saw their mission now to be one of wild growth, unrestrained by cost considerations and risk potential. Leadership now became opportunistic, rash, showy, and completely oblivious to stakeholder long-term best interests. And in the process, it seems, it became unethical.

INVITATION TO DISCUSS

Critique this position: "Mission statements are a waste of time. Our executives are going to try to make the most profit they can. That is all investors need be concerned with."

---

for schemers and eager speculators in Texas. Previously, Texas regulations had limited the lending power of S & Ls to the lesser of the purchase price or the appraised value of any project. But the new federal regulations overrode this requirement, permitting S & Ls to lend 100 percent of appraised value, even if the actual purchase price was much lower. And it was not difficult to find appraisers who would greatly inflate the value of property.

At this point, using federal deposit insurance, developers got low-rate debt to put into their housing and shopping center developments. If the projects were successful,

9. John A. Pearce II, "The Company Mission as a Strategic Tool," *Sloan Management Review* (Spring 1982), p. 17.

fortunes were made. If unsuccessful, the Federal Home Loan Bank Board and the FSLIC absorbed the loss. As Art Soter, a bank analyst at the Morgan Stanley investment banking firm, noted: "What regulators failed to see is that the current system of deposit insurance increases the propensity to take risks."[10]

A further error of deregulation occurred: equity capital standards were lowered. For years, thrifts had to have capital equal to at least 6 percent of their deposits. Then, as industrywide losses caused capital to deteriorate (in only two years, between 1980 and 1982, the value of capital in the industry fell from $32 billion to less than $21 billion), thrifts were allowed to expand by taking as many deposits as they could.

Soon, brokered deposits moved in. These are funds collected by stockbrokers and sent in large amounts to the highest-yielding thrifts. With such brokered deposits, there was nothing to slow the growth of the reckless S & L operations. Phenomenal growth was possible, as described in the following example.

American Diversified Savings was a small thrift in a rural town, Lodi, California. In June 1983, it had $11 million in assets. In only eighteen months its assets totaled $792 million, mostly from brokered deposits attracted by its high-yielding certificates of deposit. The owner, Ranhir Sahni, a former commercial pilot, put the money into his favorite projects: geothermal plants, wind-driven electric generators, as well as a venture to supply local manure to a fertilizer business. In 1988, the government had to find $1.1 billion to pay off the depositors and liquidate the thrift.[11]

So the seeds for disaster were laid. Washington aggravated the problem and the potential for disaster by failing to hire adequate regulatory staff or replenish the reserves of the Bank Board or FSLIC. All this time, S & Ls in the Southwest continued to slide into bankruptcy.

THE GOVERNMENT BAILOUT

Thus, there were thrifts with billions of dollars of losses while the governmental agencies responsible for them had not nearly enough resources to bail out the insolvents. In August 1989, a costly bailout measure was enacted by Congress and signed by the president. Upward of $166 billion was expected to have to be spent to close or sell hundreds of insolvent S & Ls over the next decade.

One obvious solution was to attract would-be acquirers to take over the dead and dying thrifts and rejuvenate them. So Congress allowed acquirers to use the great bulk of the accumulated tax losses of the previous owners. Thereby, federal income and other taxes would be greatly reduced, while taxpayers absorbed the losses through a larger deficit, reduced government services, and new taxes. The Federal Home Loan Bank Board made the deal even better. Not only would it guarantee the losses on the nonperforming portfolios, but is also guaranteed the performing portfolios against losses. For example, should interest rates move adversely and lower the value of the performing assets (i.e., those assets still viable and paying interest), the Bank Board would make up the loss if the S & L later found itself illiquid. This was an El Dorado for acquirers. As *Barron's* noted:

10. Curran, p. 188.
11. *Ibid.*

From the moment an acquirer signed the papers, he would be able to deduct already acquired losses of, say, $1 billion. Against a combined corporate tax rate of about 40 percent, he would be saving about $400 million in year one. For his out-of-pocket outlay of $50 million, he would have made a return of eight times.[12]

In December 1988, Robert Bass, a forty-year-old Texas billionaire, took over the crippled American Savings and Loan of Stockton, California. This represents perhaps the consummate gilt-edged deal to one of America's richest men.

American Savings was once the largest thrift in the United States, but it got into the same trouble as many others, with brokered deposits and high-risk loans. The Bank Board seized American in 1984 and installed fresh management. But the new team gambled and failed, and the Bank Board eventually granted exclusive bargaining rights to Bass.

In the deal, American Savings was split into two entities: a healthy S &L with $15.4 billion of good assets and a "bad" one that would liquidate $14.4 billion in sour loans. For a total investment of only $500 million, the Bass Group got 70 percent ownership of the good thrift, a huge, healthy S & L with 186 branches. As another sure thing, more than half of this thrift's assets consisted of a $7.8 billion loan to the "bad" S & L that was fully guaranteed by FSLIC to pay a handsome 2 percent more than the cost of the funds. Also as part of the deal, Bass was rewarded with some $300 million in tax benefits.

Taking all this into account, Bass stood to make $400 to $500 million in straight profits over the next four years, which was roughly equal to his original investment of $500 million.[13]

DID THE S&Ls FACE AN IMPOSSIBLE ENVIRONMENT IN THE 1980S?

More than one-third of the nation's S & Ls were either insolvent or on the verge of insolvency by 1988. In 1987, losses were so high for 730 thrifts—$7.5 billion—that these were half again as much as the meager earnings of the other 2,500. In such a catastrophic environment, can we find any success stories, any S & Ls that effectively bucked the trend? Yes, we can! Their keys to viability and success? Careful growth without wild speculation; staying with traditional products and services; austerity in facilities and operations; good and better customer service—in essence, a controlled growth through sound marketing and management.

Suncoast Savings and Loan Association

Suncoast of Hollywood, Florida, is one of the largest originators and servicers of mortgages in the Southeast. Its strategy has been to reduce the interest-rate risk inherent in rate fluctuations. As we have seen before, many of the devastated S & Ls blamed their demise on rising interest rates in which the costs of funds increased while the return remained low because of long-term mortgage commitments.

12. Described in Benjamin I. Stein, "Steal of the Century?" *Barron's* (February 20,1989), p. 7.
13. Described in S. C. Gwynne, "Help Your Country and Help Yourself," *Time* (February 20, 1989), p. 72.

How did Suncoast reduce such risks? By the purchase and resale of mortgages complemented by its loan-servicing capability. Suncoast and its subsidiaries purchased and originated mortgage loans for resale into the secondary market. In the process of reselling, however, Suncoast retained servicing rights on these mortgages, and these fees made up a major part of its income. These two activities—purchase and resale of mortgages, and its loan servicing capability—are complementary, and they continue to be the strength behind Suncoast's success. For example, when interest rates are declining, mortgage lending increases, because more people buy property during such favorable conditions. But when interest rates rise and loan volume decreases, loan servicing increases in importance as more borrowers hold on to their existing mortgages.

Suncoast gains further risk reduction by contracts in which major Wall Street investment banks purchase mortgage-backed securities on specific dates at agreed-on interest rates and discounts. Although this conservative approach is costly, the risk protection from higher interest rates is deemed worth it. The conservative operating strategy resulted in the company's assets more than doubling between 1987 and 1988, while net income rose from 60 cents per share in fiscal 1987 to 98 cents a share one year later. By December 31, 1988, $2.7 billion was serviced in mortgage loans, versus $1.1 billion a year earlier. And the return on equity was 14 percent in 1988.[14]

The Boston Bancorp

Boston Bancorp's management consciously decided not to pursue diversification into nontraditional activities. It reasoned that the historical focus on retail deposit accounts and home mortgages could be profitable if costs were kept low.

And this Boston Bancorp did. It limited investment in *bricks and mortar,* having only four branches serving middle-income communities in metropolitan Boston. A long-established bank-by-mail program eliminated the need for an extensive branch system. Use of funds primarily was in single-family mortgage, commercial mortgages in apartment buildings, and high-quality government obligations and corporate stock—conservative and far from risky. With this approach, Boston Bancorp's return on equity exceeded 18 percent, and it grew to $1.4 billion in assets.[15]

Austerity also paid off for other S & Ls—for example, TCF Banking and Savings. New management took over during the turbulent mid-1980s. The first thing to go was a luxurious suite of executive offices, as well as thirty-five of the association's top brass.[16]

USA Today, in a 1989 feature story, described a number of thrifts that bucked the trend and were success stories during a time of turmoil in the industry. The common denominators for all of these was careful growth, dedicated commitment to pursuing home mortgages rather than commercial deals and brokeraged deposits, and a creativity in bettering customer service.[17]

14. Robert Chaut, "The Well-Managed Thrift: Five Success Stories," *The Bankers Magazine* (July–August 1989), pp. 35 and 38.
15. *Ibid.*
16. Harlan Byrne, "Practicing Thrift, Austerity Pays Off for a Midwestern S & L," *Barron's* (September 21, 1987), p. 15.
17. David Elbert and Harriet Johnson Brackey, "Slow Growth Was the Key to Survival," *USA Today* (February 15, 1989), pp. B1 and B2.

CONCLUSIONS

The S & L industry in the 1980s represented the greatest industry debacle since the Great Depression of the 1930s. The disaster engulfed hundreds of savings and loans in all types of communities, from the very small rural communities to the largest cities, from areas of depressed growth to those with the greatest growth. The taxpayers' bill to salvage what can be salvaged will be in the hundreds of billions of dollars.

How could this have happened? Could it have been avoided? What, if anything, can we learn from all this that might be transferable to other situations and other times, that in effect may lessen the probability of such happenings occurring again?

Some have attributed the blame for the S & L crisis to external circumstances that S & L executives had no control over. They were simply victims, so these "experts" would lead us to believe. Government has received much of the blame. In its desire to help the industry during a time of high and increasing interest rates, it promoted a dangerous deregulation by permitting S & Ls wide latitude to invest their funds far beyond the traditional home mortgage lending, as well as by relaxing equity restraints. No one could foresee that the wild boom in oil prices and land values would so abruptly deflate. Yet, such "excuses" for the debacle rest on unsubstantial foundations. Although hundreds of S & Ls failed, hundreds more maintained viability and even showed strength and growth. The common denominator of uncontrollable environmental factors does not hold the valid answer of who or what to blame and how disaster could have been avoided. Furthermore, it was the height of imprudence to expect boom conditions to be everlasting.

Where, Then, Lies the Blame?

As with most mistakes, management cannot escape primary responsibility. In this case, the fault lies with a management that violated the trust it owed its shareholders and depositors through undisciplined leadership. (See the Information Box, "Discipline in Leadership.") The violation occurred in two respects: (1) letting expenses get out of control during a time when the profitable spread of traditional mortgage business was narrowing, and (2) embarking on a wild spree of highly risky undertakings, once governmental regulation was loosened. To this we must add a good dash of white-collar crimes: outright fraud, asset-stripping, and corruption. (Of course, the inability of government inspectors to monitor closely enough permitted some of the worst excesses. But we are concerned here with management violations of the public trust, not governmental mistakes.)

WHAT CAN BE LEARNED?

Is reckless gambling of a firm's assets ethical? Let us review the first Information Box: "The Responsibility of Managers."

Managers are well paid. Isn't responsibility for protecting assets a condition of management? Even if these assets are somewhat protected by government? Is

---

INFORMATION BOX

DISCIPLINE IN LEADERSHIP

Leadership is vulnerable to abuses—abuses in overreaching, in not carefully assessing rewards versus risks, in operating beyond reasonable means, in simply not keeping a tight rein on costs, and, most important, not guiding the organization with the best interests of the stakeholders in mind. Such abuses are especially tempting in times of wild optimism, such as was occurring in the Southwest during the oil and land booms. Discipline needs to be imposed when the inclination is to run amuck.

Discipline implies controlled behavior and careful evaluation of actions and opportunities, not growing beyond resources and management capabilities. In the quest for the fine line between disciplined and undisciplined growth, the executive faces the dual risk of being too conservative or too aggressive. The first risk may be of missed opportunities and giving competitors an advantage, but this generally is less risky than jeopardizing the company with too much high-stakes leadership. Continued viability has to receive top priority. Gambling the company is hardly acceptable stakes, even in Las Vegas.

INVITATION TO DISCUSS

Discuss how disciplined leadership can be imposed on a top executive with wilder leanings.

---

there not a responsibility to the enterprise, that it not be liquidated or merged into extinction? Are not managers custodians of shareholder trust?

These are some of the troubling questions that arise when management has been completely oblivious to the greater good of the corporation and its shareholders, depositors, and employees. Ancillary questions also arise: Can selfish greed be tolerated in managers who we trust not to abdicate their responsibility? Can recklessness be tolerated? What should be the penalties for fraud?

In the S & L case, we see mistakes on a grand scale. Perhaps managers guilty of gross misconduct in connection with the public trust should face stronger penalties than simply ouster from a well-paying job, with most of their assets intact. What do you think? Can we learn from some of these mistakes?

Adversity creates opportunities. We are left with the growing recognition that adversity—in this case, a supposedly inhospitable environment—can also create opportunities for those who would adjust, adapt, and plan creatively in this environment, even embrace it with gusto—but without reckless abandon. The S & L situation created great opportunities for firms and individuals who had the resources and skills to "rescue" the troubled thrifts, with substantial government largess. And for the healthy competitors, new growth opportunities were also created, albeit the bad image of the failures cast all S & Ls in suspicious light.

The fallacy of aggressive and conservative extremes. The failed thrifts were victims of their own aggressive recklessness. The dangers of a speculative frenzy date back at least to 1634 in Holland, when individual tulip bulbs were bid up to fantastic prices in a wild but doomed speculation. The extremes of conservatism have dangers, too. To stand pat, to not even take minor risks regardless of potential opportunities, to not make needed adjustments to a changing business climate—

these can hardly be praised. The extreme example here is the buggy whip manufacturer unwilling to adapt to the new environment of horseless carriages. In general, a middle ground between extreme risk-taking and ultraconservatism usually leads to the most durable success.

How much adaptability to change is appropriate? It is useful to consider a continuum of behavior to change:

Degree of Responsiveness to Environmental Change

| Inflexible/Unchanging | Adaptive | Innovative | Reckless/Gambling |

Thus, a firm can be viewed as occupying a certain point along this continuum: the more conservative and rigid firm toward the left, the more progressive firm that is constantly developing new ideas toward the right, until we reach the extreme of reckless gambling.

The two terms, adaptive and innovative, are somewhat different, although related. Innovative may be defined as originating significant changes, implying improvement. Adaptive implies a better coping with changing circumstances, but a response somewhat less significant than an innovative reaction.

In a sense, the failed thrifts were adaptive to a changed environment, that of greater deregulation. They adapted by forsaking any plans of judicious expansion in favor of a freewheeling strategy of high risks and opportunism. Then they found themselves unable to cope with the suddenly menacing environment of drastically falling real estate prices and a newly concerned regulatory climate.

Austerity wins out over high living. Nowhere is the contrast between high living and a lack of cost constraints, on the one hand, and relative austerity, on the other, more evident than here. Reckless spending is a trap. Conspicuous examples of this were lavish entertainment, grand facilities, fleets of airplanes, and even expensive art collections. (This sounds like the Enron case, and WorldCom, Tyco, and others, hardly a decade later. Will we ever learn?) Admittedly, when things are going well, when prospects seem boundless, the temptation is to open the spending floodgates, both at the corporate level as well as for personal aggrandizement. Some would argue that lavish spending created a public image of great success, thus winning new business, but we know it now as only foolish waste.

On the other hand, we saw examples of firms that owed their viability to their austerity. They kept themselves lean, controlled costs, and were able to survive and prosper and even be in position to take over their extravagant competitors.

A government "crutch" is a destructive delusion. Knowing that depositors' accounts were insured up to $100,000 by the federal government undoubtedly motivated some of the reckless investments and other dealings of the failed thrifts. But those who felt entirely shielded were to learn to their dismay that while depositors were protected, management faced ouster and even the possibility of legal prosecution of sound legislation. The government has no great history of sound legislation.

CONSIDER

Can you add any additional learning insights?

QUESTIONS

1. Would you recommend changing an S & L's mission in the early 1980s, with most government restraints relaxed? If so, what should the mission be changed to?

2. How would you respond to an S & L executive who carefully points out to you that if land and oil prices had not collapsed without warning, his portfolio of high-interest loans would have brought great profitability to the firm?

3. "S & Ls no longer serve a useful purpose, and they should be phased out." Evaluate this statement.

4. You may want your students to discuss several of the questions raised earlier, such as: How should recklessness be punished—by dismissal, or worse? What should be the penalties for fraud? When does an executive violate the public trust?

5. Can the CEO escape prosecution for the unethical and illegal deeds of his subordinates by contending that he knew nothing of such deeds? Why or why not?

6. Would you conclude that Edward McBirney's greatest flaw was that he liked ostentatious high living?

7. A thin line seems to exist between aggressive opportunism and outright fraud. Where do you think the line should be drawn? Or are both to be criminally condemned?

8. After the examples described in the case, would you conclude that an "edifice complex" (i.e., building prestigious physical facilities) is ill-advised and even, from the viewpoint of an investor, something to encourage divestment?

HANDS-ON EXERCISES

1. You are the controller of a medium-size S & L in the mid-1980s. Your CEO is a flamboyant individual who has just announced his intention of building a new home office on a rather lavish scale. He claims this is necessary to convey the desired image of the firm. Develop a systematic analysis to disprove this idea.

2. You are the top executive of an S & L in a medium-size town in the mid-1980s. Despite the federal deregulation, you have continued to lend conservatively. Your competitor down the street has acted much more aggressively. Accordingly, he is paying depositors considerably higher interest rates than you can. Your firm is suffering, and the board is exhorting you to "loosen up." Without the benefit of hindsight, what would you do?

TEAM DEBATE EXERCISES

1. Debate this issue: The aggressive growth of lending and promoting development would have been the greatest service ever rendered to many parts of the country, except for the collapse of real estate prices. And who could have foreseen that?

2. Debate this issue: There is always risk in new ventures at the cutting edge of technology. but we must not be timid in embracing innovation and expanding to grasp it.

INVITATION TO RESEARCH

What is the state of the S & L industry today? Do you see any dangers to it on the horizon?

CHAPTER NINE

WorldCom/MCI: Massive Accounting Fraud

By Cindy Claycomb, Wichita State University

INTRODUCTION

At a hearing before the House Financial Services committee, Bernard J. Ebbers made a statement professing his innocence, then invoked the Fifth Amendment of the U.S. Constitution to protect himself against self-incrimination. One congressman told Ebbers, "Your silence may have saved you today but we're going to get answers. If you flush down the drain the retirement savings of millions of investors, you will and you should go to jail."[1]

Bernard Ebbers was once known as the person who set the tone for the global telecommunications industry. He attained cult-like devotion among shareholders for his takeover ability and his passion for making investors wealthy. But on April 30, 2002, he was forced to resign as CEO of WorldCom, the company he founded as a small reseller of long-distance telephone service, and built to a $40-billion-a-year telecom giant by piecing together more than five dozen companies.[2] The scandal that followed set the stage for a loss of a half a million jobs in the United States, three of the ten largest bankruptcies in U.S. history, and more than $1 trillion in market value wiped out.[3] WorldCom, the nation's second largest long-distance company, imploded under the scandal. How could this happen?

BACKGROUND

Bernard J. Ebbers was born in 1942 in Edmonton, Alberta. After flunking out of college and working as a bar bouncer, he ended up leaving his native Canada to get a fresh start in Mississippi, where he attended Mississippi College, a small Baptist college in

1. Pulliam, Susan, Deborah Solomon, and Randall Smith, "WorldCom is Denounced at Hearing," *Wall Street Journal*, (July 9, 2002), p. A3, Leading the News.

2. Mehta, Stephanie N., "Can Bernie Bounce Back?" *Fortune* (January 22, 2001), http://www.fortune.com/fortune/subs/print/O,15935,36996,00.html.

3. Mehta, Stephanie N., "Telecom: Birds of a Feather," *Fortune* (October 2, 2002), http://www.fortune.com/fortune/subs/print/O, 15935,372075,00.html.

Clinton, Mississippi. After college, he bought several hotels, and by the early 1980s he owned eight hotels, including several Hampton Inns and Courtyards by Marriott. His motel management company operated out of a converted Texaco station in Brookhaven, Mississippi. He discovered telecommunications when one of the hotels he bought had a side business reselling long-distance telephone service. In 1983, he and some friends had an idea to take advantage of the AT&T breakup and started a long-distance telephone company named LDDS (which stands for Long-Distance Discount Service, a name suggested to Ebbers and his partners by a waitress).[4] Ebbers was a passive investor in LDDS until the company began to lose money in 1984. The founders pushed Ebbers to step in as CEO, which he did in early 1985. After that, there was little doubt about who ran the company and the board of directors.

In 1995, LDDS bought Williams Telecommunications Group Inc. for $2.5 million and changed its name to WorldCom Inc. Ebbers, as WorldCom's CEO, specialized in buying up and merging with other companies related to telecommunications. Other major acquisitions included MFS Communications Company, a company that ran fiber-optic lines directly into office buildings; Brooks Fiber Properties Inc., a company that owned networks in big cities; UUNet, the largest Internet backbone company that carried traffic for online businesses (a backbone is a high-speed network that carries Internet traffic around the world); and Compuserve's and AOL's Internet backbones. Ebbers's mode of operation was to buy a company principally for its customer base and sales force, and drive profits by cutting overhead and transferring the customers and their traffic onto WorldCom's network. That meant new sales force, more customers, and lower costs. [5]

The beginning of the telecom boom was marked by Bernie Ebbers's success with investors. But his escalating series of thrusts and parries led to its crash. Every time Ebbers announced one of his acquisitions, Wall Street rewarded WorldCom; over the course of the 1990s, WorldCom stock rose substantially.[6] (See Figure 9.1 for a History of WorldCom Stock Price.)

Purchase of MCI

In 1998, WorldCom bought MCI for $37 billion. This was the largest deal in business history. MCI, a consumer long-distance carrier and wholesaler, had almost three times WorldCom's revenues and nearly four times the number of employees. The merger was somewhat of a surprise. British Telecommunications PLC had made an initial offer for MCI, but then had cut its offer when MCI announced a financial set-back. WorldCom pounced on the opportunity with a counteroffer, and then fended off a rival bid from GTE Corporation. [7]

With the MCI acquisition, Ebbers believed he could overcome the lock the Baby Bells had on local phone service, control the cellular airwaves across the United States,

4. *Ibid.*, Mehta, "Telecom: Bird of a Feather." and Lewis, Mark, "WorldCom: Is Bernie Still Bulletproof?" *Forbes.com* (February 6, 2002), http://www.forbes.com/2002/02/06/0206ebberstrike.html.

5. Mehta, "Can Bernie Bounce Back?"

6. Mehta, "Telecom: Bird of a Feather."

7. Kupfer, Andrew, "MCI WorldCom," *Fortune* (April, 27, 1998), http://www.fortune.com/fortune/subs/print/0,15935,379117,00.html., and Shawn Young and Eva Perez, "Finance Chief of WorldCom Got High Marks on Wall Street," *Wall Street Journal* (June 27, 2002) p. Bl.

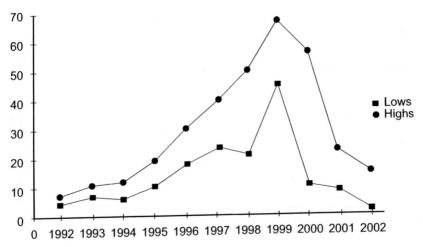

Figure 9.1 History of WorldCom Stock Price

Sources: Susan Pulliam, Deborah Solomon, and Carrick Mollenkamp, "Easy Money: Former WorldCom CEO Built an Empire on Mountain of Debt," *Wall Street Journal* (December 31, 2002), A1; Net-Advantage (2004), *Standard & Poor's:* Retrieved March 10, 2004 from index.do; Anonymous(April 13, 2003), *The Clarion-Ledger:* Retrieved February 1, 2004 from http://www.clarionledger.com/news/0304f13/b01b.html; WorldCom Annual Reports.

Commentary: Investors rewarded WorldCom during the 1990s. WorldCom's stock hit a high of $64.50 a share in 1999. The price slid to $45 a share in July 2000, and then to $33.50 in September 2000. The stock continued to tumble, and by the time Bernie Ebbers was ousted in April 2002, WorldCom's battered shares had fallen to $4.03 a share. WorldCom's lowest stock price in 2002 was $0.06 per share.

and show the Europeans how to sell phone service in Europe. The purchase of MCI meant that Ebbers would control 30 percent to 50 percent of the Internet backbone, the high-speed network that carries data around the country. Ebbers would now rely less on the other Internet companies, but they would need him more.[8]

Following the merger of WorldCom and MCI, Ebbers cut costs. He sold off corporate jets; he cut expense accounts; he cut 2,000 jobs. The biggest chunk of savings—$1.2 billion—was to come from shifting phone traffic to WorldCom's proprietary network rather than leasing outside lines. He also focused on the hottest areas in telecom—such as local and international calling and data—to guarantee long-term revenue and profit growth. Market analysts believed these actions provided strong evidence that Ebbers was delivering the kind of savings and synergies he promised when WorldCom prevailed over British Telecom and GTE to acquire MCI.[9]

8. Kupfer, Andrew, "Fortune 500: Bernie's Big Gamble," *Fortune* (April 17, 2000), http://www.fortune.com/fortune/subs/print/0,15935,370882,00.html, and Andrew Kupfer, "Why Bernie Ebbers Wants to be the Internet's Mr. Big," *Fortune* (December 8, 1997), htm://www.fortune.com/fortune/subs/print/0.15935.376902.00.html.

9. Schwartz, Nelson, "How Ebbers is Whipping MCI WorldCom into Shape," *Fortune* (February 1, 1999), http://www.fortune.com/fortune/subs/print/0,15935,378233,00.html.

WorldCom didn't know it at the time, but this would be their last major acquisition before scandal hit.

THE BEGINNING OF PROBLEMS

After the purchase of MCI, WorldCom's dial-around and consumer long-distance businesses eroded as price-conscious consumers switched among competitors and increasingly used their wireless phones to make long-distance calls. Even worse, WorldCom's wholesale revenues from selling service to other carriers fell by 16 percent.[10] WorldCom's long-distance wholesale business—once the very heart of the company—was shrinking. Even its data business faced stiff competition from carriers such as Level 3 and Qwest, which had newer technology and lots of extra capacity, and thus priced their products and services aggressively. Amid this bleak outlook, WorldCom slashed revenue and cash-earnings estimates.[11]

Attempted Purchase of Sprint

Facing this dismal scenario, in late 1999, WorldCom tried to buy Sprint for $129 billion. How would this benefit WorldCom? Global corporate customers were being wooed by most of the telecom firms, and WorldCom had an advantage because it owned its own international high-speed network. However, wooing global corporate customers had become a marketing game rather than a network game. That's where Sprint came in. Sprint was stronger than WorldCom in marketing to corporate customers and already had a presence in Latin America. WorldCom also needed consumers. Ebbers estimated that the cost of beefing up the network with electronics and software by 2005 would cost WorldCom $100 billion. He needed residential customers who make most of their calls after business hours to help fund this investment, and Sprint could offer access to these consumers. Finally, when WorldCom customers used cell phones to make calls, WorldCom saw none of that revenue because it had no cellular systems. Buying Sprint would have plugged this leak because it had a nationwide cellular network, Sprint PCS.[12] In 2000, however, the Justice Department, put a stop to the WorldCom/Sprint transaction, arguing that the combined company "would control an unacceptable share of long-distance voice and data traffic."[13]

After the collapse of the deal, WorldCom's situation worsened. Ebbers tried to address issues of slower than expected revenue growth and cash earnings by announcing plans to break the company into two parts, each with its own tracking stock (see Information Box: "What is a Tracking Stock?"). WorldCom would own the network, serve corporate customers, and cultivate fast-growing businesses such as data services; MCI would be a repository for slow-growing operations such as consumer long-distance, paging, and wholesale. MCI focused entirely on generating a cash

10. Kupfer, "Fortune 500: Bernie's Big Gamble."
11. Mehta, "Can Bernie Bounce Back?"
12. Kupfer, "Fortune 500: Bernie's Big Gamble."
13. Mehta, "Can Bernie Bounce Back?"

dividend for its shareholders. The WorldCom business anticipated that it would be able to achieve strong growth rates, thus attracting growth investors. [14]

Ebbers's Personal Financial Problems

By 2000, Bernie Ebbers faced serious problems. He had funded his personal stock market activities by borrowing on margin (see the Information Box: "Borrowing on Margin and Margin Calls"). When the value of those investments, including long bets on WorldCom, plunged, Ebbers had to pay up. The WorldCom board of directors came to his rescue, temporarily. By the time he was ousted in April 2002, the board had lent him $415 million. Although the money was intended to help him cover margin calls on bank loans that he had collateralized with WorldCom stock, a bankruptcy court examiner found that Ebbers used $27 million of the proceeds for other personal reasons including construction of his new house, $2 million to a family member for personal expenses, loans to his family, friends, and a WorldCom officer, and payments to his own business interests.[15]

In addition, Ebbers borrowed more than $1 billion from banks and brokerages, either personally or for his personal businesses, and the loans were secured by his WorldCom stock. He used this money to acquire businesses that he said he planned to manage when he retired (e.g., a timber operation, a Canadian ranch, a soybean farm, and a yacht builder). The banks lent him money because they did not want to lose his or WorldCom's business. Eventually, the banks issued margin calls because the value of WorldCom's stock had sunk so low. In some cases, Ebbers pledged the same stock to different lenders.[16]

Ebbers put the interests of WorldCom shareholders at risk because WorldCom's share price could plummet if he tried to sell his stock. Furthermore, by using WorldCom shares to collateralize his massive debt obligation, Ebbers placed himself under intense pressure to keep WorldCom's share price high.[17] By April of 2002, Ebbers's personal financial problems were so threatening to the company that the WorldCom board of directors asked for his resignation. They gave him a $1.5 million annual pension payment for the rest of his life, limited access to WorldCom's fleet of corporate aircraft, and a below-market interest rate of 2.32 percent on the $415 million he borrowed to be paid back in five years.[18] This was very generous when you consider the fraud and scandal that Ebbers foisted on WorldCom.

14. *Ibid.*; "Ebbers Out at WorldCom," *CNN Money* (April 30, 2002): http://money.cnn.com/2002/04/03/technology/ebbers.

15. Susan Pulliam and Jared Sandberg, "WorldCom Seeks SEC Accord as Report Claims Wider Fraud," *Wall Street Journal* (November 5, 2002), A1; and Andrew Backover, "Report Slams Culture at WorldCom," *USA Today* (November 4, 2002), http://www.usatoday.com/money/industries/telecom/2002-11-04-worldcom-report_x.htm.

16. Deborah Solomon and Jared Sandberg, "WorldCom's False Profits Climb," *Wall Street Journal* (November 6, 2002), A3.

17. *Ibid.*, Pulliam and Sandberg, "WorldCom Seeks SEC Accord as Report Claims Wider Fraud."

18. Christopher Stern, "WorldCom Battles Founder on Pension," *Washington Post* (October 17, 2003), E01.

INFORMATION BOX

WHAT IS A TRACKING STOCK?

Tracking stocks are shares issued by a company that pay a dividend determined by the performance of a specific portion of the whole company. Tracking stock differs from a spin-off in that it does not represent or require any change in business structure. A tracking stock is a separate stock created by a parent company to "track" the financial progress of a particular piece of its business. Tracking stock is often set up by companies that have several diverse divisions, both so that investors can take a share in a division of their interest, and so that the performance of these divisions can be tracked in terms of shareholder interest. Despite being part of a publicly traded entity, tracking stocks trade under their own ticker symbols. A company will sometimes issue a tracking stock when it has a very successful division that it feels is underappreciated by the market and not fully reflected in the company's stock price. Tracking stocks are meant to create opportunities for investors to buy into a fast-growing unit without investing in the whole company; however, tracking stocks do not lend shareholders ownership in the parent company, nor do they include voting rights.

WorldCom Inc. issued tracking stock for its two divisions: WorldCom and MCI. Ebbers believed that the slow-growing operations of MCI resulted in the entire company being undervalued by the market. He hoped that without the burden of MCI, the supposedly faster-growing operations of WorldCom would flourish and be rewarded by investors.

INVITATION TO DISCUSS

Do you agree with Ebbers's idea? Why or why not? Do you think it would have worked if the accounting fraud had not taken place?

Sources: investorwords.com (2004), "Tracking Stock," *Web Finance,* Retrieved February 23, 2004 from http://www.investorwords.com/5013/tracking_stock.html; Change Wave Glossary (2004), "Tracking Stock," *ChangeWave Research:* Retrieved February 23, 2004, from http://www.changewave.com/Glossary.html#T.

Fraudulent Accounting

Amid Ebbers's personal financial difficulties, rumors circulated that WorldCom might have some questionable accounting, that its debt might be downgraded, that the company was on the verge of bankruptcy, and that it was a takeover candidate for a Bell or an overseas carrier.[19] The Securities and Exchange Commission launched an investigation of WorldCom in February 2002.[20] In the meantime, a small team of WorldCom internal auditors suspected that WorldCom's financial statements were fraudulent. In secret, they began an investigation. Cynthia Cooper, the vice-president of internal audit, discovered the accounting fraud on her own initiative. (WorldCom executives initially took credit for launching an internal audit that discovered the errors.[21]) Cooper found that each quarter Scott Sullivan, WorldCom's chief financial

19. Stephanie N. Mehta, "Feature: WorldCom's Bad Trip," *Fortune* (February 19, 2002), http://www.fortune.com/fortune/subs/print/0,15935,374157,00.html.

20. Jared Sandberg, Rebecca Blumenstein, and Shawn Young, "WorldCom Admits $3.8 Billion Error in its Accounting," *Wall Street Journal* (June 26, 2002), A1.

21. Susan Pulliam, Jared Sandberg, and Dan Morse, "Prosecutors Gain Key Witness in Criminal Probe of WorldCom," *Wall Street Journal* (July 3, 2002), A1.

INFORMATION BOX

BUYING ON MARGIN AND MARGIN CALLS

Buying on margin is borrowing money from a broker to buy a stock and using your investment as collateral. Investors typically use margin trading to buy more stock than they would be able to normally afford without fully paying for it. The margin is the difference between the market value of a stock and the loan a broker makes.

To buy on margin, you need a *margin account*, not merely a cash account in which you trade just with the money in the account. By law, an initial investment of at least $2,000 is required for a margin account (some brokerages require more). This deposit is known as a *minimum margin*. With an operational margin account, you can borrow up to 50 percent of the purchase price of a stock. The portion of the purchase price that you deposit in a margin account is known as the *initial margin*. Investors do not have to margin all the way up to 50 percent. They can borrow less; say, 10 percent or 25 percent.

An Example

Let's say you buy a stock for $100 and the stock rises to $150. If you bought the stock in a cash account and paid for it in full, you will earn a 50 percent return on your investment; however, if you bought the stock on margin—paying $50 in cash and borrowing $50 from your broker—you will earn a 100 percent return on the money you invested. Of course, you will still owe the brokerage firm $50 plus interest.

The downside to using margin is that if the stock price decreases, substantial losses can mount quickly. For example, let's say the stock you bought for $100 drops to $50. If you fully paid for the stock, you will lose 50 percent of your money; however, if you bought on margin, you will lose 100 percent, and you still owe the broker firm the interest on the loan.

Margin Call

There is a restriction imposed on a margin account regarding the amount the brokerage firm needs you to maintain after you trade (i.e., a *maintenance margin*). Margin calls are concerned with the maintenance margin. In unstable markets, prices can fall very quickly. If the *equity* (value of the securities minus what you owe the brokerage firm) in your account falls below the maintenance margin, the brokerage will issue a dreaded *margin call*. A margin call requires you (the investor) to either liquidate your position in the stock or add more cash to the account. If you do not meet a margin call for any reason, the brokerage firm has the right to sell your securities to increase your account equity until you are above the maintenance margin. Your broker may not even be required to consult you before selling.

INVITATION TO DISCUSS

What are the advantages of buying on margin? What are the risks of using a margin account? Do you think Bernie Ebbers placed too much pressure on himself by buying on margin? Why or why not?

Sources: Fiscal Reference (2004), "Investor Tips: Margin—Borrowing Money to Pay for Stocks," *FiscalReference.com*, retrieved February 23, 2004 from www.fiscalreference.com/sec/margin.htm; Investopedia.com (2004); "Margin Call," *Equade Internet Ltd.*, retrieved February 23, 2004 from www.investopedia.com/tenus/m/margincall.asp.

officer, would move operating costs to capital accounts so as to keep WorldCom's profits high. Sullivan's goal was to keep line costs—the access charges and transport fees paid to local telephone carriers to use their networks to complete calls—to 42 percent of WorldCom's revenue. Any costs above that 42 percent mark were transferred to the capital accounts as prepaid capacity costs, where they were depreciated over time. This boosted cash flow and profit and transformed a net loss in 2001 into a net profit.[22] Cooper found that for five quarters covering 2001 and 2002, WorldCom had buried $3.9 billion in expenses.

When Cooper confronted Sullivan with the questionable accounting practice, he told her to delay her audit. By the end of the second quarter of 2002, Sullivan planned to wash the $3.9 billion through the company's books with a large write-down WorldCom had previously announced. Cooper decided to take her findings to Max Bobbitt, chairman of the audit committee of WorldCom's board. At that point, Bobbitt notified the newly hired accountants, KPMG LLP, of the discrepancy. On June 20, 2002, WorldCom's audit committee met at KPMG's Washington office and asked Scott Sullivan and David Myers (senior vice-president and controller) to justify their accounting treatment. Sullivan explained his position, but the KPMG partner in charge of the WorldCom account was skeptical and gave Sullivan the weekend to produce a so-called white paper that would clearly set out his justification. At a board meeting the night of June 24, 2002, at WorldCom's offices, Sullivan again made his case. A national practice specialist at KPMG said, however, that the issue was "an open-and-shut case" against Sullivan's position.[23] The board members concluded that they would have to restate earnings, and they asked Sullivan and Myers to resign. Scott Sullivan maintained that what he was doing was legitimate, and refused to resign because he did not want to imply guilt. The board then fired him. After WorldCom announced the findings, the Securities and Exchange Commission filed civil fraud charges, and the Justice Department filed criminal charges against WorldCom and several of its executives (including Ebbers, Sullivan, and Myers). An additional $3.3 billion in improper accounting was uncovered by August 9, 2002, bringing the total fraud to $7.2 billion.[24]

Consequences

By the end of 2002, four employees had pleaded guilty in the WorldCom accounting scandal. David Myers, WorldCom's former controller, pleaded guilty to three felony counts in federal court, saying he helped manufacture profits at the behest of "senior management" as part of a massive scheme to defraud investors and meet Wall Street

22. Stephanie N.Mehta, "Telecom: Is There Any Way Out of the Telecom Mess?," *Fortune* (July 8, 2002), http://*www*.fortune.com/fortune/subs/print/0,15935,367241,00.html.

23. Jared Sandberg, Deborah Solomon, and Rebecca Blumenstein, "Disconnected: Inside WorldCom's Unearthing of a Vast Accounting Scandal," *Wall Street Journal* (June 27, 2002), A1.

24. Susan Pulliam, Jared Sandberg, and Deborah Solomon, "WorldCom Board Will Consider Rescinding Webbers's Severance," *Wall Street Journal* (September 10, 2002), A1; and Jared Sandberg and Deborah Solomon, "WorldCom Board to Begin Search for New CEO," *Wall Street Journal* (September 11, 2002), A3, Leading the News.

expectations. The guilty plea, the first in the WorldCom case, came as part of his agreement to cooperate with the government's investigation into the scandal at WorldCom.[25] Also indicted by a federal grand jury in New York were the former directors of general accounting, management accounting, and legal accounting: Buford "Buddy" Yates Jr., Betty Vinson, and Troy Normandy. Federal prosecutors also won an indictment against Scott Sullivan, once one of the most celebrated chief financial officers on Wall Street. He was accused of orchestrating WorldCom's $7.2 billion fraud. Sullivan did not cooperate with officials, making it difficult to prove a link to Ebbers.[26] In April 2003, WorldCom announced plans to change its name to MCI. WorldCom had used the MCI moniker for its consumer long-distance operations after its purchase of MCI in 1998. The MCI name was seen as not suffering from the stigma associated with the WorldCom name. Creating an entirely new name would have cost hundreds of millions of dollars and would have wasted the widespread recognition that the MCI name already had. (See Information Box: "Reputation and Brand Recognition.")

But MCI still faced escalating problems. WorldCom had filed for bankruptcy court protection in July 2002. WorldCom had to disclose all of the accounting problems and create a reorganization plan for emerging from bankruptcy. By 2003, WorldCom's accounting fraud, dating back to 1999, had mounted to $11 billion.[27] It faced additional civil charges from the SEC for misleading investors for more years than previously disclosed. Competitors were claiming that MCI engaged in a variety of schemes to avoid paying access charges, including dumping calls onto AT&T's network by routing them through Canada and disguising long-distance calls as local traffic. MCI denied any wrongdoing and said that access charge disputes are routine and have existed between local and long-distance carriers for decades.[28] The company also faced charges of avoiding hundreds of millions of dollars in state taxes through a special shelter created by KPMG for WorldCom. MCI said it conducted its own review and concluded that the tax program recommended by KPMG in 1997 and 1998 was appropriate.[29]

ANALYSIS

The telecom industry of today is very different from the stable, regulated, slow-growing industry Ebbers entered in 1983. Competition is intense, prices have decreased,

---

25. Susan Pulliam and Jared Sandberg, "Two WorldCom Ex-Staffers Plead Guilty to Fraud," *Wall Street Journal* (October 11, 2002), A3, Leading the News, and Deborah Solomon, "WorldCom's Ex-Controller Pleads Guilty to Fraud," *Wall Street Journal* (September 27, 2002), A3, Leading the News.

26. Deborah Solomon and Susan Pulliam, "U.S., Pushing WorldCom Case, Indicts Ex-CFO and His Aide," *Wall Street Journal* (August 29, 2002), A1.

27. Kara Scannell, "WorldCom Ex-Chief of Finance Faces New Bank-Fraud Charges," *Wall Street Journal* (April 17, 2003), B2.

28. Almar Latour, Yochi J. Dreazen, and Laurie Hays, "MCI, Hoping to Exit Bankruptcy, Faces New Investigation of Fraud," *Wall Street Journal* (June 28, 2003), A1, A6, and "New Fraud Inquiry for WorldCom," *BBCNews* (July 28, 2003), http://news.bbc.co.uk/l/hi/business/3100975.stm.

29. Nick Baker, "Richard Thomburgh Releases Third Report on WorldCom," *Wall Street Journal Online* (January 26, 2004), http://online.wsj.com/article_print/O,BT_CO_20040126_003 920,00.htm.

INFORMATION BOX

REPUTATION AND BRAND RECOGNITION

In 1968, Microwave Communications Inc. was incorporated. Later to become MCI, this spunky little company was one of the first to attack AT&T and stop Ma Bell's dominance of the telecommunications industry. In 1969, the FCC approved an application from Microwave Communications, Inc. (MCI) to build a private-line microwave communications system between Chicago and St. Louis that competed with AT&T. Then, without quite realizing what it had done, the FCC approved MCI's actions to provide the first competitive long-distance service for U.S. businesses. These actions ultimately stimulated full competition in the long-distance phone business. The price of long-distance telephone service is one illustration of this increasing competitiveness. When MCI was first incorporated, the average long-distance telephone call was 24 cents a minute. By 1984, the price had risen to 32 cents a minute. In 2000, the price was down to 12 cents per minute. MCI had a reputation as an important private institution that engaged in competition and succeeded.

After the 1998 purchase of MCI by WorldCom, the MCI name continued to be used only for WorldCom's consumer long-distance operations. In 2003, WorldCom decided to change its name to MCI amid its image crisis associated with its accounting scandal. WorldCom believed that the MCI reputation wasn't as tarnished as the WorldCom brand. Former MCI employees say that they feel a deep sadness. "For years, we all felt like we were making a difference in the world, that we were always on the right side of competition," stated Frank Walter, former vice president of corporate relations for MCI. "I think anyone who worked for MCI is devastated" (Blumenstein, Dreazen, and Chittum 2002, A9).

INVITATION TO DISCUSS

How important is reputation? Do you think, like the WorldCom executives, that MCI's brand is still intact, or like the former MCIer that the brand has been tarnished? WorldCom could have created a new name (like Philip Morris's change to Altria Group Inc. "to better clarify its identity as the owner of both food and tobacco companies that manage some of the world's most successful brands" [see http://www.philipmorris.com]). Do you think WorldCom should have created a new name? Why or why not? How important is name recognition? Can MCI return to its former reputation?

Sources: "WorldCom to Take MCI as New Name Amid Image Crisis," *Wall Street Journal* (April 11, 2003), B6; Mitch Betts, "The Story So Far," *Computerworld* (January 20, 2003), retrieved February 25, 2004 from http://www.compuerworld.com/print-this/2003/0,4814,77644,00.html; and Rebecca Blumenstein, Yochi J. Dreazen, and Ryan Chittum, "Questioning the Books: MCI, a Company with a Cause, Has Reputation Hurt by Scandal," *Wall Street Journal* (June 28, 2002), A9.

technology is in constant flux, and the capital markets have deteriorated. It is a world that favors new products and customer care over cost cutting, and expects growth in sales as well as the bottom line. WorldCom and Ebbers never excelled at product evolution and customer care and service, partly because they didn't have to. Take customer relations. Though Ebbers's cost cutting won kudos from investors, neither Wall

Street nor Ebbers seemed concerned that slashing expense budgets made it nearly impossible for high-end sales reps to entertain customers and prospective clients. One WorldCom executive remembers meeting with Ebbers during a particularly good year for his division. Ebbers looked up from a spreadsheet and admonished him, saying, "I see you spent $3,000 taking customers to a Cubs game."[30] Customers had come to expect these types of perks, but Ebbers wasn't interested in providing them.

WorldCom was far from a leader in developing new products and services, either. For example, Ebbers formed an interest in owning wireless assets only after many purses and pockets already had cell phones in them. Even as it became the nation's number-one carrier of Internet traffic, WorldCom ignored such trends as high-end corporate Web site management.[31]

By early 2001, WorldCom's growth had started to slow. The thriving telecommunications market itself was beginning to falter after a frenzied investment in fiber-optic networks. Multibillion-dollar contracts had been signed with third-party telecommunications firms such as Baby Bells to ensure that WorldCom would be able to complete calls for its customers. WorldCom found that roughly 15 percent of these costs weren't producing revenue. But WorldCom was not alone in this situation. Suddenly, telecom firms found that there was too much fiber, too much capacity, and too much inventory across the whole telecommunications industry. How WorldCom handled the situation is what distinguished it. Instead of reducing profits by the costs of the access charges that were not producing revenue, WorldCom accounting irregularities spread those costs to a future time when the anticipated revenue might arrive. This violated one of accounting's most fundamental rules—capital costs should be connected to long-term investments, not ongoing activities.[32]

Unfortunately, WorldCom had few ways to compensate for the slowing growth. Although overcapacity in the telecom industry prevented price increases, it tried to at least maintain prices. It could cut costs, but was already running very lean—a trademark of Ebbers's management style. Consequently, WorldCom needed to sell more sophisticated and pricier services, such as Web hosting and private-line services that route calls over the Internet. However, it had been promising heady results from new services for years, but those results never materialized.[33]

WorldCom's bookkeeping abuses revealed the difficulty even large telecom firms had to make money amid a vast oversupply of network capacity and intense price competition. To competitors it seemed that WorldCom had some secret formula for producing decent margins when they could not. Such deception put additional pricing pressure on other carriers, made investors and lenders apprehensive of anything telecom related, and forced telecom firms to cut back orders and cannibalize their capital expenditure budgets to survive.[34]

30. Stephanie N. Mehta, "MCI: Is Being Good Good Enough?" *Fortune* 148 (9) (October 27, 2003), p. 117–124.

31. Mehta, "Can Bernie Bounce Back?"

32. Sandberg, Solomon, and Blumenstein, "Disconnected: Inside WorldCom's Unearthing of a Vast Accounting Scandal."

33. Mehta, "Feature: WorldCom's Bad Trip."

34. Mehta, "Telecom: Is There Any Way Out of the Telecom Mess?"

The collapse of WorldCom demonstrates how a single earnings number at the bottom of an income statement can be built on a collection of manipulations that produce deceptive results.[35] By merely tweaking assumptions, WorldCom exactly met analysts' earnings expectation, avoiding the penalty that investors were imposing on other companies that failed to meet or beat their numbers.

Did Bernie Ebbers Know?

To be found guilty of criminal charges, prosecutors had to prove that Bernie Ebbers willfully or recklessly violated securities laws that prohibit the dissemination of materially false financial statements. Prosecutors needed to demonstrate not only that Ebbers knew of the accounting in question but also that he knew it was illegal or fraudulent. That left room for Ebbers to argue that he didn't know that what Scott Sullivan was doing was wrong.[36]

Did Bernie Ebbers know what was going on? He had an eye for numbers. He cut budgets and managed minutiae. Some people close to the company said Ebbers must have known about Sullivan's actions. The two men were inseparable and had adjoining offices. Other WorldCom officials found it hard to believe that Ebbers was schooled enough in accounting to understand what Sullivan was doing.[37] Some casual observers and insiders of the telecom industry argued that Bernie Ebbers did not understand the telecom industry—he wasn't even a telecom guy, "just a stingy motel operator." But that wasn't quite true. Ebbers had been the CEO of WorldCom for seventeen years.

If no evidence directly implicating Ebbers in the fraud is uncovered, investigators could build a circumstantial evidence case against Ebbers, driven by the size of the fraud and the fact that he was in charge of the company. There is some evidence that Ebbers knew about the methods that artificially inflated the company's earnings. First, Scott Sullivan, ex-CFO of WorldCom, gave federal prosecutors a broad outline of discussions he had had with Ebbers about the company's fraudulent accounting practices. Although the outline did not directly link Ebbers to the company's fraudulent accounting practices it did make it clear that he knew about them.[38]

Accounts of meetings, e-mails, and voice mails also suggest that Ebbers knew about the accounting improprieties. While Ebbers did not use e-mail, a memo written by Ebbers to Ron Beaumont, the company's chief operating officer, indicated that Ebbers knew about the accounting entries used to meet analysts' revenue expectations. Ebbers allegedly knew about a double set of books kept by WorldCom's accountants

35. Henry Sender, "Inside the WorldCom Numbers Factory," *Wall Street Journal* (August 21, 2002), Cl, Heard on the Street.

36. Laurie P. Cohen, Susan Pulliam, and Deborah Solomon, "WorldCom Report Suggests Ebbers Knew of Accounting Irregularities," *Wall Street Journal* (March 12, 2003), A3, and Yochi J. Dreazen, Shawn Young, and Carrick Mollenkamp, "Sullivan Says Ebbers Knew of WorldCom Methods," *Wall Street Journal* (July 12, 2002), A3, Leading the News.

37. Jared Sandberg, "Was Ebbers Aware of Accounting Move at His WorldCom?" *Wall Street Journal* (July 1, 2002), A3, Leading the News.

38. Laurie P. Cohen, and Deborah Solomon, "Ex-Finance Chief at WorldCom Outlines Talks," *Wall Street Journal* (December 20, 2002), A3.

and made it clear that he wanted sales commissions paid on the true revenue figures rather than the adjusted ones.[39]

Who Can Be Blamed?

Many share the blame. Richard Thornburgh, former U.S. Attorney General, was appointed the bankruptcy court examiner in charge of investigating the WorldCom fraud. Thornburgh's three reports describe a company culture rampant with conflicts of interests and lacking proper controls. With the speedy acquisition of more than seventy companies, WorldCom's management and internal controls could not keep pace. He found fault with WorldCom's board of directors, external accountants, lawyers, and investment bankers.

The board of directors and its audit committee were ineffective and abdicated many of their responsibilities to Ebbers. Consequently, they were often kept in the dark. The board agreed to extend more than $400 million in loans to Ebbers at rates far below commercial interest rates without checking his ability to repay the loans.[40] Ebbers argued that stockholders benefited from these loans. He had already agreed to sell 3 million WorldCom shares to meet a margin call, and the loans kept him from having to sell even more, which would have hurt the share price. Critics of such corporate loans, however, protested that they diverted company resources to benefit executives at the expense of shareholders.[41]

Arthur Andersen, the company's external auditor, somehow missed WorldCom's senior management's override of internal controls to hide its true financial condition. This was despite warnings from suspicious WorldCom employees as far back as 2000. Andersen stated that they brought the issue to the attention of senior financial management at WorldCom and were informed that the issue would be corrected in the third quarter of 2000.[42] This suggests, however, that Arthur Andersen was too lackadaisical, especially given its own maximum-risk client label for WorldCom.[43] WorldCom executives kept Andersen in the dark by altering crucial documents and denying access to a database in which the most sensitive financial numbers were stored. Why didn't Andersen complain to the company's board or its audit committee? Instead, the accounting firm kept signing off on WorldCom's numbers, which company executives used to silence questions from its critics about its financial situation.

Criticism of WorldCom general counsel, Michael Salsbury, occurred because of his lack of advice which allowed the fraud to occur in the first place.[44] In most corporate contexts, counsel takes the responsibility of advising management and a board of directors on corporate governance structure. Salsbury did not see this as his

39. Cohen, Pulliam, and Solomon, "WorldCom Report Suggests Ebbers Knew of Accounting Irregularities."

40. Nick Baker, "Update: WorldCom Report Critical of KPMG Plan, Citigroup," *Wall Street Journal* (January 26, 2004), http://online.wsj.com/article_print/0,BT_CO_20040126_006195,00.htm.

41. Mehta, "Can Bernie Bounce Back?"

42. Yochi J. Dreazen, and Deborah Solomon, "WorldCom Alerts about Accounting Went Unheeded," *Wall Street Journal* (July 15, 2002), A3.

43. Pulliam and Sandberg, "WorldCom Seeks SEC Accord as Report Claims Wider Fraud."

44. Rebecca Blumenstein and Jesse Drucker, "MCI's Treasurer, Counsel Resign after Disclosures," *Wall Street Journal* (June 11, 2003), A3, A12.

responsibility and did not advise on such matters. The board hence did not benefit from expert advice that might have helped to avoid some of the monitoring and governance problems WorldCom faced.

Conflicts of interest were prevalent in WorldCom's relationship, and more specifically Bernie Ebbers's relationship with its investment banker Salomon Smith Barney. There is substantial evidence that Ebbers steered investment banking business to Salomon Smith Barney in return for personal financial favors. Ebbers dominated the selection of WorldCom's investment bankers, steering the group to Citigroup's Salomon Smith Barney division. Over a six-year span ending in 2002, WorldCom paid Salomon more than $100 million in fees. During the same time, Salomon allowed Ebbers to buy huge stakes in several companies before shares were sold on the open market. The deals allowed Ebbers to garner a personal profit of $12 million.[45]

EPILOGUE

At its peak, shareholders of WorldCom held stock worth $118 billion. These shareholders who lost money as a result of the massive accounting fraud at WorldCom will receive $750 million in compensation under a plan to settle fraud charges filed against WorldCom by the Securities and Exchange Commission. The settlement includes a $500 million cash payment and an additional $250 million in shares of the company once it emerges from bankruptcy-court protection. Investors who are compensated through the fund will still be able to pursue separate legal action against the company in court. In addition, MCI was mandated ethics training and stringent accounting controls. WorldCom's reorganization plan, approved on October 31, 2003, by U.S. Bankruptcy Judge Arthur J. Gonzalez reduced WorldCom's total debt from $42 billion to about $5.5 billion. It was also freed of interest payments during 2003, allowing it to hoard cash. When WorldCom entered bankruptcy, it had about $200 million in cash on hand. In late 2003 it had more than $5 billion in the bank. The company also used the bankruptcy process to get out of onerous contracts with other companies. For example, WorldCom got out of contracts for tens of thousands of square feet of office space around the country.[46]

When WorldCom emerges from bankruptcy court protection, using the revived name of MCI, it will have a smaller debt load than many of its competitors. (See Figure 9.2: MCI's Debt versus Debt of Competitors.) Its debt will be about $5.5 billion compared to others. SBC's chief financial officer summed up the feelings of rivals, by saying, "We're appalled." Verizon's chairman echoed this by saying, "Crime pays."

---

45. Christopher Stern, "Report Reveals More WorldCom Problems," *Washington Post* (January 26, 2004), http://www.washingtonpost.com/ac2/wp-dyn/A49019-2004Jan26?language=printer., and Christopher Stem, "WorldCom May Owe Millions in State Taxes," *Washington Post* (January 27, 2004), E01.

46. Mehta, "MCI: Is Being Good Good Enough?"; Deborah Solomon and Shawn Young, "MCI to Pay Investors $500 Million," *Wall Street Journal* (May 20, 2003), A3, A13; Shawn Young, "MCI Boosts Payout to Shareholders," *Wall Street Journal* (July 3, 2003), A3, A5; and Christopher Stem, "Judge Backs WorldCom's Bankruptcy Reorganization Plan," *Washington Post* (October 31, 2003), http://www. washingtonpost.com/ac2/wp-dyn/A48350-2003Oct3?language=printer.

Figure 9.2 MCI's Debt versus Competitor's Debts (dollars in billions).

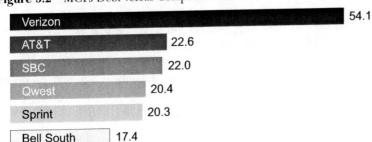

Verizon 54.1
AT&T 22.6
SBC 22.0
Qwest 20.4
Sprint 20.3
Bell South 17.4
WorldCom 5.5

Source: Rebecca Blumenstein and Gregory Zuckerman, "WorldCom: Hold the Heavyweight's Requiem," *Wall Street Journal* (April 15, 2003), C1, C3.

Commentary: Note that WorldCom's $5.5 billion debt is post-bankruptcy. WorldCom's stock will be "cancelled" when the reorganization is completed. Shareholders of WorldCom will be allocated $250 million in shares of the new MCI stock. Their WorldCom holdings-worth $118 billion at their peak-will be wiped out and replaced by the much lower amount of MCI stock.

Competitors continue to object to the $750 million settlement, saying "it is little more than a slap on the wrist for a company that perpetrated the biggest accounting fraud in U.S. history." MCI is still the nation's second largest long- distance company with 20 million customers. Businesses and government agencies continue to be the backbone of its customer base and the evolution of the Internet a focus for its growth. The only major asset sold during bankruptcy protection was an ailing wireless division.[47]

New Leadership

Michael Capellas took over as CEO of WorldCom on December 2, 2002. He was the former CEO of Compaq and president of Hewlett–Packard (when the two merged). Capellas was viewed as a straight-talking operational professional who thrives on adversity and can soothe the fears of employees, customers, and Wall Street. But, it wasn't clear whether those skills could reverse WorldCom's destruction of its public image.

Capellas signed a three-year contract valued at $20 million. He will receive an annual salary of $1.5 million, a signing bonus of $2 million, a further $1.5 million bonus if he meets certain performance targets, and $12 million in restricted stock with a vesting period of three years. If he exercises any stock options, he cannot sell the WorldCom stock for a twelve-month period.[48]

47. Young, "MCI Boosts Payout to Shareholders,"; Stem, "Judge Backs WorldCom's Bankruptcy Reorganization Plan"; Rebecca Blumenstein and Gregory Zuckerman, "WorldCom: Hold the Heavyweight's Requiem," *Wall Street Journal* (April 15, 2003), C1, C3, Heard on the Street; and Grant Gross, "Critics Slam WorldCom Bankruptcy Plan," *Network World Fusion* (July 22, 2003), http://www.nwfusion.com/cgi-bin/mailto/x.cgi.
48. Colleen DeBaise, "Judges Approve WorldCom CEO's New Pay Package", *Wall Street Journal* (December 17, 2002), B7, Technology.

To fix MCI, Capellas must integrate various units that his predecessor bought, keep the cutthroat competition at bay, and align MCI's costs with those of top rivals (e.g., AT&T's operating profit margins are about 26 percent, while MCI's are about 10 percent). Capellas' theory: The company did some cost cutting around mergers but did not culturally absorb all the acquisitions to benefit from the integration savings. He believes that the restructuring of WorldCom will require more layoffs and deeper cuts in cost structure. He urges employees to place more emphasis on new products and winning small and medium-sized business customers.[49]

UPDATE

After two years of trying to build a case against Ebbers, federal prosecutors indicted him on March 2, 2004, and he was led away in handcuffs. Former WorldCom CFO, Scott Sullivan, pleaded guilty to devising a massive accounting fraud that pushed WorldCom into bankruptcy. He agreed to cooperate with the federal prosecutors in the continuing investigation of WorldCom. Ebbers was charged with conspiracy to commit securities fraud and filing a false statement with the U.S. Securities and Exchange Commission. The government alleged that the two men were well aware of what they were doing. Reid Weingarten, an attorney for Ebbers, stated that Ebbers never intended to mislead investors or to improperly manipulate WorldCom's numbers. In addition, he believes that a "fair-minded jury" will find that Ebbers never acted with criminal intent. Both men face up to twenty-five years in prison.[50]

WHAT CAN BE LEARNED?

Fear and intimidation set the climate for corporate wrongdoing. A few employees challenged Scott Sullivan's actions. For example, Steven Brabbs, who ran a WorldCom international division, reported his suspicions about accounting improprieties to Arthur Andersen. He was reprimanded by his boss and got nowhere with his complaint. Other employees did not disclose accounting problems they discovered because they felt intimidated and feared for their jobs. Bankruptcy court reports indicated that while dozens of people knew about the fraud, it remained hidden from auditors and investors because employees were afraid to speak out. If employees do not have the confidence to challenge their boss when they believe activities are wrong or unethical, corporate wrong-doing is likely to go unchecked.

49. Stephanie N. Mehta, "WorldCom: Can Mike Save WorldCom?" *Fortune* (December 3, 2002): http://www.fortune.com/subs/print/0,15935,395214,00.html; Shawn Young, "WorldCom Plans Deeper Cost Cuts," *Wall Street Journal* (January 15, 2003), B5, Technology; and Neil Weinberg, "Screaming Match," *Forbes.com* (October 13, 2003), http://www.forbes.com/forbes/2003/1013/062_print.html.

50. WorldCom's Ebbers Pleads Not Guilty," *Wichita Eagle* (March 4, 2004), 4B, *Business & Money;* Aude Lagorce, "Ex-World Com CEO Bernie Ebbers Indicted," *Forbes* (March 2, 2004), http://forbes.com/commerce/2004/03/02/cx_al_ 0302ebbers.html; and Michael Rapoport and Janet Whitman, "Former WorldCom CEO Ebbers Indicted on 3 Counts," *Wall Street Journal* (March 2, 2004), http://online.wsj.com/article_print/0,BT_CO_20040302_004483,00.html.

Overly optimistic or conservative investment decisions can be disastrous. WorldCom overinvested in telecom equipment and services. This led to too much fiber, too much capacity, and too much inventory. However, WorldCom did not invest in corporate computer systems needed to monitor its huge, far-flung business. Bernie Ebbers used to loudly criticize his competitors, bragging about how he spent so little on information technology in his operations—just half what Sprint and AT&T spent.[51] Eventually he paid for his arrogance.

Adequate oversight of accounting requires checks and balances. Scott Sullivan, WorldCom's CFO at the time of the fraud, and a small group of executives were legendary for keeping tight control over WorldCom's books. Lots of corporations allow individual units to do their own accounting, and then consolidate those results for the overall corporation. Sullivan, however, eager to slash costs from the more than seventy companies WorldCom acquired since 1983, decided to centralize all of the U.S. accounting at the corporation's Mississippi headquarters. The centralization proved beneficial early on, as WorldCom did manage to aggressively cut costs. But that tight control resulted in very few checks and balances within WorldCom, and encouraged fraud.

Accounting deception will eventually be found out. It took awhile to find the accounting deceptions and abuses practiced by WorldCom's executives. Auditors could have employed industry diagnostics (not just accounting diagnostics) to recognize that Sullivan disguised operating expenses as long-term investments. Anyone who understood telecom industry norms for capital expenditures should have noticed investments were far out of usual bounds. Eventually, it did catch up with WorldCom, even though the external auditors were not the ones that discovered the fraud.[52] Rather, an astute group of internal auditors who had a sense of ethical purpose uncovered the accounting fraud. A company or individuals can only get by for so long with unethical (or criminal) actions before someone discovers their deceit.

Be wary of matching competitors' actions when their results seem too good to be true. Ken Sichau, president of business sales for AT&T, stated, "It was a mystery to us how WorldCom could report the numbers they did. It just didn't add up. We knew we were performing well in the marketplace, aggressively managing expenses, and pricing prudently. But we were determined to be more competitive with WorldCom's pricing and apparent results, so we made some tough decisions."[53] AT&T's (and other WorldCom rival's) reactions to WorldCom's actions ended up hurting them. When things seem too good to be true, they usually are.

CONSIDER

Can you add any additional learning insights?

51. David Kirkpatrick, "Fast Forward: Savvy Telecom Execs Outpaced Sleepy Auditors," *Fortune* (July 11, 2002), http://www.fortune.com/fortune/subs/print/O,15935,372759,00.html.

52. *Ibid.*

53. Mehta, "Telecom: Bird of a Feather."

QUESTIONS

1. "Crime pays" was stated by an executive of an MCI rival. Discuss.

2. It looks like WorldCom will resurrect itself—under the MCI brand name—from the largest accounting scandal ever, with $36 billion less debt. Do you think MCI should use price as a competitive weapon? Discuss the influence of a price-war on the telecommunications industry.

3. MCI's competitors are particularly bothered by the fact that MCI is scheduled to emerge from bankruptcy with most of its debt cleared off its books. MCI's rivals believe that MCI should be liquidated because it isn't fair for MCI to emerge from bankruptcy nearly debt free and able to create unfair price competition that other companies cannot afford. What do you think?

4. Do you think Bernie Ebbers knew about the accounting fraud? Do you think he should go to jail?

5. Was the $750 million settlement between the SEC and MCI fair?

6. Do you think Michael Capellas can turn around MCI, or will the company be sold off to a competitor?

7. Do you think MCI was guilty of rerouting long-distance calls to illegally reduce costs, or do you think it is sour grapes on the part of MCI's rivals?

8. Who was most to blame for WorldCom's implosion?

HANDS-ON EXERCISES

1. You are the new chief ethics officer for MCI and report directly to CEO Michael Capellas. Design a strategy to ensure ethics compliance by all employees.

2. It is 2002, and Troy Normand, an internal auditor for WorldCom, has discovered that line costs and prepaid capacity have been booked as capital expenditures when they should have been booked as operating expenses. As of yet, he has not received a satisfactory answer to his question about the practice of improperly booking operating expenses. Mr. Normand is concerned about losing his job (he has a family to support). What would you suggest Mr. Normand do in this situation?

TEAM DEBATE EXERCISES

1. It is July 2002. WorldCom has just disclosed that it has uncovered accounting improprieties for 2001 and 2002 of $3.9 billion. John Sidgmore, the CEO of WorldCom, believes that the best course of action for WorldCom is to declare bankruptcy and clear up problems through bankruptcy proceedings. Two vocal WorldCom board members believe that the best course of action for WorldCom is to sell the company to another telecommunications concern. Debate the two sides.

2. U.S. Bankruptcy Judge Arthur J. Gonzalez said that "Congress and the courts have recognized that the chief function of the bankruptcy process is to prevent the liquidation of a company for the greater economic good of saving jobs and the continued production of goods and services."[54] MCI's rivals and critics object to the SEC settlement ($750 million), saying it is little more than a slap on the wrist for the company that perpetrated the biggest accounting fraud in U.S. history. They believe that WorldCom/MCI should be liquidated. Debate the two sides.

INVITATION TO RESEARCH

1. What is the influence of the "Do Not Call" federal legislation on the telecommunications industry, and, in particular, MCI?

2. MCI's CEO Michael Capellas promised new products. He stated that there were many products and services that MCI had developed, but they had not been introduced to the market. In addition, he said that a new market for MCI would be computer and network security for business customers. Has MCI been successful at bringing new products and services to market?

3. WorldCom was scheduled to emerge from bankruptcy protection by a court-imposed deadline of February 28, 2004.[55] Did MCI emerge from bankruptcy as planned? What has happened to the company since that time?

4. Have customer care and product innovation become more important at MCI after the collapse of WorldCom? If so, what evidence supports this?

5. In July 2003, rivals AT&T, Verizon, and SBC claimed MCI engaged in a variety of schemes to avoid paying access charges, including dumping calls onto AT&T's network by routing them through Canada and disguising long-distance calls as local traffic to avoid paying access fees for use of other operators' networks.[56] Under Federal Communications Commission rules, rerouted calls are not to have the jurisdiction or status of a call changed. These allegations, if proven, would certainly raise questions about the clean-up of MCI's business ethics and practices. What was the outcome of these allegations?

6. Has the introduction of Voice Over Internet Protocol (VOIP) influenced MCI? If so, how? If not, why not?

54. Christopher Stern, "Judge Clears WorldCom's Exit from Bankruptcy," *Washington Post* (November 1, 2003), A01.

55. Christopher Stern, "WorldCom Wraps Up Restatements," *Washington Post* (January 12, 2004), E03.

56. Latour, Dreazen, and Hays, "MCI, Hoping to Exit Bankruptcy, Faces New Investigation of Fraud"; and Stephanie N. Mehta, "Spats: Fighting over the Phone," *Fortune* (August 11, 2003), http://www.fortune.com/fortune/subs/print/O,15935,474476,00.html.

CLASSIC ETHICAL VIOLATIONS

CHAPTER TEN

General Motors' Corvair versus Ralph Nader: Triggering the Age of Consumerism

*R*alph Nader precipitated a new era in business–society relations. His best-selling book *Unsafe at Any Speed* was an indictment of the safety of General Motors' rear-engine Corvair. Spawned in an age of apathy by carmakers toward highway deaths, the book had two enduring consequences.

1. It fanned consumer resentment toward certain business practices, a militancy that came to be known as *consumerism* and that was to have major implications for marketers and business in general (see the Information Box discussing consumerism).

2. It compelled General Motors to eventually withdraw the Corvair from the market when the company realized that carmakers could no longer escape blame for downplaying safety using the old rationale that drivers, not cars, caused accidents.

Nader has been a major force for change, but GM contributed to Nader's influence by not only disregarding customer safety but also attempting to discredit and intimidate him.

HORROR SCENARIOS

John Bortolozzo was a California Highway Patrol officer. In 1961, while patrolling in Santa Barbara, he noticed a Chevrolet Corvair approaching in the opposite lane. Approvingly, he noted the driver's observance of the 35-mile-per-hour speed limit. Suddenly he stiffened. The Corvair suddenly veered to the left and then turned over!

He rushed to the wreck and saw an arm with a wedding band and a wristwatch lying on the ground. He extricated an injured woman while trying to stop the blood gushing from the stub of her arm. He remembered that the woman was calm, only murmuring, "Something went wrong with my steering."[1]

---

1. This is described in Ralph Nader's *Unsafe at Any Speed* (New York: Grossman, 1965), p. 5.

INFORMATION BOX

HISTORICAL PERIODS OF CONSUMER MILITANCY (CONSUMERISM) IN THE UNITED STATES

Dates	Precipitator	Consequence
Early 1900s	Harvey W. Wiley and "poison squad" of twelve healthy young men who were fed adulterants daily with marked deterioration of health publicized dangers of preservatives then being used in food.	Law forbade adulteration and misbranding of foods and drugs sold in interstate commerce.
	Upton Sinclair's book, *The Jungle,* depicted unsanitary conditions in meat-packing plants.	Law provided for federal inspection of slaughtering, packing, and canning plants that shipped across state lines.
1930s	Drug elixir sulfanilamide was introduced without adequate safety testing, and 100 people died.	Food, Drug, and Cosmetic Act of 1936 was passed.
Mid-1960s	Ralph Nader's book, *Unsafe at Any Speed,* and Rachel Carson's *Silent Spring* were published.	A plethora of consumer protection and environmental laws passed at all levels: federal, state, and local.

INVITATION TO DISCUSS

The period of consumer militancy starting in the mid-1960s has lasted far longer than those of earlier periods and it is still evident today. Why has it had such staying power?

Officer Bortolozzo later testified in a suit brought by the driver, Mrs. Rose Pierini, against GM that, in his opinion, the design of the Corvair caused it to go out of control and flip over. At that point, GM decided to settle the case. Mrs. Pierini was awarded $76,000.

In 1962, Doreen Collins was driving her fiancé's 1960 Corvair on a narrow, two-lane highway. Suddenly it swerved out of control and hit a sixteen-ton truck head-on. Her fiancé and a child were killed. She brought suit claiming that the car was "inherently defective." Although the judge seemed sympathetic, GM lawyers argued that the fault lay with Miss Collins, who was an inexperienced driver. She had driven the Corvair for only four months and had only a learner's driving permit. They claimed that she had panicked and that the accident had nothing to do with any defect in the car. The jury acquitted GM of responsibility.

In a celebrated Florida case, two state legislators were driving on U.S. 19 when their 1962 Corvair overturned and killed one of them. In a trial that lasted six weeks,

General Motors was again acquitted of any negligence. More suits were to follow. By mid-1969, 150 had been brought against GM, with most of these settled out of court.

GENERAL MOTORS AND THE CORVAIR

In the mid-1960s, General Motors was the behemoth of American industry. In 1966, it employed 734,600 people in the United States, with a payroll of $5.1 billion. That year its net profit was $2.1 billion after taxes, the highest profit ever recorded by a U.S. firm. This came from sales of $20.7 billion, representing 5,348,568 cars sold. The Chevrolet Division led the company, with sales of 2,417,177 cars.

Chevrolet introduced the Corvair in 1959. The car featured an aluminum air-cooled engine mounted in the rear, with a swing-axle independent rear suspension. The Corvair gave the U.S. consumer an affordable sports car reminiscent of European sports cars, in particular the Porsche, but without their huge price tags. It was hailed as the most exciting innovation since automatic transmissions.

In designing the car, General Motors wanted a small, lightweight car with good fuel economy that would seat six passengers comfortably while giving a ride comparable to a standard Chevrolet sedan. With the rear-engine, rear-drive design, the floor hump for the drive shaft could be eliminated. Engineers chose the swing-axle rear suspension for lower cost, ease of assembly, ease of service, and greater simplicity of design. Production costs were thereby lowered.

However, the design had a potential hazard. On the 1960–1964 Corvairs, the rear wheel was mounted on the control arm, which hinged and pivoted on an axis near the center of the vehicle. In a sharp turn, this could cause the outside wheel to tuck under and cause steering difficulties. Until the 1964 Corvair, only the shock absorbers limited this problem, but this is not a function shock absorbers are designed to perform. Tire blow-outs, wind gusts, cornering maneuvers, and the second leg of S-shaped curves could cause the wheels to tuck under. At this critical point, it took an expert driver to take the corrective action to avoid trouble. But the Corvair was promoted as a sports car particularly appealing to youth. In trying to take curves at high speeds, the young and inexperienced drivers were especially vulnerable.

Yet, these cars were tested on proving grounds, in laboratories, and otherwise analyzed by engineers to provide information about any design limitations before being put into production. Actually, a considerable internal controversy arose among GM engineers about what some felt were serious design flaws. But Ed Cole, Chevrolet's general manager, who was also an engineer and product innovator, was "enthralled with the idea of building the first modern, rear-engine American car."[2]

The problem with the Corvair suspension was so bad that several enterprising companies realized that money was to be made from the flawed design. For example, EMPI, a California company, developed and marketed an accessory specifically for installing beneath the rear control arm of Corvairs. This stabilizer was quite effective in keeping the rear wheels in optimum contact with the roadway.

---

2. J. Patrick Wright, *On a Clear Day You Can See General Motors* (Grosse Pointe, Mich.: Wright Enterprises, 1979), p. 54.

Ford, which was also considering a rear-engine compact to compete with the Corvair, had suspicions that the Corvair design was flawed. In 1959, it acquired a Corvair that it tested on the Ford proving ground for comparison with the Ford Falcon. The engineering report stated:

> These pictures have shown only that the Corvair exhibited instability under extreme cornering conditions, under which the Falcon remained stable . . . While the average driver of the Corvair will not encounter difficulty under most normal driving conditions, there are frequently encountered emergency conditions such as slippery pavement or emergency maneuvering in which the Corvair falls considerably short of our handling standards.[3]

MOUNTING CRITICISM

By the early 1960s, criticism was mounting. The legal department at GM was inundated with lawsuits. GM executives and associates were also becoming victims. The son of the general manager of the Cadillac Division was killed in a Corvair. The son of an executive vice president was critically injured. So was the niece of Semon (Bunkie) Knudsen, head of the Pontiac Division. And the son of an Indianapolis dealer was killed in the car.[4]

Still, nothing was done to make the car safer until the 1964 models. Then, at the insistence of Knudsen, then head of Chevrolet, top management of GM relented and authorized installation of a stabilizing bar in the rear that counteracted the tendency of the car to flip. John DeLorean, former GM executive, noted that the cost of the modification was about $15 per car. But for years the top brass refused to permit this because it was "too expensive."[5] What price is a human life worth?

In May 1965, Dr. Seymour Charles, a General Motors stockholder and founder of Physicians for Automobile Safety, made a plea to management to recall all remaining 1960–1963 Corvairs so that the stabilizing parts could be installed. This was the first time a shareholder had ever publicly raised the question about unsafe vehicle design. Charles estimated that the recall would cost $25 million, equivalent to one-half of one day's gross sales, or less than five days' net profits to GM at that time.[6] But GM refused to act. The book, *The Investigation of Ralph Nader,* reported that the attorney in charge of general litigation for GM was in favor of recalling the 1960–1963 Corvairs. He had driven the car on the proving grounds at General Motors, and it had rolled over, although he was apparently not injured. However, three weeks later, at the age of fifty-four, he died of a cerebral thrombosis. It is not known if the accident contributed to his death. One can only speculate on what might have happened if this attorney had lived and pressured for recall.[7] It remained for the power of the press, in particular the soon-to-appear bestseller of Ralph Nader, to stimulate corrective action.

3. "Corvair's Second Case," *Time* (September 10, 1965), p. 37.
4. Wright, p. 55.
5. *Ibid.* p. 56
6. "Profits vs. Engineering: The Corvair Story," *Nation* (November 1, 1965), p. 295.
7. Thomas Whiteside, *The Investigation of Ralph Nader* (New York: Arbor House, 1972).

RALPH NADER'S INDICTMENT OF THE CORVAIR

Ralph Nader was born in 1934, so he was not much more than thirty years old when he came to national prominence. He was six feet, two inches tall, slender, and unmarried. He graduated from Princeton University magna cum laude in 1955, and from Harvard Law School with distinction in 1958.

He served a six-month tour of active duty in the Army Reserve and then entered private law practice in Hartford, Connecticut. After four years, he left commercial law and went to Washington to pursue the cause of what he liked to call "public interest law." He was particularly interested in automobile safety, but the field was not very lucrative. He supported himself by occasional lectures and articles on auto safety for the *New Republic* and the *Nation*. In 1963, he also began writing on auto safety for the *Christian Science Monitor*. Then he came to the attention of Daniel P. Moynihan, who was assistant secretary of labor. Nader began consulting for him as a writer and researcher. Just before the end of 1964, Senator Abraham A. Ribicoff's Subcommittee on Executive Reorganization invited Nader to become an unpaid adviser during the preparation of upcoming safety hearings.

During the summer of 1964, Richard Grossman, a book publisher, was looking for a writer to prepare a book on auto safety. Nader was mentioned as someone very knowledgeable about this subject. The resulting book, *Unsafe at Any Speed*, was published in 1965.

In his book, Nader accused the auto industry, as well as the traffic safety establishment, of failure to protect the public from poorly designed automobiles and charged the government with failing to set adequate safety standards for cars. Although others had written on the subject of auto safety, Nader cast blame on the entire industry's concerted negligence in depriving the public not only of safe vehicles but also of basic information concerning the vast numbers of defective cars capable of causing highway deaths. He focused his attack on one particular car: the 1960 through 1963 models of the Corvair. He accused GM of "one of the greatest acts of industrial irresponsibility in the present century," in describing the Rose Pierini suit against GM.[8]

> A great problem of contemporary life is how to control the power of economic interests which ignore the harmful effects of their applied science and technology. The automobile tragedy is one of the most serious of these man-made assaults on the human body. The history of that tragedy reveals many obstacles which must be overcome in the taming of any mechanical or biological hazard which is a by-product of industry or commerce. Our society's obligation to protect the body rights of its citizens with vigorous resolve and ample resources requires the precise, authoritative articulation and front-rank support which is being devoted to civil rights.[9]

The press quickly disseminated the allegations in the book; Nader was immediately thrust into the limelight, with frequent interviews and television appearances. On January 6, 1966, he held a press conference in Detroit concerning auto safety and

---

8. Ralph Nader, *Unsafe at Any Speed* (New York: Grossman, 1972), p. 4.
9. *Ibid.*

his criticisms of the auto manufacturers. He had invited each of the four major auto firms to send representatives to debate him. None showed up.

The next day he went to Des Moines, Iowa, to participate in a hearing conducted by State Attorney General Lawrence Scalise. During these proceedings Nader became suspicious that he was being followed. He informed Scalise, who assigned state officials to investigate. No evidence could be found to support Nader's uneasiness, but this was the beginning of General Motors' harassment of Ralph Nader, an action that was to backfire on GM and lend credence and support to Nader's allegations.

GM's Investigation of Ralph Nader

Written in late 1965, a memorandum to investigators instructed:

> Our job is to check his life and current activities to determine what makes him tick, such as his real interest in safety, his supporters, *it* any; his politics, his marital status, his friends, his women, boys, etc., drinking, dope, jobs—in fact, all facets of his life.[10]

The principals were Aloysius Power, General Motors' general counsel, and Vincent Gillen, a former FBI agent who ran a detective agency in New York. James Roche, the president of General Motors, was thought to be implicated but was able to convince later congressional investigations that he knew nothing about the extent and direction of the probe of Nader. Roche admitted to hiring detectives to investigate Nader but stated that it was only to determine whether Nader was involved in any of the Corvair cases still pending. The harassment of Nader began in January of 1966 and continued until March. It included surveillance, late-night telephone calls, and apparent efforts to lure Nader into compromising situations with young women. Nader's friends and associates from his Connecticut hometown of Winsted were questioned about his drinking habits, driving record, sex life, attitudes toward Jews, political beliefs, and credit rating, His unlisted Washington, D.C, telephone would ring in the middle of the night and "ominous-sounding voices" would ask him, "Why don't you go back to Connecticut, buddy-boy?" Gillen admitted to the Senate subcommittee that he had been told "to get something, somewhere on this guy to get him out of their hair and shut him up."[11] The press was quick to side with Nader and to criticize the "intimidation." They raised the question of the right of General Motors to pry into a person's private life.[12]

After the hearing information came out, Nader sued GM for $26 million in an invasion-of-privacy suit; he also sued Vincent Gillen for $100,000 on the same charge. Immediately, GM abandoned Gillen, but this proved to be a serious blunder on GM's part. Gillen decided to cooperate with Nader's attorneys, as long as the civil suit would be dropped. Gillen had taped all conversations he had with GM's executive

10. "GM Hired the Dick," *New Republic* (March 19, 1966), pp. 8–9.

11. "Auto Safety: Nader Again," *Newsweek* (February 20, 1967), pp. 85–86.

12. For example, James Ridgway and David Sanford, "The Nader Affair," *New Republic* (February 18, 1967), p. 9; Elinor Langer, "Auto Safety: Nader vs. GM," *Science* (April 1, 1965), p. 48; and "Private Eyes vs. Public Hearings," *Newsweek* (April 4, 1966), pp. 77–78.

counsel and proved that GM was indeed trying to harass and discredit Nader. In 1970, Nader accepted a settlement out of court for $425,000, which, according to Nader's attorney, was the largest such settlement for an invasion-of-privacy action. After legal fees, Nader was left with $284,000, which he put into consumer advocacy programs, including a renewed attack on the Corvair.[13]

Thus, General Motors' inept handling of the Nader affair put the company back into the villain's role it had been trying to shake off regarding product safety and made a hero of one of its most determined critics.

Consequences for General Motors

The publicity given the Corvair case and Ralph Nader brought General Motors a tarnished image, a reputation of deceit, dishonesty, and unconcern for customer safety. Sales and profits were affected. And lawsuits by Corvair owners proliferated.

In May 1969, ten years and 1,710,018 sales later, the last Corvair came off the assembly line at General Motors' Willow Run, Michigan, plant. During 1960, its first full year of production, 229,985 cars had been sold. By 1964, Corvair sales were down to 193,642 cars. In 1965, Nader's book was published, and in 1966 only 88,951 Corvairs were sold. By 1968, sales had dropped to 12,977. Also during this time, competition was increasing from European and Japanese imports, as well as from other sporty cars such as Ford's Mustang, but more than anything else, Corvair was done in by the attacks of Ralph Nader.

In view of Corvair's plummeting sales after 1965, why did General Motors continue to manufacture the car as long as it did? Legal reasons may have accounted for this. Dropping the car might have been construed as an admission of guilt in view of all the pending court cases and public and congressional questions of the automobile's safety.

The Corvair blunder had far-reaching repercussions. President Lyndon Johnson proposed the Traffic Safety Act, authorizing the secretary of commerce to set safety standards. Detroit was to be given two years to increase safety or the government would step in. The act was passed by the Senate on June 23, 1966, and signed into law by the president on September 5, 1966, as the National Traffic and Motor Vehicle Safety Act of 1966. The new law required that (1) the secretary of transportation establish appropriate federal automobile standards, (2) civil sanctions be imposed on manufacturers who produce vehicles or parts of vehicles not meeting these standards, and (3) the manufacturer be required to notify its customers of any defects or flaws later discovered in the vehicle.

Thus, an important initial step was taken to improve automobile safety for the general public. This was to lead to other advances, such as padded dashes, passive restraints, antilock brakes, and air bags.

FACTORS BEHIND THE DEBACLE

We can identify these major factors that led General Motors down the path of the Corvair disaster:

13. Ed Cray, *Chrome Colossus: General Motors and Its Times* (San Francisco: Mc Graw-Hill, 1980), p. 427.

Ignoring or Condoning the Risks

Here we see a classic disregard for the customer, except as a source of revenue. The objective was to design cars to make sales and to maximize profits. Safety was not a top priority; keeping costs down and maximizing profits was.

In the late 1950s, GM wanted to build a car that could compete with the smaller, lighter, European cars, yet be priced low enough for widespread demand. By 1959, four years after the initial decision, the Corvair was introduced. Perhaps this was too short a time to develop an innovative product as complex as a car. The profit motive persuaded the company to rush the car to market, despite "a few imperfections."

Since its beginning, the automobile industry had had no standard safety regulations. The automakers primarily depended on the Society of Automotive Engineers to set safety standards. But one might suspect that this body was not entirely objective, since members were employed by the key automakers, who were eager to produce vehicles at the lowest possible cost. Stringent safety standards would increase manufacturing costs, and the jobs of SAE members might even be in jeopardy. Perhaps there was a crucial lack of communication between the engineers and the top-level executives most interested in bottom-line results. We are left to wonder why no engineer spoke out or became a whistleblower, given driving-test evidence of product instability and possible danger. (See the Information Box discussing *whistleblowing.*)

Intimidation of Ralph Nader

GM added immeasurably to its problems by its injudicious investigation of its major critic. Perhaps such an investigation could have been supported *if* it had been a routine attempt to ensure that no conflict of interest existed between Nader and one or more plaintiffs in lawsuits against GM. But it went too far—beyond the bounds of the ethical to the point of invasion of privacy and harassment. The rationale behind the overzealous probe was to protect General Motors' reputation and discredit Ralph Nader. In fact, the investigation tarnished GM's reputation and made Ralph Nader a hero.

Lack of Top Executive Communication and Control

The president, James Roche, apparently relied on the general counsel to handle the matter of Nader. Roche claimed he did not know what the general counsel was really doing, and apparently he received no progress reports concerning the investigation. The general counsel, Aloysius Powers, did not exercise close restraints on the chief investigator, Vincent Gillen. So we have a situation of a president of a major corporation and his chief attorney not being on top of what was actually happening in the field, until too late.

Perhaps the directives by top management were unclear or were poorly understood. On the one hand, the increasing popularity of Nader and his mounting criticisms may have been interpreted by subordinates as pressure to intensify this probe, so that they went beyond the bounds of what was proper and expected by management. On the other hand, protestations of ignorance by top executives may have simply been buck-passing, an attempt to escape blame.

INFORMATION BOX

WHISTLEBLOWING—AGAIN!

A whistleblower is an insider in an organization who publicizes alleged organizational misconduct. Such misconduct may involve unethical practices of all kinds, from fraud, restraint of trade, bribes, coercion, to unsafe products and facilities, as well as violations of other laws and regulations. Presumably, the whistleblower has exhausted the possibilities for changing the questionable practices within the organizational channels and as a last resort has taken the matter to the public officials and/or the press, which is often panting for sensational evidence of misconduct.

Since whistleblowing may result in contract cancellations and lost jobs, those who become whistleblowers may be vilified by their fellow workers and ostracized by their firms. This makes whistleblowing a course of action only for the truly courageous whose concern for societal best interest outweighs their concern for themselves. (However, there is sometimes a thin line between an employee who truly believes the public interest is jeopardized and the individual who has a gripe or is a fanatic. There are some who believe management is condoning misconduct when, in fact, such misconduct may be isolated and without awareness or acceptance.)

Ralph Nader, in a 1972 book on whistleblowing, suggested that corporate employees have a primary duty to protect society that exists over and above secondary obligations to the corporation. He gives examples of whistleblowing heroes, as well as courses of action for other would-be whistleblowers.[14]

INVITATION TO DISCUSS

Do you think you could ever be a whistleblower? Under what circumstances?

UPDATE ON RALPH NADER

After beating giant General Motors, and receiving international acclaim with his best-selling book *Unsafe At Any Speed*, Ralph Nader pursued his calling to be the pre-eminent consumer watchdog. In the 1970s, he founded such groups as Public Citizen, a consumer-protection group; Aviation Consumer Action project, advocating tougher airline safety and consumer-rights measures; and the Center for Auto Safety, a watchdog for motorists' rights. He has remained active with them ever since.

In December 2000, the Supreme Court ruled that a ballot recount in Florida must be statewide to satisfy the equal protection clause, effectively making George W. Bush the winner of the presidential election in Florida by 537 votes. Nader, who was a long-shot presidential candidate, won 97,488 votes in Florida. Ever since, organizations affiliated with Nader have been reeling from the backlash of onetime supporters who

---

14. Ralph Nader, Peter Petkas, and Nate Blackwell, *Whistleblowing* (New York: Bantam Books, 1972).

accuse Nader of luring voters away from the Democratic party in 2000 and vaulting Bush to the presidency. One former supporter publicly said, "Ralph Nader is a name that shall live in infamy." Although his public citizen's activities are "admirable," Nader's impact on the 2000 campaign "is such a capital offense that it outweighs everything else."[15]

Nader tried to dispute the argument that he cost Gore the election, citing exit-poll data indicating that many of his supporters would have stayed home, while some 25 percent would have voted for Bush in Florida had he not been on the ticket.

Still, memberships in his various organizations dropped 20 to 25 percent and contributions plummeted. In 2004, some of the organizations were threatening to take Nader's name off their letterheads as he positioned himself to run again in 2004.

WHAT CAN BE LEARNED?

One person can make a difference. Since the notorious Corvair case, we have come to realize that business cannot be relied upon to protect us from safety deficiencies in its own products. The government has thus become actively involved. Ralph Nader is not single-handedly responsible for the changes in product safety regulations, but his well-researched book and his consumer-interest efforts have helped bring this about. Even General Motors back in 1965 must have realized his potential influence, or they would have ignored him.

The example of Ralph Nader shows us that the small can successfully shake the mighty. Our importance in the scheme of things has suddenly achieved a new meaning and vitality—because of Nader. Exercising the power of the individual, however, is not for the weak and timid but for the courageous and persevering.

Apathy toward society promotes governmental intervention. For decades, automobile manufacturers ignored many car safety considerations—even though it was technologically possible to make cars safer—because adding safety features would raise production costs. Furthermore, the industry had the mindset that safety did not sell, that customers would not pay extra to lower their risk of injury or death. That mindset was not totally unfounded. We see even today that some people resent the requirement that vehicles carry airbags, which add to the sticker price and carry their own, albeit smaller, risks. Eventually, business and public apathy toward the best interests of society is often violently overcome, perhaps by best-selling books such as *Unsafe at Any Speed* and Rachel Carson's *Silent Spring* (which took on the chemical industry) or by investigative reporters. As public apathy shifts into a smoldering, and then more vehement resentment, government eventually imposes regulations on the industry. The following diagram illustrates the common progression:

| Public apathy | Media attention | Public resentment and outcry | Imposition of government regulations |

→

Time

15. Stephen Power, "Reeling From Nader Backlash," *Wall Street Journal* (January 14, 2004), p. A10.

We see this classic pattern in the Corvair case, which resulted in the National Traffic and Motor Vehicle Safety Act of 1966.

What can a firm do about this scenario? The obvious answer is to be fully responsive to *serving* the customer. Serving implies several things.

1. Meeting customers' needs as efficiently as possible, both to hold costs down without sacrificing reasonable quality standards and safety and also to maximize customer utility from the product or service
2. Protecting the general public—society—from unsafe or environmentally dangerous products or manufacturing facilities

For the auto industry, an unsafe product, such as a Corvair that is uncontrollable under certain circumstances, endangers not only the customer who bought the car but innocent people who are exposed to an accident-prone situation.

The threat of litigation should motivate most firms today to exercise reasonable prudence in their products and operations. But the final motivation to correct any inherently dangerous situation should be the threat of governmental intervention. Such intervention is not always objective or most effective. It may vary from the extremes of punitive and bureaucratic nit-picking to weak and inadequate protection. At the very least, government regulation involves compliance, red tape, and constraints. Yet, many would see this as the just desserts of firms who are careless with the public welfare.

Emphasis on maximizing short-term profits can lead to flawed business practices. While a firm needs to make a profit in order to survive and prosper, the single-minded pursuit of maximizing immediate profits can be perilous. It often is incompatible with the customer's best interest, as well as the long-term success of the firm. We saw this starkly with the Corvair. We will encounter other cases in which short-term concern with maximizing or protecting profits has led to abusive practices and cover-ups, as well as public disgrace.

Most firms are in the business for the long haul; such business depends on continued customer satisfaction and protection. Such a mission might mean sacrificing some profits and increasing some costs in order to solidify relationships and ensure customer satisfaction in the future.

Top management is ultimately responsible. Top management is ultimately responsible and accountable for what goes on within the organization no matter how large the organization may be. This is a sacred principle of leadership and authority. Top management is quick to take credit—and be rewarded with huge bonuses—for a firm's success; to repudiate any responsibility for the organization's failings or misdeeds is hardly appropriate. So, the protestations of ignorance of the Corvair–Nader affair by top GM brass should in no way excuse them. (We will encounter other buck-passing by top executives in some of the cases that follow.) But while top management may not know the details of any misdeeds, they are instrumental in fostering a climate in the organization of unconcern for customer welfare and scrupulously honest conduct, subordinating everything to short-term profit maximization. Yes, the ultimate responsibility for corporate violations of the public trust should rest with top management.

Mechanistic attitudes sometimes prevail in executive suites. Something seems to happen to the conscience and the moral sensitivity of top executives. They commission actions in their corporate personas that they would hardly dream of doing in their private lives. John DeLorean, former GM executive, was one of the first to note this dichotomy:

> These were not immoral men who were bringing out this car [the Corvair]. These were warm, breathing men with families and children who as private individuals would never have approved this project for a minute if they were told, "You are going to kill and injure people with this car." But these same men, in a business atmosphere, where everything is reduced to terms of costs, profit goals, and productive deadlines, were able to approve a product most of them wouldn't have considered approving as individuals.[16]

We encounter this same mechanistic mindset, devoid of a human context, in a number of other cases. We have to raise the question: Why this lockstep obsession with sales and profit at all costs? See the following Information Box for a discussion of this question.

CONSIDER

Can you think of other learning insights?

QUESTIONS

1. Can the president or CEO of an organization disavow himself or herself of the illegal or unethical actions of subordinates?

2. How can an organization's orientation be changed from short-term to long-term profit maximization? Be as specific as possible.

3. How do you account for the fact that the engineering staff of GM was negligent in revealing the dangerous deficiencies of the Corvair? How could a better customer orientation be fostered?

4. How do you account for the way the Ralph Nader investigators exceeded the bounds of moral and ethical conduct? How would you design controls to prevent such abuses from occurring again?

5. The two earlier periods of consumer militancy were short-lived. The present one has lasted over twenty years, even though it is not as well-publicized today as in the past, perhaps because the worst of the perceived problems have been corrected. How do you account for the long-lasting consumerism of today compared to the short-lived agitation at the turn of the century and in the 1930s?

16. *On a Clear Day,* pp. 5–6.

INFORMATION BOX

WHY THE QUESTIONABLE ETHICAL DECISIONS OF GROUPTHINK?

The callousness regarding the Corvair, despite increasing evidence that it was a "killer" car, would, as John DeLorean pointed out, probably never have prevailed if an individual was making the decision outside the corporate environment. But bring in *groupthink*, which is decision by committee, and add to this a high degree of organizational loyalty (versus loyalty to the public interest), and such callousness can manifest itself. Why can the moral standards of groupthink be so much lower than individual moral standards?

Perhaps the answer lies in the "pack mentality" that can characterize certain committees or groups highly committed to organizational goals. All else then becomes subordinate to these goals, being a single-minded perspective. Within any committee, individual responsibility for decisions is diluted since this is a committee decision. Furthermore, without the contrary arguments of a strong "devil's advocate" (i.e., one who argues the opposing viewpoint, sometimes simply to be sure that all sides of an issue are considered), a follow-the-leader syndrome can take place, with no one willing to oppose the majority views.

But there is more to it than that. Chester Barnard, a business executive, scholar, and philosopher, noted the paradox: People have a number of private moral codes that affect behavior in different situations, and these codes are not always compatible. Codes for private life, regarding family and religion, may be far different from codes for business life. Throughout the history of business, it has not been unusual to find that the scrupulous and God-fearing churchgoer is far different when he or she conducts business during the week: a far lower ethical standard prevails during the week than on the Sabbath. Nor has it been unusual to find that a person can be a paragon of love, understanding, and empathy with his or her family but be totally lacking in such qualities with employees or customers. (Even tyrants guilty of the most extreme atrocities, such as Hitler and Saddam Hussein, have been known to exude great tenderness and consideration for their intimates.)

It takes a strong personal code of ethics to control one's conduct in the presence of strong contrary desires or impulses.[17]

INVITATION TO DISCUSS

What does it take for a person to resist and not accept the majority viewpoint? What do you think would be the characteristics of such a person? Do you see yourself as such a gadfly?

HANDS-ON EXERCISES

1. Place yourself in the role of an engineer at Chevrolet's Corvair unit. You have strong reasons to believe the car is unsafe, but higher management is unresponsive to your concerns. What do you do now?

17. Chester I. Barnard, *The Functions of the Executive* (Cambridge, Mass.: Harvard University Press, 1938), p. 263.

2. Place yourself in the position of James Roche, the president of GM. You want to instill in your massive organization greater concern for the customer. Discuss how you would go about fostering and controlling such an orientation and commitment among your executives and workers. What problems do you see?

TEAM DEBATE EXERCISES

1. Debate the decision to try to discredit Ralph Nader. Do not be swayed by what actually happened—maybe the situation demanded doing everything possible to blunt his charges.

2. Debate the decision to continue the Corvair after Nader's book came out. Do not be swayed by lawyers' arguments that dropping the car would be an admission of guilt.

3. Debate Nader's decision to run in the 2000 presidential election.

INVITATION TO RESEARCH

1. Review Nader's book on whistleblowing and, in particular, his recommendations for would-be whistleblowers. In your opinion, how practical is this advice today?

2. Did Nader continue his run for the presidency in 2004? If so, what did he accomplish?

CHAPTER ELEVEN

Union Carbide: Assault on the Ohio Valley

Ralph Nader also became involved in an environmental dispute concerning a major polluter, Union Carbide Corporation. Nader helped pressure the company and governmental bureaucracy toward remedial action after some twenty years of worsening air pollution and after a Nader-sponsored book, *The Vanishing Air*, published in 1970, highlighted this and other national environmental concerns.

THE OHIO VALLEY POLLUTION PROBLEM

The Ohio River between Ohio and West Virginia flows through a relatively narrow valley with rounded hills rising 200 to 300 feet above the valley floor on either side. The scenic valley is partially protected from strong winds, but this tends to cause pollutants to accumulate in high concentrations. The valley had become a home to large metal-processing and chemical plants. And these have created pollution, both from their manufacturing processes and from the combustion of coal used to meet their energy requirements.

Union Carbide began its operations in the Ohio Valley in 1950, with the opening of an electrometallurgical plant in Riverview, Ohio. This was shortly followed by plants in Alloy, West Virginia; Anmoore, West Virginia; Marietta, Ohio; and Institute, West Virginia. Although the plants made a major contribution to the economy of this area, it was not long before pollution problems became evident. As early as 1951, a citizens' committee was formed to fight air pollution, and in 1954 it pressured Union Carbide to install dust control equipment. However, air pollution grew worse as the industry expanded, and in 1964 a county health department complained that Union Carbide was causing a major problem to local residents with its emissions of heavy soot.

In March 1967, officials from the Department of Health, Education and Welfare (HEW) convened an interstate conference in Parkersburg, West Virginia, to examine air pollution problems in the area around Parkersburg and Marietta. During the conference, federal officials presented a fifteen-year documentation of high air pollution levels (high enough to cause injury to vegetation and property), soot and ash, foul odors, and high incidences of cardiorespiratory disease. Local citizens pleaded for help. But in spite of strong evidence, the question of emissions was never resolved, and the first Parkersburg conference proved to be fruitless. As the Nader-sponsored book described the result:

> The agency [the National Air Pollution Control Administration (NAPCA)] had allowed itself to be hornswoggled by the Union Carbide Corporation, the region's number one environmental enemy, the Ohio State Department of Health, and Ohio Congressman Clarence Millart. The indifference of the Secretary and the timidity of the West Virginia Air Pollution Control Commission helped to make the "take" complete.[1]

UNION CARBIDE INTRANSIGENCE

From the beginning, Union Carbide had exhibited a cavalier attitude and apparent lack of concern about environmental degradation. The company repudiated any assumption of social responsibility for the worsening Ohio Valley contamination. But the battle lines were being drawn. By 1970, environmentalists were to label Union Carbide's ferro-alloy plant in Alloy, West Virginia, "the world's smokiest factory." Dense layers of soot-laden smoke streamed constantly from the plant, dumping masses of black grit on nearby communities. In all, it was alleged that the factory poured out more health-endangering particles in one year than the total emitted by all of New York City.[2]

Eventually, Union Carbide was to become a symbol of corporate resistance to pollution controls. It was to find itself the center of a controversy that pitted one of the nation's largest corporations against local citizens, environmentalists, and the federal government. It was to receive national attention after it denied agents of the federal government's National Air Pollution Control Administration (NAPCA) entry into its Marietta plant.

The Runaround

On August 29, 1967, five months after the first Parkersburg conference, NAPCA sent a letter to Union Carbide plant manager G. G. Borden asking for permission to inspect the Marietta plant. Borden replied on September 7, 1967, that he was "giving the matter careful consideration, but with vacations, etc., [he was] unable to help at that time."[3] Four months went by with no further reply. NAPCA repeated its request on January 11, 1968. Union Carbide replied twenty days later that at this time they were already spending a considerable amount of money on antipollution devices. However, no specifics were mentioned, and NAPCA's request for an inspection was completely ignored.

---

1. John C. Esposito and Larry J. Silverman, *Vanishing Air* (New York: Grossman, 1970), p. 123.

2. "Union Carbide's Big Cleanup Job," *Business Week* (November 9, 1974), p. 184.

3. As reported in *New York Times* (July 6, 1970), p. 26.

NAPCA then sent its request to Union Carbide's chief executive officer. The company responded by sending Dr. J. S. Whitaker, its coordinator for environmental health, to meet with NAPCA in April 1968. Whitaker informed the agency that the requested information already had been supplied to the Ohio State Department of Health, and that it would be more appropriate to obtain this information from them. But the Ohio State Department of Health denied all knowledge. So the runaround continued. In October 1969, a second conference was held at Parkersburg. Studies cited there noted that emissions of particulate matter from the Union Carbide plants alone had increased substantially. Increasing complaints from local residents were primarily focused on Union Carbide. The firm was accused of emitting 44,000 pounds per day of particulates and 22,000 pounds per hour of sulfur oxides. However, Carbide boycotted the conference on the grounds that it was working with state authorities, not federal agencies.[4]

Pressure Mounts

In the fall of 1970, a series of severe air-pollution episodes brought Union Carbide once again to national attention. The *New York Times* began running articles describing the controversy between Union Carbide and the local residents. People in the Ohio Valley were beginning to publicly voice their indignation and fears. In Anmoore, West Virginia, site of Union Carbide's Carbon Products Division, Mr. and Mrs. O. D. Hagedorn started a newsletter devoted exclusively to Union Carbide's activities, or lack thereof. The newsletter was distributed to local citizens through merchants, and copies were sent to the West Virginia Air Pollution Control Department, the local plant manager, company offices in Charleston, West Virginia, and the chairman of the board of Union Carbide in New York City. Still no response. Then the Hagedorns took matters one step further and filed a class-action suit against Union Carbide and federal and state air pollution control officials. The complaint was joined by fifty other families from a town of 1,000. They contended in the $100,000 suit that they had been denied their constitutional right to a decent place to live because of the pollution created by Union Carbide.[5]

Now Ralph Nader became involved. He wrote letters and organized citizen meetings in Union Carbide factory towns. He was also successful in getting higher taxes levied against Union Carbide by these towns in an effort to make the firm pay for some of the damage caused. In 1970, *Vanishing Air,* a book by a Nader study group, condemned with specific examples the growing environmental problem and the lack of sufficient concern across America.

In 1970, the government's power against polluters was strengthened by the Clean Air Act of 1970 and the newly formed Environmental Protection Agency (EPA). The administrator of the EPA, William D. Ruckelshaus, singled out Union Carbide as a test case in the government's efforts to get industry to comply with the Clean Air Act. The state of West Virginia also joined in setting stringent standards and regulations on the emissions of particulate matter from many manufacturing processes.

4. "Along the Ohio: A Test of Will," *Chemical Week* (February 10, 1971), p. 47.

5. As reported in *New York Times* (January 9, 1971), p. 11.

Eventually, Union Carbide yielded to federal and state pressure. On January 14, 1971, it agreed to clean up the pollution caused by the Marietta plant in compliance with government requirements. This was the first major victory for the new EPA and the end of a six-year dispute.

The EPA set three requirements:

1. Immediate procurement of low-sulphur coal so as to achieve a 40 percent reduction in sulphur oxide emissions.

2. Construction of taller smokestacks no later than April 1972 to eliminate the downwash by wind of soot, sulphur dioxide, and other emissions.

3. Installation of scrubbers by September 1974 to further reduce sulphur oxide emissions by 74 percent.[6]

However, even at this late date, Union Carbide still resisted compliance. Now it turned its attention to stimulating public pressure against such compliance. On January 19, 1971, the date set by the EPA for a written commitment to meet the prescribed requirements, the company announced the impending layoff of 625 employees at its Marietta plant in order to comply with the federal requirements. Union Carbide claimed that the only way it could meet the fly-ash reduction was to shut down one boiler, and thus the need to layoff 125 employees. Furthermore, the company saw no way to meet the April 1972 deadline for reduction of sulphur emissions other than by cutting production, which would result in the layoff of 500 additional workers.

This was an extremely sensitive issue: jobs. (See the Information Box for a discussion of clean air versus jobs.) Most of the workers at the Marietta plant lived in West Virginia, where per-capita income was the lowest in the nation and the unemployment rate was nearly twice the national average. For many people living there, smokestacks meant jobs and income. Factory smoke was even called "gold dust."

Then Ralph Nader entered the picture again, calling the job threat environmental blackmail in a letter to Senator Edmund Muskie, chairman of the Senate subcommittee on air and water pollution. Senator Muskie expressed deep concern and promised an investigation. The Securities and Exchange Commission also became involved. A petition had been brought before it alleging that Union Carbide was misleading stockholders regarding its pollution record, thus violating securities laws.

UNION CARBIDE CRIES "UNCLE"

The mounting pressure began to have an effect. At Union Carbide's annual meeting in April 1971, pollution and what to do about it was the main order of business. Moreover, in an attempt to improve public relations and its public image, Carbide announced a massive reorganization. Chairman Birney Mason Jr. and Vice-Chairman Kenneth H. Hannan resigned; F. Perry Wilson became chairman of the board. Dr. J. S. Whitaker, coordinator of environmental health, and the man many blamed for holding back the data and locking out government inspectors, was subordinated to a new environmental director, Philip Huffard, and the ferro-alloy division received a new president.

6. *Ibid.*

INFORMATION BOX

CLEAN AIR VERSUS JOBS

A major issue in the environmental arena is the question of jobs versus clean air (or water). When the costs of complying with government standards are too high, facilities either have to shut down or downsize. This means lost jobs. Making the issue particularly troubling is that often such decisions involve a small town where the factory in question is the major employer. If it is forced to shut down because of stringent environmental standards, the economy of the town can be devastated. The closing can have a powerful multiplier effect: many other businesses, retail and service, depend on support by factory workers. So do city tax revenues, thus affecting the school system and other city services. Real estate values plummet as the economic base is eroded. In such small towns, often no alternative employer exists.

So, there is a lot at stake when any government agency comes down hard on polluters. Does this mean that economic protection should carry a higher priority than environmental protection? The issues should be viewed in terms of relatives rather than absolutes. Perhaps the EPA and other agencies and pressure groups have sometimes been guilty of thinking too much in terms of absolutes. Demanding a certain level of air or water purity might exact too high an economic toll and thus might be unreasonable in terms of preserving a community's way of life. Likewise, refusing to make any technological improvements because of costs might be unreasonable on the part of the industry. Legitimate environmental concerns should not be thrust aside because there is a cost to addressing those concerns.

The issue is so complex that reasonable people often disagree profoundly. Yet perhaps we should shy away from extreme positions on either side. To have a bit more air purity at the cost of many jobs and many millions of dollars may be unreasonable. But our planet must be protected for ourselves, our children, and future generations. Jobs may have to be sacrificed when environmental degradation has become extreme. Diehards would support the polluting that Union Carbide did in the 1960s because it protected jobs, but the majority would see this as going too far in savaging the environment. Of course, Union Carbide was a well-heeled corporation, not some marginal firm. It could afford the costs of pollution-control equipment and lower-sulphur coal. Public support for Carbide's position faded greatly in this dispute.

INVITATION TO DISCUSS

Given the situation of a plant being the major employer in a small town, how might the issue of jobs versus cleaner air be resolved? What options do you see?

By spring 1972, Union Carbide had apparently reversed its intransigent position. It committed itself to spending some $50 million over the next several years to clean up pollution from its plants in Anmoore, Alloy, and Marietta. At the Marietta plant, $10 to $15 million had already been invested in abatement. This plant was now burning low-sulphur coal and had shut down one of its boilers. The shutdown was attributed to decreased demand for the plant's products, which included ferro-chrome, electrolytic chromium, ferromanganese, vanadium alloys, and silicon. Layoffs claimed 250 employees, not the threatened 625, and these layoffs were all attributed to the slowdown in demand. At the Alloy plant, $30 million was now committed to antipollution devices, which represented 95 percent of all plant investment over a five-year span. And in Anmoore, the Hagedorns had discontinued their newsletter. Now, Union Carbide's new chairman stated: "[Environmental considerations] have become a part of every corporate business decision from site selection to production, sales, and distribution."[7]

ANALYSIS

The Union Carbide affair in the Ohio Valley was of immense proportions. It involved a wide range of governmental agencies, from the EPA and HEW to the SEC, as well as agencies from two states, Ohio and West Virginia. It brought much bad publicity to the corporation, both locally, in the form of the Hagedorn newsletter, and nationally, from the *New York Times* to *BusinessWeek*. By polluting the air with 45,000 tons of emissions of sulphur dioxide alone, not to mention the tons of soot and fly ash spewed into the air every year, the lives and health of the area's 220,000 residents were seriously endangered. Marked increases from earlier years were found not only in respiratory illnesses but also in skin disorders, allergies, headaches, eye irritations, and psychological depression. Greater costs were also incurred in maintaining homes and other properties because of the grime and the corrosive attributes of the pollutants.

Why the Long Delay in Correcting the Situation?

The plants were almost thirty years old before they were brought into compliance. How was Union Carbide able to delay a crackdown for so long? Four key factors accounted for the insensitive procrastination:

1. At the time the plants were initially constructed and became operational in the 1950s, the environment was by no means the issue it was later to become. Not until the mid-1960s, triggered partly by Rachel Carson's *Silent Spring,* did the general public and the government fully begin to realize the current and potential dangers of the various kinds of pollution. And while pollution was occurring in the 1950s and before, it became much more serious with increased production and prosperity.

2. Although Union Carbide's sales were in excess of $3 billion, only 20 percent of its sales consisted of consumer items such as antifreeze, batteries, and plastic kitchen bags. This suggested less vulnerability to consumer pressures for reform. The company appeased its stockholders with self-flattering pronouncements. And it used evasive tactics in dealing with the government.

3. Before 1970, no federal regulatory agency had the power to coordinate environmental-protection matters; these were diffused in a number of agencies, with most efforts uncoordinated and toothless. Only in 1970, with the Clean

7. Fred C. Price, Steven Ross, and Robert L. Davidson, *Business and the Environment* (New York: McGraw-Hill, 1972), p. 49.

Air Act and the establishment of the Environmental Protection Agency, was serious regulatory power put in place. Since the EPA was a new organization, not yet having won a major confrontation, Union Carbide apparently underestimated its authority. This soon changed: the EPA won its first major confrontation—against Union Carbide.

4. Not only did Union Carbide underestimate the power of federal regulation, it also underestimated the impact of the media, the influence of consumer groups and Nader, and the determination of the local population.

Was Union Carbide the Complete Villain?

Union Carbide had been one of the first chemical firms to install an emission-control system. In 1951, when the Marietta plant opened, its smelting furnaces were equipped with scrubbers that trapped about 75 percent of the particulate emissions. And it continued to invest in new pollution-control technology during the 1960s.

We can wonder whether a more honest and direct approach by Carbide, explaining to the public and the governmental agencies about the serious costs and technological problems involved with meeting the EPA's deadlines, might have avoided much of the controversy. Both costs and technology were problems for Union Carbide at that time. Since 1965, pressures on company profits had been intensifying. It was just coming out of one of the worst financial periods in its history. Part of this was due to a major capital expansion program that had begun in 1965. By 1969, Carbide had spent $1.5 billion on new facilities. Yet, despite increased sales, earnings during this time had plummeted nearly 22 percent because of an untimely combination of factors: faulty construction, an extremely poor operating performance, and a squeeze on chemical prices.

Union Carbide was naturally reluctant to assume any additional financial burdens at that time, particularly ones that would not produce earnings. Compliance with EPA's recommendations promised to run into the millions of dollars, despite the smelting furnaces having already been equipped with scrubbers: after more than a decade, this equipment needed upgrading. Then, too, the real pollution problem was not the smelting furnaces but the generating plant that fired the furnaces. Every day, it poured out thousands of pounds of sulphur dioxide, which came from the high sulphur coal that Carbide, in order to keep costs down, mined from its own nearby coal fields and burned at the rate of a million tons per year.[8]

By switching to a low-sulphur coal, Carbide's $4.5 million annual coal bill, which was 20 percent of total production costs, would increase 50 percent. Raising the height of the stacks would cost another $1 million, and the new scrubbing system for the power plant would cost between $8 million and $10 million.[9] However, Carbide's corporate capital expenditures for the 1971–1975 period were projected at $225 million. In light of this, the projected expenditures for emission controls were hardly daunting. Untried technology was another problem. At that time, no scrubbing system

8. A Corporate Polluter Learns the Hard Way," *BusinessWeek* (February 6, 1971), p. 53.

9. Union Carbide to Shut Part of Power Plant in Pollution Dispute," *Wall Street Journal* (January 20, 1971), p. 1.

had been developed that would curtail sulphur dioxide emissions on such a large scale. Carbide was experimenting with such a system but still needed time to work out the problems. The EPA, however, was unyielding. Ruckelshaus, the EPA administrator, decided to take a tough stance with Carbide because of its irresponsible behavior in the past; he refused to grant any more delays. (See the Information Box for a discussion of the *cost–benefit analysis* that theoretically should guide requirements for pollution-control expenditures.)

INFORMATION BOX

CLEAN AIR VERSUS JOBS

A cost–benefit analysis is a systematic comparison of the costs and benefits of a proposed action. Only if the benefits exceed the costs would we normally have a "go" decision. The normal way of making such an analysis is to assign dollar values to all costs and benefits, thus providing a common basis *for* comparison.

Cost–benefit analysis has been widely used by the Defense Department in evaluating alternative weapons systems. And in recent years, such analysis has been sporadically applied to environmental regulation and even to workplace safety standards.

Theoretically, cost–benefit analysis is a very attractive way to determine environmental cleanup actions. For example, is it socially worthwhile for a firm to spend X million dollars to meet a certain standard of clean air or water? Such an analysis has the potential to determine how much should be spent for environmental protection or cleanup; it has the potential to show that, at some level of expenditure, costs will exceed the benefits, with further regulatory requirements not cost-effective.

Actually, using cost–benefit analysis to make environmental cleanup decision has serious flaws. Many of the costs, such as for improved scrubbers or taller smokestacks, can be specifically determined. But placing a dollar value on the anticipated benefits is often a problem. How much is a clear sky worth? A fishable lake? How many extra years of life may result; and what are these worth? (Even the value of a human life is subject to great differences of opinion.) Value judgments for such benefits can differ greatly. We are left with hard quantifiable numbers on the one hand and fuzzy subjective values on the other.

INVITATION TO DISCUSS

Let's examine the intriguing possibilities, but also the major problems, in a specific cost–benefit analysis:

Estimates place the cost of new scrubbers at $17.5 million. If the benefits exceed the cost of this investment, the company will be forced to comply by the government. Environmental engineers estimate that the scrubbers would improve air quality by 25 percent, resulting in less haze, less respiratory distress, less property deterioration (resulting in less maintenance) better all-around health, and generally a more aesthetically pleasing environment.

Discuss the specific process by which you would assign dollar values to these benefits.

WHAT CAN BE LEARNED?

Business has a symbiotic relationship with society. Despite business's preoccupation with profit, in reality a firm has a symbiotic relationship with society. Each benefits from the well-being of the other. Society can hardly allow a firm to falter and go bankrupt because of strict regulations and expenditure demands. To do so would mean the loss of jobs and economic support to the community and the state. But this is not as widely realized by business leaders as one might hope—the firm also benefits from a prosperous, safe, and pleasant community. Although the economic impact of such a pleasant environment may not be so directly calculated in terms of the bottom line, an environmentally desirable community provides a more pleasant lifestyle for the firm's executives, makes it easier to attract able employees and executives, makes for pleasant relationships with the community and the press and in general brings harmony to the business-societal relationship. The example of Union Carbide and its adversarial relationships in the 1960s and early 1970s shows the problems of a business-societal relationship that has gone sour.

Woe to the firm today that is insensitive to society's needs and demands. With the enactment of the Clean Air Act and other regulatory measures, and with the establishment of the Environmental Protection Agency, the public now has outlets for its concerns, which means it has clout. Any firm, large or small, that ignores or procrastinates on meeting the public's concern will surely be brought to heel. Our society has been more militant since the advent of consumerism in the mid-1960s. The general public is more concerned, less easily satisfied, unwilling to be put off, and quicker to voice its concerns. And not only will the government—federal, state, and local—listen to these concerns, but the press is quick to respond to a newsworthy issue and often, through investigative reporting, leads the way in uncovering abuses. The legal profession is always willing, indeed, eager to encourage complaints and damage suits, especially against those organizations with "deep pockets." The environment for business is very different today than it was a few decades ago. Woe to the insensitive or myopic firm today.

The issue of "jobs versus protection" is still unresolved. Both sides of this issue have been argued aggressively and emotionally. Logically, the answer lies somewhere in the gray area of moderation. Economic considerations are necessarily important to many communities. If a plant is closed because of regulatory demands, the community's very existence may be threatened. It may become a backwater inhabited mostly by the elderly, while younger families seek employment elsewhere. On the other hand, how much environmental degradation can we tolerate? These are decisions with big stakes. The solution often leaves neither position satisfied; each must sacrifice for the overall best recourse.

Major problems arise when one side or the other gains an advantage. And in our pluralistic society this often happens, not because of the merits of one position over another but because of that side's greater eloquence, its ability to attract media attention, its greater resources, or its militancy.

Environmental planning should be an important part of a firm's total planning process. Because of the threat of regulatory scrutiny and punitive action, or simply because of the recognition that environmental protection is an important part of our life and our children's quality of life, firms need to study the effect that their decisions will have on the environment. They must consider decisions that will minimize social and environmental injury.

This may mean that plant design and site selection should be given very careful scrutiny. If Union Carbide had not located its ferro-alloy plants in a valley, the pollution would not have been maintained in such great concentrations. Also, by raising the height of the smokestacks between 50 and 100 feet, much of the emissions would have been disseminated. And if low-sulphur coal had been used from the beginning, emission contaminants would have been greatly reduced.

Careful attention to environmental impact lowers the risk of blocked or rejected projects. Potential problems can be identified and corrected, thus minimizing unforeseen and costly surprises. Environmental planning reduces the potential for lengthy conflicts, such as the one Union Carbide experienced. Such adverse publicity can be costly in terms of community goodwill, employee morale, as well as the company's reputation with customers and the general public.

This kind of planning needs input from a variety of sources. Often, the people directly involved in the project are too close to it to see the potential problems. Workers themselves can be a source of information. (At Union Carbide's Marietta plant, for example, workers' concern for the dust within the plant itself resulted in the construction of a forty-five-foot wall on the operating floor between the air shafts to eliminate the dust problem.) Or outside consultants may need to be utilized. And governmental input may be needed, since an agency such as the EPA may be involved in monitoring and regulating.

CONSIDER

Can you think of additional learning insights?

QUESTIONS

1. "Environmentalists are going too far! Unless they are checked, they will destroy our free enterprise system." Evaluate this statement.

2. What do you think accounted for Union Carbide's intransigence? Would a firm today likely be as unyielding?

3. Do you have any criticisms of Ralph Nader in this episode?

4. In the 1960s and early 1970s, other factories in the Ohio Valley and the Kanawha Valley of West Virginia were contributing to air pollution. Do you think Union Carbide was unfairly singled out? In other words, should not all of the polluters have been confronted?

5. Given that the costs of environmental cleanup for an older plant are enough to make such a firm at a serious disadvantage in the competitive marketplace, what recourse does this firm have?

HANDS-ON EXERCISES

1. Put yourself in the position of the mayor of Marietta, or Anmoore, or Alloy in the late 1960s. Increasingly, citizens are complaining about the local Union Carbide plant. What course of action might you take? Discuss as many options and their implications as you can.

2. You are the plant manager of the Marietta plant in the late 1960s. You are being publicly condemned for the filthy air your plant is creating. How would you react to this situation? Be as specific as you can, with a full rationale for your recommendations.

TEAM DEBATE EXERCISE

The class should take two sides: (1) that of well-paid workers who see their livelihood jeopardized by agitating environmentalists, and (2) other people in the community, as well as outsiders, who decry the degradation of the environment and the health risks involved. Each side should array as many arguments supporting their position as they can, present them persuasively, and be prepared to defend them.

INVITATION TO RESEARCH

1. Research Union Carbide's efforts with respect to the environment since the early 1970s. Has it changed? Has it been subjected to any criticisms in recent years?

2. How serious a problem is air pollution today?

CHAPTER TWELVE

Union Carbide's Bhopal Catastrophe

On the night of December 3, 1984, a Union Carbide chemical plant located near the congested streets of Old Bhopal, a low-income area north of Bhopal, India, was involved in a disaster of monumental proportions. Dwarfing Union Carbide's earlier air-pollution problems in the Ohio Valley, the Bhopal disaster resulted in the loss of life, which made it perhaps the worst industrial disaster until that time. (Less than two years later, on April 26, 1986, a much worse disaster occurred in the Russian Ukraine when the Chernobyl nuclear plant spewed radioactive material over thousands of square miles of Europe.) Union Carbide was far more caring and responsive after the Bhopal disaster than it had been during the Ohio Valley controversy. Still, the disaster occurred. How culpable was the company? How might the loss of human life have been avoided?

THE DIMENSIONS OF THE DISASTER

Some time after 11 P.M., a worker in the plant noticed that the temperature of tank 610, which stored MIC (methyl isocyanate, a toxic chemical used in the production of pesticides), was growing dangerously high. Sometime after midnight, after attempts to bring the tank's temperature under control failed, the concrete over the tank began cracking. A runaway chemical chain reaction was taking place. Suddenly, forty tons of MIC escaped, forming a dense fog of toxic gas that began to drift toward Bhopal.

The night air was cool, around 16° C (60° F), and the wind was calm. These conditions added to the disaster, preventing the fog from dissipating. Slowly, the fog made its way through the railroad station, into homes, shops, temples, up and down streets and alleyways. It left behind bodies, both human and animal, and panic.

An estimated 2,500 deaths would occur, with upwards of 300,000 people injured. "Even more horrifying than the number of dead was the appalling nature of their dying—crowds of men, women, and children scurrying madly in the dark, twitching and writhing like the insects for whom the poison was intended."[1] Thousands struggled to

1. Richard I. Kirkland, Jr. "Union Carbide: Coping with Catastrophe," *Fortune 111* (January 7, 1985), p. 50.

hospitals and clinics for relief from burning eyes and searing lungs, resulting in a medical chaos that made record keeping well-nigh impossible. Severe environmental damage also occurred to the land and livestock, with an estimated 20,000 cattle killed.

Long-term repercussions awaited. Thousands were no longer able to put in a full day's work. Children suffered from breathing problems and memory lapses. Some experienced months of severe vomiting. Among pregnant women, nearly a fourth of whom were in their first trimester at the time of the disaster either miscarried or had premature or disfigured babies. Psychological problems—depression and anxiety—were common.

Beyond the physical were the economic consequences. In the year following the leak, the Indian government spent about $40 million on the victims. This included food, medical attention, new hospitals, research projects, and individual payments of $835 to the 1,500 families who lost members to the disaster and $125 to the 12,000 families with incomes below $40 a month.[2] Training was offered to women who had lost their providers, but little was done to find jobs for the thousands of men who could no longer spend long hours at manual labor: many of them were doomed to be permanent welfare dependents. The economy of Bhopal was devastated. As people lost their source of income, merchants faced greatly decreased per-capita spending.

BACKGROUND

Bhopal is located 360 miles south of New Delhi. It is the capital of the Indian state of Madhya Pradesh, one of the poorest and least developed states. Bhopal's population of more than 700,000 people is basically divided into two areas: New Bhopal, where the city's rich live amid spacious residences, and Old Bhopal, the congested, low-income district.

After the accident, questions were raised as to why such a dangerous plant was located so close to a densely populated area. However, at the time the location was selected, more than seventeen years before the accident, the area was not densely populated. In India, the people looking for jobs and economic gain tend to gravitate toward areas that contain manufacturing facilities. Over the years, housing spread until it reached the very fences that surrounded the plant. The population of Bhopal had tripled since the plant was opened.

Union Carbide of India, Ltd. operates the chemical plant. It is 50.9 percent owned by Union Carbide and 49.1 percent by Indians. Management links between the Indian subsidiary and Carbide's corporate headquarters in Danbury, Connecticut, were few. Although Carbide was the majority owner, the plant was essentially an Indian operation. Most of the other investors, as well as all the managers and workers, were Indian.

Union Carbide is not a newcomer to India, having had facilities there since 1905. By 1983, its Indian subsidiary was one of India's largest industrial concerns, with fourteen plants scattered throughout the country. In 1985, this subsidiary had sales of $202 million and profits of $8.8 million.

---

2. Judith H. Dobrzynski et al., "Bhopal, A Year Later: Union Carbide Takes a Tougher Line," *BusinessWeek* (November 25, 1985), 96.

Union Carbide was the third-largest U.S. chemical company. It is a true multi-national firm, operating plants in thirty-eight countries and manufacturing a wide range of products, from industrial chemicals and powerful pesticides to such consumer goods as Glad trash bags and Prestone automotive products. Of Carbide's 1984 sales of $9.5 billion, more than 14 percent came from international operations, which contributed 21.6 percent of total profits. Carbide was the only U.S. manufacturer of MIC. MIC was first manufactured commercially in the United States in the mid-1960s. It is a highly volatile, highly flammable, toxic chemical that is stored in liquid form in refrigerated stainless steel tanks. Refrigeration is necessary, since MIC vaporizes into a gas at 38° C. As a gas, the pressure begins to build, and a relief valve is essential to vent the gas in order to prevent the tanks from rupturing.

A number of U.S. pesticide manufacturers buy MIC from Carbide as an intermediate to make pesticides. U.S. consumption of MIC reached 23 to 28 million pounds in 1982, with production capacity believed to be close to 50 million pounds.[3] Carbide also produces MIC at its plant in Institute, West Virginia, a facility nearly identical to the one in Bhopal.

WHY DID THE ACCIDENT OCCUR?

The exact details of how the disaster occurred are to this day a matter of great controversy. Carbide and the Indian government do agree that the cause of the accident was the entry of 1,000 to 2,000 gallons of water into the MIC storage tank, resulting in a runaway reaction. The resulting rapid rise in pressure caused a relief valve to open, releasing the poisonous gas for about two hours. During the release, pressure probably averaged 180 psig (pounds per square inch gauge), and maximum temperature probably exceeded 200° C. MIC is normally stored at 0° C at a pressure of between 2 and 25 psig. The relief valve opens at 40 psig to avoid excessive pressure buildup.[4] Further investigation revealed that the following problems existed and presumably were not known by corporate headquarters:

1. The MIC unit's refrigeration system had been shut down for more than five months. As a result, the MIC temperature in the tank was 15 to 20° C instead of 0° C, a temperature that would have retarded reaction rates.

2. The tank temperature alarm had not been reset when the refrigeration unit was shut down. When the water reacted with the MIC, temperature and pressure rose, but there was no alarm to signal the change.

3. The unit's vent gas scrubber was on standby for more than a month and had to be restarted manually after the release was discovered. The scrubber releases caustic material meant to destroy the escaping gas automatically as it is sensed entering the containment area.

4. The flare tower, which is intended to incinerate any of the highly flammable gas that escapes the scrubber, was out of service.

3. "Carbide's Search for Answers," *Chemical Week* 135 (December 19, 1984), p. 34.

4. "Bhopal Disaster: Union Carbide Explains Gas Leak," *Chemical & Engineering News* 63 (March 25, 1985), p. 4.

The possibility of sabotage became a major controversy between Union Carbide and the Indian government. The company maintained that the cause of the disaster was a "deliberate act" by a disgruntled plant worker. Water was introduced directly into the MIC tank with the intention, said Carbide, "not to create a hideous disaster, but to ruin the batch of MIC as an act of mischief."[5] The Indian government disagreed, stating that the disaster was brought about by the plant's dangerous location, the unsafe production and storage of MIC, inadequate safety systems, operating mistakes, and preventable employee problems.

COMPANY REACTION

With such an overwhelming disaster, Carbide's management had to decide how best to aid the victims, how to be sure that whatever happened at Bhopal could not happen again somewhere else, how to help employees keep up morale, how to assure investors and creditors that the company was financially stable, and, last but by no means least, how to protect the company from expensive legal liability that could endanger the survival of their firm. On the day of the disaster, Carbide halted production of MIC in its plant at Institute, West Virginia. To prevent any further problems at the Bhopal plant, it went back into production there to neutralize the remaining 15,000 tons of MIC. Until the exact cause of the disaster was determined, Carbide stopped all shipments to customers. Operations were not resumed at the Institute MIC plant until the spring of 1985.

Initially, Carbide's management was skeptical about the accuracy of the burgeoning estimates of dead and injured, which seemed beyond the limits of possibility. Help was quickly sent to India—medical supplies, respirators and similar equipment, and a doctor with extensive knowledge of the effects of the chemical. Still, the company was operating with imperfect information. Shortly, a team of technical experts was sent to examine the plant.

On the evening of December 4, with the death toll still mounting, Warren Anderson, the chairman of Union Carbide, took the company jet and followed the technical team. Unfortunately, his journey accomplished nothing. Indian officials, still stunned by the disaster, arrested Anderson upon his arrival. They held him briefly before releasing him on $2,500 bail, then sent him to New Delhi, the capital of India. There, officials told Anderson to leave the country for his own good. Government officials refused his offer of $1 million in immediate aid and the use of the company's guesthouse in the hills above Bhopal to orphans of the victims. Anderson's dash to India was dismissed by some as an empty gesture. Still, the trip showed Carbide's concern in a way no other action could. That it accomplished nothing during a time of crisis and wild emotionalism does not detract from the top executive's good intentions.

The team Anderson took with him was denied access to the Bhopal plant, and the Indian government seized all of the plant's records and arrested the plant supervisors. As a result, facts were hard to come by, and rumors were rampant. With only two phone lines to Bhopal and the plant supervisors there under arrest, Carbide was

5. Wil Lepkowski, "Union Carbide Presses Bhopal Sabotage Theory," *Chemical & Engineering News* (July 4, 1988), p. 8.

reduced to relying on Indian news reports relayed by phone from employees at its subsidiary in Bombay.

Carbide's attempts to administer financial and medical aid were initially rejected by government officials. Anderson believed that "if we try to do something with our name on it, the Indian government turns it down. They're worried that if they take anything it would have negative implications on the lawsuit."[6]

CONSEQUENCES

Image Problems

On Wall Street, nervous investors, scrambling to unload their stock, drove the price down by more than 11 points to about $37 a share, a total loss in market value of nearly $900 million. This plunge in Carbide stock led the company to begin stressing its financial soundness in press releases and briefings. However, these actions had the unwanted side-effect of making the company seem bottom-line oriented rather than compassionate. According to a Harris poll taken a few weeks after the event, 44 percent of Americans who had heard of the accident believed that Carbide had done only a "fair" or "poor" job of telling the truth about what happened, as opposed to 36 percent who judged it to have done an "excellent" or "good" job. Of those surveyed, 31 percent declared that they would be "less likely" to buy Carbide products if it turned out that either company or employee negligence was responsible. Normally, only about 20 percent of the public can identify a company of Carbide's size; yet, 47 percent of those polled, without prompting, were able to name Carbide as the company involved in the accident.[7] These results caused Carbide concern: Bhopal might be the only thing many people knew about Carbide. Its image appeared to be in the pits.

Impact on Sales and Profits

Table 12.1 shows Union Carbide sales and net income during the 1980s. We see that Carbide's business was very cyclical, the two years preceding Bhopal not nearly as good as 1980 and 1981. The huge deficit of 1985 directly reflects the impact of Bhopal, with write-offs and reserves set aside for future settlements. The much lower sales figures in the latter part of the decade reflect company streamlining and divestiture of certain operations. In the process, earnings again reached toward the peak years of 1980 and 1981.

The company has bounced back from its Bhopal adversity. As we will see in the next section, the litigation essentially favored Carbide, and the viability of the company was fully preserved.

Legal Effects

Like hungry vultures, U.S. lawyers flocked to India. They saw representing the victims as an excellent opportunity for financial gain. Some felt that each individual victim

6. Dobrzynski et al., p. 97.

7. Stuart Jackson, "Union Carbide's Good Name Takes a Beating," *BusinessWeek* (December 31, 1984), p. 40.

Table 12.1   Union Carbide's Sales and Profits, 1980–1989

	Sales	Net Income
	(millions)	
1980	9,994	673
1981	10,168	649
1982	9,061	310
1983	9,001	79
1984	9,508	341
1985	9,003	599 deficit
1986	6,343	130
1987	6,914	232
1988	8,324	662
1989	8,744	573

Source: Company annual reports.

should be represented separately; others saw a class action lawsuit against Union Carbide as the best strategy for their clients and themselves. A famous and flamboyant San Francisco attorney, Melvin Belli, along with four other lawyers, filed a $15 billion suit on charges of negligence and defects in the company's design and construction of the Bhopal MIC storage facility. The complaint also alleged that Carbide failed to warn the citizens of Bhopal and the Indian government about the dangerous nature of MIC and MIC storage. Further, the Belli complaint stated that Carbide did these things "knowingly, willfully, and wantonly, or with utter disregard for the safety of the residents of Bhopal, India."[8]

The U.S. lawyers thought the trial should be held in the United States because the victims could win more money. Carbide held that since the accident occurred in India and the victims and witnesses were Indians, the trial should be held there. Some of the Indian attorneys also maintained that the case should be tried in their country. The stakes were huge on this particular issue: the viability of Union Carbide was even at stake, given the multibillion-dollar awards U.S. juries were likely to dispense.

A major ruling was made in May 1986, a year and a half after the actual accident. All claims in U.S. federal courts against Union Carbide were dismissed, and the trial was to be kept in India. This effectively put an end to the involvement of U.S. lawyers and preserved Union Carbide. In February 1989, the company paid $425 million to settle all litigation arising from the 1984 leak. Union Carbide of India Ltd. also paid a rupee equivalent of $45 million. Now the company was finally freed from its legal encumbrances.

Update

As a result of the Bhopal disaster, enforceable international standards that defined the best practices for designing and operating hazardous facilities were developed.

8. "Bhopal: The Endless Aftershocks," *Chemical Week* (December 19, 1984), p. 42.

The National Academy of Sciences focused on extensive testing for new and old chemical products, while belatedly noting that of 65,000 chemicals in common use, we knew very little about 90 percent of these.[9]

Overall, the lax regulation of occupational safety and environmental laws was of great embarrassment to India when the accident occurred. As a result, the laxity in developing countries began to reverse. Brazil, for example, tightened its safety regulations considerably after Bhopal.

ANALYSIS

Due to the backward state of the Indian economy, much of the technology of the Bhopal plant was imported. Union Carbide of India paid a technical service fee to the parent for its technology, patents, and training. Consequently, Union Carbide of India was dependent on the parent to provide the information necessary to use this technology effectively. But the question can be raised: Was the technology too complex for an undeveloped country?

The employees' low educational and technical level, coupled with a lack of "safety mentality," may have greatly contributed to the accident. Insufficient technical competence among both managers and workers is by no means unique to India. It is a problem many multinational firms face as they export advanced technologies to less developed countries. (See the Issue Box: "Responsibility for Worker Competence in Third-World Countries.")

A major incentive for building manufacturing facilities in underdeveloped countries is the high rate of return on investment, higher than often can be achieved in more advanced economies. Labor costs, of course, are typically lower. But another irresistible incentive is avoiding costly, safety-related measures—especially in the absence of government-prescribed safety standards. (See the Issue Box: "Flawed Incentives for Building Plants in Less-Developed Countries?") Instituting the same safety standards prescribed in the United States would make such foreign investments far less attractive.

As underdeveloped countries understandably increase their safety standards, they will also have to create more incentives to attract firms that will now find the costs of doing business in these countries just as high as in more developed countries—but with the higher risks that come from less-educated workers. Perhaps this situation will place a new responsibility on the governments of these countries to bring their local laborers and managers to a higher level of technical and workplace competence. This is a new challenge for education in such environments.

India did receive substantial benefits from the Bhopal plant. Pesticides are estimated to have saved 10 percent of the Indian food crop, enough to feed 70 million people. The Green Revolution, started in India under the Ford Foundation in the early 1960s, increased the life expectancy of the average Indian citizen from thirty to fifty years, prevented many deaths from starvation, and alleviated much malnutrition.[10]

9. Ward Morehouse and M Arum Subramanian, *The Bhopal Tragedy* (Council of International and Public Affairs, 1986), p. 112.

10. Larry Everest, *Behind the Poison Cloud* (Chicago: Banner Press, 1985), pp. 107–117.

ISSUE BOX

RESPONSIBILITY FOR WORKER COMPETENCE IN THIRD-WORLD COUNTRIES

Manager and worker incompetence at Bhopal showed up both in the build-up to the disaster and in the mishandling of the crisis itself. Their training and monitoring by the parent company left something to be desired. But a major issue is raised for multinationals as they extend their operations to less-developed countries.

Are these people trainable to acceptable standards of technical knowledge, work ethics, and careful adherence to safety and quality?

Some would argue that the multinationals should be able to train and develop native workers to acceptable standards, and if they do not, the blame is solely on the big corporation. But it can also be argued that the governments of such countries are at least partially to blame in not providing sufficient education to their people so that they are fully trainable in modern technology.

The two positions sound very much like passing the buck—"blame the other guy." But both arguments have merit. For the multinational corporation, however, the Bhopal experience should raise concern about exporting advanced technology to developing countries, especially when health and safety are involved, without very careful and continuous monitoring and the tightest controls.

INVITATION TO DISCUSS

Take a position on either side of this issue. Collect as many arguments as you can to support your position. Be sure and cover difficulties in implementation. What would your compromise be?

So, how culpable was Union Carbide? Was there a blatant disregard of human consequences? Was the company calloused and uncaring? Was it criminally negligent?

A terrible accident happened. With the benefit of hindsight, it need not have happened. The company did not deliberately disregard safety measures. But it did not exercise the close controls needed for a dangerous product in a distant and less technically proficient land. Management should have known better. But, of course, no one expected a catastrophe of such magnitude—and yet it happened. Then, company officials, particularly the chief executive, Warren Anderson, acted with compassion and deep concern. At the same time, he had to protect the company from a multitude of lawsuits, no matter how much compassion he felt for the suffering victims and their families.

Anderson summed the situation up in this way in a January 1985 interview by *Chemical & Engineering News:*

> Union Carbide had a good reputation for health, safety, and the environment;
> We're a company that has resources; and we can cope with an issue like this
> one. Maybe out of this will come a whole new approach to this issue of
> health, safety, and environment. Not only in developing countries, but in the

ISSUE BOX

FLAWED INCENTIVES FOR BUILDING PLANTS IN LESS DEVELOPED COUNTRIES?

It is common practice for multinational firms to locate plants within developing countries such as India. Labor costs are lower. Usually industrial safety standards are lower than those in the United States. Often these governments, eager for the economic benefits of such plants, provide incentives, including development costs and natural resources. Thus, profits can be greater than with domestic operations. For a company with an altruistic bent, the prospect of raising living standards in another country is a nice rationale.

But in the production of hazardous substances, the dangers at these plants are extremely high. Although Union Carbide and other multinational firms contend that the plants they build abroad are identical to those built in the United States, the operations may be far more lax and imprudent. As Peter Thatcher, former deputy executive director of the United Nations Environmental Program, noted: "You have to assume that in a developing country, people will not be as careful in terms of inspection, quality control, and maintenance. And you must assume that if a problem occurs, it will be more difficult to cope with."[11]

INVITATION TO DISCUSS

In the absence of adequate safety and environmental-protection standards in many developing countries, how might a multinational lessen risks of accidents?

United States as well. If it had happened to a company that didn't have Carbide's capabilities, maybe not as much would have been learned. So we have a commitment and an obligation to lead the way if we can. The world's going to be a better place. It's a hard way to learn a lesson, but if we went through a disaster like this and didn't learn anything, that would be the worst.[12]

WHAT CAN BE LEARNED?

Expect and prepare for a worst-case scenario. There are those who preach the desirability of positive thinking, of confidence and optimism—whether it be in personal lives, athletics, or business practices. But expecting and preparing for the worst has much to commend it, since a person or a firm is then better able to cope with adversity, not be overwhelmed, and therefore make prudent decisions.

11. Peter Thatcher, "The Lesson of Bhopal: The Lure of Foreign Capital Is Stronger Than Environmental Worries," *Atlantic* (March 1987), pp. 30–33.

12. "Carbide's Anderson Explains Post-Bhopal Strategy," *Chemical & Engineering News* (January 21, 1985), p. 15.

Certain industrial activities carry with them a potential risk so large as to threaten the organization's very survival. With such high-potential risk, managers, employees, and community residents need to be coached on safety procedures in the event of an accident. Local governmental bodies and hospitals should be well-prepared to treat any local industrial accident victims and should stock appropriate drugs and equipment—just in case of the worst scenario. Mock accident drills could be conducted from time to time.

A side benefit of such active accident awareness might well be that people might not be so eager to live near such dangerous plants, thus minimizing the potential for massive injuries and deaths.

Should multinationals follow U.S. safety standards worldwide? The risk of a catastrophe on the scale of Bhopal is remote; accidents on a smaller scale involving workers and perhaps some environmental degradation are more likely. But the consequences of a Bhopal-like disaster are almost as life-threatening to the corporation as to the population, with litigation becoming ever more costly in defense and in settlement. Prudent companies dealing with hazardous products or processes can no longer afford to tolerate less-stringent safety standards than those in the United States. Indeed, the argument can be raised that standards ought to be even more strict because of the caliber of the workforce. It is myopic thinking to do otherwise, rather akin to Russian roulette.

Cost-cutting must not have the highest priority. The Bhopal plant design focused on cost-cutting measures that would enhance profitability. For example, the storage tanks were oversized to save money. Other manufacturers of MIC use many smaller storage tanks instead of a few large ones: Bayer's West German facility, for example, had tanks with a 10-ton capacity, in contrast to the 100-ton capacity of Bhopal's tanks.

Many of the safety systems at Bhopal were manual. The only computers were those used for accounts payable and payroll applications. None were used in instrumentation and controls. Any leaks were investigated when workers noticed odors or when their eyes became irritated.[13]

Admittedly, it will be more costly to shift toward safer methods of processing, storing, and manufacturing hazardous substances. But Bhopal should be an object lesson on the dangers of cost-cutting with such products and processes.

A laissez-faire decentralization is not appropriate in underdeveloped countries when safety and environmental degradation are at stake. Complete "hands-off" decentralization of subsidiary operations in foreign countries (leaving only financial and capital expenditures directly controlled by corporate management) is far from adequate when hazardous products are involved. Clear, ongoing lines of communication are vital to such operations. The corporate headquarters can no longer act as an "ivory tower," performing only high administrative functions. The same social responsibility criteria must be used for home-country and foreign-country decisions. Corporate officials need to more closely monitor foreign operations and react to inefficiencies as they would if the problem had occurred in their home country. Unfortunately for Union Carbide, this lesson was a costly one.

13. Everest, pp. 33–40.

CONSIDER

Can you add any learning insights?

QUESTIONS

1. Do you agree with the decision to legally try the case in Indian courts rather than the U.S. ones? Why or why not?
2. "Union Carbide is guilty of such a terrible crime against humanity that it should be dissolved and no longer be permitted to exist as a complete entity." Discuss and give your rationale for your position.
3. Should Warren Anderson and other high-level corporate executives have been prosecuted and even jailed? How about the Indian plant employees and managers? Discuss these issues.
4. Could the company be blamed for the population growth around its plant's perimeter? How might this have been prevented?
5. Do you think the public image of Union Carbide was heavily damaged in the United States? Why or why not?

HANDS-ON EXERCISES

1. You are the assistant to the vice president of overseas facilities. From your position at corporate headquarters in Danbury, Connecticut, how might you have prevented the Bhopal disaster?
2. Place yourself in the position of Warren Anderson, CEO of Union Carbide at the time of the disaster. You are determined to fly to Bhopal. What agenda do you propose having? What would you hope to accomplish?
3. You are a worker at the Bhopal plant. Several months before the accident, you notice that your eyes were burning around tank 610. What, if anything, would you do, and why? Assess the possible consequences.

TEAM DEBATE EXERCISE

Debate Warren Anderson's plan to visit Bhopal shortly after the tragedy. If you are on the team against his going, would you send someone else in his place, and what type of executive?

INVITATION TO RESEARCH

Is the Bhopal plant operating now, or has it been closed? If still operating, is it still producing MIC? Did any local employees receive prison sentences?

CHAPTER THIRTEEN

Nestlé's Infant Formula: Pushing An Unsafe Product In Third-World Countries

When a firm is a huge international conglomerate, with diversification into many product lines, bad publicity and negative public reactions about a single product seemingly should be no particular cause for alarm. The inclination is to ignore such a "minor" problem, assuming it will go away.

But the expectations of Nestlé went awry. The attitudes of the general public toward the firm continued to worsen, exacerbated certainly by a negative press and vocal protesters. Far from diminishing over a few weeks and a few months, the situation worsened over years. And far from affecting only the particular product involved—infant formula marketed to underdeveloped countries—other products and other divisions of the company became the object of virulent protests. Nestlé had for too long ignored assaults on its public image, and now the road back to public acceptance was slow and rocky.

BACKGROUND

The Trouble Begins

By the early 1970s, there were suspicions that powdered infant formula manufacturers were contributing to the high infant mortality in developing countries by their aggressive marketing efforts directed at people unable to read the instructions or use the product properly. The possible link between infant formulas and mortality through product misuse began to be discussed by medical professionals, industry representatives, and government officials at a number of international conferences, but public awareness of the problem had not yet surfaced.

Then, in 1974, a British charity organization, War on Want, published a twenty-eight-page pamphlet, *The Baby Killer.* In it, two multinationals, Nestlé of Switzerland and Unigate of Britain, were criticized for engaging in ill-advised marketing efforts in Africa. With the printing of this short publication, the general public became not only aware of the problem but increasingly concerned.

This concern was to intensify less than a year later. The German-based Third World Working Group reissued a German translation of *The Baby Killer* but with a few changes. Whereas the British version criticized the entire infant formula industry, the German activists singled out Nestlé for "unethical and immoral behavior" and retitled their version *Nestlé Kills Babies*.

The accusation enraged executives at Nestlé headquarters, and they sued the activists for defamation. The trial lasted two years and focused worldwide attention on the issue. Though Nestlé won the lawsuit, the court advised the firm to review its current marketing practices. "We won the legal case, but it was a public-relations disaster," one Nestlé official admitted. "The baby-killing accusation was a natural for antiwar groups and others looking for a cause. The company was dealing with the situation on a scientific and nutritional level, but the protesters were dealing on an emotional and political level."[1]

The Nestlé Company

The Nestlé Company, formally known as Nestlé Alimentana, S.A., is headquartered in Vevey, Switzerland. It is a giant worldwide corporation, with sales of $12.5 billion in 1983. It owns or controls extensive interests in numerous companies in the food and cosmetics industries in various parts of the world. Products include instant drinks (coffee and tea), dairy products, cosmetics, frozen foods, chocolate, and pharmaceutical products. In addition, it holds interests in catering services, as well as restaurant and hotel operations such as the Stouffer Corporation, which was acquired in 1973. By 1980, Nestlé was marketing its products in Europe, Africa, North America, Latin America, the Caribbean, Asia, and Oceania. Its three top product groups were dairy products, instant drinks, and culinary/sundry products. Infant foods, including the controversial infant formula, and dietetic products accounted for less than 10 percent of total conglomerate sales.

Nestlé's appetite for acquisitions continued unabated. In 1975, it purchased food processor Libby, McNeill & Libby. In 1979, it acquired Beech-Nut, the baby-food producer. Other purchases of note include CooperVision, a contact lens maker; such well-known candy brands as Chunky, Bit-O-Honey, Raisinettes, Oh Henry!, Goobers, Sno Caps, Hills Bros. Coffee Company and Carnation.

The Infant Formula Industry

Nestlé first developed and marketed a milk food used to nourish premature infants in 1867. This was in response to the urgent need of a premature infant who was unable to take any food. Borden introduced a similar sweetened and condensed milk.

Infant formula foods are somewhat more recent, having been developed in the early 1920s as an alternative to breast milk. Infant formula is a specially prepared food for infants (under six months) and is based on cow's milk. It is scientifically formulated to approximate the most perfect of all infant foods, human breast milk. Today, a number of different artificial milk products are available for infants, and these range in

1. "Infant Formula Protest Teaches Nestlé a Tactical Lesson," *Marketing News* (June 10, 1983), p. 1.

nutritional value from very high (humanized infant formula) to very low (various powdered, evaporated, and sweetened condensed milks).

Sales of infant formula had increased sharply after World War II and hit a peak in 1957, with 4.3 million births in developed countries. After this time, births started a decline that continued into the 1970s. The result was a steep downturn in baby formula sales and profits. Therefore, the industry began searching for new business. This was found in developing countries where the population was still increasing: the less developed countries of Africa, South America, and the Far East.

Total industry sales for infant formula alone, excluding all other commercial milk products, was about $1.5 billion. Of this, an estimated $600 million came from developing countries. Hence, this market segment represented a significant total market potential.

Nestlé maintained a strong market share—40 to 50 percent—of the market in developing countries for baby formula. Competitors included three U.S. firms, American Home Products, Bristol Myers, and Abbott Labs, which shared 20 percent of the market. Foreign firms accounted for the remainder. In 1981, the market was estimated to be growing at 15 to 20 percent per year.[2]

THE ISSUE: MISUSE OF THE PRODUCT AND MARKETING PRACTICES

> If your lives were embittered as mine is, by seeing day after day this massacre of the innocents by unsuitable feeding, then I believe you would feel as I do that misguided propaganda on infant feeding should be punished as the most criminal form of sedition, and that these deaths should be regarded as murder.[3]

This lone indictment from a doctor in 1939 evolved from a single cry into a crescendo of protest against the infant formula industry.

Incapability of the Market to Use the Product Correctly

A large number of consumers in developing countries live in poverty, have poor sanitation, receive inadequate health care, and are illiterate. Therefore, the misuse of infant formula would seem inevitable. Water is obtained from polluted rivers or a common well and is brought back in contaminated containers. A refrigerator is considered a luxury item, and fuel is very expensive.

Consequently, powdered formula may be mixed with contaminated water and put into unsterilized bottles and nipples. In addition, the mothers are tempted to dilute the formula with excess water so that it will last longer. An example was cited by one physician at a Jamaican hospital of the malnutrition of two exclusively bottle-fed siblings, four months and eighteen months old. A can of formula would adequately feed a four-month-old baby just less than three days. However, this mother so diluted the formula

2. Kurt Anderson, "The Battle of the Bottle," *Time* (June 1, 1981), 26.

3. As quoted in Cicely D. Williams, "The Marketing of Malnutrition," *Business and Society Review* (Spring 1980-1981), 66.

as to feed the two infants for fourteen days. This mother was poor and illiterate, had no running water or electricity, and had twelve other children.[4]

Studies have given three reasons for the trend to less nursing and more bottle feeding in the developing countries.[5]

First, the sociocultural environment was changing. This consists of urbanization, changing social mores, and increased mobility in employment. Infant formula was seen as representing social mobility, one of the highly regarded modern products, and medical expertise. The smiling white babies pictured on the fronts of formula tins suggested that rich, white mothers fed their babies this product and that therefore it must be better. The high-income consumers in these less-developed countries were the first to use infant formula in imitation of Western practices. Bottle feeding was looked upon as a high-status practice, and the lower-income groups readily followed along.

Second, healthcare professionals were a factor in the switch to bottle feeding. Many hospitals and clinics endorsed the use of infant formula. A woman's first experience with a hospital may be to deliver a baby. Consequently, any products or gifts she receives there carry medical endorsement. Also, hospital practices are perceived as better and deserving of emulation. Babies are routinely separated from their mothers for twelve to forty-eight hours and are bottle fed, whether or not the mothers plan to breast-feed.

A third factor was the marketing and promotional practices of infant formula manufacturers, which we will discuss shortly.

In 1951, approximately 80 percent of all three-month-old babies in Singapore were being breast-fed; by 1971, only 5 percent were. In 1966, 40 percent fewer mothers in Mexico nursed six-month-old babies than had done so six years earlier. In Chile, in 1973, there were three times as many deaths among infants who were bottle-fed before three months of age than among wholly breast-fed infants. Other statistics of increased illnesses and higher death rates of bottle-fed infants are plentiful.[6]

Quality Control Problems

Nestlé had some serious quality-control problems in its production of the formula in its far-flung plants:

In April 1977, the Colombian General Hospital encountered an increase in deaths in the premature ward. Bacteria was traced to a Nestlé factory, but twenty-five deaths occurred before the cause was found.

Also in 1977, the Australian Department of Health reported that 134 infants had fallen seriously ill as a result of being fed contaminated infant milk formulas produced by Nestlé. Government officials estimated 20 million pounds of contaminated milk

4. U.S. Congress, Senate, Committee on Human Resources, Subcommittee on Health and Scientific Research, *Marketing and Promotion of Infant Formula in the Developing Nations,* Hearing, 95th Congress, 2nd Session, May 23, 1978 (Washington, D.C.: Government Printing Office, 1978), p. 6.

5. Prakash Sethi and James E. Post, "Public Consequences of Private Action: The Marketing of Infant Formula in Less Developed Countries," *California Management Review* (Summer 1979), 35–48.

6. For more such statistics, see Leah Margulies, "Bottle Babies: Death and Business Get Their Market," *Business and Society Review* (Spring 1978), 43–49.

had been exported to Southeast Asian counties. The Australian story started in 1976. The Nestlé Tongala plant noticed an increase in bacterial counts in samples of infant milk powder. Inspection revealed cracks in the spray drier used to turn liquid milk into powder form. The bacteria was found to be a variant of salmonella that causes severe gastroenteritis. The State Health Department was not informed. Nestlé attempted to sterilize the equipment without halting production, but the bacteria continued to be discovered. The drier was kept in operation for a full eight months after the contaminants were found.[7]

Criticisms of Misuse

In fairness to Nestlé, the critics who condemned the company and other infant-food manufacturers for even attempting to market in the developing countries disregarded any benefits of such products over the alternatives. The problem of water contamination also affects the alternatives to the commercial infant foods, which are various alternative cereal gruels of millet and rice used as weaning foods. The nutritional quality of these gruels tends to be low, and this deficiency is in addition to contamination of the water and containers used to cook the material. Furthermore, the millet or flour often has microbial contamination. Although it is true that infant formula mixed with contaminated water and containers presents dangers, the commercial formulas are more nutritious than local foods and are closer to breast milk than native weaning foods and are therefore easier to digest. A further rebuttal to the critics is that not all people in developing countries face water contamination. Millions can safely mix powdered formula with local water without fear of water contamination.[8] (See the Issue Box for a discussion of *good versus evil.*)

Criticisms of Nestlé's Marketing Practices

Nestlé has undoubtedly been an aggressive marketer in many developing countries. Its promotional efforts have been directed to physicians and other medical personnel as well as consumers. Direct consumer promotion of infant formula has taken many forms. Media have included radio, newspapers, magazines, and billboards—even vans with loudspeakers have been used. Nestlé has widely distributed free samples, bottles, nipples, and measuring spoons. In some countries, direct customer contacts have been made through *milk nurses*, and these have been the subject of particular criticism.

Nestlé employed about 200 women who were registered nurses, nutritionists, or midwives. These professionals were often nicknamed *milk nurses*. Critics maintained that these milk nurses were actually sales personnel in disguise who visited mothers and gave product samples in an attempt to persuade mothers to stop breast-feeding. With their uniforms giving them great credibility, the nurses were criticized for being too persuasive for naive consumers.

7. Reported in Douglas Clement, "Nestlé's Latest Killing in Bottle Baby Market," *Business and Society Review* (Summer 1978), 60–64.

8. John Sparks, *The Nestlé Controversy-Anatomy of a Boycott*, Public Policy Education Fund (June 1981).

Promoting these products to physicians and other medical personnel has also been controversial. This type of promotion has generally involved the use of detail people who discuss product quality and characteristics with pediatricians, pediatric nurses, and other related medical personnel. (The use of *detail people*, who are a type of missionary sales representative, is common practice, as we will describe in the accompanying Information Box.) Materials such as posters, charts, and free samples were made available to physicians, hospitals, and clinics without charge. Physicians and other hospital personnel have also received company-sponsored travel to medical meetings.

ISSUE BOX

THE COEXISTENCE OF GOOD AND EVIL— HOW TO RECONCILE?

In some situations, good and evil exist simultaneously; they are inextricably bound. And while the press and vocal critics invariably focus on the evil, the good should not go unnoticed. Such was the case with Nestlé and its infant formula.

It could hardly be disputed by even the harshest critics that the formula led to saving of infants' lives when the mother was not available or the infant could not be breast-fed. Furthermore, the dietary supplement could lead to much healthier babies when used properly. Conversely, when used improperly, it could lead to deaths as mothers mixed the powdered food with contaminated water and their babies died of dysentery.

How can this issue of good and bad intermixing be resolved? There is no simple solution acceptable to all sides. Emotions, and publicity, tend to run high on issues such as this. Should a firm abandon a product because of some misuse? The implications of such a position can become ludicrous. For example, should cars be banned because of careless use and hundreds of thousands of accidents, injuries, and deaths?

It is but a short step to other raging issues. Should pesticides be banned because they contribute to environmental pollution and possible injury to wildlife and fishes? Should utility plants be closed because they contribute to acid rain? More realistically, should the public be made to pay greatly increased utility rates so that acid rain can be virtually eliminated by the most stringent emissions controls? Should lawn mowers be banned because a few people use them incorrectly? Should all guns be banned because of their escalating misuse?

You can see that there is no easy solution to such issues that will satisfy all interested parties. The tides of pressure seem to swing from one position to the other; too much environmental influence versus too much "business self-interest." Unfortunately, these issues are highly emotional and easily fanned by press, politicians, and the public relations efforts of special interest groups.

INVITATION TO DISCUSS

A simple solution to such issues would be to choose the way that offers "the greatest good for the greatest number." Discuss the problems with such a simplistic solution. Can these be reasonably resolved?

Critics felt that the promotion of infant formula had been too aggressive and had contributed to the decline in breast feeding. Despite increased criticisms, however, sales of infant formula in poor countries continued to escalate. It had become the third most advertised product in these countries, after tobacco and soap, and it was generally recognized that new mothers in such countries were most susceptible to advertising. A 1969 study of 120 mothers in Barbados found that 82 percent of those given free samples later purchased the same brand—regardless of whether the samples were received from the hospital or at home.[9]

In summary, the criticisms of promotional practices were that:

- Bottle-feeding contributes to infant mortality in developing countries.
- Baby booklets ignore or de-emphasize breast-feeding.
- Media promotions are misleading in encouraging poor and illiterate mothers to bottle-feed rather than breast-feed their infants.
- Advertising portrays breast-feeding as primitive and inconvenient.
- Free gifts and samples are direct inducements to bottle-feed infants.
- Posters and pamphlets in hospitals and milk nurses are viewed as "endorsement by association" or "manipulation by assistance."
- The prices of formulas at the milk banks are still too expensive for many consumers, who are tempted to dilute the formula.

THE SITUATION WORSENS FOR NESTLÉ

After the publication of the two articles, *The Baby Killer* and *Nestlé Kills Babies*, and the subsequent lawsuit by Nestlé, which received worldwide publicity, two groups were formed: The Interfaith Center on Corporate Responsibility and the Infant Formula Action Coalition (INFACT). The opposition of these organizations eventually led to a boycott of Nestlé products and services.

Since the early 1970s, various agencies had been trying to reduce the promotion and advertising practices of infant formula companies. These agencies included the Protein Advisory Group in 1970 and 1973, the World Health Assembly in 1974, and the World Health Organization (WHO) in 1978.

As a byproduct of the growing condemnation of the industry, Nestlé and other firms began to make changes in their promotional practices, at least on paper. The changes were brought about through the auspices of the International Council of Infant Food Industries (ICIFI), which was formed in 1975 by nine infant food manufacturers, including Nestlé. The changes included the following: product information would always recognize breast milk as best; infant formulas would be advertised as supplementary, and ads would recommend that professional advice should be sought; nurse uniforms would be worn only by professional nurses.

But the self-regulation apparently did not work sufficiently to allay the criticisms. Documentation by the International Baby Food Action Network confirmed more

9. Reported in "A Boycott over Infant Formula," *BusinessWeek* (April 23, 1979), 137–140.

than 1,000 violations of the "code" from 1977 to 1981. Some critics scoffed that "asking for self-regulation was like asking Colonel Sanders to babysit your chickens."[10]

After continued reported violations, a boycott was organized in the United States in July 1977 and soon spread to nine other countries. It was to last until January 26, 1982, in the United States and Canada, with other countries ending their boycotts over the next two years.

Nestlé was singled out as the sole object of the boycott because of its 50 percent worldwide market share and the fact that it had attracted more adverse publicity than had other firms that were engaged in the same business practices.

INFACT and the boycotters had four demands:

1. Stop altogether the use of milk nurses.

2. Stop distributing all free samples.

3. Stop promoting infant formula to the health care industry.

4. Stop consumer promotion and advertising of infant formula.

The boycott soon had the support of more than 450 local and religious groups across America, and proponents claimed it was the largest nonunion boycott in U.S. history. Boycott activity was strongest in Boston, Baltimore, and Chicago, where INFACT established an office with five full-time staffers. Thousands of signatures were gathered on various petitions urging removal of Nestlé products from supermarket shelves. Some grocers acquiesced, agreeing to remove such products as Taster's Choice. The boycott also hit college campuses. With the slogan "Crunch Nestlé," boycotts were encouraged on products ranging from milk chocolate to tea, coffee, and hot chocolate. The college boycott reportedly began at Wellesley College and soon spread to others, such as Colgate, Yale, and the University of Minnesota.

This boycott was undoubtedly effective, not only directly in causing lost business and profits for the company but also indirectly in crystallizing public opinion against the company and in invoking governmental response. For example:

> The government of New Guinea enacted stringent laws to curb the artificial feeding of babies in the summer of 1979. Bottles and nipples now could only be obtained by prescription. Other countries also began introducing legislation to reduce the marketing and advertising of breast-milk substitutes.

> The World Health Organization (WHO), in May 1981, adopted a restrictive ad code that applied only to the infant food industry. A portion of Article 5 of the code states: "There shall be no advertising or other forms of promotion to the general public of products within the scope of this code."[11] The products covered were infant food formulas and other weaning foods.

The European Parliament in France voted overwhelmingly for strict enforcement of the WHO code throughout the ten-nation European Community. The European Parliament also placed responsibility on firms of member nations for the actions of their subsidiaries abroad in observing the WHO code.

---

10. "Killer in a Bottle," *Economist* (May 9, 1981) 50; "Nestlé's Latest Killing," pp. 60–64.
11. "World Health Organization Drafts Restrictive Ad Code," *Editor & Publisher* (April 11, 1981), p. 8.

INFORMATION BOX

THE USE OF MISSIONARY SALESPEOPLE (DETAIL PEOPLE)

Missionary salespeople—these are called *detail people* in the drug industry—are commonly used by many firms to provide specialized services and cultivate customer goodwill. The generally do not try to secure orders.

Missionary salespeople are employed by manufacturers to work with their dealers. They may put up point-of-purchase displays, train dealer salespeople, provide better communication between distributor and manufacturer, and in general try to have their brand more aggressively promoted by the dealer. In the drug industry, the detail people leave samples and explain research information about new products to the medical professionals so as to encourage prescriptions and recommendations for their brands.

INVITATION TO DISCUSS

Do you think the critics were unfair in condemning the milk nurses, a type of missionary salespeople? Do you think Nestlé should have bowed to this criticism and discontinued the milk nurses?

Nestlé Fights Back

Nestlé's first efforts to combat vituperative accusations resulted in more harm than good, as we have seen. As its public image continued to worsen, the worldwide boycott finally surfaced in 1977. Now Nestlé could no longer ignore the protests and hope they would go away. Obviously they were not going to go away. Initial strategy at this point was to treat the boycott and widespread protests as a public-relations problem. The public relations department of the firm was upgraded into the Office of Corporate Responsibility. The world's largest public-relations firm, Hill & Knowlton, was hired to assist. More than 300,000 packets of information were mailed by Nestlé to U.S. clergymen, informing them that they were wrong in their denunciations of Nestlé. Finally, Daniel J. Edelman, a renowned public relations specialist, was hired. He advised the company to keep a low profile and try to get third-party endorsement of its actions.

Finally, in 1981, after failing to improve its image and mute the critical cries against it, Nestlé dismissed its two public-relations firms and took upon itself the task of reestablishing its reputation. Ignoring the situation had not helped; public outcries, rather than lessening, had increased. And efforts to angrily denounce the critics had only exacerbated the situation. Now the firm was ready to try a new tack in efforts to establish its credibility as a humane and responsible corporate citizen.

One of the first steps was to endorse the World Health Organization's Code of Marketing for Breast Milk Substitutes—a step that three other U.S. manufacturers did not make until two years later. Compliance with the code was voluntary. It banned advertising to the general public, as well as distribution of samples to mothers.

Next, Nestlé sought an ethical group to vouch for its compliance with the code and settled on the Methodist Task Force on Infant Formula. Nestlé's relations with the press had been abysmal. For example, in the first six months of 1981, the *Washington Post* published ninety-one articles critical of Nestlé. In the company's multifaceted attempt to rebuild its image, the policy for dealing with the media was changed to an "open-door, candid approach."[12]

The most effective restorative strategy finally adopted was the establishment of a ten-member panel of medical experts, clergy, civic leaders, and experts in international policy to publicly monitor Nestlé's compliance with the WHO code and to investigate complaints against its marketing practices. This Nestlé Infant Formula Audit Commission (NIFAC) gained credibility with the acceptance of the chairmanship by Edmund S. Muskie, former secretary of state, vice presidential candidate, and Democratic senator from Maine. The commission was established in May 1982.

The Muskie Commission worked with representatives of WHO, the International Nestlé Boycott Committee (INBC), and UNICEF to resolve conflicts in four areas of the WHO code. Points of contention were educational materials, labels, gifts to medical and health professionals, and free or subsidized supplies to hospitals. These were resolved, and Nestlé agreed that on educational material it distributed, the social and health aspects of formula versus breast-feeding would be addressed. Its infant formula labels would clearly state the dangers of using contaminated water and the superiority of mother's milk. Personal gifts to health officials (which smacked of bribery and seeking preferential treatment) were banned. Finally, free samples of formula distributed to hospitals were to be limited to supplies that go to mothers incapable of breast-feeding their children.

At last, after years of Nestlé's adversarial posture, which had only resulted in a growing crescendo of criticisms, boycotts, and bitter accusations that the company was causing the deaths of millions of babies in developing countries because of its marketing practices, the situation was improving. "We have all learned a lesson, . . ." said Rafael D. Pagan, Jr., president of the Nestlé Coordination Center for Nutrition. "Companies should be sensitive and listen carefully to what consumers and members of the general public are saying. When problems surface, they should seek a dialogue with responsible leaders and try to work out the problems together."[13]

After a decade of confrontation with protesters and seven years of boycotting, early in 1984 most groups agreed to a suspension of their boycott. While some diehards refused to accept the conciliatory efforts of Nestlé, several large groups—for example, the American Federation of Teachers, the American Federation of Churches, the Federation of Nurses & Health Professionals, the United Methodist Church, and the Church of the Brethren—had either withdrawn from the boycott or decided not to join it. Nestlé admitted, however, that perhaps twenty obdurate boycott leaders and 50,000 followers in the United States may never stop ostracizing the company no matter what Nestlé does.[14]

12. "Fighting a Boycott," *Industry Week* (January 23, 1984), p. 54.

13. "Nestlé Gains Formula Accord: Product Boycott Is Suspended," *Marketing News* (February 17, 1984), p. 5.

14. "Fighting a Boycott," p. 55.

The results in lost business for Nestlé are difficult to pinpoint. Company estimates ranged up to $40 million in lost profits as a direct result of the boycotts. However, lost business was probably far greater than this, with some coming in the years before the boycotts began as consumers turned to alternative brands from firms with better reputations. Even during the years of boycotts, not all consumers were militant protesters, but they could certainly take their business elsewhere, as a silent protest. Admittedly, infant food business accounted for only 3 percent of total Nestlé sales worldwide, but other Nestlé products were blackened to an unknown degree by the destroyed public image of this one minor part of the total business. One of the most obvious negative consequences of the boycotts was the loss of meetings and convention business at Stouffer facilities, with some planners choosing to schedule at other locations as a means of avoiding any association with negative publicity.

Table 13.1 shows the sales and profits for the Nestlé conglomerate during 1974 to 1983. It shows profits declining in some years, perhaps as a result of the protests. We really cannot measure how much is the direct effect of the confrontation. We can only guess at the extent of unrealized potential.

WHAT CAN BE LEARNED?

The Nestlé debacle should be sobering for many firms. It should raise some real concerns about the possibility of damage to the public image—damage that can be difficult to rebuild. Specifically, the following are major lessons to be learned from this experience.

The public image is especially at risk for large firms. A reputable image, or at least one that is neutral and not negative, can be quickly besmirched. A firm should not underestimate the power of social awareness and activist groups. Furthermore, the large firm is more vulnerable—even if other firms in the industry are engaged in the same practices—and is the most desirable target for activist groups. Large size brings with it greater visibility and public recognition than is the case with smaller competitors. This makes a large firm the target of choice: the

Table 13.1 Nestlé Sales and Profits, 1974–1983 (thousands of Swiss Francs)

Years	Sales	Profits
1975	18,286,000	799,000
1976	19,063,000	872,000
1977	20,095,000	830,000
1978	20,266,000	739,000
1979	21,639,000	816,000
1980	24,479,000	638,000
1981	27,734,000	964,000
1982	27,664,000	1,098,000
1983	27,943,000	1,261,000

Source: Company annual reports.

goal is to bring down the giant. And public sentiment, be it on the athletic field, in business, or wherever, is not on the side of the big and powerful.

Beware of the power of a hostile press. A bad press can both arouse and intensify negative public opinion. It can fan the flames. A firm cannot rely on the press to be objective and unbiased in such reporting. The press tends to be eager to find a "fault object," and when this is a large and rather impersonal firm, the likelihood is all the greater that bad actions or the negatives of a particular situation will be emphasized far more than the positive and helpful side of the issue. Although infant formulas had many benefits and were a positive health influence in many situations, publicity focused almost exclusively on alleged abuses.

A besmirched reputation is not easily overcome. Nestlé's expectations that the controversy would die out were certainly quashed by the duration and increasing virulence of the protest movement. Without constructive efforts by Nestlé in the early 1980s, the gathering strength of the protest movement probably would have resulted in ever greater boycotting and most likely in restrictive legislation by many countries. Thus, a tarnished reputation is not suddenly going to become bright and shiny just because of the passage of time. Strong positive efforts must be made by the firm to try to restore its image, or it will not be improved.

Public relations efforts by themselves will seldom improve a negative public image. Public relations is not the answer when certain aspects of a firm's operation are the focal points of criticism. The act must be cleaned up first. The public-relations efforts of Nestlé were notoriously impotent, despite hiring two of the largest and most expensive public-relations firms in the world. Without improving the operations under question, no amount of public relations statements—even mailing some 300,000 pamphlets to clergy promoting Nestlé's position—could produce positive and lasting results.

Marketing efforts tend to have the strongest impact on public image. Many of Nestlé's problems emanated from its marketing efforts in developing countries. Normally, such efforts would be viewed as effective; under different circumstances, they could even have been lauded as models for introducing a new and improved product. Here, however, they were seen as far too effective in swaying a naive population in not wholly desirable directions. A firm's marketing efforts are the most visible aspects of its operation. This visibility can sometimes be a curse, as it was with Nestlé.

Suggested responses to a darkening public image. The Nestlé example gives us helpful insights as to how best to respond to smears and protests. Ignoring the problem seems ill-advised if the protests are severe enough and the issue is inflammatory. And certainly, alleged culpable loss of life—whether from chemical dumps or spills or from the ill-advised use of infant formula—is inflammatory enough.

Direct confrontation and an adversarial stand is seldom effective, either. As Nestlé found out the hard way, a court case, even if you win, only increases the negative publicity and fuels the protestations. Even if the weight of evidence is on the firm's side, the propaganda and one-sided criticisms of the opposition will likely win over the general public.

So it seems more prudent for the firm that falls into the snare of public image problems regarding its social role to approach the situation with a spirit of cooperation and constructive participation with opposing groups, despite some diehard activists who may refuse all efforts at conciliation. We cannot fault the efforts of Nestlé in 1981 to 1983 in working with the more reasonable critics. But we can severely fault the company for waiting so long to take such constructive actions.

Many firms need a greater sensitivity to potential problem areas involving corporate social performance. They need to try to anticipate potential problems and nip them quickly. Failing this, an organization should strive to resolve as many of the objections as it can, even if this means assuming the burden of an inequitable compromise position. The consequence otherwise may be a gradually deteriorating image, despite the fact that negative public perceptions are not fully based on facts.

A firm doing business in sensitive areas needs to prove that it is a responsible corporate citizen and not an insensitive giant organization. More attention to the public image may well prevent the type of image problems that bedeviled Nestlé for years.

CONSIDER

Can you think of any other learning insights?

QUESTIONS

1. How could the disaster have been avoided in the first place?
2. What should have been done when Nestlé first learned of the problem?
3. Faced with activist protesters, do you think a firm has any recourse but to give in to their demands? Is there any room for an aggressive stance?
4. Could the public-relations efforts of Nestlé have been used more effectively? How?
5. Do you think Nestlé was unfairly picked on? What makes you think this?
6. Did Nestlé act unethically in using milk nurses?
7. Was Nestlé guilty of severe violations of ethical standards?

HANDS-ON EXERCISES

1. As the staff assistant to the CEO of Nestlé, you have been asked to develop a position paper on the desirability of withdrawing infant formula from developing countries. Discuss the pros and cons of such a move, and then make your recommendations and support them as persuasively as you can. (*Note:* This could also be a debate exercise with another group taking a contrary position.)
2. You are the manager of a Stouffer hotel. A delegation of clergy and lay people has approached you threatening to boycott your premises. Be persuasive in trying to dissuade them from doing so.

TEAM DEBATE EXERCISES

1. Debate the issue of the boycotters. Were they earnest people with right on their side? Or were they anti-establishment agitators looking for anything to strike out against? One side in the debate should defend the protesters; the other side should condemn them.

2. Debate whether Nestlé should leave the African market now that the protests have begun.

INVITATION TO RESEARCH

Can infant formula still be found in developing countries? Have its risks in using been overcome? Have the critics been satisfied?

CHAPTER FOURTEEN

The Dalkon Shield: Ignoring User Safety

*I*t is February 29, 1984. Three company executives have been summoned to appear in federal district court before Judge Miles Lord in Minneapolis, Minnesota. They are E. Claiborne Robins Jr., A. H. Robins Company president and CEO; Dr. Carl D. Lunsford, director of research; and William A. Forrest, Jr., the company's general counsel. With them in the courtroom is a horde of lawyers.

To the three executives' acute shock, embarrassment, and anger, they hear Judge Lord publicly chastise them and their company for their conduct regarding the marketing of the Dalkon Shield, an intrauterine birth-control device.

For some months, Judge Lord had been involved with a combined suit against the company by seven women who had been seriously injured by the Shield. The investigation delved into past Dalkon Shield litigation and the legal tactics employed by Robins for more than ten years. The judge noted in his stinging rebuke:

> And when the time came for these women to make their claims
> against your company, you attacked their characters. You inquired
> into their sexual practices and into the identity of their sex partners.
> You ruined families and reputations and careers in order to intimidate
> those who would raise their voices against you. You introduced
> issues that had no relationship to the fact that you had planted in
> the bodies of these women instruments of death, of mutilation, of
> disease. Another of your callous legal tactics is to force women of
> little means to withstand the onslaughts of your well-financed team
> of attorneys. You target your worst tactics at the meek and the poor.
> You have taken the bottom line as your guiding beacon and the low
> road as your route.[1]

Judge Lord ordered a search of the company's files. Court-appointed officials found strong evidence that the company had covered up its knowledge of the Dalkon Shield's dangers.

1. Miles W. Lord, "A Plea for Corporate Conscience." Speech reprinted in *Harpers* (June 1984), pp. 13–14.

Robins's officials retaliated by bringing a lawsuit against Judge Lord—which they subsequently lost.

Between 1971 and 1975, Robins had sold more than 4 million Dalkon Shield IUDs in eighty countries of the world. In so doing, it had ignored ever-increasing concerns of physicians and others about the Shield's effectiveness and safety. In the United States alone, more than 2 million women were fitted with the inadequately tested contraceptive device by doctors who believed the optimistic claims of the company. As a result, thousands of women suffered serious damage caused by the shield—from pelvic infection to sterility, miscarriage, and even death.

This became one of the biggest business blunders of all time, made so much worse by a firm that at first blinded itself to any danger, then tried to cover it up, until finally the mess was too big to bury.

How could a respected management, one with the reputation of a multigenerational family firm at stake, have accepted such risks with an untested new product in the crass pursuit of short-term profits? And how could it, in a panic over impending lawsuits, have so deceived itself, as well as the medical profession and the general public, into believing that nothing was wrong, that others—that is, physicians themselves—were to blame?

INTRAUTERINE CONTRACEPTIVES (IUDS) AND THE DALKON SHIELD

Interest in birth control, and, in particular, IUDs as a form of contraception, goes back to ancient times, although most efforts were perilous and unreliable. Medical reports in the 1920s noted many cases of pelvic infection and inflammation with the crude IUD devices available then, and these devices were generally discredited.

In the early 1960s, interest in birth control greatly increased because of two factors. First, fears had begun to emerge of an overpopulated world. These fears seemed justified, since a billion people had been added to the world's population between 1930 and 1960. Although most of the fears centered on the developing nations of Africa, Asia, and South America, the United States was also experiencing population growth, reaching the psychological milestone of 200 million in the 1960s.

Second, the first oral contraceptive was approved by the Food and Drug Administration in 1960 and was enthusiastically received by both women and the medical profession. However, worries began to surface about the Pill. Some of these concerned its side effects, such as blood clots. Of even more concern was the possibility of long-term risks for women using the powerful birth-control hormones for as many as three decades of childbearing years.

After decades of IUDs being discredited, two developments in the 1960s spurred interest in them. One was the discovery of a new, malleable, inert plastic from which IUDs could be made, and the second was the development of a new molding process. Two new IUDs were patented in 1966: the Lippes Loop and the Saf-T-Coil.

Meantime, Hugh J. Davis, an associate professor of gynecology at Johns Hopkins, and Irwin Lerner, an inventor, came up with an idea for a new IUD—on Christmas Day, 1967. Initial results looked good, and Lerner applied for a patent in

1968. In shape, this new IUD resembled a shield and was a dime-sized, crablike plastic device with a string attached for removal by the physician.

On February 1, 1970, the *American Journal of Obstetrics and Gynecology* published an article by Davis based on his testing at Johns Hopkins Family Planning Clinic of 640 women who had worn the device, named the Dalkon Shield. Davis cited five pregnancies, ten rejections, nine removals for medical reasons, and three removals for personal reasons. He reported a pregnancy rate of 1.1 percent. The article impressed many doctors because of such favorable statistics and because it was tested at the prestigious Johns Hopkins School of Medicine. As a result, many became interested in obtaining the device for their own patients.

Davis and Lerner decided to market the device themselves, and the Dalkon Company was formed in 1969. They worked to refine the product, and by April 1970, they introduced a new, improved device, which made the Shield more flexible and thinner, with barium sulfate to strengthen the plastic, while retaining its flexibility. However, lacking a sales organization, the owners quickly realized that the Shield would have to be distributed by an established corporation.

Schmid Laboratories turned down the idea, but then Upjohn made an offer. However, at a medical meeting in Bedford, Pennsylvania, another company was attracted, A. H. Robins. On June 12, 1970, after three days of negotiating, Robins topped the Upjohn offer and bought ownership rights to the Dalkon Shield for $750,000 plus consulting fees and a royalty of 10 percent on all U.S. and Canadian net sales. (That figure ultimately came to nearly $1.2 million.)

THE A. H. ROBINS COMPANY

The A.H. Robins Company, headquartered in Richmond, Virginia, was a relatively small company ($135 million in sales at the time), but it had subsidiaries in more than a dozen foreign countries. It was best known for such products as Robitussin cough syrup, Chap Stick lip balm, and Sergeant's Flea and Tick collars. It was no fly-by-night company: for more than a century, it had been a solid business citizen.

In 1860, Albert Hanley Robins opened a small apothecary shop in downtown Richmond. In 1878, he expanded into manufacturing: while A.H. Robins handled walk-in business, selling the patent medicines of the day; his son and daughter-in-law had a small pill-rolling operation upstairs. So the mom-and-pop undertaking continued until 1933, when a grandson, Edwin Claiborne Robins, took over management with dreams of expanding. He stopped selling medicines directly to the public and turned instead to selling prescription drugs to physicians and pharmacists. The first such product was a stomach remedy, Donnatel, which is still a major product. After World War II, the company became a major manufacturer of mass-marketed prescription and nonprescription drugs. In 1963, with net sales of $47 million and profits near $5 million, the firm went public. In the process, E. Claiborne Robins Sr. turned his family into one of the wealthiest in Virginia. In 1978, E. Claiborne Robins Jr. became president and CEO.

Since 1965, the company had been interested in the birth-control market and particularly in intrauterine devices, although it had never made or sold a medical device or gynecological product before and had no obstetrician or gynecologist on its staff. It had considered buying the rights for the Lippes Loop, but then the Dalkon Shield opportunity surfaced.

The potential for IUDs as a group seemed attractive. But perhaps the biggest plus for IUDs was that they did not require filing a New-Drug Application (NDA) with the Food and Drug Administration. Since the agency only had jurisdiction over drugs and not over medical devices (which was how IUDs were classified), a manufacturer did not have to file an NDA demonstrating that it had established relative safety with reliable and sufficient clinical and animal testing. Thus, lengthy research safety testing of the Dalkon Shield could be avoided. (On May 28, 1976, the Medical Device Amendments were enacted to bring medical devices under the supervision of the Food and Drug Administration, but these amendments came five years after the Dalkon Shield was first brought to market.)

Robins quickly made plans to bring the Shield to market, and its assembly was assigned to the Chap Stick division. The company saw an urgent need to get into the market before potential competitors could rush in. In January 1971, only six months after Robins acquired the rights, the Dalkon Shield was ready for national distribution. The profitability potential was intriguing: the production cost was only about 25 cents, while the, Shield was priced at $4.35. Although there were some quality-control problems, they were deemed not to be particularly serious.

Promoting the Dalkon Shield

An aggressive marketing strategy was put in place. Several hundred salespeople were trained to contact physicians. The advertising itself was directed at both the medical professionals—physicians as well as agencies and clinics that provided IUDs—and women directly to persuade them to accept the Shield if their physicians should so recommend, and even to request and insist on the device if their physicians were skeptical. Consequently, in addition to medical journals, *Family Circle*, *Mademoiselle*, and similar magazines carried Dalkon Shield advertising.

Robins wanted to position the Shield as a superior product. In 1970, it was promoted as a modern, superior IUD, with the lowest pregnancy rate (1.1 percent), lowest expulsion rate (2.3 percent), and the highest continuation rate (94 percent). Other promotional literature stated that it was the only IUD anatomically engineered for optimal uterine placement, fit, tolerance, and retention.

In the ads in major medical journals, Dr. Davis (the original researcher and coinventor) was shown as an impressive research physician, with citations from the articles he had published. Not disclosed was his financial interest in the product and that he was hardly the objective and unbiased researcher deemed essential to sound medical research.

The Shield proved to be a popular product in the contraceptive market. By 1972, an estimated 12 million IUDs were in use worldwide, with 3 million in the United States. And the Shield was in the forefront: some 1,146,000 were sold in 1971, with an estimated market share of 40 percent. In one month, April 1972, some 88,000 women were fitted with the Shield. But the physician complaints began to mount. In the early months, many of these complaints focused on the difficulty of inserting the Shield—later, these complaints would assume a more serious nature.

Despite all objections, by August 1973, more than 5 million pieces of promotional literature had been printed. The sales pitch did not change: "No general effects on the body, blood, or brain…safe and trouble-free…the safest and most satisfactory method of contraception…truly superior."[2] A new, smaller Shield had been brought out, and this was especially directed to women who had never borne children. However, no safety and effectiveness testing was ever done with this new version.

Shield Comes under Government Investigation

In June 1973, Henry S. Kahn, a researcher working for the Centers for Disease Control, headed a study to assess the safety of IUDs in general. In a survey of physicians in the United States and Puerto Rico, some surprising and troubling things surfaced. There seemed to be a significant correlation between the Dalkon Shield and the incidence of women hospitalized for a complicated pregnancy. He suggested that a more detailed investigation was warranted. At about the same time, Representative L. H. Fountain of North Carolina was chairing a subcommittee investigating whether medical devices should be subject to the same kinds of controls as drugs.

In the months that followed, more serious problems came to light, including some Shield-related deaths. In October 1973, Robins changed its Shield package label to include the warning; "Severe sepsis with fatal outcome, most often associated with spontaneous abortion following pregnancy with the Dalkon Shield *in situ* has been reported. In view of this, serious consideration should be given to removing the device when the diagnosis of pregnancy is made with the Dalkon Shield *in situ.*"

Robins convened its own Ob-Gyn advisory panel in February 1974 to evaluate information on cases of spontaneous septic abortion among women who became pregnant with the Shield in place. The panel finally concluded that there was inadequate information to establish a cause-and-effect relationship.

But problems continued to multiply. The Shield had a multifilament tail, compared with the monofilament tails used in all other IUDs. This tail was shown in several studies to be an excellent harbor for bacteria. In a letter dated May 8, 1974, Robins informed over 125,000 doctors that the Dalkon Shield should be removed immediately if a patient became pregnant and, if this was impossible, to perform a therapeutic abortion. The letter did not advise removal of the Shield from nonpregnant women. The company also stated that it felt the problems shown with the Shield were common to all IUDs. This letter was reported in the *Wall Street Journal*, and Robins quickly issued a press release stating that it had no intention of canceling production of the Shield.

There were more deaths, and by the end of June 1974, the Food and Drug Administration asked (not ordered) Robins to cease marketing the Shield. Bowing to public pressure, the company announced it would cease marketing the Shield until FDA tests were finalized. However, it still insisted that women who were currently using the Shield were in no danger. Meanwhile, the directors of Planned Parenthood and federally funded family planning programs urged the discontinuance of the Shield.

In October 1974, a preliminary report from the FDA concluded that the Shield was as safe as any other IUD and attributed the problem to the fact that the Shield was the

2. Morton Mintz, *At Any Cost: Corporate Greed, Women, and the Dalkon Shield* (New York: Pantheon Books, 1985), 75.

newest IUD on the market and was still undergoing a "shakedown" period. In December 1974, Alexander Schmidt, then commissioner of the FDA, announced that Robins could continue to market the Shield as long as accurate records were kept of all wearers.

Lawsuits Replace Government Scrutiny

Robins was never to remarket the device. Where the FDA failed, the judicial system took over. By March 1975, 186 suits had been filed against Robins. Also in March, the first judicial award was made: $10,000 compensatory and $75,000 punitive damages against Robins. In May, a $475,000 judgment was awarded to the estate of a woman who had died while using the Shield. In August 1975, Robins formally announced that it would not remarket the Shield, but insisted that women who had had it inserted previously were in no danger.

Not until September of 1980, six years after problems with the Shield had begun to surface, did Robins finally send a letter to 200,000 doctors urging them to remove the device from all women who were still using them. The company stated that a "new" study showed that other problems, such as an infection called *pelvic actinomycosis*, were more likely the longer the device was worn. This move followed a $6.8 million judgment in Colorado in June 1980, in which $600,000 was awarded in compensatory damages and $6.2 million in punitive damages. The punitive award was of serious concern to the company since Robins' liability insurance covered only compensatory damages.

By 1980, 4,300 suits were pending against Robins. Some attorneys were spending their entire time suing Robins; this became so popular a cause that a newsletter was published covering IUD litigation, and four-day yearly seminars were held so that more experienced lawyers could instruct on how best to sue Robins.

The company's 1981 annual report noted that 2,300 cases were still pending, whereas 4,200 had been settled. Up to now, the company and its insurer (Aetna) had paid out $98 million for Dalkon Shield litigation. Lawsuits continued to multiply, and they became increasingly expensive for the company to deal with. For example, the average settlement in 1976 was $8,000; in 1984, the average was in the $400,000 range.

As 1985 approached, Robins's sales continued to climb, reflecting the strength in its other product lines and its international operations. Profits rose more grudgingly because of the heavy legal costs—until 1984. (See Table 14.1 for the trend in sales and profits, as well as a chronology of major events.)

In 1984, hounded by ever-mounting legal costs and judgments and running out of liability insurance coverage from Aetna, Robins took an extraordinary charge of $615 million as a reserve for claims. This resulted in a paper loss of $461.6 million in 1984. In August 1985, Robins filed Chapter 11 bankruptcy. Under Chapter 11 bankruptcy, all litigation against a company is stayed while the company and its creditors attempt to devise a plan to pay the bankrupt company's debts. E. Claiborne Robins Jr. said the action was necessary to protect the company's economic vitality against those who would destroy it for the benefit of a few. Attorneys for the victims found this action to be fraudulent and in bad faith, an attempt by Robins to escape responsibility for the thousands of injuries the Shield had caused.

Not even Aetna was to escape unscathed. In 1986, a group of former Dalkon Shield users sued Aetna, charging that it had conspired with Robins to keep the alleged health hazards of the IUD from the public. The women claimed that Aetna

Table 14.1   Trend in Sales and Profits, 1970–84, and Chronology of Major Events (hundreds of thousands of dollars)

	Sales	Profits	Profits as Percent of Sales	Major Events
1970	132.6	15.7	11.8	June12, 1970, Robins buys the Dalkon Shield
1971	151.4	19.1	12.6	January 1971, Robins begins to market the Shield
				April 1972, peak month for number of women fitted with the Shield
1973	189.2	25.4	13.4	October 1973, Robins put warnings on packages
				June 1974, Robins suspends Shield sales in United States
1975	241.1	26.6	11.0	April 1975, Robins suspends Shield sales in other countries
1977	366.7	26.8	7.2	
1979	386.4	44.7	11.6	June 1980, $6.8 million judgement against Robins
1981	450.9	44.2	9.8	
1983	563.5	58.2	10.3	
1984	631.9	(461.6) loss		February 1984, Judge Miles Lord chastises Robins in Minneapolis court
				October 1984, Robins urges removal of all Shields, Robins establishes $615 million reserve for claims in late 1984
				August 21, 1985, Robins files for bankruptcy

also participated in intentional destruction of evidence that would have helped the plaintiffs prove the dangers of the device.

A bidding war developed for the troubled Robins Company. Rorer Group, a Pennsylvania pharmaceutical concern, made the first offer. Late in 1987, Sanofi, a French drug maker, made another takeover proposal. A week later, American Home Products Corporation joined the fast-developing bidding war. On January 20, 1988, the bid by American Home Products was accepted. John Stafford, chairman and CEO of American Home Products, was interested in Robins because of the tax advantages and the acquisition of two popular consumer brands: Robitussin and Dimeatapp. "Franchises that powerful come along every few decades," he said.[3] And American Home could deduct its funding of Dalkon Shield liabilities from federal taxes. American Home offered Robins's shareholders $700 million in American Home stock and agreed

3. Michael Waldholz, "American Home Expects Most of its Price for A. H. Robins Will Be Tax-Deductible," *Wall Street Journal* (January 21, 1988), A1.

to pay $2.15 billion in cash to the trust fund of claims. In the final modification, the two top executives of Robins each gave $5 million in exchange for protection against being sued personally over the Shield. This plan, Robins's fourth in its twenty-nine months of bankruptcy proceedings, was the first to receive endorsement from both the company's shareholders and the committee representing the Shield claimants.

POSTMORTEM

Here we see a company in extremes. Its conduct led a well-regarded firm with a 100-year history down the road to bankruptcy, but even worse, the innocent public was brutalized. How could this have happened? After all, these were not deliberately vicious men; they were well intentioned, albeit badly misguided. Perhaps their worst sin was trying to ignore and then cover up their product's increasingly apparent serious health problems, doing this to such an extent that a federal judge castigated them for their company's corporate immorality. How could this situation—which everyone lost but the lawyers—have been permitted to get so out of hand?

It began innocently enough, and in accordance with sound business strategy. Robins recognized an emerging opportunity: the birth control market. Although competitors were already in the oral contraceptive market, the IUD sector of this market was virtually untapped yet seemed to offer enormous potential. This sector appeared to be in the early stages of development, with no serious competitors. But the likelihood of strong competitive entry could not be ignored, and Robins thus saw the need to enter this IUD market quickly and secure a major share of it—that is, beat competitors to the punch. Again, we have to recognize that this is textbook business strategy.

In accordance with the desirability of quickly entering the market, many decisions were made with little deliberation. One such decision was to assign production of the Dalkon Shield to the Chap Stick division of the company. Any similarity between the two products was remote at best, but this assignment seemed a matter of expediency and a means of offering lower labor costs. It might be argued that with such a new and unique product, there was not much more compatibility with any other division of the company.

Now we come to the point where Robins deviated from sound business strategy. It was entering a market in which it had no previous experience whatsoever, one in which health dangers ought to have been carefully evaluated. Yet Robins had not a single obstetrician or gynecologist on its staff. The company also neglected to conduct its own testing of the product, relying instead on the limited research that had been done by the Dalkon Shield's inventors. Robins did not question their research and testing, flawed though it soon proved to be. Rather, it rushed the product to market, thankful that the Food and Drug Administration did not have to be involved. Good judgment would have mandated confirmation of the safety of the product by independent parties. But this would have taken time, time that Robins was fearful of spending.

Recognizing an emerging and spectacular strategic opportunity, Robins pursued it with single-minded determination. Unfortunately, such determination ignored prudent and even ethical considerations. For example, much of the product information and advertising used was taken from Davis and Lerner's admittedly biased research, and the financial interest that these two "researchers" had in the Dalkon Shield was ignored and certainly never publicly mentioned. Physicians were thereby misled into thinking the research was objective and unbiased.

The impressive research figures cited in the ads were soon to conflict with studies done by others. As one example, Robins's ads originally claimed that the Shield had a low pregnancy rate of 1.1 percent, but later studies showed pregnancy rates varying from 5 to 10 percent. But Robins continued to use the 1.1 percent rate in its advertising until late 1973, when the claimed pregnancy rate was revised upward.

Other advertising claims attested to the safety and superiority of the Dalkon Shield, that "it was generally well tolerated by even the most sensitive women," and that no anesthetic was required. Only after many physicians complained about the difficulty of insertion was the advertising literature changed in November 1971 by removing the statement that no anesthetic was required. The claim of being safe and superior went unchanged.

Robins continued to ignore reports of major problems—such as massive bleeding, pelvic inflammatory diseases, miscarriages, and even deaths—that kept coming in over the years following the introduction of the Shield. Admittedly, the term *safety* was relative: Was the Shield as safe or safer than the Pill? After all, the Pill was known not to be completely safe—it could cause serious side effects. Still, the evidence was mounting that there were significant dangers associated with the Shield, dangers beyond reasonable risk. Robins opted to ignore these far longer than was prudent and ethical.

Robins maintained that its product was safe—and it proclaimed so publicly. But evidence suggests that the company knew otherwise. Internal memos indicated that the company knew of potential danger less than a month after it acquired rights to the Shield. And more internal company memos were to surface during subsequent litigation: two to three truckloads of incriminating papers.

The basic component of Robins's strategy now became strictly defensive: to cooperate when necessary but to spend most of its time lobbying Congress and defending itself against lawsuits. Major concern was thus with legal and not ethical considerations regarding its past actions.

So, what seemed at first to be an unassailable strategy was found seriously wanting. Was the company guilty of subordinating everything to the profit maximization goal, an end-justifies-the-means perspective? Or did it simply panic, faced with a calamity of extraordinarily severe consequences, and resort to the defense mechanism of denial?

Roger L. Tuttle, a former A. H. Robins attorney, believed the latter:

> "I've got to believe that had they known early on what they were dealing with they wouldn't have touched it with a ten-foot pole. It was just that one step led to another, until they had the grenade spinning in the middle of the floor."[4]

Nevertheless, the dire consequences to the company and to its customer-victims represent a classic example of a monumental ethical mistake that should have been handled better. (See the Issue Box, "Must Management Assume the Worst Scenario?")

---

4. Mintz, *At Any Cost,* 51–52.

ISSUE BOX

MUST MANAGEMENT ASSUME THE WORST SCENARIO?

The Dalkon Shield turned out to be an unmitigated disaster—for the thousands of women victims, and also for the company. Certainly, no company would undertake a business venture that was likely to produce such results. There should be a commonality of interests on the part of consumers and firms to prevent such happenings. Ignoring the issue of a company's culpability for not noticing and then covering up the danger, another question should be asked: Does ignorance of future dire consequences relieve a firm of much of its blame? The contentious segment of the general public—lawyers as well as politicians eager to mollify their constituents—sees a *no mercy* scenario: the corporation is guilty despite ignorance of any wrongdoing, or any danger, at the time. But is this the most equitable viewpoint?

We live in a complex world. And our products are increasingly more complex technologically; some products, such as drugs, asbestos, and cigarettes, may well have long-term consequences far beyond our ability to predict at this time. Was this the case with the Dalkon Shield?

In today's environment, firms are not able to escape the long-term negative consequences of their products. The litigious environment will not permit this, however ignorant the firm may have been. Ethically, the blame has to be more muted for a firm that could not see any dire consequences. But, does the very fact of not knowing really excuse a firm?

Does such "unknowing" absolve Robins with its Dalkon Shield? Hardly. Although knowledge of long-term consequences for any product may be limited, this does not preclude adequate and objective testing to achieve a high level of safety assurance. This Robins did not do. Furthermore, when the first suspicions were raised of possible problems, it ignored them and even concealed them. Here was Robins's great ethical and moral misdeed: it placed short-term company profits above very strong doubts of customer health and safety.

INVITATION TO DISCUSS

Robbins's executives may argue that if they had had any idea of the serious danger of the Shield, they would have jerked it from the market, but they had nothing to confirm this until too late. Therefore, they should be exonerated from any serious wrongdoing. Discuss the pros and cons of this defense.

WHAT CAN BE LEARNED?

The Robins Company's actions seemed exemplary at first:

1. Identify a business opportunity or strategic window.
2. Find or develop a product to fit this strategic window.
3. Beat competition in being the first to capitalize on this opportunity.

But there was one basic difference from other effective strategies: health and safety were more at stake with this particular product. This should have necessitated a more cautious approach to the window of opportunity to ensure that the product had no risks to customers. Yet, at Robins, health and safety considerations were ignored in a single-minded pursuit of profits. Everything else was secondary to this profit orientation. We can take several lessons from this case:

A firm today must zealously guard against product liability suits. Any responsible executive now has to recognize that product liability suits, in today's increasingly litigious environment, can bankrupt a firm. The business arena has become more risky, more fraught with peril for the unwary or the naively unconcerned. Consequently, any firm needs careful and objective testing of any product that can even remotely affect customer health and safety—and this must be undertaken even if product introduction is delayed and competitive entry encouraged.

Suspicions and complaints about product safety must be thoroughly investigated. We should learn unequivocally from this case that immediate and thorough investigation of any suspicions or complaints must be undertaken regardless of the confidence management may have in the product and regardless of the glowing recommendations from persons whose objectivity could be suspect. To procrastinate or ignore these warnings poses risks that should be unacceptable.

In the worst scenario, go for a salvage strategy. Robins faced a crossroads in 1974. Scary reports of problems and lawsuits were flooding in. How should the company react? One course of action was to tough it out, trying to combat the bad press, denying culpability, and resorting to the strongest possible legal defense. This Robins opted to do. At stake were its reputation, its economic life, and the welfare of tens of thousands of women.

The other recourse was what we might call a salvage strategy: recognition and full admission of the problem and removal of the Shield from more than 4 million women amid a full-market withdrawal. Expensive, yes, but far less risky for the viability of the company and certainly for the health of those women involved.

Neither strategy is without major costs. But the first course of action puts major cost consequences in the future, where they may turn out to be vastly greater. The second course of action poses an immediate impact on profitability but may save the company and its reputation and return it to profitability in the future.

This is an era of caveat vendidor—let the seller beware. Businesses today have to recognize that this is no longer an age of *caveat emptor*—let the buyer beware. This philosophy ruled the business environment for many decades, but now the pendulum has swung to *caveat vendidor*—let the seller beware. Products or business practices that are perceived as not in the best interest of the public are subject to reprisals—either through customer resentment and public outcry or through lawsuits. Woe to the firm that does not recognize this or underestimates the environmental constraints.

CONSIDER

Are there other learning insights that should be mentioned?

QUESTIONS

1. At what point in the Dalkon Shield's life did unethical practices first become apparent?

2. What should have been done at that point?

3. Can a firm guarantee complete product safety? Discuss.

4. Design a strategy for the Dalkon Shield that would have minimized the problems Robins eventually faced. What might be some concerns with such a strategy?

5. After this disaster, do you think Robins could ever have regained a sufficiently respected image to be a viable business under the same management? Even the same name? Why or why not?

6. Do you think prison sentences should have been the fate of top executives?

HANDS-ON EXERCISE

You are the public relations director for Robins in late 1972. Some disquieting information has come to you about far-higher-than-expected physician complaints about the Shield. Top management has so far been unconcerned about such reports, especially because of Food and Drug Administration complacency. Develop a plan of action for dealing with potential product safety problems that can be persuasively presented to top management.

TEAM DEBATE EXERCISE

The worst has happened. The Shield has been shown to be a dangerous product, and the company guilty of disregarding earlier claims of such dangers even while it continued to advertise product safety. In a congressional hearing, the issue is: (1) Was the company guilty of subordinating everything to maximizing profits, or (2) Did company officials simply panic, faced with a calamity of severe consequences, and resorted to the defense mechanism of denial. In a simulated courtroom environment, defend top management against the prosecutors' charge of sheer callousness to product safety in pursuit of big profits.

INVITATION TO RESEARCH

Were any jail sentences or huge fines meted out to corporate executives? Why do you think this is? Investigate the performance of American Home products since it took over Robins in 1988. Was this a wise acquisition?

CHAPTER FIFTEEN

Exxon's Alaskan Oil Spill: Environmental Destruction on a Giant Scale

At 12:04 A.M., in the darkness of the cold Alaskan night of March 24, 1989, a huge oil tanker, the *Exxon Valdez,* came to an unexpected and abrupt halt. At that moment, the worst maritime oil spill in U.S. history commenced. The damage to the pristine waters, fish, and wildlife of Prince William Sound, and to the people who depended on it, was feared to be profound. Exxon, the giant petroleum firm, would show ambivalent behavior about the oil spill: responsiveness and concern, then reluctance and blame shifting, finally the grudging continuation of cleanup efforts. And so, despite the $2.5 billion the company eventually spent for cleanup efforts, its image of callousness toward the environment was not dispelled. Of course, Exxon was not alone to blame for the disaster.

THE CAPTAIN

The captain of the *Exxon Valdez* was Joseph Hazelwood, a twenty-year Exxon veteran who had commanded the Valdez for twenty months. At age forty-two, he was fairly young to be captaining such a vessel, but he was regarded as a talented seaman. An honors graduate from New York Maritime College, Hazelwood was only thirty-two when he received his master's license. At home on the sea, he had displayed cool headedness, courage, and skill—qualities that helped his rapid rise. But he had a dark side as well: he was rumored to be a drinker, with a reputation for alcohol abuse.

It was never proven that Hazelwood was drunk when he captained the *Exxon Valdez* on March 24. Nine hours after the collision, his blood-alcohol level was 0.06, which is higher than the 0.04 considered acceptable for captains by the Coast Guard. Assuming a normal metabolism rate, this would put the level at 0.19 at the time of the accident; almost double the amount at which most states consider a person to be legally drunk. However, Hazelwood maintained that he had consumed a low-alcohol beverage in his cabin after the accident, the ship having been stabilized.

Fueling the suspicions about Hazelwood was the fact that he had twice been convicted of drunk driving in the preceding five years and had had his driver's license revoked three times. At the time of the accident, though he retained his license to command a super tanker, he was not permitted to drive a car. In 1985, Exxon had sent him to an alcohol rehabilitation program, but after the accident the company claimed it was not aware that his alcoholism had persisted.

After the accident, Exxon fired Hazelwood. Contrary to general belief, he was not fired for drunkenness on duty—a charge difficult to prove—but for not being on the bridge of the ship, as company regulations require. Having been convicted of negligent discharge of oil, Hazelwood was sentenced, a year after the accident, to 1,000 hours of community service helping clean up the oil spill. A jury had acquitted him of three more serious charges: criminal mischief, reckless endangerment, and operating a vessel while intoxicated.

THE ACCIDENT

Only two years old, the *Exxon Valdez* was the newest and best-equipped vessel in Exxon's fleet. It had such advanced technology as collision avoidance radar, satellite navigational aids, and depth finders.[1] Some 987 feet long, it drew 33 feet of water when loaded. It made regular trips from the Port of Valdez to the terminal at Long Beach, California, a five-day trip. On this particular trip, it was loaded with 52 million gallons of crude oil. Because of its sheer size and mass (211,000 tons) this loaded ship required a full minute to respond to any steering changes.

Still, there was no reason to expect any trouble as the *Valdez* left port at 9:12 P.M. on March 23, under the guidance of harbor pilot Ed Murphy. After all, 8,548 tankers had made the rather routine and boring trip before this, without a serious accident. When the local pilot left the tanker at 11:24 P.M., Captain Hazelwood took command. Inexplicably, he left the bridge and went below to his cabin, thus violating company policy that a captain stay on the bridge until the ship reaches open water. But the *Valdez* was still passing through the narrow waters of the Valdez Arm of Prince William Sound. Third Mate Gregory Cousins, who was not licensed to steer a vessel through the coastal waters of Alaska, was left in charge.

A short time later, the tanker radioed the Coast Guard for permission to steer a course down the empty incoming ship lane to avoid icebergs in the outgoing lane. Permission was granted, and the *Valdez* altered course. The Coast Guard lost radar contact with the tanker soon afterward. The *Exxon Valdez* had run aground on Bligh Reef in Prince William Sound, with Hazelwood still in his cabin.

By 5:40 A.M. the *Valdez* had lost more than 8.8 million gallons of oil. By 7:27 A.M. the oil slick was 100 feet wide, five miles long, and spreading. Eventually, 10.1 million gallons would be spilled, threatening the year's $100 million seafood harvest, Alaska's lucrative tourism business, $750 million a year in commercial fishing, and the entire aquatic ecosystem.

The oil slick continued to spread, soon covering more than 1,000 square miles (an area larger than the state of Rhode Island) and contaminating hundreds of miles of beaches. The slick eventually moved 100 miles out into the Gulf of Alaska.

---

1. William C, Rempel, "Disaster at Valdez: Promises Unkept," *Los Angeles Times* (April 2, 1989), 1-20.

BACKGROUND

Alaskan Oil

Oil and natural gas were discovered in January 1968 on the frozen north slope of Alaska's Prudhoe Bay. Tests indicated that at least 10 billion barrels of oil and 26 trillion cubic feet of natural gas were lurking below the surface. But for years, debate raged whether this reserve should be used and how it would be transported to processing plants. Intense lobbying by Alaska and a tie-breaking vote by Vice President Spiro Agnew cleared the way for the Trans-Alaska Pipeline and Tanker Route. An oil industry pledge that the environment would be protected at all costs was a key to congressional approval of the pipeline. Alaska agreed to create a Department of Environmental Conservation (DEC) to regulate and monitor the oil industry. In 1973, construction started on the pipeline. In 1977, the four-foot diameter, 800-mile-long pipeline and ship-loading terminal were completed. Oil started flowing.

More than 2 million barrels a day move through this pipeline, about 25 percent of America's oil needs. Alaska has benefited greatly. Valdez, where the ship-loading terminal is located, gets 94 percent of its tax revenues from oil. Oil-related money has made state income taxes unnecessary; the state even paid an annual oil dividend to each resident amounting to at least $800 per person. Other economic developments—jobs, roads, schools, libraries, and cultural activities—resulted from this oil prosperity. As one resident stated after the accident: "For twelve years we enjoyed the prosperity of our state's oil wealth without having to face its trade-offs—until the wreck of the *Exxon Valdez*."[2]

Exxon

Exxon Corporation is America's second-largest corporation and the world's third-largest oil company. In 1989, the year of the oil spill, Exxon sales were more than $86 billion, with profits close to $3 billion. However, dividends decreased when Exxon put aside funds to finance the cleanup and pay the legal and punitive costs for the spill. Table 15.1 shows Exxon operating statistics from 1986 to 1990.

Exxon has diversified beyond oil, but oil remains its major emphasis. With Exxon's worldwide organization and purchasing power, it was in a position to mobilize

Table 15.1   Exxon Operating Statistics, 1986–1990

Year	Revenues (millions)	Earnings (millions)	Dividends (dollars per share)
1986	$69,888	$5,360	$7.42
1987	76,416	4,840	3.43
1988	79,557	5,260	3.95
1989	86,656	2,975	2.32
1990	115,794	5,010	3.96

Source: Company public records.

2. Art Davidson, *In the Wake of the Exxon Valdez* (San Francisco: Sierra Club Books, 1990), xiv.

experts, equipment, planes, materials, and an army of manpower to combat the oil spill. It is unlikely that any other environmental or government agency could have done this. Yet, somehow, relief efforts were flawed.

Aleyeska

Aleyeska was born with the creation of the Trans-Alaska oil project. It is a consortium of the seven oil companies that invested in the Alaskan oil venture: Exxon, British Petroleum, Mobil, Atlantic-Richfield, Amerada Hess, Unocal, and Phillips Petroleum. Each company has a partial interest in Aleyeska, with Exxon having a 20 percent interest. Aleyeska brought unified efforts to the design, construction, planning, operation, safety, and personnel for the oil transportation from Prudhoe Bay to Valdez. The biggest part of this operation was in the city of Valdez, and Aleyeska played a big role in that city's affairs.

Aleyeska was also entrusted with preventing any adverse environmental effects that might be caused by this massive drilling and transportation operation. The consortium was heavily involved in the preliminaries, submitting plans for operations, safety, environmental impact, emergency response procedures, and readiness programs to the newly created Department of Environmental Conservation (DEC). The construction of the pipeline was even delayed until all plans were approved.

Unfortunately, when the accident occurred, Aleyeska failed miserably. Although charged with safeguarding against such an accident, and with providing the initial response if one should happen, Aleyeska proved unable to cope. It left the major part of the cleanup efforts to Exxon.

Other Participants

The DEC had the role of watchdog. It was empowered to enforce the environmental laws and regulations created for the Alaskan oil transportation system. However, the agency seemed more motivated to making sure oil flow was not interrupted than concerned with environmental safeguards.

Fishermen were the most adversely affected by the oil spill. Protecting fish hatcheries became a top priority for them. Unable to get enough oil containment booms, they made their own with logs, chains, and plastic. With financial backing from Exxon, these homemade booms helped to preserve the future of the industry.

Almost overnight, Valdez became a boomtown, with people pouring in to help in the cleanup. All the chaos and opportunism of any boomtown became the lot of Valdez.

CLEANUP EFFORTS

For a spill of this size, the cleanup technology is woefully inadequate. Add human carelessness and incompetence to the enormity of the oil spill, and a problem of monumental proportions was created. The timing of the disaster could hardly have been worse. Millions of fish were headed toward Prince William Sound for spawning, and millions of birds were migrating north. All this fueled the cry for action.

The Technology

Basically, oil spills can be controlled in four ways: containment, collection, dispersion, and burn-off. The first priority should be containment. If the slick is prevented from spreading over a wide area, it is obviously easier to collect. But containment efforts failed here. Containment booms that can be used to surround the oil at the very earliest stages of a leak were not aboard the *Exxon Valdez*; the nearest booms were in the town of Valdez. Preparedness plans called for a response within two and a half hours. However, the barge used for transporting the booms was damaged and in dry dock for repairs. It took fourteen hours for the first booms to arrive at the site, and by that time the slick was out of control, beyond the capability of containment.

Once an oil spill is contained, various methods can be used to collect the oil. In a skimmer operation, ships travel through a slick and "skim" off the thicker, lighter oil on the water surface and place it into larger storage barges. The problem with an oil slick of this magnitude is finding enough storage barges to hold the collected oil so that the skimming can be resumed.

Chemical dispersants are another possibility. These react with the oil much like dish soap does with grease. However, these chemicals do not actually remove the oil, and they are themselves toxic. There is disagreement as to which of the two evils is worse.

Finally, the oil can be set on fire, which has obvious drawbacks: controlling the fire, air pollution, and ash fallout. This alternative also requires calm waters. But although the weather cooperated at first during the Exxon oil spill, bureaucratic bungling and disagreement impeded early burn-off efforts. Then the weather worsened.

Operational Problems

A number of organizations were involved in cleaning up the spill. They all had the same objective, but they disagreed wildly on how best to cope with the problem. Besides Aleyeska, Exxon, and the DEC, other groups involved were the Department of Fish and Game, the U.S. Coast Guard, the Environmental Protection Agency, fishermen, and various conservation groups. Their vastly different viewpoints created major impediments.

Exxon assumed immediate responsibility and control. The president of the subsidiary Exxon Shipping, Frank Iarossi, was assigned the cleanup task. Because the mechanical means to contain the spill and collect it from the water were either not available or not in working order, and because of the size of the slick, Iarossi's solution was to use dispersants, fire, or both. But this met with strong disapproval by local groups and government agencies. Debate raged for four days, while the problem escalated. By the time permission was granted to use dispersants and a permit was issued for burning, the calm weather conditions had turned into gale-force winds, a blizzard, and twenty-foot waves. Planes scheduled to spray the chemicals were grounded; boats to be used for sea operations could not leave their safe harbors. The monster spill was unchecked. Before long, virtually every island in Prince William Sound was surrounded by oil, and over 800 miles of beaches were covered. The battle plan now changed from recovering the oil to protecting the fish hatcheries and cleaning up the beaches. Dissension, confusion, and a lack of unified and decisive action had allowed the monster to spread.

There was one aspect of the operation that Exxon *could* control: the lightering of the ship. *Lightering* was the process by which the ship's remaining 11 million gallons of oil were off-loaded to another tanker. Exxon feared that the ship might split, thus releasing even more oil and geometrically worsening the situation. But even lightering the ship was criticized as self-serving, since it enabled Exxon to profit by sending the oil on to Long Beach.

CONSEQUENCES

After a sixteen-month investigation into the accident, the National Transportation Safety Board issued a report on July 31, 1990. The report cited the failures of the ship's captain, its third mate, Exxon Shipping Company, the U.S. Coast Guard, and Alaskan authorities in the disaster.

The report concluded that Captain Hazelwood was not able to supervise the tanker at the time of the accident because he was impaired from alcohol, that Third Mate Cousins, the man in charge at the moment the tanker ran into the reef, was unable to avoid the accident because of fatigue and overwork. Exxon was blamed for failing to provide a fit master and a rested and sufficient crew and failing to monitor Hazelwood's drinking problems. The U.S. Coast Guard was criticized for inadequately tracking ships and icebergs in the area. And the state of Alaska was criticized for not having a pilot aboard past the dangerous reef.[3]

On October 8, 1991, a federal judge in Anchorage, Alaska, approved a settlement reached between Exxon, the Alaskan government, and the U.S. Justice Department over criminal charges arising from the accident. The judge's approval effectively ended all state and federal lawsuits resulting from the spill. Exxon agreed to pay a total of $1.025 billion in fines and restitution payments through the year 2001. The settlement guaranteed, however, the rights of native Alaskans and other private litigants to continue to bring separate lawsuits against Exxon.

The spill's immediate destruction of fish, wildlife, and unspoiled beaches shocked the nation. Pictures of oil-covered birds and animals, of beaches covered with a gooey layer of crude oil, became commonplace in the media. However, after the initial confusion and delay, Exxon employed thousands of temporary workers in a massive cleanup operation. Unfortunately, these cleanup operations were not without their downside. Beaches were left sterilized, unable to support life. Thousands of people came to collect the $16.67 an hour Exxon paid for clean-up labor, but unsanitary conditions, crime, and garbage were byproducts of these efforts.

By early May 1989, Exxon had revised its cleanup plan, leaving some of the cleanup work to wave action and nature. By the end of the summer, much of the surface pollution had been eradicated, though there was the question of how much had sunk to the ocean floor as thick black gunk. Efforts continued in the following summers, with the company spending more than $2 billion in cleanup efforts.

---

3. *Facts on File* (October 10, 1991), p. 602.

The massive cleanup seemed to pay off. By the fall of 1990, little evidence of the oil remained on beaches, although below the surface it still was a problem. By November 1990, about 85 percent of the shoreline had been adequately cleaned.

Environmentalists' worst fears were apparently not realized. Cold weather did not prevent the oil slick from disintegrating. Even the predicted destruction of fish and wildlife did not occur. Estimates were that up to 2,000 otters and some 33,000 birds may have died. More worrisome was what the long-term effects might be, especially the effects of the oil deposits that sunk to the ocean floor. Could these release harmful hydrocarbons for several years, contaminating the food chain and ruining the catches of shrimp, salmon, herring, and crabs?

The impact of the *Exxon Valdez* oil spill could have been much worse: about 10.1 million gallons were released from the accident, but the tanker was loaded with 52 million gallons. One wonders at the environmental impact if five times the volume of oil had escaped.

EXXON'S PUBLIC-IMAGE PROBLEMS

Exxon's reaction to the spill, its crisis management and handling of the publicity, did not cast it in good light. The media and the public remained hostile to the company. Environmentalists, including Ralph Nader, castigated the company. Customers were urged to boycott Exxon and cut up their credit cards. Some 40,000 cards were destroyed, but this was out of 7 million cards outstanding.

Even some business executives were critical. Responding to a survey, 200 Americans and Canadian executives said that Exxon was slow to react, attempted to shift blame on others, ducked its responsibility, failed to manage the local political scene, lacked preparation, seemed arrogant, was negligent, lost control of information processes, and ignored opportunities to build public support.[4]

Perhaps Exxon's apology was late. But it did take full-page ads in newspapers nationwide a week after the accident with a statement from its CEO, Lawrence Rawl, that the company was sorry and that it would meet all of its obligations. Rawl was criticized for not personally appearing at the site of the spill. From a public relations standpoint, this perhaps was a mistake. He defended his lack of presence in a later interview:

> The tanker went on the rocks, and visually it was perfect for TV and not too bad for pictures of oily birds in the printed media. How would those environmentalists ever let that go? If I just went up there and said I was sorry? I went on TV and said I was sorry. I said a dozen times that we're going to clean it up . . . .. [I]t wouldn't have made any difference if I showed up and made a speech in the town forum. I wasn't going to spend the summer there; I had other things to do, obviously.[5]

4. James E. Lukaszewski, "How Vulnerable Are You? The Lessons from Valdez," *Public Relations Quarterly 34* (Fall 1989), pp. 5–6.
5. Richard Behar, "Exxon Strikes Back," *Time* (March 26, 1990), p. 62.

Certainly, Exxon spent money: besides the $2 billion it spent on the cleanup itself, it reimbursed the city of Valdez, the state of Alaska, and the federal government for direct expenses, wildlife rescue, and rehabilitation. It also gave Alaskan fishermen $200 million for their merely having a fishing license and the previous year's tax return.

What it failed to do was immediate containment and cleanup. Perhaps most important, it failed to convey a public image of sufficient concern, openness, and repentance. In an accident of this magnitude, surely the CEO, as the company's figurehead, should be the company's spokesperson.[6] Lawrence Rawl's defensive mindset was perhaps best expressed by his own statements just a year later:

> There were 30 million birds that went through the sound last summer, and only 30,000 carcasses have been recovered. Just look at how many ducks are killed in the Mississippi Delta in one hunting day in December! People . . . said, "This is worse than Bhopal." I say, "Hell, Bhopal killed more than 3,000 people and injured 200,000 others!" Then they say, "Well, if you leave the people out, it was worse than Bhopal."[7]

ANALYSIS

Who Can We Blame?

The *Exxon Valdez* accident was not as simple as a drunken sailor steering a tanker onto rocks. Many events led to the shipwreck and to the disastrous handling of the situation that followed. We know how Exxon handled the situation. Would some other oil firm—British Petroleum, for example—have handled it better? Or worse? Business, government, and society all contributed to the disaster. The finger of blame cannot realistically point to just one person or one organization.

The common denominator was complacency. For twelve years, oil flowed through the pipeline and waterways without serious mishap. The few minor mishaps that happened were handled without trouble: "A decade with few major mishaps lulled oil companies and regulatory agencies into complacency, driving down demand for cleanup crews and expertise."[8]

For example, at Traffic Valdez, the Coast Guard commander requested that the tracking system be updated to add another radar station at Bligh Island. Instead, as a result of budget cuts, the existing 100,000-watt radar unit was replaced with a 50,000-watt unit. With such weakened radar, controllers were often unable to track ships well before they reached Bligh Island and the wider waters of Prince William Sound.

Budget cuts at Aleyeska also affected disaster readiness. When the pipeline system was new, equipment, procedures, and trained personnel were organized and ready. Scheduled periodic drills were conducted at considerable cost. By 1989, when the

---

6. William I. Small, "*Exxon Valdez*: How to Spend Billions and Still Get a Black Eye," *Public Relations Review 17* (Spring 1991), p. 9.

7. Behar, p. 63.

8. Kenneth R. Sheets, "Would You Believe $16.67 an Hour to Scrub Rocks?" *U.S. News & World Report* (April 17, 1989), p, 48.

accident occurred, drills had been discontinued, equipment was in disrepair, and trained personnel had been reassigned.

The Alaskan people also grew complacent. Each year, when they received their $800 windfall checks, they took oil's presence a little more for granted; any criticisms or worries were muted.

Even the Reagan administration can be faulted for creating a climate of less regulation and more reliance on businesses to govern themselves. Yet, when left to govern themselves, businesses find it difficult to balance short-run profit objectives against long-term environmental "might happens." (See the Issue Box: "The Ethics of Accidents.")

Can This Happen Again?

For more than ten years, no serious mishaps had occurred, despite thousands of trips and millions of tanker miles. Yet, somehow, the right combination of circumstances

---

ISSUE BOX

THE ETHICS OF ACCIDENTS

When an accident occurs, does it automatically mean the person or organization involved has acted unethically? The issue is often murky; less murky is the issue of legal responsibility. Damage suits on behalf of victims abound, regardless of how culpable the deep-pocketed defendant is. Ethics and legality are not always synonymous.

The ethics issue hinges on carelessness, negligence, or bad judgment, perhaps in product or plant design or in maintenance (e.g., placing victims in a risky situation). But what about acts of God or terrorists, which cannot reasonably be foreseen—the unexpected wind shear that destroys a plane, the terrorists' bomb? Hardliners will argue that these should be foreseen and avoided. But is this expecting too much, even of a prudent person?

The issue becomes more complicated when several parties are negligent, as was true in the *Exxon Valdez* situation. It can be argued that, with adequate radar, the Coast Guard could have warned the ship in time, or, that if better disaster planning and training had been in place, the spill could have been contained with far less environmental damage. If Exxon was guilty of unethical practices because of carelessness or negligence, so was the Coast Guard, Aleyeska, the state of Alaska, the Environmental Protection Agency, and others. Of course, Exxon was the organization with the "deep pockets."

INVITATION TO DISCUSS

1. If a person uses a product in a dangerous manner for which it was not intended— such as using a power lawn mower to trim a hedge—is the seller guilty of unethical behavior? Is the seller vulnerable to a damage suit?

2. If Captain Hazelwood had been completely sober and in his correct station *on* the ship and a severe and unexpected storm had forced the *Valdez* onto the rocks; would Exxon have been guilty of unethical behavior? How about legal vulnerability? Do you think Exxon should foot the major responsibility for the cleanup in this scenario?

came together. Could this happen again? The hope is that all the involved parties have learned from this experience. Better safeguards have been established, controls have been tightened, and more resources have been committed to radar and prevention training. We hope any future accidents will be less serious and more quickly controlled. Yet, it is naive to think that we have seen the last oil spill.

Safeguards Needed

After every serious accident, recriminations rage (which is not always constructive); preventative measures are proposed (which should be constructive, if followed up on). Such is certainly the case with the *Exxon Valdez* episode: What measures should be taken to minimize the chances of any future occurrence?

Obvious measures are better radar and closer monitoring of potential problems, improved and rigorously maintained disaster training, continued efforts at improving technology for coping with oil spills, well-planned and rehearsed procedures for handling any future mishaps—and, perhaps, such imposed safeguards as *double-hulled tankers*. (For a discussion of these controversial vessels, see the following Issue Box.)

Whether these ambitious safeguards could be maintained during a decade or more with no major disasters is doubtful, human nature being what it is. A further motivation to allow high levels of preparedness to slip is the fact that no human lives were lost in this worst scenario, only a few birds and animals, as the nonenvironmentalists, including Exxon Chairman Lawrence Rawl, would hasten to point out.

UPDATE

Fifteen years after the 1989 *Exxon Valdez* oil spill; the company was still facing major damage awards. In a case that had gone back and forth in appeals courts, a federal judge on January 28, 2004, ordered Exxon Mobil to pay $4.5 billion in punitive damages and about $2.25 billion in interest to 32,000 fishermen, Alaska Natives, landowners, small businesses, and cities affected by the spill. The company promised to appeal again. A lawyer for the plaintiffs said the judge's ruling should bring an end to the litigation, but "a company as big as Exxon Mobil can grind the legal process to a halt."[9]

WHAT CAN BE LEARNED

The environmental lobby is powerful today and growing stronger. Moral: business beware. It should come as no surprise to business executives that public sentiment is moving strongly toward protecting the environment, at almost any cost. Many see this as a welcome-and-needed-change from the old frontier attitude that the environment must be conquered. But the new attitudes pose new constraints on business; they lead to less tolerance, public decrying, and strong pressure on governmental bodies to take punitive and restrictive measures.

9. Thaddeus Herrick, "Judge Tells Exxon to Pay $4.5 billion," *Wall Street Journal* (January 29, 2004), p.B3.

ISSUE BOX

SHOULD DOUBLE-HULLED TANKERS BE REQUIRED?

None of the tankers using the Valdez terminal at the time of the spill were double-hulled. Double-hulled tankers had been proposed as a safeguard against spills in the initial planning of the pipeline in the 1970s, but they were not adopted.

There are some tradeoffs. Although double-hulled tankers would lower the probability of oil leakages occurring from a mishap, they cost up to 8 percent more to build, and they have only 60 percent of the capacity of a single-hulled tanker. This latter factor is the more serious limitation. To maintain the same daily flow of oil, two additional tankers would be needed for every five single hull ships, meaning much more traffic and more docking facilities.

So, although we might have safer ships, the possibility for human error would be increased. And human error is usually responsible for such mishaps, not the ships. Drug and alcohol testing and tougher personnel rules and training have been proposed for minimizing the probability or human error. But can human error ever be eliminated?

INVITATION TO DISCUSS

Do you think employees should be tested for drug and alcohol abuse? Would this eliminate human error?

This is the third case in this book in which the environment was an issue. (The other cases were Union Carbide's polluting of the Ohio Valley and its catastrophe in Bhopal.) Exxon's management may have been surprised at the public outcry over an accident that "only killed a few birds and animals." After all, the company did not deliberately set out to wreak havoc on the environment, and no human lives were lost, the company would maintain. But these attempts to defend the company were lost on a general public unwilling to accept excuses, quick to blame "insensitive corporations" and readily supported by the media and by politicians eager to gain publicity as "defenders of the environment."

In this milieu, the prudent business firm does not try to buck the tide, but instead exerts extraordinary precautions to prevent anything that smacks of environmental degradation.

Many environmental problems lend themselves to graphic portrayal by the media. This exacerbates the condemnation of the business firm involved. The polluting smokestack, the contaminated pond or stream, oil-covered birds and animals—these are easily caught on camera and transmitted to a concerned and indignant public, thus fanning cries for punishment and preventative governmental action. No other questionable business dealings lend themselves to so much graphic portrayal.

This is all the more reason for business firms to tread carefully in such matters, to seek the image of an environmental defender.

In grave public concerns, the top corporate executive must assume an active role, lest the company gain the reputation of being uncaring and arrogant. One of the harshest criticisms levied at Exxon was that it was uncaring and arrogant. Although Chairman Rawl defended his actions for not personally taking charge, this did not mollify the critics. No amount of company institutional advertising (i.e., nonproduct advertising aimed at public relations) achieved what might have been gained by Rawl's prompt and concerned presence.

An accident saddles the firm with major public image challenges, the response to which can either enhance or denigrate the firm's reputation. Although a serious environmental or product-safety accident is about the worst scenario any corporate executive can envision, what is usually overlooked is that such scenarios present an opportunity to enhance the firm's reputation as a caring and concerned presence.

To convert catastrophe into some gain is very difficult to accomplish. In Chapter 22, we encounter a firm that did this to an exemplary degree. It usually requires an out-of-the-ordinary sacrifice of short-term profits, a real unselfish commitment to correcting the situation and helping the victims regardless of cost, and an attitude of openness and caring in all public actions and statements. Even then, of course, the efforts may be misunderstood and condemned, as were the efforts of Warren Anderson, the chairman of Union Carbide during the Bhopal disaster. But there is far greater risk of a destroyed reputation when such a spirit of openness and concern is not publicly conveyed.

Firms need to plan for worst-case scenarios. We have encountered this insight before. In many of these ethical blunders, the worst-case possibilities are not considered, not planned for, not even given any thought. Yet the lesson is clear: the worst-case scenario, by some happenstance or human error or whatever, is always a possibility, even though the probability seems remote. Therefore, plan for the worst scenario, and all other mishaps should be more easily handled.

Such planning requires commitment. It is often difficult to get this, because costs are involved, and short-run profits may be somewhat curbed. But catastrophes occur just frequently enough that such contingency planning has merit. Many parties could have benefited from contingency planning before the great oil spill: Exxon, Aleyeska, Alaska's Department of Environmental Conservation, the U.S. Coast Guard, and others. Easier said than done, but our worst-case disasters would be curbed—or at least quickly and effectively reacted to—with such foresight.

CONSIDER

Can you add any learning insights?

QUESTIONS

1. Did Exxon act unethically in this disaster? Discuss.

2. Do you think the federal government should have taken over the cleanup operation rather than leaving it primarily to Exxon, with superficial help from Aleyeska and others? Why or why not?

3. How can an organization guard against culpable human error like Captain Hazelwood's? An airline pilot's error, a bus driver's, a railroad engineer's? Are your suggested measures an unacceptable invasion of privacy? Discuss.

4. Do you think Hazelwood was unfairly treated? Why or why not?

5. Do you think full-page newspaper ads saying the company was sorry would salvage the public image? What else could be done?

6. In your opinion, was too much fuss made over the loss of a few thousand birds and animals (out of millions)? Please discuss.

7. Should CEO Rawl of Exxon be forced to resign?

HANDS-ON EXERCISES

1. You are the staff adviser to Lawrence Rawl, CEO of Exxon, at the time of the spill. How would you advise him to handle this situation? Be as specific as you can, and defend your recommendations.

2. You are Captain Hazelwood, confronted with the reality of the worst oil spill in U.S. history. You were resting in your cabin when the crash occurred. You rush up on deck and survey the disaster. What do you do now? How do you defend your conduct? Can you possibly salvage your heretofore highly successful career?

TEAM DEBATE EXERCISES

1. Debate: CEO Rawl should be fired after the disaster versus he should not be fired.

2. The full measure of the oil spill catastrophe is apparent now. Debate whether to spend $10 billion to try to correct the situation, versus a much more modest expenditure, perhaps $1 or $2 billion.

INVITATION TO RESEARCH

What happened to Hazelwood after this? Have any safety regulations been enacted to prevent a similar disaster from occurring? Does the Alaskan oil spill still haunt the public image of Exxon?

CHAPTER SIXTEEN

ITT: Heavy-Handed Interference in a Foreign Government

On October 24, 1970, Dr. Salvador Allende Gossens was elected president of Chile. This election brought Chile its first Marxist regime, spearheading a socialist philosophy in a country that had once been proud of its democratic society.

On March 21 and 22, 1972, Jack Anderson, a well-respected American newspaper columnist, published an outline of a series of secret documents he had obtained from International Telephone and Telegraph Company (ITT) files. The documents revealed the efforts that ITT and the Central Intelligence Agency (CIA) had made to stop the election of President Allende in 1970, and the unsuccessful efforts they made to overthrow him in 1973.

ITT, attempting to protect its Chilean property from government expropriation, intruded in the affairs of a foreign country to an extent unacceptable by the mainstreams of business, government, and society, both here and abroad. At issue: What right does a multinational corporation have to interfere in the governance of countries in which it is doing business?

THE COMPANY

ITT (originally called IT&T) began in 1920. It specialized in the newly emerging communications industry, operating outside the United States, although its headquarters were in New York City. By 1960, it was 51st on *Fortune's* list of the country's largest 500 corporations. Growth surged even more during the 1960s, much of this through the acquisition of fifty-four U.S. companies and fifty-six companies abroad. By 1971, ITT was eighth on the *Fortune* 500. It had more than 250 divisions, business groupings, and subsidiaries operating in 80 countries. Some 350,000 people were employed by ITT in such industries as insurance, chemicals, food production, automotive parts, and hotels. Yet, the company had a checkered past, and more questions were being raised about its activities as it moved toward its half-century mark.

In 1923 founders Colonel Sosthenes Behn and his brother purchased a small Puerto Rican telephone company at a distressed price. Partly due to his Spanish background, Behn got the contract to run the Spanish telephone network from the dictator of Spain, Primo de Rivera. In the years that followed, Behn made more acquisitions around the world, turning ITT into an international conglomerate. The firm's reputation was somewhat tainted by its close ties with Nazi Germany in the 1930s and by its overall attitude of self-serving expediency—virtually out of the reach of government controls. Colonel Behn retired in 1956, but the company's mindset changed little under his successor.

Harold S. Geneen

In 1959, Harold Geneen was chosen to be ITT's president. He had previously been executive vice president of Raytheon, and when he left Raytheon, its stock dropped six points, a graphic indication of the business community's perception of his competence.

Geneen used his background as an accountant and his ambitious drive to become a veritable financial wizard. It was his habit to put in sixteen-hour workdays, and he expected the same dedication from his subordinates. His word was law, and he tended to set near-impossible goals for his top executives. He was ruthless in his demands. In his first decade at the helm of ITT, some fifty senior executives either quit or were fired.

Geneen was paid more than $800,000 in 1971, more than two-and-a-half times as much as the next-highest-paid ITT executive. He had an apartment off Fifth Avenue, a winter house at Key Biscayne, and a summer home on Cape Cod. He regularly logged 100,000 miles a year in his private jet, which was about the size of Air Force One.[1]

Geneen revamped ITT's financial system so that he could analyze each company's profitability and exert close operational control. He decided to obtain more investments in the United States in order to reduce what he saw as the increasing pressures on operations abroad. However, to expand within the United States, ITT was limited to making acquisitions, because of American Telephone and Telegraph (AT&T)'s having competitive rights to the U.S. market. Consequently, Geneen set out on an aggressive acquisition campaign, which was to add greatly to the company's growth over the coming decade.

The major acquisitions during the 1960s included Sheraton (hotels), Continental Baking (bakeries), Aetna Finance (consumer finance), Avis (car rentals), Apcoa (airport parking), Levitt (construction), Canteen (vending foods), Hartford (insurance), and Rayonier (chemicals). Geneen's acquisition spree encountered few obstacles, but the Justice Department did oppose ITT's acquisition of the American Broadcasting Company; in 1968, Geneen reluctantly backed away. In the late 1960s, the Justice Department also began contesting some of the completed acquisitions, including the Canteen, Hartford, and Avis mergers. But with top-level political connections in Washington, the company suffered no other major setbacks.

Controversy: The Dita Beard Affair

While ITT was battling with the Justice Department's antitrust investigations of the Canteen, Hartford, and Avis acquisitions, trouble was brewing over the location of the 1972 Republican National Convention. The White House wanted it to be held in

---

1. Richard J. Barnet and Ronald E. Miller, *Global Reach* (New York: Simon and Schuster, 1974), p. 52.

San Diego but was having trouble raising the money to do so. Conveniently, Bob Wilson, the key Republican congressman from the San Diego area, was a good friend of Geneen. Geneen's Sheraton division had just completed a new hotel complex in San Diego, and the promotional benefits of hosting the convention would be substantial. ITT pledged $200,000 to the Republicans, and the convention committee approved the site, despite ITT's ongoing antitrust proceedings. Dita Beard was a top lobbyist for ITT. When a highly incriminating memo written by her surfaced, it revealed a secret deal between ITT and Attorney General John Mitchell to settle the antitrust suit involving the Hartford acquisition in ITT's favor: Mitchell pledged a positive influence on the decision.

ITT IN CHILE

If the antitrust cases against ITT and the exposure of a $200,000 bribe to the Republicans in exchange for favorable treatment by the U.S. attorney general were not enough to keep Geneen occupied, he certainly outdid himself in Chile. On March 22, 1970, Jack Anderson published a column that revealed ITT's manipulations in Chilean internal affairs and its relations with the CIA and the White House in this regard. Anderson had compiled a thorough study of this affair, which was later used by a Senate subcommittee investigating the matter. According to Anderson, ITT had tried to prevent Salvador Allende from being elected in Chile, and, with the CIA, had encouraged economic chaos and a military coup in Chile, and had offered $1 million to the White House to be used against Allende.[2]

Chile

Chile is situated along South America's western coast. It is only 110 miles wide but some 2,600 miles long. It is a land of extremes. The northern third is desert; the Andes Mountains are in the east. A fertile valley dominates Chile's central region, where most of its nine million people live. South of the valley, the land breaks down into thousands of tiny islands leading to Cape Horn and Antarctica.

Chile had had stable political institutions until a 1972 military coup, which deposed and killed Allende. But great inequalities existed—3 percent of the population received 40 percent of the nation's income, while 50 percent of the working population earned just 10 percent of total income. With such extremes of wealth and poverty, it was not surprising that 40 percent of all Chileans suffered from malnutrition and one-third of all deaths were children.

ITT's Holdings in Chile

Despite Chile's small population and unpromising economic potential, ITT's global reach extended there, including the Chilean Telephone Company, the Standard Electric Company, two Sheraton hotels, and some smaller holdings. The telephone company, in particular, was highly profitable, earning some $10 million annually. By

2. Anthony Sampson, *The Sovereign State of ITT* (Briarcliff Manor, N.Y.: Stein and Day, 1974), p. 253.

1970, it employed 6,000 workers and was valued by ITT at more than $150 million. Yet, these holdings comprised only a small fraction of ITT's worldwide assets and earnings. Despite its small stake in Chile, by the end of the 1960s, ITT began to fear that its properties, in particular the phone subsidiary, would be nationalized and taken over, with the Chilean government offering ITT only a small fraction of its value. (This had already happened in Peru, a neighbor of Chile.) The reason for this newfound fear in a country noted for its stability was the political emergence of Dr. Salvador Allende Gossens, who was a Marxist.

Dr. Salvador Allende Gossens

Allende was born in 1908, the son of a well-to-do lawyer. His formal education was in medicine, but his career soon veered away from that. In 1933, Allende helped found Chile's Socialist party. Four years later, he was elected to the Chilean Congress. He was later appointed to the country's cabinet, where he gained national recognition for his humanitarian concerns. Allende's early political years were marked by strict adherence to the Constitution. This put him at odds with Chile's Communist party. After election to the Senate in 1945, he embarked on twenty-five years of unbroken political service. His rallying cry was that Chile was a nation whose promise had not been fulfilled.

He was defeated in a run for the presidency in the 1964 elections by Christian Democrat Eduardo Frei, but Allende suspected that his time had come in the 1970 elections. Reforms promised by Frei had not materialized, and in 1968 the Christian Democrats lost their popularity and their majority in Congress.

In the 1970 presidential elections, Allende, the Popular Unity Coalition candidate, won 36 percent of the votes, former President Jorge Alessandri won 35 percent, and the new Christian Democrat candidate, Radomiro Tomic, won only 17 percent. Under the Chilean Constitution, because no candidate had won a majority, the choice of president thus had to be decided by congressional elections seven weeks later. (It was during these seven weeks that most of the ITT memos revealed by Anderson were written.) On October 24, 1970, the Congress voted 153 to 35 in favor of Allende for president.

President Allende had campaigned for a program of extensive land reform and rapid nationalization of basic industries that were controlled by foreign capital. On September 29, 1971, Chile took over the telephone company (CHIL TELCO) after several months of negotiations and offers, all rejected by ITT. Chile declared that CHIL TELCO' s service was deficient, that it was charging too much, that its profits were too high, and that the country was too dependent on ITT for investment decisions.[3]

At this point, there was a sizable disagreement in the negotiations as to the value of the phone company: ITT put the value at $153 million; Chile put it at $24 million. The Chileans proposed a group of international adjudicators, but ITT would not accept this. ITT proposed an international auditing firm that the Chileans would not accept. By March 1972, the Chilean ambassador in Washington had just come up with a new formula to determine the fair value. Then Anderson's column appeared, transforming the whole situation.

3. U.S. Senate Committee on Foreign Relations, Subcommittee on Multinational Corporations, *ITT and Chile: 1970-1971* (Washington, D.C,: U.S. Government Printing Office, 1973), p. 811.

SPECIFICS OF ITT'S INTERFERENCE
IN CHILE'S AFFAIRS

For a long time, Chile was a secure base for foreign corporations, a far cry from the revolutionary nationalism of its neighbors. The election of Christian Democrat Eduardo Frei in 1964, with his pledge to reform without antagonizing the big corporations, was comforting. The likelihood was that Geneen and other industrialists had contributed to Frei's campaign fund, although this was not proven.

Anderson's publication of secret documents obtained from ITT files provided strong proof that ITT had been involved with the Central Intelligence Agency (CIA) in attempting to stop Allende's election to the presidency in 1970, as well as in his 1973 overthrow.

Two days after the first Anderson column appeared, the Senate Foreign Relations Committee formed a special subcommittee, the Multinationals Subcommittee, chaired by Senator Frank Church. On June 21, 1973, the subcommittee issued a 1,000-page report charging that ITT had "overstepped the line of acceptable corporate behavior." If the scheme to defeat leftist Dr. Salvador Allende had been fully implemented, said the report, "it could have resulted in bloodshed and possibly civil war."[4]

The subcommittee criticized Geneen for having offered $1 million to the CIA for its help in supporting the conservative candidate. If such actions came to be accepted as normal, the report said, "no country would welcome the presence of multinational corporations."[5] The subcommittee report continued: "The attitude of the company was best summed up [by ITT Senior Vice-President Edward J. Gerrity, Jr.,] when he asked, 'What's wrong with taking care of No.1?'"[6]

The report concluded:

> [T]he highest officials of ITT sought to engage the CIA in a plan to manipulate the outcome of the Chilean presidential election. In so doing, the company overstepped the line of acceptable corporate behavior...The pressures which the company sought to bring to bear on the U.S. Government for CIA intervention are incompatible with the formulation of U.S. foreign policy in accordance with U.S. national, rather than private interests.[7]

CONSEQUENCES

In Chile, the Anderson disclosures came just as negotiations between ITT and the Chilean government had reached a critical stage. Allende made the most of it. A week after Anderson's column, the Chilean Congress decided to investigate the past activities of ITT and the CIA. A month later, at a vast pro-government rally of 200,000 people,

4. "The Probers Are on ITT's Doorstep Again," *BusinessWeek* (June 23, 1973), p. 29.

5. *Ibid.*

6. *Ibid.*

7. *ITT and Chile*, p. 520.

Allende announced that he would ask the Chilean Congress to nationalize the telephone company, and the Congress duly approved. In December 1972, Allende addressed the United Nations General Assembly in New York City. ITT, he said,

> had driven its tentacles deep into my country and proposed to manage our political life. I accuse the IT&T of attempting to bring about civil war…[the big corporation has been] cunningly and terrifyingly effective in preventing us from exercising our rights as a sovereign state.[8]

The United Nations Economic and Social Council unanimously adopted a resolution calling for a study group to examine the role and impact of transnational corporations in developing countries.

The relations between the United States and Chile worsened, intensified in August 1973 by a large anti-U.S. campaign mounted by the Chilean press, radio, and television media. The United States was charged with influencing the nationwide truckers' strike and other labor strikes that were bringing the nation to economic paralysis.

World critical attention was focused even more on Chile after a military coup on September 11, 1973, which led to the death of President Allende. A military junta, headed by Army Commander General A. Pinochet Ugarte, took control.

Because of the unreimbursed takeover of the Chilean phone company, ITT filed a $92.5 million claim with the Overseas Private Investment Corporation (OPIC). On April 9, 1973, the claim was denied, presumably because of the adverse publicity from ITT's role in Chile. A lengthy court battle ensued, and on January 1, 1975, a $39 million cash settlement was reached by binding arbitration. Still, this was far short of ITT's reimbursement hopes. The image of the big U.S. multinational firm intruding on the affairs of a small developing country—including allegations that it had tried to plunge Chile into a civil war—brought worldwide criticism. This led to violent actions against some of ITT's property. For example, a building occupied by ITT in Zurich, Switzerland, was extensively damaged on September 16, 1973. Two days later, a time bomb demolished four rooms in the Latin-American section of an ITT building on Madison Avenue in New York City. Minutes before the explosion, the *New York Times* was informed by an unknown caller that it was in retaliation for crimes against Chile. On October 6, 1973, fire damaged an ITT warehouse in Milan, Italy, to the extent of $12 million.

At their annual meeting in May 1973, ITT stockholders were divided in their support of management. Some praised the company's increasing profitability. (Indeed, ITT was racking up record profits: a 45 percent increase in 1972.) Others sharply criticized Geneen. The former bishop of the Methodist Church in Chile, for example, denounced the company's role in Chile by asking Geneen, "Is it legal and ethical to throw a nation into chaos to preserve ITT's profitable ventures?"[9] (See the following Issue Box.)

The ITT Chilean "adventure" was to have longer-term consequences. Partly because of the negative publicity engendered by these actions and by other large corporations' payoff scandals, such as Lockheed (discussed in the next chapter), Congress

---

8. Tad Szulc, "ITT Under the Gun," *The New Republic* (August 6, 1977), p. 20.

9. Michael C. Jensen, "Stockholders Challenge ITT's Use of Influence in U.S. and Abroad," *New York Times* (May 10, 1973), p. 65:3.

ISSUE BOX

DO WE HAVE A RIGHT TO EXPECT THE HIGHEST MORAL CONDUCT FROM OUR BUSINESS LEADERS?

How much moral adherence, and even leadership, do we have a right to expect from our business leaders? Do they owe anything to society, or is the arena simply one of the law of the jungle or the Darwinian idea of survival of the fittest?

The Darwinian philosophy held sway during the last century. We would hope that it is passé today. Yet, some executives are dinosaurs; throwbacks to an earlier business climate. And Geneen epitomized this attitude.

Have we as a society sufficiently progressed today that we can rely on altruism and a conscience imbued with social moralism to bring out the most socially desirable actions by executives and their corporations? Even if governmental laws and regulations are slackened, it is difficult for most of us to see granting business firms unfettered scope, not even in foreign adventuring. Although some executives will see the public's best interest as completely compatible with their own and their firms', others will view the absence of constraints as opportunistic.

Furthermore, short-term bottom-line performance still prevails in most firms, and this does not always result in the best actions from society's viewpoint. Although more responsive actions might lead to greater long-term results, stockholders and creditors demand more immediate gains, as does industry stature.

INVITATION TO DISCUSS

What ideas do you have for fostering a more ethical and moral stance in U.S. corporations? (This assumes, of course, that you think improvement is desirable, and possible.)

---

passed the *Foreign Corrupt Practices Act* in 1977. This controversial act was designed to clean up business dealings between multinationals and foreign officials and politicians.

Attempts to Indict ITT and CIA Officials

In 1977, a federal grand jury in Washington, D.C., held a nine-month investigation into the activities of ITT and the CIA. Harold Geneen, Edward J. Gerrity (vice president of ITT), and former CIA Director Richard Helms were also considered for indictments for perjury during the multinationals' subcommittee hearings.

Helms was quoted as saying that, if he were indicted, he would "bring down" former Secretary of State Henry Kissinger, who was one of the architects of the American anti-Allende efforts that contributed to the bloody military coup in September 1973.[10]

In 1978, the Department of Justice brought charges of lying and obstructing against Gerrity for denials that he had done anything to try to stop Allende in 1970. But Geneen escaped being charged, and Richard Helms had already pleaded guilty to a misdemeanor charge for lying to Congress on the same matter. He got off with a small fine.

10. Szulc, p. 21.

We can speculate that Geneen had the "protection," also enjoyed by Helms, of being able to expose national security secrets if he was forced into a legal defense.[11] Prudence perhaps dictated immunity from prosecution. Despite all the information, no indictments were brought in the ITT Chile case. Essentially, Geneen and his associates escaped with only some bad publicity, although the corporation itself did not fare so well.

ANALYSIS

ITT gambled and lost when it attempted to interfere in the Chilean situation. Besides the Senate subcommittee's condemnation, the company incurred substantial property damage around the world and was penalized in its reimbursements for the financial losses it incurred during the expropriation period. The abuses of power seemed to come home to roost, especially when we consider the fate of other multinationals doing business in Chile at the same time. Xerox was not nationalized. RCA Victor settled for a minority interest in its electronics and phonographic records plants. General Tire sold its shares to the government and continued providing technical assistance. But none of these firms tried to promote sabotage or harassment of the Chilean government.

By most standards, ITT's conduct was reprehensible, resulting in a tainted public image and the loss of millions of dollars in property damage and lost insurance claims. Still, the main victims were Chile, and most of all, Salvador Allende, who lost his life. The promising future of this brilliant and dedicated public servant, even though he had Marxist leanings, can hardly be compared to the minimal losses of a multibillion-dollar corporation.

Admittedly, the blame was not all ITT's. The U.S. government—particularly the CIA, but also the offices of the secretary of state and the president—also interfered in the internal workings of a foreign government. ITT and Washington had a commonality of interest in stopping Allende—and later, removing him. Unfortunately, these efforts went beyond honorable means.

But was ITT all that culpable? Are we blaming a firm unjustly? Does a firm not have a right to protect its property, whether in the United States or abroad? As with many ethical and legal issues, it is all a matter of degree. The general consensus is that ITT overstepped the boundaries of acceptable behavior in Chile. But how much influence may a corporation, in its own interests, legitimately exert on foreign policy? The Senate subcommittee raised this question.[12]

ITT, as well as other multinational corporations, should have the right to seek its best interests through the political and legal processes. And this certainly includes lobbying, which is a fact of life, regardless of the issues involved with it. (See the following Information Box: "Lobbying.") But ITT went beyond this in attempting to influence foreign affairs in covert and intrusive ways.

As an example of the controversy of diplomatic redress of private corporative grievances, Robert G. Hawkins, of New York University's Graduate School of Business Administration, believes that parent companies should not expect "substantial sanctions" by the United States against foreign countries. But then he argues that the

11. Norman Birnbaum, "ITT, Equal Justice and Chile," *The Nation* (April 1, 1978), p. 356.
12. "The Question the ITT Case Raises," *BusinessWeek* (March 31, 1973), p. 42.

ISSUE BOX

LOBBYING

Lobbying may be defined as the efforts of a corporation, trade association, or other interest group to influence government on its behalf. Lobbyists predominantly work in Washington, with perhaps 30,000 legislative advocates, government or public relations consultants, and lawyers so engaged. Lobbying is conducted within the legislative and executive branches of government, with Congress and the administrative agencies main targets. The judicial branch, notably the Supreme Court, is generally insulated from special interest lobbying.

Lobbying has been widely condemned. Certainly, it advocates the view of the special-interest groups, which are often opposed to the "public interest." Critics maintain that in attempting to influence key legislators and government officials, it is only a short step to corrupt practices, of which the most flagrant are bribery and payola. More insidious favors are less susceptible to detection. These include helping legislators with the heavy research workloads, helping them with their speeches and public appearances, and advising them on public relations and campaign strategies. Many observers are concerned that the general public's interests tend to be subordinated because it lacks an effective lobbying presence.

Lobbyists do perform a useful function. They provide legislators with technical information about bills and with information about the attitudes of constituents and those most concerned about specific pending legislation. Of course, if a lobbyist supplies biased or misleading information, legislative decisions are compromised. But proponents of lobbying are quick to point out that lobbyists who do that are quickly shunned. Most legislators want to hear a balanced presentation regarding key issues.

INVITATION TO DISCUSS

On balance, how would you assess the growing popularity of lobbying? Do you think it should be curbed? If so, how?

U.S. government should be involved in, and even negotiate, property rights for American companies abroad since "the government is at least responsible for protecting the property rights *of* its citizens."[13] So we see the ambivalence and controversy of this aspect of business/government relations.

WHAT CAN BE LEARNED?

A multinational should be wary of assuming a heavy-handed posture in foreign environments, especially in Third-World countries. The less-developed countries, many of which are governed by dictators antagonistic to U.S. power, see multinational corporations as the embodiment of that power in their country. They look

13. *Ibid.*

on foreign businesspeople with distrust, see them as exploiters of their raw materials, and labor—in other words, as economic imperialists.

In such an environment, the U.S. multinational firm needs to tread warily, and exercise the greatest caution in order not to jeopardize its position and its property. As a result of ITT's heavy-handed activities in Chile, demands for restraints on multinational firms reached all-time highs. Just when it seemed that the suspicion and resentment were diminishing, the Bhopal accident occurred in 1984 (discussed in Chapter 12). Anti-American sentiment is an easy rallying point for those seeking power in Third-World countries, so the perceptions of the United States specifically and of multinational companies in general rise and fall, depending in large part on the political events of the time.

Corporate self-interest is vulnerable in Third-World countries. Multinationals can contribute greatly to developing countries by raising their standards of living, their level of education and employment, their social stability, and indeed, their whole quality of life. For the most part, these goals are fully compatible with the firms' goals. But they may not always be compatible with the firms' short-range goals. If a corporation sees its self-interest more tied to short-range profit goals, it may be vulnerable to hostile governments. At best, it will be doing business in an uncertain environment. Immediate self-interest may have to be sacrificed. Although there is always some risk of expropriation in Third-World environments, this risk can be reduced by an amicable posture, one that is supportive of the host country. Of course, there is always more risk than in stable societies.

U.S.-based multinationals' actions in foreign markets have a direct effect on the image on the United States itself. Like it or not, the image of the United States is affected by the practices—especially the negative practices—of its U.S.-based firms. ITT, with its unacceptable interference in foreign governance; Nestlé, with its aggressive promotion of a product that was dangerous unless properly used; and Union Carbide, with its naive acceptance of foreign subsidiary safety standards—all these deficiencies and abuses discredit the image of the United States and promote the idea of the "Ugly American."

This should infuse U.S. multinationals with an added responsibility. They are representatives of the U.S. government: their actions, good or bad, contribute to the prestige (or lack of prestige) of the United States as a whole. Such responsibility should not be treated lightly by our multinationals. They are the conveyors of the public image, not only of themselves, but also of their country of origin.

Lower management should resist top management's loose ethics, but they usually do not. So many times in this book, we have found that ethical and social responsibility abuses have been either instigated or encouraged by top management. What is lower management to do in this situation? Cotton to it, stubbornly oppose it, whistleblow? With few exceptions, lower management follows along, and even surpasses the questionable standards of higher management. Are we as individuals unable to form our own positions about questionable practices? Are we like driven sheep, swayed greatly by those in higher office? If this indeed is true, it is a sad commentary. In the corporate world, there is a vast need for those who are not willing to follow the crowd and accept the lowest common denominator of conduct. But, this is very difficult to do, as we have seen with the whistleblowers. Let us resist being "dumb, driven sheep" when the cause is right and correct conduct is at stake.

CONSIDER

Can you think of other learning insights?

QUESTIONS

1. Was ITT really acting unethically? Why or why not?
2. "A corporation doing business in a foreign country had the right to protect its investment at all costs." Comment on this statement.
3. Is it not appropriate that Marxist and communist governments should be opposed, even if such opposition is aggressive? Countries that support terrorism? Countries posing a nuclear or biological capability? Where do we draw the line?
4. Discuss the pros and cons of multinationals operating in foreign countries, from the perspective of the countries involved.
5. Do you think Geneen should have been indicted? State your rationale.
6. Do you have any problems with a corporation doing aggressive lobbying? Please discuss.
7. Do you have any problems with ITT (or any other multinational) working closely with the CIA and the State Department in its foreign markets?

HANDS-ON EXERCISES

1. As the public relations director of ITT at the time of this controversy, what would you have advised Geneen concerning his Chilean activities? How would you handle his criticism of your hands-off position?
2. Be a devil's advocate (one who takes an opposing position for the sake of considering all aspects and consequences of the issue) and argue against Geneen's plans to overthrow Allende. Be a persuasive as you can.

TEAM DEBATE EXERCISE

In the ITT boardroom the Chilean problem is at the top of the agenda. The board is divided between hawks and doves. Geneen and his group propose aggressive action. Another group seeks a softer approach, even if it means some ITT property may be expropriated. Debate the two positions.

INVITATION TO RESEARCH

What ever happened to ITT, and to Geneen?

CHAPTER SEVENTEEN

Lockheed Corporation: Overseas Bribery Gone Rampant

*I*n September, 1975, the Senate Committee Hearings on Multinational Corporations, chaired by Senator Frank Church, released the stunning news that the Lockheed Corporation had made more than $200 million in secret payments to foreign agents and government officials in the Netherlands, Italy, Japan, Turkey, and other countries. As months wore on and more and more details emerged, a sense of outage grew in the nation and the Senate. The morality of a major U.S. defense contractor was impugned, as was the morality of the entire defense industry, even U.S. corporations in general. The Foreign Corrupt Practices Act of 1977 was a direct result.

SCANDALS

A Deal with a Prince

Prince Bernhard, husband of Queen Juliana of the Netherlands, was highly respected. He had fought bravely with the Dutch Army when the Nazis invaded Holland during World War II. He commanded a Dutch brigade when the Allies retook Holland in 1944. After the war, he was a dedicated booster of the Netherlands around the world. He had founded the World Wildlife Fund, was inspector general of the Dutch Armed Forces, and was on the board of the KLM Royal Dutch Airlines, among other highly visible positions.

But he was vulnerable to temptation, temptation wielded by Lockheed. With his apparently expensive tastes, this paragon of nobility and public service succumbed to monetary inducements designed to promote the sale of Lockheed Starfighters. The total contract involved between $150 and $200 million. The contact between Prince Bernhard and Lockheed was an ex-KLM agent who had been employed by Lockheed as a salesman. The negotiated commission for the Prince was $1 million.[1]

---

1. Yerachmiel Kugel and Gladys W. Gruenberg, *International Payoffs* (Lexington, MA: Lexington Books, 1977), pp. 59–60.

The Japanese Connection

Lockheed's involvement with Japanese bribes began in 1958 when the company engaged Yoshio Kodama, who had strong ties with Japanese governmental officials. With his help, Lockheed gained the contract for a Japanese Air Force jet.

In 1972, Lockheed again hired Kodama. And he succeeded in securing a $1.3 billion contract with All-Nippon Airways, for which he asked and received about $9 million from Lockheed from 1972 to 1975. Much of the money allegedly went to then Prime Minister Kukeo Tanaka and other government officials who interceded with All-Nippon Airlines for Lockheed.

In August 1975, an investigation by the U.S. government led to Lockheed's admission that it had made $22 million in secret payoffs.[2] Senate investigations in February 1976 publicized the company's involvement with Japanese government officials. Such revelations forced Prime Minister Tanaka to resign. Japan subsequently cancelled the billion-dollar contract with Lockheed. By September 15, 1976, eighteen individuals, including Kodama and Tanaka, were arrested as a result of their involvement with Lockheed.

Other Payoffs

Lockheed's payoffs extended to a number of other countries as well, although these did not generate as much public scrutiny and shock as the disclosures from the Netherlands and Japan. Bribes in such countries as Saudi Arabia and Iran were thought to be a "way of life" in those parts of the world. But there was also evidence of payoffs to Italy ($2 million paid to land a $60 million contract for C-130s), Spain ($1.3 million), South Africa ($9 million), as well as Greece, Mexico, Nigeria, Turkey, and Columbia.[3]

MECHANISM OF PAYOFFS

Payments, whether they are bribes, kickbacks, political contributions, or donations and gratuities of various kinds, may be paid directly to the recipient who wields the desired amount of influence. However, this presents a higher degree of risk than a more indirect connection.

Payments more often are made through intermediaries. A subsidiary corporation may be used, its accounting records not being consolidated with the parent company. In this way, the payoff can be disguised as an expense for services and goods never provided. The subsidiary may be a dummy corporation established only for the payoff function. With this arrangement, the parent company pays sales commissions to the dummy, with no knowledge and no direct link to any payoffs.

Sales agents are the more common mechanism for channeling payments. They can be completely legitimate, and even when they're not, their "commissions" on large purchases such as airplanes—though a quite low percentage of the total contract—

2. "Lockheed Says It Paid $22 Million to Get Contracts," *Wall Street Journal* (August 9, 1975).

3. "Payoffs: The Growing Scandal," *Newsweek* Special Report (February 23, 1976), pp. 26–33.

can amount to a substantial dollar figure. In many foreign environments, such agents maintain their contacts through personal favors, and thereby facilitate and expedite transactions and favorable decisions. An unusually high commission, which suggests part is turned over to third parties, is suspect, but the evidence is often not clear cut whether the commission exceeded reasonable bounds for the services rendered.

THE COMPANY

During World War II, Lockheed produced 20,000 combat planes, mainly P-38 fighters. In Korea, its F-80 Shooting Stars ruled the skies. Later it built the U-4 spy plane and the F-104 fighter, the latter being the mainstay of NATO's air defense. Its Agena rocket was used in more than 200 space launchings, and the Polaris submarine-fired missile—completed two and a half years ahead of schedule—had been an essential part of our nuclear deterrent. The test firing of the more advanced Poseidon missile induced a Russian tracking ship to nearly collide with a U.S. destroyer as the Russian ship raced to pick up some hopefully tell-tale debris.

After Lockheed's history of successfully developing highly sophisticated products, its contract to build the military transport C-5A, the world's largest plane, seemed relatively simple. But the heavy weight of the plane required major new technological ground to be broken, and this, combined with inflation and other factors—there were charges of bad management—led to a 40 percent cost overrun. Lockheed stood to lose $500 million. Furthermore, the Air Force cut orders for the giant cargo plane. Lockheed experienced other problems with its defense contracting, as well. For example, its Cheyenne hybrid craft, capable of hovering like a helicopter or flying at 250 mph, developed defects, and one of them crashed. This resulted in the contract being canceled, leaving Lockheed with $124 million in unreimbursed costs and product payments.

Although economic and technological problems led to Lockheed's difficulties, political and bureaucratic factors compounded the problems. The C-5A was the first and most disastrous of the TPP (total package procurement) contracts, in which a contractor had to bid on the whole contract from designing to final production, thereby attempting to forecast costs before the product had even been invented. The political climate also hurt Lockheed: the Air Force's deviousness toward a congressional committee investigating military spending had hardened congressional opposition to costly military programs and raised further criticism of the military-industrial complex.

So, going into the 1970s, Lockheed was a financially troubled company, despite its importance to national defense. Bankruptcy itself threatened in 1971.

Lockheed had wanted to reduce its dependence on the military by entering the commercial jet aircraft market. So it developed a three-engine, wide-body jet: the L-1011. About $400 million was spent on this development, and Lockheed had to obtain an additional $400 million credit line from a group of banks. The engines were to be built by Rolls-Royce of Britain, but this company went bankrupt. Lockheed now had no engines for the L-1011, and at that late date, there was no chance to switch to another supplier and still meet its delivery schedules. Now Lockheed itself faced bankruptcy, with the heavy costs already incurred and almost $300 million in canceled orders.

The company was saved only when the government stepped in to provide a bailout: a $250 million guarantee for Lockheed's loans. With the federal government standing behind the loans, agreeing to pick up the tab in case of default, creditors would now consent to loan Lockheed the cash it needed to survive. (See the following Issue Box for a discussion of the controversy concerning *bailouts*.)

In order for Lockheed to survive, its overseas sales had to expand greatly, particularly for the C-130 Hercules transport. Foreign sales had grown nicely: from $146 million in 1970 (when the political payments began) to $650 million by 1974. Sales to Iran and Saudi Arabia were particularly high, but both countries received substantial payoffs. In the meantime, Lockheed had used $195 million of the loan guarantees provided by the U.S. government.

THE INVESTIGATION UNFOLDS

The government loan guarantee had saved Lockheed from bankruptcy. But the guarantee had a major negative consequence: all the company's operations were now open to scrutiny, and questionable acts involving international payoffs soon surfaced. This was a problem for the government, as well: Exposure of inappropriate payments to foreign officials could undermine Lockheed's ability to repay the loans.

At the time Congress was considering the loan guarantee, hearings before the Senate Banking Committee dredged up initial evidence of payoffs to win contracts. When the story first broke, Lockheed maintained its right to bribe, and refused to

---

ISSUE BOX

WAS A BAILOUT FOR LOCKHEED JUSTIFIED?

The debate by Congress on the Lockheed bailout was extensive. The two sides were divided on philosophical and practical grounds. Those opposing the bailout saw this as undermining the very purpose of a competitive economy, by sustaining a marginal firm and incompetent management.

Those in favor of the bailout argued that the bill would cost the government nothing because the government would have first claim on the company's assets should it fail. They cited the 60,000 jobs lost if the company folded, and the $500 million in lost income taxes. A further powerful argument was that the company was essential to national defense.

The practical arguments prevailed over the ideological. Lockheed survived and became profitable, and the government eventually earned $26.6 million in fees on the deal.

In early 1980, Chrysler, facing a similar situation, won $1.5 billion in federal loan guarantees. In later years, the government has stepped in to save banks and savings and loans; in some instances, as we saw in Chapter 8, these firms were riddled with scandal and mismanagement.

INVITATION TO DISCUSS

Are some companies too important to be allowed to fail? Where do we draw the line on size and importance? How small should a firm be for government aid to be denied? Is this fair?

disclose the information sought by Congress and the SEC, unless ordered to do so by the courts.[4]

In subsequent hearings before Senator Frank Church's subcommittee on multi-national corporations, the full extent of the bribery began to unfold. President Gerald Ford expressed "deep concern" about the widening scandal, and he ordered further investigation. The SEC intensified its investigation, not only of Lockheed but also of other multinationals, and so did the IRS, with 300 agents searching through corporate books as well as records in foreign countries.[5]

It soon became clear that top corporate officers of Lockheed were involved in the payoff operation. And it also became clear that although a number of multinationals were involved in overseas payments, Lockheed, with $250 million, was far and away the biggest culprit. (The biggest spenders after Lockheed were Northrop, with $30 million, and Exxon, with $27 million; other sizable spenders were Raytheon, GTE, and Gulf Oil.)[6]

The Defense Department continued to place multimillion-dollar orders with Lockheed, despite the bad press. And Congress refused to withdraw government contracts as a sanction for misconduct, thus showing the vital importance of Lockheed to the military establishment (and the government's desire to keep the firm viable so it could repay the loan). But in 1977, Congress was so moved by the unfolding of the scandal that it passed the Foreign Corrupt Practices Act, designed to clean up business dealings and ban most types of foreign payoffs. (See the following Information Box: "The Foreign Corrupt Practices Act of 1977.")

Daniel J. Haughton, chairman of the board, and A. Carl Kotchian, president, were forced to retire. A new administration and a revamped board led by outsiders sought to undo the damage and clean up the image of a tainted company.

In June 1979, Lockheed pleaded guilty to concealing the Japanese bribes by falsely writing them off as "marketing costs."[7] Under the Internal Revenue Code, no deduction is allowed for payments constituting illegal bribes or kickbacks. Lockheed also pleaded guilty to four counts of fraud and four counts of making false statements to the government. Of course, it could not be specifically charged with illegal bribery because the Foreign Corrupt Practices Act had not been enacted at the time of the misdeeds.

THE COMEBACK

Roy A. Anderson was elected chairman and CEO of Lockheed in October 1977. He had been the company's chief financial officer. In contrast to the "no comment on anything" practice of former chairman Haughton, Anderson evinced an open-door policy, with frank disclosures. He also sought to improve public relations in other ways, such as by getting the company more involved in community affairs at plant locations.

4. "Lockheed's Defiance: A Right to Bribe?" *Time* (August 18, 1975), p. 128.

5. "Payoffs: The Growing Scandal," p. 26.

6. Securities and Exchange Commission, *Report on Questionable and Illegal Corporate Payments and Practices*, Exhibits A and B, submitted to U.S. Congress, Senate, Committee on Banking, Housing and Urban Affairs, May 12, 1976. Some estimates of the extent of the illegal payments are much lower; the discrepancy seems to result from whether to consider sales-type commissions as illegal payments or as cover-ups for bribes.

7. "Lockheed Pleads Guilty to Making Secret Payoffs," *San Francisco Chronicle* (June 2, 1979).

INFORMATION BOX

THE FOREIGN CORRUPT PRACTICES ACT OF 1977

This act makes it a criminal offense to offer a bribe to a foreign government official, and it authorizes the harshest penalties ever imposed on executives and business firms. For examples, companies may be fined $1 million, and individuals face fines of $10,000 and five years in jail.

Although the law mandates high ethical standards when U.S. firms deal in foreign environments, it has been subject to strong criticism. Opponents claim that the law is too restrictive, that the accounting requirements are too burdensome, and that the penalties are so severe as to discourage many companies from attempting to do business overseas. But the biggest criticism has to do with competitiveness: U.S. firms lose to competitors of other nations who are not restrained from offering bribes or other inducements to foreign officials. And in many countries of the world, especially the developing countries, such practices are an accepted way of life. Although proponents of the law maintain that U.S. superior technology will win out over payoffs, such superiority is questionable in most industries today. Particularly hard hit by the act have been makers of heavy electrical equipment, electrical components, and consumer electronic products.[8]

INVITATION TO DISCUSS

A common defense for the practice of offering bribes in certain foreign countries is: "When in Rome, do as the Romans do!" What is your position on this attitude? Do you think our companies doing business in foreign environments should face these legal restraints?

That the company would recover from adversity was fully evident by 1982. Lockheed's earnings had increased substantially, its core business in particular had strengthened, it had won major new contracts, its capital structure had greatly improved, and, for the first time in more than a dozen years, its independent auditors were able to issue an unqualified report as to the company's financial statements.[9]

The company was now in the best position it had been in for more than a decade. Lockheed entered 1983 with an order backlog of $7.8 billion. It had increased its research and development substantially. It had also expanded the five-year capital spending program to approximately $3.5 billion.[10] All this was accomplished within the bounds of respectable business conduct.

ANALYSIS

How Guilty Was Lockheed?

Lockheed officials argued that "payments to foreign officials and political organizations are such a necessary part of its business that the U.S. government should not

---

8. "State Regulators Rush in Where Washington No Longer Treads," *BusinessWeek* (September 19, 1983).

9. 1982 *Annual Report of Lockheed.*

10. *Ibid.*

prohibit it from making them in the future."[11] Lockheed President A. Carl Kotchian strongly defended the payments:

> Such disbursements did not violate American Laws … My decision to
> make such payments stemmed from my judgment that the [contracts]…
> would provide Lockheed workers with jobs and thus rebound to the benefit
> of their dependents, their communities and stockholders of the corporation.
> I should like to emphasize that the payments…were all requested… and
> were not brought up from my side.[12]

(See the following Issue Box about the *acceptability of catering to extortion.*)

Lockheed had a host of supporters who maintained that U.S. firms would lose foreign business without payoffs. In a survey of business leaders, nearly half said they owed it to their companies to make payoffs in countries where such practices were accepted.[13]

Other proponents of payoffs in foreign environments maintained that:

- U.S. firms should not attempt to control foreign counterparts who have different standards and customs.

- Payoffs can prevent delays and expedite action, and are therefore less costly and more effective than not using payoffs. Furthermore, there are no viable alternatives to payoffs in motivating reasonable efficiency in some foreign environments.

- Without payoffs, U.S. firms will lose foreign business. They will not be able to compete with multinationals of other countries who are not so constrained; and, as a result, the continued viability of U.S. multinationals, and even the U.S. economy, will be jeopardized.

Therefore, was Lockheed guilty of the serious charge of bribery and corruption? Despite its supporters, and despite the contentions of its top management at the time, the prevailing judgment was strongly against these practices. Although bribery and corruption may be an accepted way of life in some foreign environments, and although foreign multinationals do not feel compelled to refrain from such practices, they are still anathema to the majority of U.S. citizens. Perhaps a greater factor in judging Lockheed is the incontrovertible fact of the sheer extent of Lockheed payoffs: almost ten times the amount of any other U.S. firm. What some might condone in moderation the majority cannot accept in the extreme.

There are those who view payoffs under any circumstances and in any amounts as something to be condemned:

- They decry the lack of moral leadership on the part of top executives who stoop to such means, and they condemn their failure to impose stronger moral standards on their subordinates.

- They feel that payoffs are a sign of moral decay.

11. As reported in William A. Schumann, "Lockheed Agrees to End Payouts Abroad," *Aviation Week & Space Technology* (September 1, 1975), p. 19.

12. A. Carl Kotchian, "The Payoff: Lockheed's 70-Day Mission to Tokyo," *Saturday Review* (July 9, 1977), p. 12.

13. "The Unfolding of a Torturous Affair," *Fortune* (March 1976), p. 27.

ISSUE BOX

IS CATERING TO EXTORTION AN ACCEPTABLE DEFENSE?

Whereas bribery involves offering something of value in order to influence actions, extortion is the demanding of a fee or payoff. In the first case, the initiative comes from the seller; in the second, from the buyer. Extortion is a type of blackmail.

If a firm wishes to do business in an environment where extortion is prevalent, should it not be excused from any culpability? Is it not the innocent victim? This of course, was Kotchian's defense for the Japanese payoffs. Kugel and Gruenberg argue that "once the black-bag operation starts, the roles becomes so enmeshed that it is difficult to determine where bribery ends and extortion begins."[14] And the Foreign Corrupt Practices Act makes no distinction between bribery and extortion in improper payments.

No less an authority than Peter Drucker maintains that we should condemn less strongly the firm that pays a bribe than the person or government that demands it in the first place. "There was very little difference," he concludes, "between Lockheed's paying the Japanese and the pedestrian in New York's Central Park handing his wallet over to a mugger. Yet no one would consider the pedestrian to have acted unethically."[15] Drucker however, does miss the point that the pedestrian's very life was in danger if he did not hand over his money, whereas Lockheed only stood to lose on the L-1011 contract, important though this might be to the company, its employees, and stockholders.

INVITATION TO DISCUSS

Discuss the pro and cons of an extortion defense. Which position do you see as more compelling? Why?

- They believe that the social costs of international payoffs outweigh the business benefits. Therefore, morality pays in the long run.

Circumstances Most Conducive to Payoffs

The propensity to fall into a payoff situation follows a certain identifiable pattern. Not all firms are placed in this temptation, nor would payoffs be effective in all situations. When multimillion-dollar products bought by governments rather than private corporations or individuals are involved or when government officials are the negotiators of the sales contracts, the propensity is greater. In oligopolistic markets, where only a few firms compete, international payoffs become a kind of nonprice competition.

A multinational firm with host-country production facilities is better able to resist pressure for payoffs than a firm with only distribution facilities there. The latter firm usually has to rely on foreign sales agents, and as we have seen earlier, such an arrangement has the potential for payoffs under the guise of sales commissions.

14. Kugel and Gruenberg, p. 13.

15. Peter Drucker, "There Was Very Little Difference," *The Changing World of the Executive* (Truman Talley/Times Books, 1982), p. 237.

WHAT CAN BE LEARNED?

Corporations can prevent questionable payments. Firms engaged in overseas dealings could take actions to comply with the Foreign Corrupt Practices Act and prevent questionable payments. Admittedly, this is more difficult than with domestic operations simply because of the more distant settings with less direct supervision.

Developing, clarifying, and tightening corporate policies concerning questionable dealings is a starting point. Such policies should be well communicated to employees. Internal auditing can be strengthened in order to monitor employee behavior and ensure that policies are being followed. Furthermore, top management must not be allowed to escape responsibility for questionable payments made by subordinates—or for any other unethical and/or illegal acts.

Since foreign agents tend to be a prime source of payoffs, such agents, when used, need to be thoroughly checked out and, of course, well informed of company policies. The use of foreign subsidiaries to export the company's products—especially in Western Europe, where bribery laws are less stringent—permits more flexibility, although the spirit of the law may be in danger of being violated.

Payments to expedite normal business transactions in foreign environments are not illegal. The law does not prohibit facilitating or "grease" payments that are intended, and needed, to move a transaction to its eventual conclusion where go-no go decisions are not involved. Thus, payments or gifts to a customs officer or a minor governmental official for expediting paperwork and approvals are not in violation. Such payments to relatively low-paid government people are usually small, seldom reaching more than a few hundred dollars. In the local environment, they are considered a means to supplement rather meager salaries.

Does a firm have to stoop to the lowest common denominator of ethical conduct simply because "everyone is doing it"? On the one hand, if the conclusion is "yes," then the moral conduct of an entire industry can sink to the "pits"; a follow-the-leader attitude prevails, and the firm that does not join the herd sees itself as competitively disadvantaged. This attitude has implications well beyond questionable payments. It includes deception and fraudulent acts of all kinds. In the absence of specific and enforced laws controlling such practices, the herd mentality is all the more evident.

On the other hand, cannot a firm take a stand, assume a moral stance, and go against the herd? Such a position may hurt short-term performance but may bring better long-term trusting relationships with customers. But with foreign payoffs, the situation becomes more muted. If U.S. technology and service is far above foreign competitors, a U.S. firm may disdain such payments—despite demands by buyers and competitors' willingness to make such payments—and not be hurt unduly. But is U.S. technology and service so superior to foreign competitors?

Surprising though it may be to some, a firm can prosper without payoffs. In the years after its payoff revelations, Lockheed, under new operating management and board and with a new moral corporate climate, turned itself around. The early indications of such a turnaround were appearing by late 1977, and by 1982, significant improvements in all aspects of the operation were readily evident. The stock market was quick to recognize this.

Both substantial new business and sustaining business came from U.S. government contracts. But Lockheed also kept making considerable foreign sales.

Does this turnaround mean that foreign payoffs had not been all that effective? Perhaps they were effective at the time, even if some people would argue that they were not truly needed. And perhaps the worldwide publicity given the Lockheed scandals, as well as investigations of other multinationals, brought a more sobering stance toward payoffs by all participants. Still, the Lockheed recovery lends strong support to the view of Foreign Corrupt Practices Act proponents that firms can maintain high ethical standards and still compete and be viable.

CONSIDER

Are there other learning insights for this case?

QUESTIONS

1. Are widespread global standards regarding business practices likely to be enacted and enforced in the foreseeable future? Why or why not?

2. What factors do you think led Lockheed's top executives down the perilous path of bribery and questionable practices? In your opinion, did such factors excuse these executives from condemnation?

3. In this case, unlike most others, the top executives received major blame, not lower-level executives. How do you account for top management being so visibly involved in the scandals?

4. What is the difference between bribery and extortion? Is there an ethical difference?

5. Does the judgment of unethical conduct change if payoffs are an accepted way of doing business in the particular country?

6. Should top management escape responsibility for questionable payments made by subordinates?

7. Defend Lockheed's position regarding payoffs in the early 1970s. Be as persuasive as you can.

HANDS-ON EXERCISES

1. As a special representative of Lockheed, what arguments would you present to Prince Bernhard for accepting a bribe for the use of his influence? What objections would you expect him to raise, and how would you answer them?

2. How would you advise company officials to react to extortion attempts today? How about grease money?

3. As a top executive brought into the company after the serious charges against Lockheed and the resulting negative publicity, how would you attempt to remedy the situation? Be specific.

TEAM DEBATE EXERCISES

1. Debate the government bailout of Lockheed.
2. Debate the Foreign Corrupt Practices Act.

INVITATION TO RESEARCH

What has happened to Lockheed since the scandals? Have other firms been involved in questionable payoffs in recent years?

CHAPTER EIGHTEEN

General Dynamics: Fleecing U.S. Taxpayers

*B*etween 1970 and 1986, General Dynamics Corporation became a symbol of corporate irresponsibility and opportunism in the military-industrial sector, fleecing U.S. taxpayers who were footing the bills for military hardware. During this time, General Dynamics was investigated by the Defense Department, the Internal Revenue Service, the U.S. Senate, and the Securities and Exchange Commission. A variety of charges were levied, the most serious involving billion-dollar cost overruns incurred on the Los Angeles–class submarine program. Other charges for wide-ranging programs were also levied. America's major defense contractor faced these serious allegations of wrongdoing:

- Wild cost overruns
- Fraud
- Faulty workmanship
- Questionable dealings with Washington officials
- Bill padding
- Mismanagement
- Overseas bribery
- Tax evasion

These allegations were not unique to General Dynamics. They were symptomatic of the entire defense industry. But, they reached their apogee with General Dynamics.

THE COMPANY

General Dynamics started as the Electric Boat Company, a New Jersey ship and submarine builder founded by John Holland in 1895. During World War II, the Electric Boat Company distinguished itself by producing large numbers of submarines, PT boats, and other ships. At the end of the war, faced with diminishing sales, the company adopted a strong acquisition strategy. In 1952, it merged with Canadair, forming General Dynamics.

By 1984, General Dynamics employed 92,600 people and had nearly $7.8 billion in contracts, with profits of $382 million. The nation's third largest defense contractor, it produced a wide range of major weapons systems for all branches of the armed forces, including the F-16 Fighter Aircraft, the Tomahawk Cruise Missile, the Stinger Antiaircraft System, the Phalanx Gun System, the Trident and SSN-688 class submarines, the M1 Main Battle Tank, and such defense electronics as the Army's Single Channel Ground and Airborne Radio System.

General Dynamics sold Atlas and Centaur launch vehicles for both government and commercial space launches. Its subsidiary, Cessna Aircraft, was one of the world's top makers of business jets (with 50 percent of the market). Another subsidiary, Material Service Corporation, sold building and highway construction materials, lime, and coal. Upcoming projects included the Navy's A-12 Attack Aircraft (produced with McDonnell Douglas) and the Advanced Tactical Fighter (General Dynamics was one of two contractor teams competing to produce this aircraft). The Electric Boat Division was one of the two ship-builders constructing the new Seawolf class attack submarine for the Navy.

Although General Dynamics' major customer was the U.S. military, it also did business with foreign countries. For example, the F-16 airplane has been ordered by Belgium, Denmark, the Netherlands, Norway, Israel, Egypt, Venezuela, South Korea, Turkey, Greece, Thailand, Singapore, Indonesia, and Bahrain.

EMERGING PROBLEMS

Over the years, General Dynamics had developed a close and symbiotic relationship with the Pentagon. Its products were at the heart of our defense armament during World War II and during the subsequent Cold War. However, allegations of mismanagement, illegal kickbacks, and overcharges had been surfacing for years. To be sure, General Dynamics was not the only object of such charges—the other defense contractors also had their critics—but General Dynamics got most of the spotlight, particularly regarding its Trident and SSN-688 attack submarines.

The story began in 1968. The Navy was under pressure to stay ahead of the growing Soviet submarine threat. This was at the height of the Cold War, with the Berlin Wall completed only a few years earlier (construction on the Wall began on August 13, 1961). The prospects for war brought the decision to seek defense contractors for nuclear submarines. Because of the heavy costs involved, and because this was the first nuclear-powered submarine, the bidding process was limited to what the Navy deemed the two ablest contractors. General Dynamics' Electric Boat Division won the contract and became the first firm to make the Navy's nuclear-powered SSN688 sub, armed with the most important weapon in the U.S. arsenal, the Trident ballistic missile.

The Navy insisted that the job be done under a fixed-price contract instead of the more common "cost plus" contract. This was exceedingly risky for General Dynamics, since no one knew how much it would cost to build high-speed nuclear submarines. Only years later, when the price ballooned well above the contracted price, did the problems with this arrangement become evident. In 1976, General Dynamics filed a claim for $843 million in cost overruns; this being a $46 million surcharge for each of the eighteen subs. General Dynamics claimed the cost increase was due to Navy mismanagement of the contracts, due to its constant changing of specifications. However, the Navy recoiled at paying what it claimed were totally unjustified charges due to gross mismanagement. The low-price bidding practices of the defense industry became vulnerable to intensive critical investigation.

ALLEGATIONS

In 1978, the Navy finally agreed to pay a significant portion of the heavy cost overruns on the submarines. Some people—including Admiral Hyman Rickover, the guiding force behind the nuclear navy, and Senator William Proxmire—were highly critical of the deal. They maintained that the company had falsely attributed the overruns to the thousands of engineering changes ordered by the Navy.[1]

The cost overruns were not limited to the Electric Boat Division. Other projects with major overcharges were the M1 Abrams Tank, the DIV AD Self-Propelled AntiAircraft Gun, and the F-18 Fighter Bomber. For example, the authorized cost per unit of the Abrams Tank was $2 million. But the actual production cost was $2.8 million, a 42.4 percent overcharge. Although cost overruns received the most attention, they were not the most damaging to General Dynamics. Allegations of fraud were. The Defense Department uncovered evidence that the company illegally gave Admiral Rickover $67,628 in gifts, presumably to gain his influence. Influential he was, supervising billions of dollars of top-secret work at the Electric Boat Shipyard. The Defense Department discovered other General Dynamics indiscretions, including a history of padding its bills to the Defense Department with dubious overhead charges, such as: executives' country club dues, the costs of lobbying government officials, and, a celebrated example, the cost of boarding a top executive's dog. The company was found to have billed the government for 90 percent of the $22 million in air travel costs for flights from the company St. Louis headquarters to Albany, Georgia, where General Dynamics Chairman David S. Lewis owned a farm he used as a weekend retreat.[2]

The company was accused of gross mismanagement. Numerous internal documents compiled by congressional investigators revealed the complaints managers at all levels had about the company: poor supervision, low morale, materials not ordered on time, proper records not kept. The documents also suggested that the company had long had a strategy of recouping its losses through false expense claims.[3] Other allegations concerned attempts to manipulate the value of General Dynamics' stock, illegal wiretapping, and improper reporting of income taxes.

In September 1983, more fraud charges arose when P. Takis Veliotis, a Greek shipbuilding executive brought in to straighten out the problems at Electric Boat in 1977, was himself indicted by a federal grand jury for taking kickbacks on contracts he had let while running another General Dynamics shipyard. Veliotis, a dual citizen of the United States and Greece, fled to Athens—out of reach of U.S. law—after the

---

1. Eric Gelman, "A Giant Under Fire: General Dynamics Faces Numerous Charges of Fraud," *Newsweek* (February 11, 1985), pp. 24–25.

2. Tom Morganthau, "Waste, Fraud and Abuse? The Navy Cracks Down on a Major Defense Contractor," *Newsweek* (June 3, 1986), pp. 22–23.

3. Gelman, pp. 24–25.

indictment. But, early in 1982, he sought to plea bargain with the Justice Department, providing documents and tapes to help the case against General Dynamics. Veliotis also charged that the company had bribed government officials in South Korea and Egypt in order to sell the F-16 fighter plane.

CONSEQUENCES

In May 1985, as a result of the 1984 to 1985 investigation, John Lehman, secretary of the Navy, announced a crackdown on General Dynamics. Some $22.5 million in contracts were canceled, a $676,283 fine was imposed, and a series of housecleaning measures was mandated, including the creation of a rigorous code of ethics for company employees and the settlement of some $75 million in disputed Navy billings. Lehman decried the "integrity and responsibility" of the corporation.[4]

The next day, General Dynamics' sixty-seven year-old chairman, David S. Lewis, announced his retirement. Also retiring were Finance Officer Gordon MacDonald, Vice President George Sawyer, Executive Vice President James Beggs, Division General Manager Ralph Hawes, Program Director David McPherson, and Assistant Director James Hansen. Lewis was replaced by Stanley C. Pace, who had a more upright ethical image. (See the Information Box: "Can a Beleaguered Corporate Image Be Salvaged by a Management Change?")

General Dynamics was virtually unpunished, even following convictions of wrongdoing. Although some management changes were made, the value of the cancelled contracts amounted only to 0.1 percent of the firm's billings the previous year. The partnership with the Pentagon was soon resumed, and the culpable executives received no prison sentences, merely a comfortable retirement.

How could such malpractices be so easily tolerated? Alas, they were endemic to the whole industry, not just limited to General Dynamics.

THE ETHICAL CLIMATE OF THE DEFENSE INDUSTRY

General Dynamics' questionable practices were not unique. They represented flaws "deeply embedded in defense procurement," as *Newsweek* magazine reported. "Some problems, ranging from faulty products to overcharges, seem endemic to defense contractors—especially the giant aerospace, electronics and high-tech companies that make up the bulk of what has long been known as the military-industrial complex."[5]

In the defense industry, major contracts rarely came in under budget. Other abuses were also prevalent. For example: after receiving evidence that thousands of computer chips had not been adequately tested, the Pentagon's inspector general, Joseph Sherick, launched an investigation of ten semiconductor manufacturers. Several of these were subsequently found guilty of failure to meet government standards. Congressional investigations revealed outrageous overpricing by contractors for commonplace tools and spare parts. As one example, Gould, Inc. charged the Pentagon $436 for a hammer. Subsequent analysis disclosed that the hammer and its packaging cost Gould only $8 to make; the rest was for unspecified overhead and administrative costs.[6]

4. Morganthau, pp. 22–23.

5. Susan Dentzer, "How the Pentagon Spends Its Billions," *Newsweek* (February 11, 1985), p. 26.

6. *Ibid.*, pp. 26–28.

INFORMATION BOX

CAN A BELEAGUERED CORPORATE IMAGE BE SALVAGED BY A MANAGEMENT CHANGE?

Stanley Pace, General Dynamics' new chief executive, supposedly had a strong moral background. After all, he had been long associated with the Boy Scouts of America. Taking over from retiring David Lewis in December 1985, Pace decided his main charge was to improve the company's ethical image. He quickly instituted a series of administrative procedures designed to tone up "executive-level ethics and thwart corruption in the future."[7]

On January 16, 1986, Pace appeared before the National Press Club in Washington to describe the changes he'd made and to try to improve the company's image before the nation's press. The "fixes" he described included tightened procedures for everything from government contract billing to time-card reporting. He said he'd hired a corporate ethics program director "who reports directly to me" and a team of field-based ethics directors who were represented at every General Dynamics site. Also, a twenty-page code of ethics handbook was to be distributed to all salaried employees.

Pace was shocked that the reporters did not treat his "fixes" with much respect. They peppered him with skeptical questions, such as, "Aren't you simply promising to be honest?" and "Is this what it takes to make a corporation honest?" After trying to defend his actions for half an hour, Pace hurried from the room, pleading another appointment.

The press remained unconvinced that Pace's announced changes were anything more than cosmetic, that they were symptomatic of a major turnaround in the company's dealing with the government and eventually with taxpayers.

INVITATION TO DISCUSS

Evaluate the importance cosmetic changes can have for a company beset with public image problems. Discuss their necessity and their effectiveness.

As of May 1, 1985, the Defense Department was investigating forty-five top defense contractors concerning possible criminal charges. See Table 18.1 for a listing of the thirty-six companies in open investigation and the allegations against them. General Dynamics was not alone in abusing its position with the government and with the public who pays the bills.

ANALYSIS: ASSESSING BLAME

In analyzing the abuses, identifying the contributory factors, and evaluating the defenses or explanations for what happened, we can categorize these as: (1) those within the organization that reflect directly on management and workers at General Dynamics, (2) miscellaneous external factors that motivated overruns and other temptations, and (3) the procurement process itself.

---

7. Janet Fix, "Corruption Thwarter," *Forbes* (February 10, 1986), p. 140.

Table 18.1   Defense Contractors under Open Investigation by the Defense Department and the Allegations, May 1, 1985

Washington—The Defense Dept. Inspector General's Office is conducting investigations of forty-five top defense contractors concerning possible criminal charges, including thirty-six companies listed as open investigations as of May 1 (AW&ST June 24, p.15). The list was made public by Rep. John D. Dingell (D-Mich.), chairman of the House Energy and Commerce oversight and investigations subcommittee.

Contractor	Allegation
MacDonnell Douglas Corp.	Cost mischarging
Rockwell International Corp.	Cost and labor mischarging
General Dynamics Corp.	Cost mischarging Subcontractor kickbacks Labor mischarging Product substitution Security compromise Defective pricing Cost duplication False claims
Lockheed Corp.	Labor mischarging
Boeing Co., Inc.	Cost mischarging Supply accountability Labor mischarging
General Electric Co.	False claims Defective pricing Labor cost mischarging Product substitution
United Technologies Corp.	Gratuities Subcontractor kickbacks Cost mischarging Bribery Defective pricing
Raytheon Co.	Labor mischarging Product substitution
Litton Industries, Inc.	Bribery-subcontractors Kickbacks Labor mischarging False claims Bid rigging Cost mischarging
Grumman Corp.	Cost mischarging
Martin Marietta Corp.	Subcontractor kickback Cost mischarging
Westinghouse Electric Corp.	Cost mischarging
Sperry Corp.	Labor mischarging Cost mischarging Defective pricing
Honeywell, Inc.	Diversion of government property Bid rigging

(Continues)

Table 18.1 *(Continued)*

Contractor	Allegation
Ford Motor Co.	Defective pricing-labor mischarging Falsification of performance records
Eaton Corp.	Conflict of interest-gratuities Cost mischarging
TRW, Inc.	Defective pricing Cost mischarging
Texas Instruments	Product substitution
Northrop Corp.	Labor mischarging False progress payments
Avco Corp.	Subcontractor kickbacks Cost mischarging
Textron, Inc.	Cost mischarging
Allied Corp.	Conflict of interest
Tenneco, Inc.	Cost mischarging
GTE Corp.	Unauthorized acquisition and utilization of classified data Labor mischarging
Sanders Associates, Inc.	Unauthorized release of contract information
Motorola, Inc.	Labor mischarging
Congoleum Corp.	Mischarging Gratuities/theft
Harris Corp.	Defective pricing
Gould, Inc.	Cost mischarging
Emerson Electric Co.	Cost mischarging Gratuities-cost mischarging
John Hopkins University	Civilian health and medical program of the uniformed services fraud
Tracor, Inc.	Product substitution
Lear Siegler, Inc.	Product substitution
Fairchild Industries, Inc.	Gratuities Product substitution Cost mischarging False statements
Dynalectron Corp.	Cost mischarging
Todd Shipyard Corp.	Noncompliances with contract

Source: "Defense Dept. Lists Contractor Investigations," *Aviation Week & Space Technology* (July 15, 1985), p. 89.

Internal Contributing Factors

General Dynamics' management was undoubtedly responsible for a great number of poor management decisions. Former senior executive James Ashton contended that the problems at the Electric Boat Shipyard during the 1970s had been caused by mismanagement. He also testified before a House subcommittee that General Dynamics made such an unrealistic bid to win the Los Angeles–class contract that it could not afford to hire the engineers needed to cope with the design revisions. Numerous memos from managers at every level of the company complained of poor supervision, low morale, ineffective inventories of goods needed, and improper recordkeeping.[8]

Top management cannot be exonerated for the deficiencies of subordinates, of course. In this case, one wonders whether the inability to effectively control their large operation caused upper managers to panic and attempt to hide mistakes. Top management seemed willing to embrace opportunities to recoup losses through false claims. From there, it was but a short step to ever more serious instances of fraud.

Admittedly, the demands on management and on the entire organization were severe on some of these projects. For example, Newport News Shipyard, which had received the contract to design the subs, had never drawn up plans for a nuclear-powered submarine before and was therefore late getting the blueprints to Electric Boat. The Navy was also late delivering construction specifications. Meanwhile, General Dynamics' Electric Boat Division had to grow very rapidly in order to do the mammoth job as quickly as the Navy demanded. Its shipyard labor force grew from 12,000 workers in 1971 to almost 30,000 by the middle of 1977. The proportion of skilled workers plummeted from 80 percent of the work force in 1972 to 35 percent four years later.

It quickly became apparent that Electric Boat was in deep trouble. "Its rapidly hired work force, lacking necessary expertise, wasn't up to the task. Welders couldn't weld, managers couldn't manage, and quality controllers couldn't control the quality of materials or workmanship."[9] A Navy inspector reported that 2,772 welds had to be repaired. The wrong kind of steel was used in 126,000 locations in the Trident subs, and much of it had to be replaced. A faulty turbine was installed in the *U.S.S. Ohio*, first of the Trident subs, and had to be taken out piece by piece.[10]

External Contributing Factors

General Dynamics' officials were quick to contend that thousands of design changes initiated by the Navy and Air Force caused, not only delays in the construction of the various defense weapons, but also massive additional expenditures to expedite corrective measures. Undoubtedly, there was merit to this excuse; at least, the blame was not all General Dynamics. A major external factor in widespread defense industry fraud *was* the ineptitude of government watchdog agencies:

> [E]vidence is mounting that Justice's Defense Procurement Fraud Unit hasn't lived up to its billing… [C]ritics say most of its prosecutions, which have recovered only $8.2 million, involve penny-ante charges that didn't require much expertise. The unit, they complain, is plagued by inadequate resources and has handled poorly its few major cases.[11]

8. Gelman, pp. 24–25.

9. O. Kelly, "Inside Story of the Trident Debacle," *U.S. News & World Report* (March 30, 1981), p. 21.

10. *Ibid.*

11. Paula Dwyer, "Is Justice Bungling the Defense Fraud Crackdown?" *BusinessWeek* (April 21, 1986), p. 75.

After a probe into the Sperry Corporation for cost overruns and labor mischarging was called off because of the fraud unit's ineptitude in pursuing the case, Senators William Proxmire, of Wisconsin, and Charles Grassley, of Iowa, were shocked, publicly stating: "It is abundantly clear we do not have efficient and effective enforcement against defense fraud."[12]

Such ineffective enforcement resulted in an inability to maintain any accountability of defense contractors. As a consequence, they were allowed to indulge in unchecked spending, wild cost overruns, and fraudulent claims—easy temptations for most firms, large and small, to succumb to.

Another major factor leading to a climate of opportunism and grab-what-you-can is the scarcity of real competition in this industry. These firms are in the cat-bird seat. Defense-sanctioned monopolies that spawn waste, inefficiency, and fraud predominate in the absence of true competition. In other business environments, the customer who is taken advantage of simply shifts to another supplier. But this is not easily done with major defense firms. As Stanley Pace of General Dynamics summed it up:

> We (GD) have the major heartland programs with each of the armed services. And we have the balance sheet and cash flow to make the investments for the weapons of the future. We are now working both sides of the street.[13]

The Procurement Process

The defense procurement process lends itself to abuses and taxpayer fleecing. To begin with, not all contracts are subject to competitive bidding. General Dynamics holds a monopoly on the building of Trident submarines, the M1 tank, and the F-16 fighter. Undoubtedly, this enabled it to escape serious punishment for all of its problems with the government. With competitive bidding, or even with split-sourcing (having more than one company bid for the contract, the company with the lowest bid receiving 60 percent of the contract, and the losing company receiving the rest), the government's dependence on a single vital supplier would be reduced. The possibility of punitive actions that more closely matched the abuses should act as a deterrent. And price gouging should be tempered.

The number of layers in the procurement process promotes inefficiencies. Each of the military branches has its own separate group for acquisitions (Air Force Command, Army Material Command, etc.). At least 165,000 people have been directly employed by the Pentagon for research, development, and logistics; thousands more work for aerospace corporations at the government's expense. Each layer has its own reviews, which call for bureaucratic meetings and paperwork. This adds to the cumbersomeness of the process, the costs, and the fragmentation of control.[14] Invoice auditing poses another problem. In the mid-1980s, the Defense Contract Audits Agency had a backlog of $70 billion worth of invoices. For years, many of the

---

12. Janice Castro, "Probe Scuttled—A Three-Year Inquiry Ends," *Time* (June 1, 1987), p. 51.

13. Robert Wrubel, "Gunning It," *Financial World* (March 8, 1988), p. 25.

14. Gregg Easterbrook, "Sack Weinberger, Bankrupt General Dynamics, and Other Procurement Reforms," *The Washington Monthly* (January 1987), pp. 33–46.

fraudulent billing claims were allowed to slip through the audits because of a flaw in the process. The auditor's job is tied to the companies audited. If expenditures with a company are reduced, auditing positions are eliminated. This creates a disincentive for auditors to severely scrutinize and follow-up on questionable activities. The solution here would be to evaluate how much waste auditors uncover and eliminate.[15]

Adding to the Defense Department's motivations for continuing questionable programs and hiring questionable contractors is the military career syndrome. Rotations and transfers are so extensive among officers involved with procurement that dozens of people may have been involved in purchasing a single system. Such turnover and "new perspectives" often result in ever-changing specifications and add-ons, thus greatly increasing costs. Furthermore, officers advance their careers far more by acquiring weapons systems than by killing projects. Hence, procurement officers often have as much interest in seeing a weapon developed as the manufacturer does:

> Procurement officials and contractors effectively become co-conspirators; both sides may understate the costs of a weapon while its purchase is still being contemplated in an effort to secure the final order.[16]

Add to all this a good dash of politics: "[O]nce politics enters the picture, procurement decisions may not be made on the basis of economics or military decisions, but on the need to satisfy constituents."[17] Woe to the member of Congress who does not protect the major employers in his or her district, no matter how unneeded the output is, or how inefficient or corrupt this large employer may be.

WHAT CAN BE LEARNED?

There should be a balanced view of the defense industry. There's a temptation to regard General Dynamics' dismal record—and that of the rest of the defense industry—as yet another indictment of a capitalist system fraught with inefficient and self-seeking workers and managers. However, the facts do not totally support this easy, finger-pointing conclusion. Certainly, General Dynamics can be criticized—and perhaps should have received harsher penalties. But the whole system by which the Pentagon procures new weapons systems is flawed.

Every major cost overrun, scandal, and engineering or production mistake stimulates two powerful political reactions. The first is that Congress, the media, and the public are quick to look for wrongdoers. Extensive investigations are undertaken, some of which result in grand jury indictments, and the press pounces on any suspicions of corruption and greed. Usually, the charges are eventually dropped for lack of sufficient evidence of criminal intent, or else watered-down plea bargains defuse the public's criticism and blame seeking. The second powerful reaction is pressure put on the Pentagon to add more checks and balances, more auditors and

15. *Ibid.*

16. Tony Kay, "It's Waste and Fraud as Usual at the Pentagon," *The Nation* (June 15, 1985), pp. 734–738.

17. Dentzer, p. 27.

inspectors—in other words, to burden the procurement process with even more red tape, paperwork, and bureaucracy. For example, the Defense Department, responding to scandal of the $436 hammer, the $600 toilet seat, and the $7,000 coffee makers, "added 7,000 additional staffers to solve such problems."[18]

Neither investigations nor inspections are the solution. What is needed is a better recognition of what defense contractors can do well. Crash programs to build whole new fleets (of nuclear submarines, for example) and weapons systems invite trouble. The huge numbers of new workers that the Electric Boat Division needed to build the Trident sub invited trouble: Technicians, managers, workers—none could cope well with the timetable, resulting in poorly built and wildly expensive products. Of course, "the sheer size of the stakes, $100 million or more for a single sub, was enough to excite the greed and test the integrity of even the most well-meaning contractor."[19] The bigger and more complex a project is, the fewer the prime contractors who will be able to bid on it. Relying on a single firm in such a monopoly situation provides a great opportunity for abusive practices, suspicions and distrust by the government, and it lessens the likelihood that there will be sufficient penalties to deter management's darker leanings. (See the Issue Box: "How Tolerant Can We Be with Firms Vital to Our National Security?")

The bureaucratic procurement process invites abuses. The relatively few major defense contractors competing for multimillion— and even billion—dollar projects present an environment fraught with temptations for abuses of all kinds. Influence seeking and peddling can become major factors in procurement decisions and with politicians involved in seeking the fruits of massive governmental contracts for the benefit of their own constituents, the decision-making process can become muddled, and not always objective. The sheer complexity of these major techno-logical projects defies close control and monitoring, despite government attempts to do so. At the same time, the virtual monopoly position that the winner of a major defense contract assumes tends to deaden the effort to maximize efficiency and keep a tight rein on costs.

So we have mighty cost overruns, quality control problems, the temptation to pad bills and throw in extravagant and irrelevant expenses, as well as other fraud-ulent practices, even including bribery. While, as we saw in the Lockheed case, the defense industry at one time became notorious for its bribery of foreign govern-mental officials to win contracts, certainly bribery on a lesser scale was far from unknown domestically. However, it often assumed more subtleties. These might include high-level executive positions for retiring generals and admirals, as well as key procurement officers. They might include lucrative consulting and speaking engagements for politicians and government administrators.

In the normal competitive business environment, such practices and looseness of operations would be little tolerated and would be competitively vulnerable. But in the folds of bureaucracy, and with the cloak of highly complex technologies, the actions of General Dynamics were far from unique, as we have seen.

18. Jack Robertson, "Currie: Contractors on Tightrope," *Electronic News* (July 1989), p. 35.

19. Charles P. Alexander, "General Dynamics Under Fire," *Time* (April 1985), p. 57.

ISSUE BOX

HOW TOLERANT CAN WE BE WITH FIRMS VITAL TO OUR NATIONAL SECURITY?

This is a crucial issue, with major implications for how we tolerate discrepancies in cost, quality, and deadlines—not to mention improper and unethical conduct. Theoretically, because national security is at stake, we expect the highest operational and ethical standards. But is this realistic?

Unfortunately, the answer is no. Because of the crucial roles such contractors play in national defense, and because of the lack of acceptable alternative contractors, we may have to tolerate conduct that would not be acceptable in other industries. Because of the monopoly position such firms as General Dynamics have, we can hardly refuse to do further business with them, despite their misdeeds. We should not penalize them so severely as to curtail their viability and performance. Beyond publicly decrying their misdeeds and giving them a "slap on the wrist," there is little we can do in the way of punitive measures. So, the firm's risks from overcharging, committing fraud, and currying favoritism are minimal. Even a discredited public image—which could be devastating to firms in other industries—can be disregarded by these firms, since their role is so vital and since the government is their primary customer, not the general public.

So despite our druthers, these firms' transgressions will continue to be less severely punished—in fact, will be tacitly accepted.

Is there any recourse? The major recourse would appear to be monitoring more closely, seeking to develop competitive options, and avoiding the worst of the crash programs that have plagued the military-industrial complex in the past. Perhaps our defense contractors, with fewer crash programs, could diversify into civilian markets rather than relying totally on government business.

INVITATION TO DISCUSS

Are punitive threats the best way to curb abuses in the defense industry? Discuss, and present any other recommendations.

Is there any solution to this waste in the defense industry? It is questionable if such abusive practices can be completely eliminated, especially during periods of national emergency when defense efforts are intensified. During periods of calm and reduced defense expenditures, closer controls should be possible. Government auditing can be improved, as was discussed in the section on the procurement process. Other constraints would be the encouragement of whistle-blowing, and also of investigative reporting.

Rationalizing excesses is easy when the burden is spread over millions of taxpayers. This situation of millions of taxpayers footing the bill has undoubtedly fueled more excesses than any other single factor. With the burden of extravagance, inefficiency, and bureaucratic expansion spread over the masses, the impact is minor for any individual taxpayer. Hence, the temptation. The great faceless mass is seen as somehow amorphous and hardly to be considered, and certainly unable to exercise restraints, even in election years, when more than 95 percent of incumbents are reelected.

CONSIDER

Can you think of more learning insights?

QUESTIONS

1. Top executives of General Dynamics were given only a slap on the wrist after the disclosure of improprieties: they were able to retire comfortably. Do you think punishment should have been more severe?

2. Discuss how the government could be charged $436 for a hammer when it cost only $8 to make.

3. How might the Defense Department bring more competition into the defense industry? Is this feasible?

4. How might government auditing of defense contractors be improved? Would this likely correct most of the misdeeds? Why or why not?

5. On balance, who do you think was more culpable in the defense-industry misdeeds: the firms or the government? Why?

6. Compare and contrast General Dynamics and Lockheed from the previous chapter, as to their relative culpability.

7. How did domestic bribery compare with overseas bribery?

HANDS-ON EXERCISES

1. You are an assistant to the top executive of the Electric Boat Division. Your division has just received the contract for the Trident sub. This will require a massive buildup of personnel. How would you plan for an orderly assimilation so as to meet the timetable while maintaining reasonable quality? Be as specific as you can, making any needed assumptions.

2. You are a staff assistant to the Secretary of Defense. You are charged with developing a framework for improving the procurement process. What recommendations would you make? What objections would you anticipate?

TEAM DEBATE EXERCISE

Debate this complaint by a politician about the seeming inability of the Defense Department: "We have no club to use against these defense contractors to assure their integrity and efficiency." One team should roughly take the position that the problem of waste, and so on, is so endemic that not very much can be done about it. The other team should take the position that fraud and mismanagement can be shut down.

INVITATION TO RESEARCH

1. Is General Dynamics still a major player in the defense industry today?
2. Have there been any well-publicized instances of mismanagement, illegal kickbacks, and overcharges by defense contractors in recent years?

PART THREE

QUESTIONABLE
ETHICAL CONDUCT

CHAPTER NINETEEN

Wal-Mart: A Big Bully?

*I*n March 1992, Sam Walton passed away after a two-year battle with bone cancer. Perhaps the most admired businessman of his era, he had founded Wal-Mart Stores with the concept of discount stores in small towns, and had brought it to the lofty stature of the biggest retailer in the United States—ahead of the decades-long leaders, Sears and Penney—and in 1990 pushed ahead of an earlier great discount-store success, Kmart.

Walton's successors continued his legacy well. By the end of fiscal 1998, Wal-Mart's sales of $137.6 billion made it one of the largest corporations in the world; by 2002 sales were $217.8 billion, and it had knocked ExxonMobil out of first place.

Yet, a growing number of people were questioning how Wal-Mart was using its gargantuan power, some seeing it becoming the antithesis of fair competition through questionable practices toward suppliers, competitors, employees, and communities themselves.

THE EARLY YEARS OF SAM WALTON

Samuel Moore Walton was born in Kingfisher, Oklahoma, on March 29, 1917. He and his brother, James, born three years later, were reared in a family that valued hard work and thrift. They grew up in Missouri in the depths of the Great Depression.

By the time Walton entered eighth grade in Shebina, Oklahoma, he was already exhibiting the character traits that would dominate his future life: quiet and soft spoken, but a natural leader who became class president and captain of the football team. He even became the first Eagle Scout in Shebina's history.

At the University of Missouri, Walton excelled in academics and athletics. He worked his way through college by delivering newspapers, working in a five-and-dime store, lifeguarding, and waiting tables at the university.

After his graduation in 1940, Walton went to the J. C. Penney Company and became a management trainee at the Des Moines, Iowa, store. There he applied his work ethic, competed to become Penney's most promising new man, and became imbued with the Penney philosophy of catering to smaller towns and having "associates" instead of employees or clerks. He also met J. C. Penney himself and was intrigued with his habit of strolling around stores and personally meeting and observing customers and salespeople. After eighteen months, Walton left Penney's for the U.S. Army, but what he had learned in the Penney store in Des Moines was to shape his future ideas.

WAL-MART'S GROWTH TO THE BIGGEST RETAILER

Sam Walton was discharged from the Army in August 1945. By chance he stumbled on an opportunity to buy the franchise of a Ben Franklin variety store in Newport, Arkansas, and he opened it a month later. The lease arrangement with the building's owner did not work out, so Walton eventually relocated to Bentonville, Arkansas in 1950. During the 1950s and early 1960s, Walton increased his number of Ben Franklin franchises to fifteen. In the winter of 1962 he proposed at a Ben Franklin board meeting that the company should aggressively turn its efforts to discounting, citing the great potential of this emerging retail phenomenon. The company refused to consider such an innovative idea, so Walton and his brother went ahead anyway. They opened a Discount City in Rogers, Arkansas in 1962; and they opened a second store in Harrison, Arkansas in 1964. They incorporated the business as Wal-Mart Stores on October 31, 1969, and it became a publicly held company a year later. In 1970, Walton also opened his first distribution center and general office—a 72,000-square-foot complex in Bentonville, Arkansas. In 1972, Wal-Mart was listed on the New York Stock Exchange.

In 1976 Walton severed ties with Ben Franklin in order to concentrate on expanding Wal-Mart. His operations now extended to small towns in Arkansas, Missouri, Kansas, and Oklahoma. The essence of Walton's management philosophy during these building years was that of an old-fashioned entrepreneur; Walton personally roamed through his own stores, as well as those of competitors, always looking for new ideas in mass merchandising to maximize sales at attractive prices.

Rather than confronting the major retailers—department stores, chains such as Penney's and Sears, and the strong discounters such as Kmart—Walton confined his efforts to the smaller cities, ones major retailers shunned as having insufficient market potential. But he saw these small markets as a strategic window of opportunity, untapped by any aggressive firms.

Growth accelerated. By the end of 1975 Walton had 104 stores with nearly 6,000 employees and annual sales of $236 million, which generated $6 million net profit. The next year, the number of stores increased to 125, employees to 7,500, and sales to $340 million, with $11.5 million in profit.

Table 19.1 compares the growth of sales and number of stores of Wal-Mart with Kmart, its major competitor, from 1980 to 1990, the decade that ended with Wal-Mart forging ahead to become the biggest retailer. By the end of 1990, Wal-Mart had 1,573 stores located in thirty-five states.

Some of these new stores were Wal-Mart SuperCenters, considerably larger than regular Wal-Marts, having a warehouse-style food outlet under the same roof as the discount store. While such food stores carried items comparable to products in a regular urban supermarket, the assortment and service were superior to most direct

TABLE 19.1. **Comparison of Growth in Sales and Number of Stores, Wal-Mart and Kmart, 1980–1990**

	Kmart		Wal-Mart	
	Sales (millions)	Number of Stores	Sales (millions)	Number of Stores
1980	$14,204	1,772	$1,643	330
1981	16,527	2,055	2,445	491
1982	16,772	2,117	3,376	551
1983	18,597	2,160	4,667	642
1984	20,762	2,173	6,401	745
1985	22,035	2,332	8,451	859
1986	23,035	2,342	11,909	980
1987	25,627	2,273	15,959	1,114
1988	27,301	2,307	20,649	1,259
1989	29,533	2,361	25,810	1,402
1990	32,070	2,350	32,602	1,573

Source: Company annual reports.

Commentary: Several of these statistics are of particular interest. First, the comparison of the sales from 1980 to 1990, slightly more than one decade, of Wal-Mart and Kmart, show the tremendous growth rate of Wal-Mart, starting at little more than 10 percent of Kmart sales figures to forge ahead by 1990. And Kmart was no slouch during this period.

Second, Wal-Mart achieved its leadership in total sales with almost 800 fewer stores than Kmart had. This means that Wal-Mart's stores were achieving much higher sales volume than Kmart's, a fact that is further borne out by the statistics in Table 19.3.

competitors in the smaller cities. The key advantage of adding food stores to general-merchandise discount stores was greater traffic: Because customers shop weekly for groceries, they are exposed far more to other merchandise in the stores than would otherwise be the case.

Wal-Mart, by now was also opening another category of stores: Sam's Wholesale, also known as Sam's Clubs. These stores were first introduced in 1984, and by 1991 there were 148. This wholesale club concept came about as regular discount stores seemed to be reaching saturation in some locations. The wholesale warehouse went a step further in discounting.

Sam's Clubs were large, ranging up to 135,000 square feet. Each store was a membership-only operation, and qualified members included businesses and members of certain groups, such as government employees and credit union members. Although the stores were huge, they carried less than 5 percent of the total variety of items carried by regular discount stores. Assortments were limited to fast-moving home goods and apparel, generally name brands, with prices 8 to 10 percent over cost, well under those of discount stores and department and specialty stores. Sam's Clubs were the initial entry for Wal-Mart into the big metropolitan markets it had avoided in its early years.

In December 1987, Wal-Mart opened its newest merchandising concept, Hypermart USA, in Garland, Texas, a suburb of Dallas. The hypermart offered a combination of groceries and general merchandise in over 200,000 square feet of selling space. The stores also included a variety of fast-food and service shops, such as beauty shops, shoe repair, and dry cleaners. Thus, an atmosphere was created of one-stop shopping. But despite optimistic beginnings, the hypermarket idea proved unsuccessful; it was replaced with a scaled-down version, the SuperCenter.

For a comparison of sales and profitability of Wal-Mart with Kmart, Sears, and Penney from 1980 to 1990, see Table 19.2. Note that profitability comparisons include both operating profit as a percentage of sales, and the more valid measure of profitability, the return on equity, i.e., the return on the money invested in the enterprise. From this table we see the awesome growth of Wal-Mart in sales and profitability compared with its nearest competitors. Table 19.3 shows another operational comparison, this time in the average sales per store for Wal-Mart and Kmart. And again, the comparison shows the great growth performance of Wal-Mart.

THE FUTURE WITHOUT SAM WALTON

On March 17, 1992, President Bush awarded Sam Walton the Medal of Freedom—a capstone among his other honors, which included Man of the Year, Horatio Alger Award in 1984, and "Retailer of the Decade" in 1989. Unfortunately, Walton did not live long to enjoy this high honor; he died of cancer nine days later, on March 26, 1992, just four days short of his seventy-fifth birthday and only months after guiding Wal-Mart to becoming the world's biggest retailer.

David Glass, fifty-three years old, assumed the role of president and chief executive officer. Glass was known for his hard-driving managerial style. He had gained his retail experience at a small supermarket chain in Springfield, Missouri, and joined Wal-Mart as executive vice president for finance in 1976. He was named president and chief operating officer in 1984, while Sam Walton kept the position of chief executive officer. About the transition, Glass said:

> There's no transition to make, because the principles and basic values he (Walton) used in founding this company were so sound and so universally accepted... We'll be fine as long as we never lose our responsiveness to the customer.[1]

A new generation now was entrusted to continue the successful growth as Wal-Mart entered tougher competitive environments of U.S. metropolitan areas and then the world. By 1995, sales were $82 billion and only three *Fortune* 500 companies had higher sales: General Motors, Ford, and Exxon.

INTO THE NEW MILLENNIUM

In 2001 Wal-Mart knocked off ExxonMobil to become the biggest firm in revenues, with sales of $217.8 billion to ExxonMobil's $187.5 billion. General Motors sales were $177.3 billion, and Ford in fourth place had sales of $162.4 billion.[2] Table 19.4 shows

1. Susan Caminiti, "What Ails Retailing," *Fortune* (January 30, 1989), p. 61.
2. "Sales Super 500," *Forbes* (April 15, 2002), p. 168.

TABLE 19.2 Ten-Year Comparison of Gross Revenues, Percentage of Operating Margin, and Return on Equity for Wal-Mart and its Competitors*

Year	Wal-Mart Gross Revenue	% Operating Profit Margin	Equity Return %	Kmart Gross Revenue	% Operating Profit Margin	Equity Return %	Sears Gross Revenue	% Operating Profit Margin	Equity Return %	J.C. Penney Gross Revenue	% Operating Profit Margin	Equity Return %
1981	$2,445.0	5.6	25.6	$16,527.0	2.2	9.0	$27,357	7.2	8.2	$11,860	7.5	13.2
1982	3,376.3	7.8	25.4	17,040.0	4.3	10.1	30,020	8.8	10.1	11,414	8.3	13.3
1983	4,666.9	8.3	26.6	18,878.9	6.0	16.7	35,883	9.7	14.4	12,078	8.7	13.1
1984	6,400.9	8.5	27.5	21,095.9	6.7	15.4	38,828	10.5	14.1	13,451	7.8	11.4
1985	8,451.5	7.2	25.6	22,420.0	6.2	14.4	40,715	9.5	11.5	13,747	7.7	9.8
1986	11,909.1	7.1	26.6	23,812.1	5.7	14.5	44,282	9.1	10.4	15,151	8.6	11.0
1987	15,959.3	6.8	27.8	25,626.6	5.8	15.7	48,439	8.5	12.1	15,747	9.1	14.6
1988	20,649.0	6.4	27.8	27,301.4	6.5	16.0	50,251	9.2	3.0	15,296	8.3	20.4
1989	25,810.7	6.5	27.1	29,532.7	5.8	6.5	53,794	9.2	10.6	16,405	9.2	18.4
1990	32,601.6	6.0	24.1	32,070.0	5.4	14.0	55,971	7.4	7.0	16,365	2.4	15.6

* Gross revenue is in $ billions.

Source: Company annual reports.

Commentary: The comparison with major competitors shows Wal-Mart far exceeding its rivals in revenue growth. The operating profit percentage exceeds Kmart's for most years, but Sears and Penney look better here. However, the true measure of profitability is return on equity, and here Wal-Mart shines: It indeed is a very profitable operation, while offering consumers attractive prices.

TABLE 19.3   Average Sales per Store, Wal-Mart and Kmart, 1980–1990

	Kmart	Wal-Mart
1980	$8,015,801	$4,978,788
1981	8,042,338	4,979,633
1982	7,922,532	6,127,042
1983	8,609,722	7,269,470
1984	9,554,533	8,591,946
1985	9,448,970	9,838,184
1986	9,835,611	12,152,040
1987	11,274,527	14,325,852
1988	11,833,983	16,401,111
1989	12,508,682	18,409,415
1990	13,646,808	20,726,001

Source: Computed from Table 19.1

Commentary: The great increase in sales per store for Wal-Mart is particularly noteworthy. In 1980 Wal-Mart's average store's sales was hardly one-half that of an average Kmart. By 1990 the average Wal-Mart store was generating more than 50 percent more sales than an average Kmart.

selected statistics of Wal-Mart's operating performance at the beginning and end of the decade 1992–2002. Wal-Mart's former closest retail rivals had been left in the dust by 2002, as can be starkly seen below:

	2002 Revenues ($billion)	% Change since 2001
Sears	$ 41.1	0.3
Target	39.9	8.1
Kmart	36.9	1.1
Penney	32.0	0.5
Wal-Mart	217.8	13.8

Its nearest rival up to 1990, the one that dominated the retail environment in the early days of Wal-Mart, was Kmart. But now Kmart was operating under Chapter 11 bankruptcy, with its very survival in doubt.

As it approached the millennium, and was only a short step away from becoming the world's largest firm, Wal-Mart turned to other growth opportunities. It bought Asda Group PLC, a large British supermarket chain, thereby greatly expanding its international presence. In the United States it not only accelerated the building of discount-grocery SuperCenters but also expanded its smallish (40,000 square foot) Neighborhood Markets, designed to fill the gaps between convenience stores and Wal-Mart's big SuperCenters. Wal-Mart also bought a small savings bank in Oklahoma that could pave the way for bringing to banking its low prices for such services as check cashing, credit cards, and loans.

TABLE 19.4   Wal-Mart Selected Growth Statistics, 1993–2002

	2002	1993
Net sales (millions)	$217,799	$55,484
Net income (millions)	6,671	1,995
Number of associates	1,383,000	434,000
Number of U.S. Wal-Mart stores	1,647	1,848
Number of U.S. SuperCenters	1,066	34
Number of U.S. SAM'S CLUBS	500	256
International Units	1,170	10

Source: Wal-Mart annual reports.

Commentary: Here we see a four-fold increase in sales in these ten years. Income had only a little more than a three-fold increase, but this was still impressive. Of particular interest is the decrease in the number of U.S. Wal-Mart stores in producing these increases, but the big growth was in SuperCenters and Sam's Clubs, and the biggest of all was in international units.

Overseas expansion created the most waves. European merchants and labor unions ran scared, but consumers stood to benefit enormously: "Its low-pricing policies and customer-friendly attitude is likely to change the face of British retailing and its reputation for high prices and surly service," one scribe wrote.[3]

Threat of Wal-Mart led two rival French retailers to merge in a $16-billion-dollar deal, though the combined company would still be far smaller than Wal-Mart. The battle was perhaps fiercest in Germany, where Wal-Mart had ninety-five stores. Competitors began staying open longer and improving customer courtesy. However, regulators in Germany closely monitored whether prices were too low, while powerful trade unions worried that price wars would result in store closures and job losses.

To reduce costs, Wal-Mart began buying globally, negotiating one price for stores worldwide. In so doing, it changed the organization to combine some domestic and international operations including buying, new store planning, and marketing.[4]

INGREDIENTS OF SUCCESS

Management Style and Employee Orientation

Sam Walton cultivated a management style that emphasized individual initiative and autonomy over close supervision. He constantly reminded employees that they were vital to the success of the company, that they were essentially "running their own business," that they were "associates" or "partners" in the business, rather than simply employees.

3. Ernest Beck, "The Wal-Mart Is Coming! And Shopping for the British May Never Be the Same," *Wall Street Journal* (June 16, 1999), p. A23.

4. Emily Nelson, "Wal-Mart Revamps International Unit to Decrease Costs," *Wall Street Journal* (August 10, 1999), p. A6; David Woodruff and John Carreyrou, "French Retailers Create New Wal-Mart Rival," *Wall Street Journal* (August 31, 1999), p. A14; Ernest Beck and Emily Nelson, "As Wal-Mart Invades Europe, Rivals Rush to Match Its Formula," *Wall Street Journal* (August 6, 1999), pp. A1, A6; "European Retailers Brace for Wal-Mart," *Cleveland Plain Dealer* (August 31, 1999), pp. 1-C, 3-C.

In his employee relations philosophy, Walton borrowed from James Cash Penney, founder of the J. C. Penney Company, and his formulation of the "Penney idea" in 1913. The Penney idea also stressed the desirability of constantly improving the human factor, of rewarding associates through participation in what the business produces, and of appraising every policy and action to see whether it squares with what is right and just.

Walton emphasized bottoms-up communication, thereby providing a free flow of ideas throughout the company. For example, the "people greeter" concept (described in the Information Box: "Greeters") was implemented in 1983 as a result of a suggestion received from an employee in a store in Louisiana. This idea proved so successful that it has been adopted by Kmart, some department stores, and even shopping malls.

Another example of listening to employees' ideas came when an assistant manager in an Alabama store ordered too many marshmallow sandwiches, or Moon Pies. The store manager told him to use his imagination to sell the excess, so John Love came up with an idea to create the first World Championship Moon Pie Eating Contest. It was held in the store's parking lot and became so successful that it became a yearly event, drawing spectators not only from the community but from all over Alabama, as well as surrounding states.[5]

In 1972 Wal-Mart instituted a profit-sharing plan in which all associates share in the company's yearly profits. As one celebrated example of the benefits of such profit sharing, Shirley Cox had worked as an office cashier earning $7.10 an hour. When she retired after twenty-four years, her profit sharing amounted to $220,127.[6] In addition, associates may participate in a payroll stock purchase plan with Wal-Mart contributing part of the cost.

INFORMATION BOX

GREETERS

All customers entering Wal-Mart stores encounter a store employee assigned to welcome them, give advice on where to find things, and help with exchanges or refunds. These "greeters" thank people exiting the store, while unobtrusively observing any indications of shoplifting.

Many retailers staff exits and entrances; what makes Wal-Mart's greeters unique is their friendliness and patience. Wal-Mart has found that retirees supplementing pensions usually make the best greeters and are most appreciated by customers. As noted earlier, the greeter idea originated as a suggestion from an employee (associate); Sam Walton liked the idea, and it became a company-wide practice.

INVITATION TO DISCUSS

Do you personally like the idea of a store employee greeting you as you enter and leave an establishment? On balance, do you think the greeter idea is a plus or a minus? Explain.

5. Don Longo, "Associate Involvement Spurs Gains," *Discount Store News* (December 18, 1989), p. 83.

6. Example cited in Vance H. Trimble, *Sam Walton: The Inside Story of America's Richest Man* (New York: Dutton, 1990), p. 233.

The Sam Walton philosophy was to create a friendly, down-home, family atmosphere in his stores. He described it as a "whistle while you work philosophy," one that stressed the importance of having fun while working because you can work better if you enjoy yourself. He was concerned about losing this atmosphere: "The bigger Wal-Mart gets, the more essential it is that we think small. Because that's exactly how we have become a huge corporation—by not acting like one."[7]

Another incentive spurred employees to reduce shrinkage (that is, the loss of merchandise due to shoplifting, carelessness, and employee theft). Employees were given $200 each per year if shrinkage limits were met, and they became detectives watching shoppers and each other. In 1989, Wal-Mart's shrinkage rate was 1 percent of sales, well below the industry average.[8]

A rather simple way to make employees feel part of the operation was regular sharing of statistics about the store's performance, including profits, purchases, sales, and markdowns. Many employees thought of Wal-Mart as their own company.

Not the least of the open and people-oriented management practices was what Walton called MBWA, Management by Walking Around. Managers, from store level to headquarters, walked around the stores to stay familiar with what was going on, to talk to the associates, and to encourage associates to share their ideas and concerns. Such interactions brought a personal touch usually lacking in large firms.

Not surprisingly, unions have not fared well at Wal-Mart. Walton argued that in his "family environment," associates had better wages, benefits, and bonuses than any union could get for them. In addition, the bonuses and profit sharing were inducements far better than those a union could negotiate.

State-of-the-Art Technology

The decentralized management style led to a team approach to decision making. A huge telecommunications system permitted headquarters to easily communicate with stores. In addition, home-office management teams, using company airplanes, visited stores to assess their operations and any problems and to coordinate needed merchandise transfers among stores. A master computer tracked the company's complex distribution system.

Small-Town Invasion Strategy

Adopting a strategy similar to that used by the J. C. Penney Company more than half a century before, Wal-Mart for many years shunned big cities. Instead, the firm opened stores in smaller towns where competition consisted only of local merchants and small outlets of a few chains such as Woolworth, Gamble, and Penney.

These merchants typically offered only limited assortments of merchandise, had no Sunday or evening hours, and charged substantially higher prices than would be found in the more competitive environments of bigger cities. Larger retailers, especially discounters, had shunned such small towns as not affording enough potential to support the high sales volume needed for the low-price strategy.

7. *Ibid*, pp. 104, 105.

8. Charles Berstein, "How to Win Employee and Customer Friends," *Nation's Restaurant News* (January 30, 1989), p. F3.

But Wal-Mart found potential in abundance in these small-town markets, as customers flocked from all the surrounding towns and rural areas for the variety of goods and the prices. (In the process of captivating small-town and rural consumers, Wal-Mart wreaked havoc on the existing small-town merchants. See the Issue Box: "Impact of Wal-Mart on Small Towns" for a discussion of the sociological impact of Wal-Mart on small-town merchants.) The company honed its skills in such small towns, isolated from aggressive competitors, and then flexed its muscles and moved confidently into the big cities, whose retailers were as fearful of Wal-Mart as the thousands of small-town merchants had been.

Controlling Costs

Sam Walton was a stickler for holding down costs in order to offer customers the lowest prices. Cost control started with vendors, and Wal-Mart gained a reputation of being hard to please, of constantly pressuring suppliers to give additional price breaks and advertising money, and to provide prompt deliveries. In further efforts to buy goods at the lowest possible prices, Wal-Mart attempted to bypass middlemen and sales reps and buy all goods direct from manufacturers. In so doing, a factory presumably would save money on sales commissions of 2 to 6 percent, and was expected to pass this savings on to Wal-Mart. Understandably, this practice aroused a heated controversy from groups representing sales reps.

Wal-Mart achieved great savings with its sophisticated distribution centers and its own fleet of trucks that enabled it to buy in bulk directly from suppliers. Most

---

ISSUE BOX

IMPACT OF WAL-MART ON SMALL TOWNS

During most of its growth years, Wal-Mart pursued a policy of opening stores on the outskirts of small rural towns, usually with populations between 25,000 and 50,000. Attractive both in prices and assortment of goods, a Wal-Mart store drew customers from miles around; and it was often the biggest employer in the town, with 200–300 local employees.

But the dominating presence of Wal-Mart was a mixed blessing for many communities. Small-town merchants were devastated and unable to compete. Downtowns became decaying vestiges of what perhaps a few months previously had been prosperous centers. But consumers benefited.

Wal-Mart brought trade-offs and controversy: Was rural America better or worse off with the arrival of Wal-Mart? On balance, most experts saw the economic development brought on by Wal-Mart as more than offsetting the business destruction it caused. But few could dispute the sociological trauma.

INVITATION TO DISCUSS

What is your assessment of the desirability of Wal-Mart coming into a rural small town? How might your assessment differ depending on your particular position or status in that community?

goods were processed through one of the company's distribution centers. For example, take the distribution center in Cullman, Alabama, situated on twenty-eight acres with 1.2 million square feet. Some 1,042 employees loaded 150 outbound Wal-Mart trailers a day and unloaded 180. On a heavy day, laser scanners routed 190,000 cases of goods on an eleven-mile-long conveyor.[9]

Each warehouse used the latest in optical scanning devices, automated materials-handling equipment, bar coding, and computerized inventory. With a satellite network, messages could be quickly flashed between stores, distribution centers, and corporate headquarters in Bentonville, Arkansas. Handheld computers assisted store employees in ordering merchandise. These advanced technologies cut distribution expenses to half those of most chains.

Wal-Mart had previously been able to achieve great savings in advertising costs, compared to major competitors. While discount chains typically spent 2 to 3 percent of sales for advertising, Wal-Mart held it to less than 1 percent of sales. Some of this difference reflected low media rates in its small-town markets. But advertising costs were also kept low in larger markets by using very little local advertising, relying instead on national TV institutional commercials showing prices being slashed and Wal-Mart as a good and caring firm. See the Issue Box: "Should We Use Institutional Advertising?" for a discussion.

Wal-Mart's operating and administrative costs reflected a rigidly enforced, spartan operation. A lean headquarters organization and a minimum of staff assistants compared with most other retailers completed the cost-control philosophy and reflected the frugal thinking of Sam Walton that dated back to his early days.

"Buy American" and Environmental Programs

As foreign manufacturers increasingly took market share away from American producers—in the process, destroying some American jobs—public sentiment mounted for import restrictions to save jobs. In March 1985, Walton became concerned about what seemed to him a national problem. He ordered his buyers to find products that American manufacturers had stopped producing because they couldn't compete with foreign imports. Thus began Walton's "Buy American" program, which became a cooperative effort between retailers and domestic manufacturers to reestablish the competitive position of American-made goods in price and quality. This program showcased the power of the huge retailer. Magic Chef, 3M, Farris Fashions, and many other manufacturers joined Walton's crusade, as Wal-Mart pledged to support domestic production for items ranging from film to microwave ovens to flannel shirts and other apparel.

Wal-Mart also became a leader in challenging manufacturers to improve their products and packaging in order to protect the environment. As a result, manufacturers made great improvements in eliminating excessive packaging, converting to recyclable materials, and getting rid of toxic inks and dyes.

Other environmental activities included participation in Earth Day events, with tree plantings, information booths, and videos to show customers how to improve their environment. Wal-Mart has also been active in fund-raising for local environmental

---

9. John Huey, "America's Most Successful Merchant," *Fortune* (September 23, 1991), p. 54.

ISSUE BOX

SHOULD WE USE INSTITUTIONAL ADVERTISING?

Institutional advertising is nonproduct advertising designed to create goodwill for the firm rather than immediate and specific product sales. While the intent is laudable, the payoff is murky since it is difficult to measure goodwill and its effect on sales. With specific product advertising, of course, a retailer can determine the effectiveness of an ad by the specific sales it produces compared to previous periods when the product was not advertised. We suggest that most institutional advertising is based on faith—faith that enough people will see the ad or commercial and gain a favorable attitude toward the company, the assumption being that a favorable attitude translates into more sales.

Wal-Mart's heavy use of institutional commercials on TV was two pronged: (1) showing its employees as friendly and helpful people, not only to customers but to the community at large; and (2) showing prices enthusiastically being slashed. The objectives of presenting Wal-Mart in the most favorable light were in keeping with its Buy American campaign and environmental responsiveness efforts described in the previous section. Such institutional advertising reinforced the image of Wal-Mart as a good citizen in the tradition of Sam Walton.

INVITATION TO DISCUSS

Be a devil's advocate (one who argues a contrary position for the sake of testing a decision). Argue as persuasively as you can that, while Wal-Mart's institutional advertising helped with a positive image, this did not conclusively translate into additional sales.

and charitable groups, and in "adopt-a-highway" programs, in which store personnel volunteer at least one day every month to collect trash and clean up local highways and beaches.

THE DARKER SIDE

Despite the good-citizen image that Walton sought to cultivate, Wal-Mart has provoked controversy almost from its beginnings. As it honed its skills and resources, and moved into more and more small towns, its impact on these local communities was profound. As we have discussed in a previous box, many downtowns were devastated as local merchants could not compete with this giant newcomer opening on the outskirts of town. Still, most people thought Wal-Mart brought more good than bad to their community—although some communities voted to keep Wal-Mart out.

Today, Wal-Mart is arguably the most powerful firm in the world with its size and buying clout, and this invites allegations that it may be crossing the line of unfair competition. Suppliers have felt the power of Wal-Mart and the price and service demands that it imposes on those who wish to do business with it. For many of these suppliers, losing Wal-Mart's business is life-threatening, they have to meet its dictates, or else.

Wal-Mart led the retail industry in "partnering" with its vendors. If this were truly a two-way relationship, it would be of mutual benefit and would be an example of a symbiotic relationship in which both parties gain from the success of each other. However, Wal-Mart's partnering more often meant that vendors had to assume most of the inventory management and merchandising costs associated with their products in Wal-Mart stores; it also compelled them to guarantee fast replenishment, often saddling them with huge costs, so that the stores could maintain lean stocks. The power position of Wal-Mart made some of these demands on vendors a do-it-or-else situation: "If you can't do it, we'll find another vendor."

In 1998, Wal-Mart entered grocery retailing, and in only four years, by 2002, became the nation's largest grocer with its over $53 billion in grocery sales. Its nonunionized workforce and legendary efficiency enabled it to drive prices down in all markets it entered—good for customers, but deadly for rivals. In the decade of the 90s, twenty-nine grocery chains sought bankruptcy-court protection, with Wal-Mart the catalyst in twenty-five of these cases.[10]

In recent years, Wal-Mart found toys to be a big traffic generator, especially at the important Christmas season, and expanded its emphasis on toys until it bested Toys "R" Us to become the biggest toy retailer.

During Christmas 2003, Wal-Mart moved to increase its market share even more. It drastically reduced prices on many of the hottest toys in late September, long before the peak selling season. This essentially denied its smaller competitors a profitable Christmas season as they were forced to match these low prices or lose most of their customers. As a result, two major toy chains, famed FAO Schwarz, along with its Zany Brainy and Right Start stores, and KB Toys filed for bankruptcy protection, unable to profitably match Wal-Mart's prices. Wal-Mart could afford to sell these popular toys at a loss to generate traffic for its other merchandise. But its smaller competitors could not. Toys "R" Us, the nation's second largest toy chain behind Wal-Mart, also suffered.[11]

Despite Wal-Mart's profit sharing and bonuses, scattered allegations surfaced about dictatorial employee relations and refusal to pay earned overtime. Wal-Mart led in pruning employee health benefits by requiring a six-months wait for hourly workers to be eligible for benefits, while deductibles ranged up to $1,000, triple the norm. It refused to pay for flu shots, eye exams, child vaccinations, and numerous other treatments normally covered by other employers, nor would it pay for treatment of preexisting conditions in the first year of coverage. As a result, Wal-Mart spent 40 percent less per employee for healthcare than the national average. To Wal-Mart's credit, some saw its approach to healthcare as a positive influence at a time when healthcare costs were soaring.[12]

10. Patricia Callahan and Ann Zimmerman, "Price War in Aisle 3," *Wall Street Journal* (May 27, 2003), pp. B1, B16.

11. Lias Bannon, "An Icon's Last Christmas?" *Wall Street Journal* (December 12, 2003), pp. B1, B2.

12. Bernard Wysocki Jr. and Ann Zimmerman, "Wal-Mart Cost-Cutting Finds a Big Target in Health Benefits," *Wall Street Journal* (September 30, 2003), pp. A1, A16.

In late 2003, Wal-Mart faced serious allegations of subcontracting its daily clean-ing chores in many stores to firms that employed illegal immigrants at low wages with no overtime or benefits, and without collecting payroll taxes. The illegalities purport-edly saved the company millions. If company executives knew of such practices, they could be indicted. In a company so tightly controlled, one wonders if company exec-utives could have been oblivious.[13]

Commentary

Wal-Mart is a success story of no small moment. It has certainly been good for con-sumers and for the country, and is a symbol of one man's vision. Yet, we may raise the question: Has it gotten too big? In its quest for providing customers with the lowest prices, has it become guilty of predatory practices, of crossing the line in coercing suppliers, and using its size to deliberately drive out less efficient competitors? Have its executives been guilty of going too far in hard-nosed cost cutting?

UPDATE

Going into 2004, Wal-Mart faced increasing criticisms and lawsuits. These had been granted class-action status in Massachusetts, California, Indiana, and Minnesota, and thirty-five similar lawsuits were pending. Allegations were that Wal-Mart understaffed its stores, banned overtime, and consequently required workers to continue to work after their shifts, as well as during rest and meal breaks, without compensation. Wal-Mart denied that it required workers to work without pay.

The Los Angeles City Council was trying to prevent Wal-Mart from opening its SuperCenters in the city. Similar bans on these giant stores had been approved in the San Francisco Bay area, as well as communities from Atlanta to Albuquerque. City lead-ers feared that such stores would drive down local wages as rival businesses struggled to survive; wipe out more jobs than they created; and leave more people without health insurance, thereby putting additional burden on overtaxed public hospitals and clinics.

Wal-Mart was fighting back aggressively by taking the battle to ballot. A spokesman declared, "The reality is that this is not some huge grass-roots uprising. Most communities in the state do not believe the government should be restricting the shopping choices of their residents."[14]

WHAT CAN BE LEARNED?

Take good care of people. Sam Walton was concerned with two groups of people— his employees and his customers. By motivating and even inspiring his employees,

---

13. Dan K. Thomasson, "Underpriced and Overgrown," *Cleveland Plain Dealer* (November 15, 2003, p. B7).

14. "Wal-Mart Suit Gets Glass-Action Status in Massachusetts," *Wall Street Journal* (January 19, 2004), p. A2; and Rene Sanches, "L.A. Isn't Buying Wal-Mart's Sales Job," *Washington Post*, reported in *Cleveland Plain Dealer* (February 4, 2004), p. C2.

he found that customers also were well served. Somehow in the exigencies of business, especially big business, this emphasis on people tends to be pushed aside. Walton made caring for people common practice. But is Walton's philosophy eroding?

By listening to his employees, by involving them, by exhorting them, and by giving them a real share of the business—all the while stressing friendliness and concern for customers—Walton fostered a business climate almost unique in any large organization. In addition to providing customers with the friendliest of employees, his stores also offered honest values and great assortments and catered to the concerns of many middle-income Americans for the environment and American jobs.

Go for the strategic window of opportunity. Strategic windows of opportunity sometimes come in strange guises. They represent areas of potential business overlooked or untapped by existing firms. But in the formative and early growth years of Wal-Mart, no window could ever have seemed less promising than the one Walton unlocked and threw open to great growth. Small towns and cities in many parts of rural America were losing population and economic strength, partly because of the decline in family farms and the accompanying infrastructure of small businesses. It was therefore not surprising that the major discount chains focused their growth efforts on large metropolitan areas. Although many small cities had Penney's and Sears outlets as well as Woolworth, Gamble, and Coast to Coast stores, they were usually small stores—often old, marginal, and rather in the backstream of corporate consciousness. This retail environment was one of small stores with limited assortments of merchandise and relatively high prices.

In this environment, Sam Walton seized his opportunity. He saw something that no other merchants had: that the limited total market potential meant a dearth of competition. He also saw that the potential was far greater than the population of the small town and its immediate surroundings. Indeed, a Wal-Mart store in a rather isolated rural community could draw customers from many miles away.

Do such windows of opportunity still exist today? You bet they do—for the entrepreneur with vision, an ability to look beyond the customary, and the courage to follow up on his or her vision.

Consider the marriage of old-fashioned ideas and modern technology. Walton embraced this strategy and made it work throughout his organization, even as it grew to large size. At the forefront of retailers in the use of communication technology and computerized distribution, Walton still was able to motivate his employees to offer friendly and helpful customer services to a degree that few large retailers have consistently achieved.

Other firms can benefit from the example of Wal-Mart in cultivating homespun friendliness with awesome technology, and competitors are trying to emulate it. The particular difficulty that many are finding, however, is in achieving consistency.

Showing environmental concern can pay dividends. Today many people are concerned about the environment. It seems high time that we have such concern, while much of the environment can still be salvaged and protected. The firm that takes a leadership role for environmental protection stands to benefit in customer relations and, not the least, from positive media attention.

Another issue important to many Americans involves foreign inroads to the detriment of many U.S. manufacturers and jobs. Regardless of the great controversy over the desirability of free trade, many middle-class Americans have applauded the leadership of Wal-Mart in its widely publicized Buy American policy.

What is the moral for other businesses catering to consumers? Be alert to the increasing concerns of the public, and, where possible, act on them in a leadership role.

Can a firm be too big? We cannot answer this. But we can warn of the dangers of bigness as far as the public interest and trusting relationship are concerned. The phrase, "arrogance of power," describes the temptation of bigness. Some would even see this as a natural evolution of size. Years ago, such major firms as General Motors and Standard Oil were broken up because enough people believed they had become too big. Could Wal-Mart be approaching this as it increasingly dominates certain sectors of the retail scene? When it can tyrannize its suppliers, drive competitors in the food and toy industry into bankruptcy, bring fear to others as it searches for new areas to assert its power? When it may be in danger of losing its humanity?

CONSIDER

Can you identify additional learning insights that could be applicable to firms in other situations?

QUESTIONS

1. How might you attempt to compete with Wal-Mart if you were: (a) a small hardware merchant? (b) a small clothing store for men? (c) a supermarket? (d) a toy store?

2. Do you think Wal-Mart is vulnerable today, and if so, in what way? If you do not think it is vulnerable, do you see any limits to its growth?

3. When you shop at Wal-Mart, do you usually find the employees far superior in friendliness and knowledge to those of other retailers? If not, what are your conclusions regarding Wal-Mart's employee relations programs?

4. What weaknesses do you see Wal-Mart as having, either now or potentially? How can the company overcome them?

5. Can discounting go on forever? What are the limits to growth by price competition?

6. Discuss Wal-Mart's business practices (especially in regard to unions, invading small towns, and supplier relations) in view of their ethical ramifications for the industry and for society. Should students be encouraged to emulate these practices?

7. Do you think Wal-Mart today is a benevolent and humane firm? Why or why not? It it completely ethical?

INVITATION TO ROLE PLAY

1. *Be a Devil's Advocate* (one who argues a contrary position). The decision is being made to phase out the hypermarkets. Argue as persuasively as you can that Wal-Mart is being too hasty and that the hypermarket concept should be continued, if necessary with some changes.

2. You are an ambitious Wal-Mart store manager. Describe how you might design your career path to achieve a high executive position. Be as creative as you can.

3. You are the principal adviser to David Glass, who replaced Sam Walton as chief executive. Even though Wal-Mart has expanded aggressively overseas in recent years, Glass still thinks the greatest potential lies in foreign markets. He has charged you to develop a strategy to make greater inroads. What do you advise, and why? (Hint: You may need to do some research on Wal-Mart's overseas presence at this time, i.e., how many stores and in which countries.)

TEAM DEBATE EXERCISES

1. Debate the notion of Wal-Mart aggressively seeking to enter small communities, such as in rural New England, where many people oppose this incursion. Should Wal-Mart bow to the public pressure (which the company deems to be from a small minority of vehement agitators), or should it carry on with "right on its side"?

2. Can the great growth of Wal-Mart continue indefinitely? Debate the pros and cons of this question.

3. It Wal-Mart today in danger of losing its humanity?

INVITATION TO RESEARCH

Has Wal-Mart faltered since 2002? Are there any ominous signs on the horizon? Have the management style and employee relations changed since that described in the case? Are any stores unionized? Is the Buy American program still in effect? What has been the resolution of the subcontracting daily cleaning chores?

CHAPTER TWENTY

Nike: Is Using Cheap Overseas Labor Ethical?

On August 27, 1996, the sports world was intrigued with what was in store for Tiger Woods, the twenty-year-old golfer who had just won his third consecutive U.S. Amateur championship. He decided to begin his professional career and dropped out of Stanford in what would have been his junior year.

Tiger's pro-golf career started with a contract from Nike worth $40 million. After signing, he was flown in a Gulfstream IV owned by the founder of Nike, Phil Knight, to play in the Greater Milwaukee Open. All this for a young man who had always flown coach and had to count his meal money. He had played amateur golf for the last time. Before the year was over, he was to win two tournaments and be named by *Sports Illustrated*, "Sportsman of the Year." This was only the beginning, as next spring he won the prestigious Masters on April 13, 1997, by the biggest margin ever achieved, in the most watched golf finale in the history of television.

In 2003, Nike gave a teenage basketball player, just finishing high school, a $90 million contract, more than any other basketball player in history except Michael Jordan. Knight saw in LeBron James another Michael Jordan. Nike spent two years building a relationship with James before signing him, "We have to spend the money or we'll regret it the rest of our lives."[1]

With what some thought was a commodity product, one that "could command little" brand uniqueness, and one that many others saw as only a short-term fad phenomenon, Phil Knight had fashioned for Nike a strategy that put it in the forefront of growth firms and brought it to become one of the world's great brand names. Among the 1,200 U.S. brands tracked by Young & Rubicam, Nike ranked among the top ten, alongside Coke, Disney, and Hallmark. In the process, Knight in 1996 became one of the richest Americans, worth $5.3 billion, behind only Bill Gates of Microsoft, Warren Buffett, the investor supreme, and three others.[2]

Unfortunately, Nike became bedeviled about using so-called sweatshops in poor countries of the world to make its shoes more cheaply. Despite many other firms doing

1. Kurt Bademhauser, "Slam Dunk," *Forbes* (February 16, 2004), p. 68.
2. Randall Lane, "You Are What You Wear," *Forbes* (October 14, 1996), p. 42.

the same thing, *outsourcing*, Nike became the focal point for criticisms of all kinds. Was it truly an ogre? Was it acting unethically, as vocal critics maintained? Such critics also derided Nike's targeting ghetto youth with its expensive celebrity shoes.

PHIL KNIGHT AND THE INVENTION OF THE WAFFLE SOLE

The founder of the great Nike running machine was himself only a mediocre runner, a miler of modest accomplishments. His best time was a 4:13, hardly in the same class as the below-4:00 world-class runners. But he had trained under the renowned coach Bill Bowerman at the University of Oregon. In late 1950, Bowerman had put Eugene, Oregon, on the map by turning out world-record-setting long-distance runners year after year. Constantly experimenting with shoes, Bowerman had a theory that an ounce off a running shoe might make enough difference to win a race.

In the process of completing his MBA at Stanford University, Phil wrote a research paper based on his theory that the Japanese could do for athletic shoes what they were doing for cameras. After receiving his degree in 1960, Knight went to Japan to seek an American distributorship from the Onitsuka Company for Tiger shoes. Returning home, he took samples of the shoes to Bowerman.

In 1964, Knight and Bowerman went into business. They each put up $500 and formed the Blue Ribbon Shoe Company, sole U.S. distributor of Tiger running shoes. They put their inventory in Knight's father-in-law's basement, and sold $8,000 worth of these imported shoes that first year. Knight worked by days as a Cooper & Lybrand accountant, while nights and weekends he peddled these shoes, mostly to high school athletic teams.

Knight and Bowerman finally developed their own shoe in 1972 and decided to manufacture it themselves. They contracted the work out to Asian factories, where labor was cheap. They named the shoe Nike after the Greek goddess of victory. At that time they introduced the "swoosh" logo, a highly distinctive emblem that was subsequently placed on every Nike product. See the Information Box: "The Nike Swoosh Logo" for more details. The Nike shoe's first appearance in competition came during the 1972 Olympic trials in Eugene, Oregon. Marathon runners who had been persuaded to wear the new shoes placed fourth through seventh in the trials, whereas Adidas wearers finished first, second, and third. On a Sunday morning in 1975, Bowerman tinkered with his wife's waffle iron and some urethane rubber. He fashioned a new type of sole, a "waffle" sole whose tiny rubber studs made it springier than other shoes currently on the market. This product improvement—seemingly so simple—gave Knight and Bowerman an initial impetus, helping to bring Nike's 1976 sales to $14 million, up from $8.3 million the year before, and only $2 million in 1972.

NIKE GOES PUBLIC

Now Nike was off and running, and was to stay in the forefront of the industry with its careful research and development of new products. By the end of the decade, Nike employed almost 100 people in research and development. It offered more than

---

INFORMATION BOX

THE NIKE SWOOSH LOGO

The Nike "swoosh" is one of the world's best-recognized logos. In the very early days of Nike, a local design student at Portland State University was paid $35 for creating it. The curvy, speedy-looking blur turned out to be highly distinctive and has from then on been placed on all Nike products. Phil Knight even had the Swoosh logo tattooed on his left calf. Because it was so familiar, Nike no longer adds the name Nike to the logo. A well-known logo makes Nike's sponsorship of famous athletes unusually effective as they wear shoes and apparel displaying it in their sports exploits.

INVITATION TO DISCUSS

In your judgment, do you think Nike could have achieved its current success without this unique but simple logo? In other words, how important is a good logo to a firm?

---

140 different models, many of these the most technologically advanced on the market. Such diversity came from models designed for different foot types, body weights, running speeds, training schedules, sexes, and skill levels.

In 1980, Nike went public and Knight became an instant multimillionaire, reaching the coveted Forbes Richest 400 Americans with a net worth of just under $300 million.[3] Bowerman, who at age seventy had sold most of his Nike stock and owned only 2 percent of the company, was worth a mere $9.5 million.

By 1981, Nike led all athletic shoemakers, with 50 percent of the total market. Adidas, the decades-long market leader, saw its share of the market fall well below that of Nike. Demand for Nikes was so great that 60 percent of its 8,000 department stores, sporting goods, and shoe store retailers gave advance orders, often waiting six months for delivery.

In the January 4, 1982, edition of *Forbes* in the *Annual Report on American Industry*, Nike was rated number one in profitability over the previous five years, ahead of all other firms in all other industries.[4]

CHALLENGE FROM REEBOK

By the latter 1980s, however, Reebok had emerged as Nike's greatest competitor, and threatened its dynasty. Nike had underestimated an opportunity. Consequently, it was late with shoes for the aerobic dancing craze that was sweeping the country, fueled by best-selling books by Jane Fonda and others. Reebok was first with an athletic shoe designed especially for women. Between 1986 and 1987, Nike's sales dropped 18 percent, with profits sinking more than 40 percent. Figure 20.1 shows the sales growth of Reebok and Nike from their beginnings to 1995. Of particular note is the

---

3. "The Richest People in America—The *Forbes* Four Hundred," *Forbes* (Fall 1983), p. 104.

4. *Forbes* (January 4, 1982), p. 246.

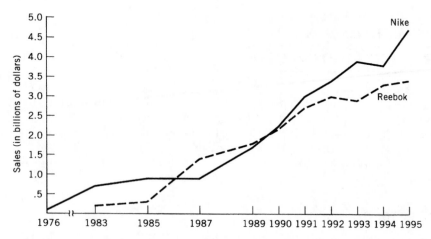

Figure 20.1   Sneaker Wars: Sales, Nike, and Reebok 1976–1995 (billions $).

Source: Company annual reports.

Commentary: Here we can graphically see the charge of Reebok in the later 1980s that for a few years surpassed Nike, but then faltered by 1990 as Nike surged ever farther ahead.

great growth of Reebok in the mid-1980s, in only a few years surpassing Nike, which had plateaued as it missed the new fitness opportunity. Then, as can be seen graphically, Reebok began slowing down, while Nike again surged. Table 20.1 shows the net income comparisons. Both firms had somewhat erratic incomes, but the early income promise of Reebok relative to Nike could not be sustained. This is confirmed with later revenue and income figures from 1995 to 1998, shown in Table 20.2.

FACTORS BEHIND NIKE'S REJUVENATION

Usually when a front runner loses momentum, reversing the trend is difficult. But Phil Knight and Nike were not ready to surrender. Knight attacked Reebok's weakness: dealer relations. Nike cultivated its customers, especially the larger dealers such as Foot Locker, while Reebok was surprisingly nonchalant and even arrogant in such dealings.

The Struggle to Win Foot Locker

In 1995, Woolworth's Foot Locker, a chain of 2,800 stores, had become the biggest seller of athletic footwear, accounting for $1.5 billion of the $6.5 billion U.S. sales. In 1993, Nike's sales in Foot Lockers were $300 million, while Reebok was slightly behind with $228 million. Two years later, Nike's Foot Locker sales had risen to $750 million, while Reebok's dropped to $122 million.[5]

Reebok was mostly to blame for this. Paul Fireman, CEO of Reebok, seemed to resent the demands of Foot Locker almost from the beginning. For example, in the

5. Joseph Pereira, "In Reebok-Nike War, Big Woolworth Chain is a Major Battlefield," *Wall Street Journal* (September 22, 1995), p. A1.

TABLE 20.1   Sneaker Wars: Net Income Comparisons, Nike and Reebok 1985–1994 (billions $)

	Nike	Reebok
1985	$10.3	$39.0
1986	59.2	132.1
1987	35.9	165.2
1988	101.7	137.0
1989	167.0	175.0
1990	243.0	176.6
1991	287.0	234.7
1992	329.2	114.8
1993	365.0	223.4
1994	298.8	254.5

Source: Company annual reports.

Commentary: Note how much more profitable Reebok was than Nike in the late 1980s. In one year, 1987, it was almost five times more profitable. But then in 1990 the tide swung strongly in Nike's favor. Note also that Nike's profitability was far steadier than Reebok's during this period.

TABLE 20.2   Nike versus Reebok Comparative Operating Statistics, 1995–1998 (millions $)

	Nike	Reebok	Nike % of Total
Revenues:			
1995	$4,761	$3,481	57.8%
1996	6,471	3,478	65.0
1997	9,187	3,644	71.6
1998	9,553	3,225	74.8
Net Income:			
1995	400	165	70.8
1996	553	139	79.9
1997	796	135	85.5
1998	400	24	82.2

Source: Calculated from company reports.

Commentary: In this comparative analysis, the further widening of the gap between Nike and Reebok is clearly evident. In revenues, Nike's market share against Reebok has grown from 57.8 percent to 74.8 percent in these four years—a truly awesome increase in market dominance. In net income, Nike's comparative performance is even more impressive, despite the poor 1998 profit performance partly due to poor economic conditions in the Asian markets. Nike's profits were down, but not nearly as much as Reebok's.

1980s when Reebok aerobic shoes faced exuberant demand, Foot Locker wanted exclusivity—that is, special styles solely for itself. It saw exclusive lines as one of its major weapons against discounters, and was getting such protection from other manufacturers. But not from Reebok, which persisted in selling its shoes to anybody, including discounters near Foot Locker stores.

In contrast, Nike had worked with Foot Locker for some years, and by 1995, had a dozen items sold only by the chain. Another aspect of Reebok's poor relationship with Foot Locker was its carelessness in getting samples on time to Foot Locker buyers. Because of the chain's size, buying decisions had to be made early in the season. Late-arriving samples, or no samples, virtually guaranteed that such new items would not be ordered in any appreciable quantity. See the Information Box: "Importance of Major Account Management" for a discussion of the importance of major customers.

Still, in 1993, Nike did not look very much a winner though it had wrested market dominance from Reebok. Share prices plummeted in February to the mid-50s. The reason? Nike's sales were up only 15 percent and earnings just 11 percent, nothing outstanding for a once-hot stock. So Wall Street began questioning: How many pairs of sneakers does the world need? (Critics had earlier assailed McDonald's under the same rationale: How many hamburgers can the world eat?)

Knight's response was that the Nike mystique could sell other kinds of goods: outdoor footwear from sandals to hiking boots; apparel lines, such as uniforms, for top-ranked college football and basketball teams—from pants and jerseys to warm-up jackets and practice gear, even golf clothing and equipment. And these same products would be eagerly sought by the general public.

INFORMATION BOX

IMPORTANCE OF MAJOR ACCOUNT MANAGEMENT

Recognizing the importance of major customers has come belatedly to some sellers, probably none more belatedly than Reebok. These very large customers often represent a major part of a firm's total sales volume, and satisfying them in an increasingly competitive environment requires special treatment. Major account management should be geared to developing long-term relationships. Service becomes critical in cementing such relations. To this end, understanding and catering to customer needs and wants is a must. If this means giving such important customers exclusivity, and making them the absolute first to see new goods and samples, this ought to be done unhesitatingly.

Such account management has resulted in changes in many organizations. Separate sales forces are often developed, such as account managers who devote all their time to one or a few major customers, while the rest of the sales force calls on smaller customers in the normal fashion. For a customer the size of Foot Locker, senior executives, even firm presidents, need to become part of the relationship.

INVITATION TO DISCUSS

Given that you think the demands of a major retailer are completely unreasonable, what would you do if you were the CEO of a major manufacturer?

In his quest to remain the dominant player, Knight recalled what he learned from his old coach and Nike cofounder, Bill Bowerman: "Play by the rules, but be ferocious."[6]

Creating an Image

Knight came to realize that shoes were becoming a disposable consumer good, almost a commodity, with little difference in quality or style among shoemakers. The challenge for success would come from transforming shoes into status symbols, with frequent model changes. Then if you could combine a fashion image, of being "in" or being "cool," with an aura of entertainment, this ought to powerfully appeal to impressionable consumers, especially those under thirty. So Knight reasoned.

Nike began introducing new models for every season: baseball shoes in the spring, tennis shoes in the summer, hiking shoes in the fall. Basketball and running shoes were revamped quarterly. Nike averaged more than one new shoe style every day.

The tie-in with entertainment combined with sports heroes suggested a new advertising theme—promoting shoes for what they represented. Knight saw people rooting for a favorite team or courageous athletic, and so Nike would sell not shoes but the athletic ideals of determination, individuality, self-sacrifice, and winning.[7]

Nike had always sponsored athletes, but now it increased that budget to $100 million a year for athletes to use and pitch Nike products. Nike started this in 1973, when it paid star runner Steve Prefontaine to wear Nike shoes—he was brilliant, fiercely competitive, a nonconformist, and the model athlete persona Knight was seeking. Unfortunately, Prefontaine died in a car crash in 1975. Eventually, Michael Jordan took his place in Nike promotions, and the Chicago Bulls star became recognized as the best basketball player in history and perhaps the most popular athlete in the country.

As Nike sought to rejuvenate itself, Knight recruited other top athletes: John McEnroe and Andre Agassi in tennis; Nolan Ryan in baseball; Deion Sanders in football; Carl Lewis and Alberto Salazar in track; football/baseball star Bo Jackson; as well as such basketball players as Charles Barkley and Scottie Pippen. Later, it added Tiger Woods, LeBron James, and Serena Williams, the dominant women's tennis star. Nike headquarters in Beaverton, Oregon, became a shrine to athletes, with hundreds of bronze plaques and giant banners.

The use of athletes from different sports enabled Nike to segment the market, all under the umbrella of a single brand. The average American teenager bought ten pairs of athletic shoes a year, six for specific sports, four for fashion, resulting in 6 million teenagers buying more than $1 billion worth of Nike shoes.[8]

"You don't win silver, you lose gold," was the theme of Nike TV spots and billboards throughout Atlanta during the summer Olympics in 1996. Rather than being a sponsor firm and paying up to $40 million to the Olympic committee, Nike furthered its visibility with hundreds of individual athletes and teams wearing the swoosh on their uniforms and shoes.

6. Fleming Meeks, "Be Ferocious," *Forbes* (August 2, 1993), p. 41.

7. "You Are What You Wear," p. 44.

8. *Ibid.*, p. 45.

Knight aimed the company in three new directions as he sought to make Nike a $12 billion company by the end of the century (it was $6.5 billion in fiscal year ending May 31, 1996). These were women's sports, foreign markets, and Nike Town stores.

Dozens of top women athletes were signed up and heavily promoted. In non-conformist advertising, little girls were depicted imploring their parents to give them a ball instead of a doll.

While Nike had tried to crack international markets, results were far below what might be reasonably expected. For example, in the United States the average consumer spent $12 a year on Nike products; in Germany, only $2. To improve this imbalance, Nike began signing up the best athletes in each country—baseball player Hideo Nomo in Japan, the Boca Juniors soccer team in Argentina, and Germany's Formula 1 race car champion, Michael Schumacher.

In 1993, Nike opened a Nike Town superstore in Chicago. It soon ranked with the Navy pier and the Lincoln Park Zoo as one of the city's top tourist attractions. The seventh Nike Town, a 90,000-square-foot store, opened on 57th Street in New York in November 1996. The landlord was Donald Trump, and rent was about $10 million a year.[9]

These huge sports stores featured the broad range of Nike products, as Nike expanded into in-line skates, swimwear, hockey equipment, even sports sunglasses. They also offered sports apparel for toddlers. Of course, hundreds of different shoes. Each sport had its own room in the stores. Nike Town's invited hands-on experiencing, such as basketball courts allowing customers to tryout various shoes. There were also sports shrines with odes to Nike athletes and displays of their autographed goods. Multiscreen TVs gave a subtle (or perhaps not so subtle) commercial touch. Some customers bought three and four pairs of shoes, as well as other paraphernalia, at a single visit.

CHARGES OF UNETHICAL PRACTICES

In the summer of 1996, critical publicity surfaced about U.S. manufacturers operating sweatshops in poor countries of the world, particularly in Asia. Indeed, most Nike footwear was produced primarily in Asia by independent subcontractors working according to Nike specifications.

In the onslaught of criticisms, even Kathie Lee Gifford was compelled to confess tearfully on her television show that she didn't know that her line of clothes sold by Wal-Mart was made by Honduran girls paid 31 cents an hour. Hundreds of multinational firms in almost every industry had outsourced in recent years in order to reduce manufacturing costs, but footwear and apparel makers faced the strongest criticisms. Nike became the target of Made in the U.S.A. Foundation, an organization funded in part by organized labor with the goal of bringing jobs back home. After failing to get a Gifford-like reaction from Michael Jordan, the premier Nike symbol, Made in the U.S.A. shifted attention to Phil Knight.

Negative publicity was fueled by prominent exposes of Asian child labor in magazines, then by the "Foul Ball" campaign of Labor Secretary Robert Reich, who led an effort to ban soccer balls, including Nike's, stitched by boys and girls in Pakistan. Several members of Congress as well sought to ban imports of all goods made with

9. *Ibid.*, p. 46.

child labor. Even the enormously popular Jordan was criticized for his professing igno-rance of the matter by *New York Times* columnist Ira Berkow.[10] On the night of October 17, 1996, Dan Rather and *48 Hours* criticized Nike on primetime network TV.

Criticisms of Nike continued into 1997. Activists charged that not only were fac-tory workers in Vietnam paid low wages, but that some were even limited to one trip to the bathroom and two drinks of water per shift, as well as being subjected to ver-bal abuse, sexual harassment, and corporal punishment, such as being forced to stand for long periods in the hot sun. A Nike company executive promised to work to improve working conditions overseas: "Bring us information we can use, and we'll do our damnedest to correct any situations that are wrong."[11]

In early April 1997 another episode denigrated Nike's image. Thirty-nine mem-bers of the Heaven's Gate cult committed suicide in a California mansion. All were wearing new black Nike's, with the swoosh logo readily visible on TV and pictures in the print media. The "Just Do It" slogan of Nike was trumpeted as being entirely apt, and some even spoofed that Nike's slogan should be changed to "Just Did It."

Consequences

At first, the criticisms seemed to have little impact on sales, with most customers not upset by working conditions in the Far East. The association of Nike with the sordid cult suicides, while misplaced brand loyalty, attested to the pervasiveness of the logo and the slogan.

Early in April 1997, a presidential task force reached an agreement to banish cloth-ing sweatshops worldwide. The eight-month-old White House task force was composed of labor unions, human-rights groups, and such apparel and footwear firms as Nike, Reebok, and Liz Claiborne, with other U.S. companies urged to join the crusade.[12]

The greatest boost to Nike's image seemed to be young Tiger Woods. His winning of the Masters Tournament before a vast worldwide TV audience and, in the process, breaking or tying nine records including those of being the youngest winner and the first minority to win this most prestigious of all golf tournaments, all while wearing the conspicuous swoosh, focused favorable attention on Nike as perhaps not even Michael Jordan had been able to do. The day after the Masters, ABC News reported that Nike's sales of golf clothing had risen 100 percent since the signing of Tiger.

Storm Clouds Won't Go Away

The troubles besetting Nike did not go away, however. In addition to continuing bad press about labor conditions in Asia, other environmental factors tormented Nike. Demand in Asia was drastically reduced due to a deep recession there. Estimates were that in Japan alone, two million pairs of Nikes went unsold because of the country's economic prob-lems.[13] Forecasts for how long this malaise would last ranged from months to years.

10. Mark O'Keefe and Jeff Manning, "Firms Find Ways to Share the Guilt," *Cleveland Plain Dealer* (July 28, 1996), pp. 1-I, and 3-I.

11. "Nike Workers in Vietnam Suffer Abuse, Group Says," *Wall Street Journal* (March 28, 1997), B15.

12. Wendy Bounds and Hilary Stout, "Sweatshop Pact: Good Fit or Threadbare?" *Wall Street Journal* (April 10, 1997), p. A2.

13. Bill Saporito, "Can Nike Get Unstuck?" (March 30, 1998), p. 49.

Another troubling portent was the public's growing disenchantment with athletes. The first inkling came in the fall of 1998, when the great home-run heroes, Mark McGwire and Sammy Sosa, found their exploits were not generating much endorsement money. Reports now surfaced that firms had become skeptical about the cost/effectiveness of most athletes in promoting products: were they worth it? Fan interest in pro sports seemed to be dropping, perhaps reflecting a growing tide of resentment at overpaid athletes proving to be selfish, arrogant, and decadent—these the very role models that Nike had spent millions to enlist. Indicative of the "public be damned" attitude of owners and players was the labor strife in the fall and winter of 1998 between the NBA and their multimillionaire players that led to weeks of game cancellations.

Nike slashed its endorsement budget by close to $100 million. Even Tiger Woods was not doing it for Nike. His product line of shoes and apparel introduced in early 1998 met with lukewarm response at best, perhaps because these products were overpriced.

Several other environmental changes bedeviled Nike now. Sporting-goods retailer consolidations closed hundreds of stores and lessened the number of outlets for Nike. The sneaker business was diversifying beyond simply running, basketball, and aerobics shoes into what some called a brown-shoe phenomenon, as demand extended to outdoor brands such as Timberland.

In addition to Timberland, Nike faced increased competition in its basic core business. Adidas, the market leader in Europe that Nike had vanquished from the U.S. market several decades earlier was resurging, with sales increasing 92 percent in North America in one quarter of 1998. Reebok and New Balance were also aggressively pursuing the athletic shoe market. Furthermore, fashion brands, such as Tommy Hilfiger, intruded into the sneaker market.

Another disturbing possibility was emerging. Had Nike grown too big? Was its swoosh logo too pervasive, to the point that it turned some people off? Was even its tag line, "Just Do It," becoming counterproductive?

Concerned about such questions, Nike began reassessing. It sought to act smaller by developing categories such as golf, soccer, and women's as separate business units. A new advertising campaign had the softer tag line, "I Can." Nike even began toning down its use of the swoosh, removing it from corporate letterheads and most advertising, and substituting a lowercase "nike."

Still, Nike could not escape the vicious comparisons of some critics regarding the rich-man, poor-man image of Knight's wealth—$3.5 billion—and the millions paid Michael Jordan for his endorsements, set against an overseas factory worker's earnings.

Performance results for the fiscal year ending May 31, 1998, showed net income decreasing for the first time in four years, dropping 49.8 percent. This was the lowest net income since 1995. Refer back to Table 20.2.

Things improved with the new millennium. The critics' outcries had become muted, as more and more firms, and even such firms as banks and hospitals, joined the wave of outsourcing. The economies in Asia were improving, and the public's disenchantment with athletes was also waning, despite well-publicized episodes of individual misdeeds. Table 20.3 shows operating comparisons for Nike and Reebok from 1999 through 2002. Nike's dominance continued to increase both in revenues and especially in income, although it did not meet Knight's goal of $12 billion in revenue by 2000; it only made about $9.5 billion.

TABLE 20.3   **Nike versus Reebok Comparative Operating Statistics, 1999–2001 (millions $)**

	Nike	Reebok	Nike % of Total
Revenues:			
1999	$8,9951	$2,872	75.8%
2000	9,449	2,865	76.7
2001	9,893	2,993	76.8
Net Income:			
1999	579	11	98.1
2000	590	81	87.9
2001	663	103	86.6

Source: Calculated from company reports.

Commentary: In this latest comparative analysis, Nike dominance has grown well beyond that during 1995–1988 (see Table 20.2). In revenues, Nike's market share against Reebok averaged 76.4 percent in those three years, while Nike has over 90 percent of the combined profitability of the two firms.

ANALYSIS

Going back to its beginnings, undoubtedly Nike faced an extraordinarily favorable primary demand in the 1970s. But Nike's success went far beyond simply coasting with the new running movement. Nike outstripped all its competitors, including the heretofore-dominant Adidas. Nike was able to overcome whatever mystique such foreign producers as Adidas, Puma, and Tiger had had. And this at a time when foreign brands—for all kinds of goods—had an aura of being better, in fashion, quality, and dependability, than American brands.

Nike, as it began to reach for its potential, offered an even broader product line than Adidas, the pioneer of the strategy of having many shoe styles. A broad product line can have its problems: It can be overdone and hurt efficiency, create consumer confusion, and greatly add to costs. Most firms are better advised to pare their product lines, to prune their weak products so that adequate attention and resources can be directed to the winners. Here we see the disavowal of such a policy.

Although Nike violated product-mix concepts, we should recognize what it accomplished. By offering a great variety of styles, prices, and uses, Nike was able to appeal to all kinds of runners. It was able to convey the image of the most complete running-shoe manufacturer of all. In a rapidly evolving industry in which millions of people of all kinds and abilities were taking up the sport, such an image became very attractive.

Furthermore, in a rapidly expanding market, Nike found that it could tap the widest possible distribution with its breadth of products. It could sell to conventional retailers, such as department stores and shoe stores, and it could continue to do business with the specialized running-shoe stores. It could even offer some models to discounters since there were certainly enough styles to go around—different models for different types of retail outlets, and everyone could be happy.

Short production runs and many styles generally add to production costs, but in Nike's case this was less a factor. With most of the production contracted out, short production runs were less an economic deterrent.

Early on Nike placed heavy emphasis on research and technological improvement. It sought ever more flexible and lighter-weight running shoes that would be protective but also would give the athlete—world-class or slowest amateur—the utmost advantage. Many R&D employees had degrees in biomechanics, exercise physiology, engineering, industrial design, chemistry, and related fields. Nike also engaged research committees and advisory boards, including coaches, athletes, trainers, equipment managers, podiatrists, and orthopedists to review designs, materials, and concepts for improved athletic shoes. Activities included high-speed photographic analyses of the human body in motion; using athletes on treadmills, wear testing, and continual study of new and modified shoes and materials. Even back in 1981, the budget was about $4 million, a major commitment to research and development for such an apparently simple thing as a shoe.

Nike at first attempted no major deviation from the accepted strategy norm of the industry that had been established several decades earlier by Adidas. It involved testing and development of better running shoes, a broad product line to appeal to all segments of the market, a readily identifiable trademark or logo prominently displayed on all products, and the use of well-known athletes at prestigious athletic events to show off the products in use. Even outsourcing production to low-cost foreign factories was not unique to Nike. But Nike used these proven techniques far better than its competitors.

This was particularly true in developing its public image. The great identification of Nike with athleticism, "Just Do It," and its association with the greatest names in sports, maximized the appeal of Nike products especially with younger customers. Diversifying to non-shoe products, while still staying in the athletic realm, opened great growth possibilities and permitted an effective transference of image.

THE ETHICS CONTROVERSY OF USING FOREIGN CHILD LABOR

Was Nike—and other U. S. manufacturers as well—guilty of violating accepted moral standards in outsourcing production to foreign subcontractors often using child labor? Critics maintained this violated corporate ethics in exploiting underpaid workers to maximize profits back home. But while long hours in a smelly shoe or garment factory might be less than idyllic, defenders saw it as preferable to subsistence farming and laboring in even harsher conditions.

Knight believed that Nike was a force for positive change in Asia: "…good corporations are the ones that lead these countries out of poverty. When we started in Japan, factory labor there was making $4 a day, which is basically what is being paid in Indonesia and being so strongly criticized today. Nobody today is saying, 'The poor old Japanese.' We watched it happen all over again in Taiwan and Korea, and now it's going on in Southeast Asia."[14]

Many of the 120,000 Indonesian workers who produce Nike shoes come from impoverished rural backgrounds. These factories provide a chance not only to earn but also to save money and to send the extra cash back to families. The workers are daughters of rural farmers, village schoolteachers, and shop clerks. They live together in factory towns, a dozen to a dormitory room, sleeping on bunk beds. Would they be better

---

14. "Nike's Indonesian Operations Facing Scrutiny and Criticism," *Cleveland Plain Dealer* (August 27, 1996), p. 10-C.

off without these jobs? Would some of them be homeless or have to turn to prostitution otherwise? Indeed, should we try to impose our value system on other societies?

WHAT CAN BE LEARNED?

The right image can bring great psychological product differentiation. Granted that technological differences in running shoes had narrowed with little tangible advantages among brands, what made Nike stand out? It was the image and the "swoosh" that identified the brand: a psychological uniqueness, with the brand very visible. For many youth, the sight of famous and admired athletes actively using this brand brought the desire to emulate them even if only in using the same brand... and maybe to dream a little. This is known as reference group influence, and is described in the following Information Box.

Nike fostered this image of celebrity users more than any other firm. With its financial resources it could afford the enormous sponsorships demanded by the best of these celebrities. For many people—especially youth—the popularity of the brand became a further attraction. Wearing Nike products was seen as being "cool", belonging to the "in" crowd. How long is this attraction to athletes and athletics likely to last? To the end of time? Or will the ever-increasing huge compensations demanded by professional athletes and the selfishness and arrogance of some eventually sour the general public?

INFORMATION BOX

REFERENCE GROUP INFLUENCE

Reference groups are those individuals and groups with whom an individual identifies. These become a standard or point of reference for forming one's lifestyle and aspirations. Such groups can be ones that a person does belong to, but they can also be ones that a person would like to belong to but does not. Regardless of whether membership or aspirational, these groups influence product and brand purchases, and even store patronage, under certain circumstances. Nike, by sponsoring famous athletes provided a potent reference group for many of its youthful customers. With their peers also wearing Nike products, the buying influence was doubly strong.

Two things are necessary for a product or brand to be susceptible to reference group influence. First, the product must be visible so that other people can see it being worn or used. Second, the product must be conspicuous—that is, it must stand out and not be so common that practically everybody has it. Of course, the Nike logo provided both visibility and conspicuousness, and the identification with athletes was unmistakable.

INVITATION TO DISCUSS

Would you expect a car to be susceptible to reference group influence? A brand of beer? A TV set? Why or why not?

Is Nike's success in building its image transferable to other firms whose products cannot be identified with use by the famous? Do such firms have any possibilities for developing image-enhancing qualities for their brands? They certainly do.

Nike's use of reference group influence represents one way to use image to great advantage. But there are other approaches for image building that can be very effective. Consider the long-advertised lonesome Maytag repairman. Maytag has been highly successful in building a reputation, an image, for dependability and assured quality. In so doing it has been able to sustain a price advantage over its competitors. For many firms, a carefully nurtured image of good quality, dependability, reliable service, being in the forefront of technology or fashion can bring a firm great success in its particular industry.

No one is immune from mistakes: success does not guarantee continued success. Many executives delude themselves into thinking success begets continued success. It is not so! No firm, market leader or otherwise, can afford to rest on its laurels, to disregard a changing environment and aggressive but smaller competitors. In the mid-1970s, Adidas had as commanding a lead in its industry as IBM once had in computers. But it was overtaken and surpassed by Nike, a rank newcomer, and a domestic firm with few resources in an era when foreign brands (of beer, watches, cars, electronics, and cameras for examples) had a mystique and attraction for affluent Americans that few domestic brands could achieve. But Adidas let down its guard at a critical point. A decade later, Nike then lagged before an aggressive Reebok because it underestimated the growing interest in aerobic dancing.

Growth can be maintained in a saturated industry. Apparently Nike has been able to do this, to continue and even increase its growth trend, while facing the reality of how many running shoes can a market absorb year after year and still be a growth industry. Nike has done this by expanding its horizons from running shoes to all kinds of athletic and outdoor footwear, to athletic apparel and uniforms, to women's and children's wear. A greater penetration of international markets offers opportunity, as well as the Nike Town superstores.

This is a unique growth plan for Nike; it would not work for every firm. On one hand, the key element, however, is that diversification into related areas complementing the already strong image of a firm have a higher probability of successful growth. On the other hand, diversification that has little relationship to the strengths and image of the firm is far more questionable. In Nike's case, the diversifications came internally.

Beware of blemishes on the public image; not all are serious, but some may truly be. The criticisms surfacing in the summer of 1996 about the labor practices in Third-World factories at first seemed to have little impact on Nike's fortunes or its image. Partly, this was due to Nike being only one of many firms subcontracting production to foreign factories. It also reflected that the typical Nike customer was hardly concerned with underpaid foreign workers who probably would be worse off without Nike's business, and was more interested in getting the best value for his or her money.

However, as the criticisms continued into 1998 a backlash against Nike began developing. Nike even felt it desirable to put a few of the negative letters it had received on the cover of its 1998 annual report. One of them vowed, "No more Nike for me!" Another said, "Your actions so disgust me that I will never buy one of your products again. I hope my attitude proved to be universal." The Associated Press reported a soccer coach at St. John's, who quit rather than wear the swoosh as part of an endorsement deal with Nike, "I don't want to be a billboard for a company that would do these things."[15]

Don't underestimate the importance of catering to major customers. A firm should seek to satisfy all its customers; but it is especially important to satisfy the needs and wants of the larger ones. In few cases is the stark contrast between effective and ineffective dealings with larger customers more obvious than between Nike and Reebok in their relations with the huge Foot Locker retail chain. Even though a manufacturer may resent the demands made by a powerful retailer, the alternatives are either to meet these demands or to lose part or all of the business to someone else. A better course of action is to work closely with the large customer in a spirit of cooperation and mutual interest, not in an adversarial power struggle.

There is a point of diminishing returns with celebrity endorsements. Athlete celebrities demand big bucks. Are their endorsements worth the price? Perhaps only in moderation, and only with the best of the best. But one cannot predict with certainty the future exploits of any athlete, even someone as talented as a Tiger Woods or LeBron James. There is the always-present risk that the athlete celebrity in contact sports may have a career-ending injury, or be guilty of some nefarious activity that destroys his or her image. Or fade into mediocrity. Although some would criticize Nike for the huge sums it offers some athletes in a bidding war with its competitors, the right role models can have a big payoff. And the great size of Nike compared to its competitors gives it a powerful advantage in any bidding war.

CONSIDER

Can you think of any other insights coming from this case that have transferability to other firms and other situations?

QUESTIONS

1. "The success of Nike was strictly fortuitous and had little to do with great decision making." Evaluate this statement.

2. In the case we offered the possibility that Nike may be becoming too big in its industry, that there are too many "swooshes" to be seen; that its slogan, "Just Do It" may have been advertised too much, that even the name Nike is everywhere you look. Can a firm become too dominant in its industry?

3. "Nike's major problem is that it's too much of a profit monger. It charges obscene prices for shoes and clothing that cost it very little. Unless Knight

15. William McCall, "Nike Fights Bad Press to Regain Old Image," reported in *Cleveland Plain Dealer* (October 11, 1998), p. 1-H.

changes his mindset and offers more modest prices, the glory days of Nike are over." Evaluate this statement.

4. "A great image is very transitory. It can go anytime." Evaluate this statement.

5. Do you think Nike can continue to be a growth stock, or has it become a more conservative holding? Give your opinion and rationale.

6. Can celebrity advertising be overdone? How would you attempt to ascertain whether you are getting your money's worth from paying some athlete millions to wear your products?

7. Should Nike be concerned that some ghetto youths have such an attachment to the Nike image that they will strong arm and even kill to get an Air Jordan shoe, for example? If so, can Nike combat this overzealousness?

8. Do you think the United States is wrong to try to impose its values on Third World societies?

HANDS-ON EXERCISES

1. Phil Knight has charged you with developing a plan to more fully tap the female market for shoes and athletic equipment. Be as specific as you can in your recommendations and defend them as well as you can.

2. The public criticism of Nike's subcontracting most of its production to Asian factories has reached a point where Nike must do something to try to counteract the bad publicity. What would you advise Knight to do about this public image problem? Consider the consequences of your recommendations.

TEAM DEBATE EXERCISES

1. "Nike is unethical and corrupt in its tempting ghetto youth with its high-priced celebrity shoes that they can ill afford to buy and may have to resort to criminal activities to satisfy their cravings." Debate this issue.

2. Debate the issue of endorsements of athletes. How much is too much? Where do we draw the line? Should we go only for the few famous? Or should we gamble on lesser stars eventually making it big and offer them long-term contracts? Argue the two sides of the issue: aggressive and conservative.

3. Debate the contentious issue of Nike's use of overseas sweatshop labor in its production.

INVITATION TO RESEARCH

Has the sweatshop issue died out, or has it become stronger and more compelling? Are the Nike Town superstores achieving the success expected? How has golf clothing and equipment fared?

CHAPTER TWENTY-ONE

DaimlerChrysler: Flagrant Misrepresentation of a Merger

*I*t was supposed to be so right, almost a merger made in heaven, some said at the beginning. Chrysler was the smallest but since 1994 the most efficient U.S. auto producer, with the highest profit margin. Now its productivity and innovative strength would be blended with the prestige of Daimler's legendary Mercedes-Benz. Furthermore, Chrysler during one of its periodic crises had sold off its international operations to help raise needed money, and this merger would increase international exposure in a big way and mate it with a rich partner. The instigator, Jürgen Schrempp of Daimler, was lauded for his intentions of building a new car company that would have global economies of scale.

Of course, there were two cultures involved, German and American. But in the executive offices, decision making would be shared, with Chrysler's CEO, Robert Eaton, being a co-chairman with Schrempp.

The expectations of Chrysler management of equality with its prestigious merger partner were soon dashed. Schrempp, as it turned out, never intended equality. He had flagrantly misrepresented the merger package, and quickly got rid of Chrysler top management. Was this deception unacceptable ethical conduct, or was it rather a hard-nosed negotiating ploy that Chrysler management should have recognized?

In any case, in November 1998, this merger of "equals" was finalized. And the s___ hit the fan.

CHRYSLER BEFORE THE MERGER

During the previous several decades, Chrysler had had a checkered history.

Some said Lee Iacocca performed a miracle at Chrysler. He became president of an almost-moribund firm in November 1978. It was so bad he turned to Washington to bail out the company, and obtained federal loan guarantees of $1.5 billion to help it survive. By 1983, Iacocca had brought Chrysler to profitability, and then to a strong performance for the next four years. He paid back the entire loan seven years before

285

it was due. Like a phoenix, the reeling number-three automaker had been given new life and respectability. Some said Iacocca should be president of the United States, that his talents were needed in the biggest job of all.

Iacocca turned to other interests in the latter half of the decade, and by 1988, the company was hurting again. To a large extent the new problems reflected capital deprivation: sufficient money had not been invested in new car and truck designs. This lack of funds was the result of a 1987 acquisition of American Motors Corporation (AMC). The crown jewel of this buyout was the Jeep line of sport-utility vehicles that appealed to younger, more affluent buyers than the older, lower-income customers of Chrysler. Still, Chrysler found itself saddled with the substantial inefficiencies that had bedeviled AMC.

An aging Iacocca again turned his full attention back to the car business, now seven years after retiring his company's horrendous bank debt. He staked company resources on four high-visibility cars and trucks: a minivan, the Jeep Grand Cherokee, LH sedans, and a full-size pickup. Fearful that the company might not survive until the new models came out, especially if a recession were to occur before then, Iacocca instituted a far-reaching austerity program, which cut $3 billion from the company's $26 billion annual operating costs.

By 1992, the company was riding high. Iacocca retired on December 31, 1992, with a job well done. As he said on TV, "When it's your last turn at bat, it sure is nice to hit a home run."[1] Robert Eaton, formerly with GM of Europe, replaced Iacocca as Chrysler chairman.

As it moved to the millennium, Chrysler prospered because of a combination of innovative designs, segment-leading products, and rising sales throughout the auto industry. See Table 21.1 for the sales and net profit statistics of these golden years for Chrysler relative to its two U.S. competitors, General Motors and Ford.

AFTER THE MERGER

Seldom has a merger turned out worse, and so quickly. Perhaps because of morale problems and too much attention given to smoothing relations between Detroit and Stuttgart, the bottom line of Chrysler was wracked. Or maybe the problems at Chrysler had been latent, below the surface, and only needed the disruption of a massive takeover to emerge. Or could the problems have been triggered by an unwise dictatorship by the company's German master?

On November 16, 1998, Daimler-Benz issued an additional $36 billion of its stock to buy Chrysler. This when added to the $48 billion value of its existing stock brought total market value of DaimlerChrysler to $84 billion. Early in December 2000, barely two years later, a collapsing DaimlerChrysler stock had a market value of only $39 billion, less than Daimler alone was worth before the deal.

Chrysler was bleeding money. During the second half of 2000, Chrysler lost $1.8 billion and went through $5 billion in cash, this at a time when GM and Ford were still doing well.

---

1. Alex Taylor III, "U.S. Cars Come Back," *Fortune* (November 16, 1992), p. 85.

TABLE 21.1 **Sales and Profit Comparisons, Big Three U.S. Automakers, 1993–1998 (millions of dollars)**

	1993	1994	1995	1996	1997	1998
Ford						
Sales	108,521	128.439	137,137	146,991	153,637	144,416
Net Profit	2,529	5,308	4,139	4,371	6,920	6,579
	2.3%	4.1%	3.0%	3.0%	4.5%	4.5%
GM						
Sales	138,220	154,951	168,829	164,069	173,168	161,315
Net Profit	2,466	5,659	6,933	4,668	5,972	3,662
	1.8%	3.7%	4.1%	2.8%	3.4%	2.3%
Chrysler						
Sales	43,600	52,235	53,195	61,397	61,147	NA
Net Profit	(2,551)	3,713	2,025	3,529	2,805	NA
	(5.9)%	7.1%	3.8%	5.7%	4.6%	

Sources: Company public records. NA=Not applicable because of merger with Daimler.

Commentary: After a poor year in 1993—a $2.5 billion loss—Chrysler really bounced back, making a profit of $3.7 billion, which was over 7 percent of sales, far above that of its two major competitors. Chrysler continued the strong showing with multibillion-dollar profits from 1994 on. In 1995, its 3.8 percent profit was well above Ford, but slightly less than GM; in 1996 and 1997 its profit margin again was the best. While we do not have specific figures in 1998, we know that this was also a good year. The collapse came in 1999.

Note: These are total company sales, the bulk of which are autos/trucks. But with nonvehicle diversifications, the sales will be somewhat overstated for autos/trucks.

By 2000, Eaton was long gone, along with nine other top Chrysler executives, including the renowned designer, Thomas Gale. Then in November 2000, Eaton's successor, James Holden, a Canadian, the last high-level non-German remaining, was also given the ax. His replacement was Daimler executive Dieter Zetsche, forty-seven, a tall German with a walrus mustache. Zetsche brought with him Wolfgang Bernhard, thirty-nine, an intense young man, an engineer with an MBA from Columbia who was a stickler for cost-cutting, as chief operating officer. It could have been worse: Zetsche could have brought a big team from Germany instead of only one other man. Still, indignation surfaced at this putting German executives in top positions at this old American firm—a firm that had played an important part in defeating the Germans in World War II.

Eaton and the rest of the Chrysler hierarchy had found to their dismay that this was not a merger of equals, despite Chairman Schrempp's 1998 statements to the contrary not only to Chrysler top management but also to the SEC (Securities and Exchange Commission), and the inclusion of the Chrysler name in the corporation name. In reality, Chrysler had become only a division of Daimler. In interviews with the media, Schrempp admitted that such subjugation of Chrysler had always been his intention, this a duplicity of no small moment.[2]

2. For example, "A Deal for the History Books: The Auto Takeover May Be Remembered for All of the Wrong Reasons," *Newsweek* (December 11, 2000), p. 57.

Later we will analyze why the merger so quickly proved a disaster, at least in the short and intermediate term. In the longer term, maybe: maybe not.

Jürgen Schrempp

DaimlerChrysler Chairman, Jürgen Schrempp, a trim fifty-six, had an untarnished reputation going into the Chrysler merger. He began his career with Mercedes as an apprentice mechanic nearly forty years before, and had moved steadily upward. Now he acknowledged that he faced "outstanding" challenges with Chrysler. But he pointed out, "Five years ago in 1995, Daimler-Benz posted a loss of six billion marks [$3 billion]. We turned it around in a matter of two years. I think we have the experience and know-how to attend to matters, and if necessary we'll do that at Chrysler … Our aim is to be the No. 1 motor company in the world."[3]

Still, there were those who thought he destroyed Chrysler, that "he didn't realize it was the people who counted, not the factories, which were old, or the sales and profits, which could come and go."[4] So, Schrempp either forced or encouraged key people to leave, and some would say these departures were of the heart and soul of Chrysler. His duplicity in misleading top Chrysler management and shareholders that this was to be a merger of equals could hardly be viewed as anything but ambitious conniving.

During the merger finalization, it was predicted that Chrysler would earn more than $5 billion in 2000, this being what it earned in 1998. In late 1999, however, Chrysler President James Holden reduced this prediction to only $2.5 billion because of having to spend billions retooling for new model introductions at a time when an economic slowdown seemed to be looming.

The reduced profit expectation coming so soon after the merger was unacceptable to Schrempp, and he pressured Chrysler to pump up earnings for the first half of the year by building 75,000 more cars and trucks than could readily be sold, with these quickly shipped to dealers. (The accepted accounting practice was to consider a car as revenue to Chrysler when it reached a dealer's lot, not when it was sold by the dealer.) As a result, Chrysler was just short of its $2.5 billion target in the first half of 2000.

Not surprisingly, the inventory buildup resulted in showrooms overflowing with old model minivans, just as new models began arriving in August. With car sales in general now slowing because of the economy, Chrysler had to cut prices even on popular minivans, and it was necessary to increase rebates up to $3,000 on the old models. These price cuts destroyed the profitability of Chrysler all the more since the company in its optimism after record profits in the 1990s had upgraded its cars and trucks, expecting to charge more for them. But with competition increasing and car pricing turning deflationary, such price hikes did not hold up, and this and the rebates severely affected profits in the third and fourth quarters. (See the following Information Box for a discussion of rebates.)

3. Williams J. Holstein, "The Conquest of Chrysler," *U.S. News & World Report* (November 27, 2000), p. 54.

4. Jerry Flint, "Free Chrysler!" *Forbes* (October 30, 2000), p. 132.

INFORMATION BOX

REBATES

A rebate is a promise by a manufacturer to return part of the purchase price directly to the purchaser. The rebate is usually given to consumers, although it can be offered to dealers instead in the expectation that they will pass some or all of the savings along to consumers.

Obviously, the objective of a rebate is to increase sales by giving purchasers a lower price. But why not simply reduce prices? The rebate is used instead of a regular markdown or price reduction because it is perceived as being less permanent than cutting the list price. This can give more promotional push by emphasizing the savings off the regular price, but only for a limited time. Rebates can be effective in generating short-term business, but they may affect business negatively once the rebate has been lifted.

INVITATION TO DISCUSS

Do you see any dangers with rebates from the manufacturer's viewpoint? As a consumer, would you prefer a rebate to a price reduction, or does it make any difference?

Schrempp Takes Action

With the huge losses in the second half of 2000, Schrempp sent Zetsche to Detroit with simple instructions: "My orders were to fix the place."[5] On his first day Zetsche fired the head of sales and marketing. Then in two months he developed a three-year turnaround plan. It called for cutting 26,000 jobs (29 percent of the workforce), reducing the cost of parts by 15 percent, and closing six assembly plants. Zetsche projected a breakeven point by 2002 and an operating profit of $2 billion in 2003.[6] This would still be well below the operating profit of Chrysler in 1993–1997, before the merger, as shown in Table 21.1.

His colleague from Stuttgart, Wolfgang Bernhard, organized engineers and procurement specialists into fifty teams to find ways to save money on parts. Suppliers were told to reduce prices by 5 percent as of January 2001, with a further 10 percent reduction over the next two years. Some companies such as Robert Bosch GmbH, the world's second-largest parts maker, and Federal Mogul, said they would not cut prices. Zetsche observed, "If they do not support us to get to the 15 percent, we have to consider that in our future decisions."[7]

Bernhard also focused attention on improving quality as a way to cut costs. In particular, the four-wheel drive trucks showed up poorly on quality surveys. The

5. Alex Taylor III, "Can the Germans Rescue Chrysler?" *Fortune* (April 30, 2001), p. 109.

6. *Ibid.*

7. "Daimler Threatens to Drop Some Suppliers," Bloomberg News as reported in *Cleveland Plain Dealer* (February 28, 2001), p. 6C.

company began rigorously evaluating new models for quality while they were still in the design stage, so that parts or manufacturing processes could be changed before too much money had been committed.

Zetsche began to direct much of his attention to bringing back standout designs that Chrysler had been noted for in the 1990s. Of late, design and engineering efforts, such as the 2001 minivan and the 2002 Ram, seemed more evolutionary than revolutionary, with leadership allowed to slip while Toyota and Honda became stronger competitors.

Despite increased competition, Zetsche had a unique asset that should help his company regain the edge: the prestige and competence of Mercedes-Benz technology. Mercedes previously had feared diluting its premium brand, but now it was directed to share components with Chrysler. New rear-wheel versions of the Chrysler Concorde and 300M coming out in 2004 and 2005, for example, were planned to make use of Mercedes electronics, transmissions, seat frames, and other parts. "If Zetsche can sprinkle some Mercedes magic on the Chrysler brand without damaging the premium status of Mercedes, Chrysler has a shot at doing well in the future."[8]

To his credit, Zetsche worked hard to overcome the anti-German feelings that initially followed his and Bernhard's arrival. To stem the potential brain drain, he persuaded many senior Chrysler executives to stay. And the drastic cutback of workers and closing of factories before long came to be viewed as necessary cost-cutting to keep the company viable. Even UAW President Steve Yokich endorsed these actions: "[Otherwise] I don't think there would be a Chrysler."[9]

Other Problems for Schrempp

Two other major problems confronted Schrempp. In October 2000, despite misgivings by Chrysler executives, he acquired 34 percent of Mitsubishi Motors, with the option to up that to 100 percent after three years. Hardly had the deal been finalized than Mitsubishi admitted it had misled consumers about product quality for decades. It also announced that losses for the last six months had nearly doubled. Schrempp reacted by installing a turnaround expert as chief operating officer at Mitsubishi and he was accompanied by dozens of Japanese-speaking Daimler executives. All the while the new chief executive, Takashi Sonobe, was quoted as saying that he, not the German team, remained in charge and that he saw no need for big changes. This was a contest of wills.[10]

DaimlerChrysler's Freightliner, the leading North American heavy-truck maker, was also struggling as the North American market hit one of the steepest slumps in a decade. After an aggressive growth policy that involved acquisitions of other truck makers and a heavy investment in a facility for reconditioning used trucks to sustain Freightliner's sale-buyback strategy, demand for new and used heavy trucks plummeted

8. Detroit manufacturing consultant Ron Harbour, as reported in *Fortune* (April 30, 2001), p. 110.

9. Taylor, p. 107.

10. Holstein, "The Conquest of Chrysler."

50 percent, and prices fell sharply. It was expected that Schrempp would install a German national as head of this unit.[11]

PROGNOSIS

As of mid-2001, many observers were pessimistic of the probabilities of Schrempp resurrecting Chrysler any time soon. In the long term, perhaps; but they questioned whether creditors and shareholders would tolerate a long period of profit drain by Chrysler and low share prices for DaimlerChrysler stock. Rumors were that Deutsche Bank, DaimlerChrysler's largest shareholder, was getting ready to oust Schrempp, and that Chrysler would be broken up into smaller pieces and sold off.[12]

Still, friendly German banks and shareholders might be more patient than Wall Street. DaimlerChrysler was the first German company to be listed on the New York Stock Exchange, and such a listing subjected Schrempp to the impatience of the international financial markets and the markets' obsession with meeting quarterly earnings expectations. In an age of volatile markets, failure to meet such expectations often resulted in a company's stock price collapsing. This bothered Schrempp: "I don't think [it] is advantageous: focusing on quarterly results. It might well be that because we increase our spending, investment, whatever, for a very good reason, that I might occasionally miss what they [investors] expect from me."[13]

Schrempp could have another worry imperiling his job if Chrysler did not improve soon. The third largest holder of DaimlerChrysler stock was the Las Vegas takeover tycoon Kirk Kerkorian, a powerful man with a reputation for being easily offended. Rumors were that Schrempp did not make himself available to see Kerkorian, but instead went to his ranch in South Africa.[14]

Chrysler executives, much as they might dislike Schrempp, could be worse off if he should be ousted. Mercedes executives ruled in the headquarters at Stuttgart, and without Chrysler's main supporter, Schrempp, Chrysler could not be sure it would receive the resources needed to make a comeback. It could be broken up and sold, or left withering within DaimlerChrysler's empire.[15]

ANALYSIS

This case illustrates the downside of mergers and acquisitions.[16] The causes of these problems are diverse, although certain commonalities occur time and again.

---

11. Joseph B. White, "Head of Truck Maker Freightliner Is Leaving Post," *Wall Street Journal* (May 25, 2001), p. A4.

12. "Can the Germans Rescue Chrysler?," pp. 106–107.

13. Holstein, p. 69.

14. Reported in "A Deal for the History Books," p. 57.

15. See Robyn Meredith, "Batman and Robin," *Forbes* (March 5, 2001), pp. 67, 68; and Jerry Flint, "Free Chrysler," *Forbes* (October 30, 2000), p. 132 for more discussion of these scenarios.

16. We use the terms *mergers* and *acquisitions* somewhat similarly, but will consider *merger* as closer to the idea of equals coming together, while *acquisition* suggests a larger firm absorbing a smaller one.

We will examine the salient factors that led to the collapse of Chrysler soon after the merger under (1) those mainly Daimler's fault, (2) those Chrysler's fault, and (3) the externals that made the situation worse. Then we will examine this whole concept of a "merger of equals." Can there really be a merger of equals?

Daimler's Contribution to the Problem

The Morale Factor

Different cultures are often involved when a merger or acquisition takes place, even among seemingly similar firms. For example, one business culture may be more conservative and the other aggressive and even reckless; one may be formal and the other informal; one culture may insist on standard operating procedures (SOPs) being followed, while the other may be far less restricted; one may be dominated by accountant or control mentalities, which emphasize cost analysis and rigidity of budgets, and the other by the sales mentality, which seeks maximum sales production and flexibility of operations even if expenses sometimes get out of line. Such differences impede easy assimilation.

This assimilation challenge for divergent corporate cultures becomes all the more difficult when different nationalities are involved, for example, Germanic versus American. National pride, and even prejudice, may complicate the situation.

It is hardly surprising that this mammoth merger of a proud German firm and an American firm with a long heritage should present morale problems. Especially with one party misled as to the sharing of leadership, the seeds were laid for extreme resentment. Some of this resentment among rank-and-file workers could even go back to World War II.

But there were other obstacles to a smooth melding of the two firms. Daimler had to adjust from being an old-line German firm to becoming a huge international firm confronted with a diversity of cultures. "The German instinct is for hierarchy, order, planning. Daimler executives use Dr. or Prof. on their business cards. Many wear dark three-piece suits. Chrysler, by contrast, was known for a freewheeling creativity."[17]

Chrysler's company culture had been highly successful in the very recent past, as shown in Table 21.1 and in Table 21.2, which presents the gain in market share or competitive position during the 1990s. This rather unrestrained-by-rules culture seemed to many to be the key to innovative thinking and technical leadership. With the merger it was not only being challenged but repudiated and supplanted by Germans who little appreciated the contributions of designers like Bob Lutz, who came up with products customers wanted that were not engineered at great cost and research. "The daring and imagination of the old Chrysler [is] buried under German management."[18]

Schrempp's Major Blunder

A miscalculation by Schrempp little more than a year after the merger was to have drastic consequences. His order to produce and ship out 75,000 more older-model

17. Holstein, p. 56.
18. Flint, p. 132.

TABLE 21.2 Chrysler's Market Share of the Big Three U.S. Automakers, 1991–1998

	Chrysler's Sales Percentage of U.S. Car/Truck Automakers
1991	12.2
1992	13.7
1993	15.0
1994	15.6
1995	14.8
1996	16.5
1997	15.8
1998	NA

Sources: Calculated from publicly reported sales figures; 1998 figures not applicable due to merger in November.

Commentary: The improvement in Chrysler performance in the middle and late 1990s is clearly evident. Market share improvement of even 0.05 percent translates into a gain in competitive position. And here we see a gain of more than 4.0 percent in 1996 and 3.6 percent in 1997. You can see how the improving performance of Chrysler in the latter years of the 1990s would be attractive to Daimler.

vehicles than could reasonably be sold before the new models came out, thus beefing up sales and profits for the first half of the year, resulted in huge imbalances of inventories in the last half and destroyed year-2000 results as well as the early months of 2001. This overproduction was perhaps the trigger that brought Chrysler its huge losses and even jeopardized the soundness of Schrempp's acquisition decision.

Chrysler's Contribution

Arguments could be raised that Chrysler had grown fat and inefficient after its years of success in the last half of the 1990s, that it was on the verge of a drastic decline in profits even if Daimler had not come on the scene to stir things up. By 1999, Chrysler showrooms were saddled with aging models, including the important minivans that were in their fifth year. While still the leader in minivan sales, Chrysler was losing market share to competitors with newer models, including the Honda Odyssey.

The prosperity of Chrysler in the mid-1990s may have reflected not so much inspired management as a combination of good luck factors: innovative designs and segment-leading products, yes, but also rising sales throughout the auto industry and a groundswell of demand for high-profit minivans and pickup trucks. Maybe the success of those years paved the way for the disaster that came shortly after Daimler took over. The great demand for vehicles like the Ram pickup truck, Jeep Grand Cherokee, and Dodge Durango brought a heady confidence that these good times would be lasting. Accordingly, Chrysler projected market share to increase to 20 percent by 2005, far above anything ever attained before. (See Table 21.2 for market share achievements during the heady days in the 1990s. You can see from this that attaining a 20 percent market share was not very close.) So Chrysler spent heavily on refurbishing plants and buying new equipment. It went from having the fewest workers per point of market share in 1996 to the most by 1999. It was spending money extravagantly and its entrepreneurial culture was operating unchecked. "The company lost its purpose and lost its direction," former chief engineer François Castaing said.[19]

The uncontrolled entrepreneurial culture led to poor communication and coordination, with each team buying its own components such as platforms and parts for the different cars, and thus not taking advantage of economies of scale. For example, the Durango and the Jeep had different windshield wipers, and Chrysler's five teams specified three different kinds of corrosion protection for the rolled steel used to reinforce plastic bumper surfaces.[20]

Other lapses of good judgment included continuing production of old-model minivans as it was switching production to the new one, thus flooding the market. This yielding to the pressure of Schrempp was, as we have seen earlier, a major factor in the disastrous 2000 results. Could Chrysler executives have protested more vigorously? The practice of the old management to introduce new models in batches rather than spreading them over several years brought a feast or famine situation: very good years, and rather bad years in between.

External Factors

Certainly the merger was consummated at a time when the auto industry, and the economy in general, was on the threshold of a downturn. Chrysler apparently miscalculated such an eventuality, spending heavily for costlier models just before demand turned down, and its brands were not strong enough to command higher premiums from customers. By early 2001, Chrysler was outspending all other major automakers on rebates and other incentives.

Chrysler also seemed to be oblivious to the threat of competitors during its golden years. Despite this heavy use of incentives, Chrysler lost market share for the first three months of 2001: a 14.2 percent market share versus 15.1 percent for the same three months in 2000.

CAN THERE REALLY BE A MERGER OF EQUALS?

In reality there is seldom a merger of equals. Unless the two parties actually recapitalize themselves with new stock—and this is seldom done—there is always an acquirer and an acquiree. Even if both parties to the merger have equal seats on the board of directors, still the acquiring firm and its executives are more dominant. Even if the name of the new, combined firm is completely changed, this does not assure a merger of equals. For example, in a well-publicized merger "of equals" in 2000 between Bell Atlantic and GTE, the name *Verizon* was created. But no one was fooled: Bell Atlantic was in

---

19. As quoted in "Can the Germans Rescue Chrysler?," p. 109.
20. *Ibid.*

charge. Furthermore, there can be no true merger of equals if one firm owns more of the consolidated stock (usually reflecting its larger size) than the other, and this is almost always the case. Daimler was certainly the larger firm in this merger, having paid $36 billion for Chrysler while its own shares just before the merger had a market value of about $48 billion.

How important is this merger of equals to the executives of acquired firms? Apparently to many it is not of major consequence as long as they get a good price for their stake, or as long as they believe the acquiring firm will honor their importance. Occasionally a merger negotiation will fall apart over the issue of who will be in charge. Take the example of Lucent and Alcatel of France, two of the world's biggest makers of communications equipment: At the last minute on May 29, 2001, Henry B. Schacht, chairman of Lucent, called off the merger talks. "It started to feel more like an acquisition than a merger," one of the Lucent participants explained. They could not accept the probability that Alcatel would be in charge.[21]

UPDATE

At the beginning of 2002, Chrysler reported it had lost a staggering $2 billion in 2001, and this brought a new wave of criticism of the merger—after all, it was four years after the deal. For the first years after the merger, Mercedes closely guarded its parts and designs for fear of eroding the Mercedes mystique. Now headquarters in Stuttgart, Germany, finally began forcing its far-flung operations to begin working together. In the Spring of 2003, Chrysler introduced two models that reflected more German engineering: the Pacifica, a cross between a station wagon and an SUV; and the Crossfire, a sleek sports car. Waiting in the wings were an LX sedan and an SUV called the Magnum. Headquarters also began bringing engineers from its Mitsubishi subsidiary to Stuttgart in order to integrate some ideas for smaller cars.[22] High time that assimilation efforts should begin, in this now five-year merger.

A trial was to begin December 1, 2003, on a lawsuit brought by billionaire investor Kirk Kerkorian, who claimed he was deceived about the 1998 merger of Daimler-Benz and Chrysler. Kerkorian is seeking $3 billion in damages. He contended that he and other investors were misled into thinking the combination was a "merger of equals." Such a merger would be more acceptable to U.S. antitrust officials and to Chrysler shareholders; it would also avoid paying a $10 billion takeover premium. CEO Jürgen Schrempp and Chief Financial Officer Manfred Gentz would be testifying.[23] At long last, this questionable "merger of equals" would be tested in the courts.

21. For more details, see Seth Schiesel, *New York Times*, reported in *Cleveland Plain Dealer* (June 3, 2001), p. 1H.

22. Neal E. Boudette, "At Daimler Chrysler, a New Push to Make Its Units Work Together," *Wall Street Journal* (March 12, 2003), pp. A1 and A15.

23. "DaimlerChrysler CEO Will Testify in Lawsuit," Bloomberg News, as reported in *Cleveland Plain Dealer* (November 25, 2003), p. C2.

WHAT CAN BE LEARNED?

Was the flagrant deception that this would be a merger of equals unethical? Outright deception and lies would seem the essence of unethical behavior, and perhaps illegal as well. It is when it comes to deceiving consumers. But in the hard negotiating climate of a merger, is a less truthful and trusting stance more the norm? Should we define ethical standards differently than when the hapless consumer is involved?

The situation is indeed different. The consumer is substantially disadvantaged before the greater product knowledge of the seller, and can easily be deceived by false claims. In a business-to-business situation, one would think that information would be shared equally, unless some fraud was involved. And even this should be uncovered if a careful audit was made before the transaction was finalized.

But verbal promises of sharing the administration? Even if written, such promises may be difficult to enforce. Kirk Krekorian's lawsuit against DaimlerChrysler may bring out what merger of equals really means—Is it a "genuine business model, or is it a takeover cloaked in the high-toned language of amity?" as Rober Bruner of University of Virginia's Darden Graduate Business School phrases it.[24]

Chrysler's top management should have suspected that its position might be temporary. After all, there is precedence for top management displacement in mega-"mergers of equals": for example, David Coulter of Bank of America, and John Reed of Citigroup, due to political infighting and disappointed expectations.

Mergers are no panacea. For years, in recurrent cycles of exuberance and caution, businesses have tried to solve the problem of growth with mergers and acquisitions. What you didn't have you could acquire, faster and better than developing it yourself, so the reasoning went. The term *synergy* became widely used, especially in the 1980s, to tout the great benefits and advantages of such mergers and acquisitions. (The following Information Box describes in more detail this concept of synergy.)

Wall Street dealmakers, investment bankers, and lawyers reap the bonanza from merger activities, but many of these mergers do not work out as well as expected, and some are even outright disasters.

We have seen the cultural conflict in the DaimlerChrysler merger. But this is just one of the things that can go wrong. Many acquisition seekers are so eager to get the target company because it has strength in market share or access to strategic technologies, or because it will make their firm so much bigger in its industry (with all the glamour and prestige of large size for the executives involved) that they are prepared to pay well, and often too much. Funds for such borrowing are usually readily available, heavy debt has income tax advantages, and profits may be distributed among fewer shares so that return on equity is enhanced. But all too often the best of the acquired human assets are soon sending out resumes to prospective

INFORMATION BOX

SYNERGY

Synergy results from creating a whole that is greater than the sum of its parts, that can accomplish more than the total of individual contributions. In an acquisition, synergy occurs if the two firms, when combined, are more efficient, productive, and profitable than they were as separate operations before the merger. Sometimes this is referred to as $2 + 2 = 5$.

How can such synergy occur? If duplication of efforts can be eliminated, if operations can be streamlined, if economies of scale are possible, if specialization can be enhanced, if greater financial, technical, and managerial resources can be tapped or new markets made possible—then a synergistic situation is likely to occur. Such an expanded operation should be a stronger force in the marketplace than the individual single units that existed before.

The concept of synergy is the rationale for mergers and acquisitions. But sometimes combining causes the reverse: negative synergy, where the consequences are worse than the sum of individual efforts. If friction arises between the entities, if organizational missions are incompatible, if the new organizational climate creates fearful, resentful, and frustrated employees, then synergy is unlikely, at least in the short and intermediate term. Furthermore, if because of sheer optimism or an uncontrolled acquisitive drive more is paid for the acquisition than it is really worth, then we have a grand blunder. Could that have been the case with the Chrysler acquisition, in addition to the culture problem?

INVITATION TO DISCUSS

Do you think a typical committee or group has more synergy than the same individuals working alone? Why or why not?

---

new employers, and the assimilation and effective consolidation of the two enterprises may be years away. Furthermore, acquiring companies may be left with mountains of debt from overambitious mergers and acquisitions, thus greatly increasing the overhead to cover with revenues before profits can be realized.

Cultural differences should be considered in mergers and acquisitions. These differences—in perceptions, in customs, in ways of doing things, in prejudices—often are not given enough heed. The acquiring firm expects to bulldoze its culture on the acquired firm (despite how this may affect pride and willingness to cooperate). As we saw with the Daimler merger with Chrysler—in reality a merger of unequals—arrogance and resentments surfaced.

Should the acquiring company express its dominance quickly, or should it try to be as soothing as possible? Morale will probably not be savaged in a soothing takeover, but there can be serious problems with this approach also. Permitting an acquisition to continue operating with little control can be a disaster waiting to happen, especially if the acquisition is a foreign firm.

How much can you trust? Both parties to a merger negotiation may express a commitment to equality. But such lip service may prove a façade. Even if executive positions are as evenly balanced as possible, one person may be a more dominant personality than the other, perhaps by dint of bigger stock ownership. Consequently, the merger of equals becomes in name only, with any equal standing of the acquired firm existing only at the convenience of the acquirer.

The danger of cannibalization. Cannibalization occurs when a new product takes away sales from an existing product. This is likely to occur whenever a new product is introduced, but flooding the market with the old product just before a new model introduction, as Daimler pressured Chrysler to do, is asking for problems. DaimlerChrysler found that it took both massive rebates of the old models and well as substantial price reductions of the new ones to move the inventory—all of this destructive to profitability. The same scenario had confronted computer makers and other firms at the cutting edge of new technology. When do you let go the old model without jeopardizing sales in the interim?

We do not advocate stopping production of the older model when the new model is first announced. But it seems judicious to reduce production in the months after the announcement. Then the newer, technologically advanced model should command a higher price than the older version? DaimlerChrysler's problems in 2000 were aggravated in that the new models were not so much technologically superior, as having expensive options that some buyers found not worth the extra money.

Let us not denigrate the desirability of cannibalizing. As products are improved, they should be brought to the marketplace as soon as possible, and not held back because there may be some cannibalization. The temptation to hold back is there, especially when the new product may have a lower profit margin than the product it is supplanting, perhaps because of competition and higher costs. Invariably, the firm that restrains an innovation because of fear of cannibalizing a high-profit product winds up making the arena attractive for competitors to gain an advantage. *Fear of cannibalization should not impede innovation.*

CONSIDER

Can you think of other learning insights?

QUESTIONS

1. Do you think Schrempp was wise to replace the top Chrysler executives? Why or why not?

2. How could Chrysler boss Robert Eaton have been so naive as to permit himself to be ousted from power in a negotiation that he actively campaigned for and accepted? Do you see any way he might have protected his position in the merger?

3. How specifically can a firm protect itself from the extreme risks of cannibalization?

4. Do you think the cultural problems could have been largely avoided in this merger? How?

5. Dieter Zetsche was sent from Stuttgart headquarters to fix all-American Chrysler, after a disastrous year 2000. On his first day in Detroit he fired the head of sales and marketing. Discuss the advisability of such a quick action, considering as many ramifications and justifications as possible.

6. Evaluate the desirability of rebates rather than regular markdowns or price cuts.

7. Do you personally think the use of Mercedes parts in Chrysler vehicles would diminish the prestige of the Mercedes brand? Would it help Chrysler that much?

8. Do you think good times can ever be lasting in the auto industry? Why or why not?

HANDS-ON EXERCISES

1. You are one of Chrysler's largest suppliers of certain parts. You are shocked at the decree by the new management of Chrysler that you must cut your prices by 5 percent immediately, and another 10 percent within two years. What do you do now? Discuss and evaluate as many courses of action as you can. You can make some assumptions, but spell them out specifically.

2. Place yourself in the position of Robert Eaton, CEO of Chrysler before the merger, and now "co-chairman" with Jürgen Schrempp. You have just been told that your services are no longer needed, that the co-chairman position has been abolished. What do you do at this point? Try to be specific and support your recommendations.

3. You are Steve Yokich, president of the United Auto Workers. You had initially endorsed the plans of Dieter Zetsche to cut costs severely, including laying off 26,000 workers and closing six plants. You had been convinced that such downsizing was necessary to save Chrysler. Now many of your union members are storming about such arbitrary cuts. They are castigating you for supporting these plans, and you may be ousted. Discuss your actions.

TEAM DEBATE EXERCISES

1. In this case we have the great controversy of German top executives replacing American ones. Debate the desirability of such replacements versus keeping most of the American incumbents. I would suggest dividing into two groups, with one being as persuasive as possible in arguing for bringing in fresh blood from German headquarters, and the other strongly contesting this. Be prepared to attack your opponents' arguments, and defend your own.

2. Debate the ethics of the flagrant deception by Daimler of this being a "merger of equals."

INVITATION TO RESEARCH

What is the situation with DaimlerChrysler today? Has the DaimlerChrysler stock bounced back to values before the merger? Are Chrysler cars and trucks gaining market share? Is Jürgen Schrempp still Chairman? Is Zetsche still heading up the Chrysler operation?

PART FOUR

PARAGONS OF GOOD
ETHICAL PRACTICES

Johnson & Johnson's Tylenol Scare—The Classic Example of Responsible Crisis Management

*I*n one of the greatest examples of superb crisis management, James Burke, CEO of Johnson & Johnson, in 1982 handled a catastrophe that involved loss of life in the criminal and deadly contamination of its flagship product, Tylenol. The company exhibited what has become a model for corporate responsibility to customers, regardless of costs.

PRELUDE

It was September 30, 1982. On the fifth floor of the Johnson & Johnson (J&J) headquarters in New Brunswick, New Jersey, Chairman James E. Burke was having a quiet meeting with President David R. Clair. The two liked to hold such informal meetings every two months to talk over important but nonpressing matters that they usually did not get around to in the normal course of events. That day both men had reason to feel good, for J&J's sales and earnings were up sharply and the trend of business could hardly have been more promising. They even had time to dwell on some nonbusiness matters that sunny September morning.

Their complacency and self-satisfaction did not last long. Arthur Quill, a member of the executive committee, burst into the meeting. Consternation and anguish flooded the room as he brought word of cyanide deaths in Chicago that were connected to J&J's most important and profitable product, Extra-Strength Tylenol capsules.

THE COMPANY

Johnson & Johnson manufactures and markets a broad range of health care products in many countries of the world. Table 22.1 shows the various categories of products and their percent of total corporate sales. In 1981, J&J was number sixty-eight on the *Fortune* 500 list of the largest industrial companies in the United States, and it had sales of $5.4 billion. It was organized into four industry categories: professional, pharmaceutical, industrial, and consumer. The professional division included products

TABLE 22.1   **Contribution to Total Johnson & Johnson Sales of Product Categories, 1983**

Product Classification	Sales (millions)	Percent of Total Company Sales
Surgical and First-Aid Supplies	$1,268	21%
Pharmaceuticals	1,200	20
Sanitary Napkins and Tampons	933	16
Baby Products	555	9
Diagnostic Equipment	518	9
Tylenol and Variants	460	8
Other (includes hospital supplies, dental products, contraceptives)	1,039	17
Total	$5,973	100%

Source: "After Its Recovery, New Headaches for Tylenol," *BusinessWeek* (May 14, 1984), p. 137.

such as ligatures, sutures, surgical dressings, and other surgery-related items. The pharmaceutical division included prescription drugs, and the industrial area included textile products, industrial tapes, and fine chemicals.

The largest division was the consumer division, consisting of toiletries and hygienic products such as baby care items, first aid products, and nonprescription drugs. These products were marketed primarily to the general public and distributed through wholesalers and directly to independent and chain retail outlets.

Through the years, J&J had assiduously worked to cultivate an image of responsibility and trust. Its products were associated with gentleness and safety—for all customers, from babies to the elderly. The corporate sense of responsibility fully covered the products and actions of any firms that it acquired, such as McNeil Laboratories.

THE PRODUCT

The success of Tylenol, an acetaminophen-based analgesic, in the late 1970s and early 1980s had been sensational. It had been introduced in 1955 by McNeil Laboratories as an alternative drug to aspirin, one that avoided aspirin's side effects. In 1959, Johnson & Johnson had acquired McNeil Laboratories, and the company ran it as an independent subsidiary.

By 1974, Tylenol sales had grown to $50 million at retail, primarily achieved through heavy advertising to physicians. A national consumer advertising campaign, instituted in 1976, proved very effective. By 1979, Tylenol had become the largest selling health and beauty aid in drug and food mass merchandising, breaking the eighteen-year domination of Procter & Gamble's Crest toothpaste. By 1982, Tylenol had captured 35.3 percent of the over-the-counter analgesic market. This was more than the market shares of Bayer, Bufferin, and Anacin combined. Table 22.2 shows the competitive positions of Tylenol and its principal competitors in this analgesic market.

TABLE 22.2 Market Shares of Major Brands—Over-the-Counter Analgesic Market, 1981

Brand	Percent of Market
Tylenol	35.3
Anacin	13.0
Bayer	11.0
Excedrin	10.1
Bufferin	9.0

Source: "A Death Blow for Tylenol?" *BusinessWeek* (October 18, 1982), p. 151.

Total sales of all Tylenol products went from $115 million in 1976 to $350 million in 1982, a whopping 204 percent increase in a highly competitive market. As such, Tylenol accounted for 7 percent of all J&J sales. More important, it contributed 17 percent of all profits.

Then catastrophe struck.

THE CRISIS

On a Wednesday morning in late September 1982, Adam Janus had a minor chest pain, so he purchased a bottle of Extra-Strength Tylenol capsules. He took one capsule and was dead by midafternoon. Later that same day, Stanley Janus and his wife also took capsules from the same bottle—both were dead by Friday afternoon. By the weekend four more Chicago-area residents had died under similar circumstances. The cause of death was cyanide, a deadly poison that can kill within fifteen minutes by disrupting the blood's ability to carry oxygen through the body, thereby affecting the heart, lungs, and brain. The cyanide had been used to contaminate Extra-Strength Tylenol capsules. Dr. Thomas Kim, chief of the critical care unit of Northwest Community Hospital in Arlington Heights, Illinois, noted, "The victims never had a chance. Death was certain within minutes."[1]

Medical examiners retrieved bottles from the victims' homes and found another ten capsules laced with cyanide. In each case the red half of the capsule was discolored and slightly swollen, and its usual dry white powder had been replaced with a gray substance that had an almond odor. One of the capsules had 65 mg of cyanide—a lethal does is considered to be 50 mg.

The McNeil executives learned of the poisonings from reporters calling for comment about the tragedy—calls came from all the media, and then from pharmacies, doctors, hospitals, poison control centers, and hundreds of panicky consumers. McNeil quickly gathered information on the victims, causes of deaths, lot numbers on the poisoned Tylenol bottles, outlets where they had been purchased, dates when they had been manufactured, and the route they had taken through the distribution system.

1. Susan Tifft, "Poison Madness in the Midwest," *Time* (October 11, 1982), p. 18.

After the deaths were linked to Tylenol, one of the biggest consumer alerts ever took place. Johnson & Johnson recalled batches and advised consumers not to take any Extra-Strength Tylenol capsules until the mystery had been solved. Drugstores and supermarkets across the country pulled Tylenol products from their shelves; it soon became virtually impossible to obtain Tylenol anywhere.

Those tracking down the mysterious contamination quickly determined that the poisoning did not occur in manufacturing, either intentionally or accidentally. The poisoned capsules had come from lots manufactured at both McNeil plants. Therefore, the tampering had to have happened in Chicago, since poisoning at both plants at the same time would have been almost impossible. The FDA suspected that someone unconnected with the manufacturer had bought the Tylenol over the counter, inserted cyanide in some capsules, then returned the bottles to the stores. Otherwise, the contamination would have been widespread, and not only in the Chicago area.

At this point, Johnson & Johnson was virtually cleared of any wrongdoing, but the company was stuck with having one of its major products publicly associated with poison and death, no matter how innocent it was. Perhaps the task of coping with the devastating impact of the tragedy would have been easier for Johnson & Johnson if the perpetrator were conclusively identified and caught. This was not to be, despite a special task force of 100 FBI agents and Illinois investigators who chased down more than 2,000 leads and filed 57 volumes of reports.[2]

COMPANY REACTION

Johnson & Johnson decided to elevate the management of the crisis to the corporate level and a game plan developed that company executives hoped would ensure eventual recovery. The game plan consisted of three phases: Phase I was to figure out what had actually happened; Phase II was to assess and contain the damage; and Phase III was to try to get Tylenol back into the market.

The company that had always tried to keep a low profile now turned to the media to provide it with the most accurate and current information, as well as to help it prevent a panic. Twenty-five public relations specialists were recruited from Johnson & Johnson's other divisions to help McNeil's regular staff of fifteen. Advertising was suspended at first. All Tylenol capsules were recalled—31 million bottles with a retail value of more than $100 million. Through advertisements promising to exchange tablets for capsules, through 500,000 telegrams to doctors, hospitals, and distributors, and through statements to the media, J&J hoped to demystify the situation.

With proof that the tampering had not occurred in the manufacturing process, the company moved into Phase II. Financially it experienced immediate losses amounting to over $100 million, the bulk coming from the expense of buying unused Tylenol bottles from retailers and consumers and shipping them to disposal points. The cost of sending the telegrams was estimated at $500,000, and the costs associated with expected product liability suits were expected to run in the millions.

2 . "Tylenol Comes Back as Case Grows Cold," *Newsweek* (April 25, 1983), p. 16.

Of more concern to the management was the impact of the poisoning on the brand itself. Many predicted that Tylenol as a brand could no longer survive. Some suggested that Johnson & Johnson reintroduce the product under a new name to give it a fresh start and thus rid itself of the devastated brand image.

Surveys conducted by Johnson & Johnson about a month after the poisonings seemed to buttress the death of Tylenol as a brand name. In one survey 94 percent of the consumers were aware that Tylenol was involved with the poisonings. Although 87 percent of these respondents realized that the maker of Tylenol was not to blame for the deaths, 61 percent said they were not likely to buy Tylenol in the future. Even worse, 50 percent of the consumers said they would not use the Tylenol tablets either. The only promising result from the research was that 49 percent of the *frequent* users answered that they would eventually use Tylenol.[3]

The company found itself in a real dilemma. It wanted so much to keep the Tylenol name; after all, the acceptance had been developed by years of advertising. Now, was it all to be destroyed in a few days of adversity? On the one hand, if J&J brought Tylenol back too soon, before the hysteria had subsided, the product could die on the shelves. On the other hand, if the company waited too long to bring the product back, competitors might well gain an unassailable market share lead. The marketing research results were not entirely acceptable to Johnson & Johnson executives. One manager expressed the company's doubts: "The problem with consumer research is that it reflects attitudes and not behavior. The best way to know what consumers are really going to do is put the product back on the shelves and let them vote with their hands."[4] But what was the right timing?

Johnson & Johnson decided to rebuild the brand by focusing on the frequent users and then to expand to include other consumers. It hoped that a core of loyal users would want the product in both its tablet and capsule forms. In order to regain regular user confidence, J&J ran television commercials informing the public that the company would do everything it could to regain their trust. The commercials featured Dr. Thomas Gates, medical director of McNeil, urging consumers to continue to trust Tylenol: "Tylenol has had the trust of the medical profession and 100 million Americans for over twenty years. We value that trust too much to let any individual tamper with it. We want you to continue to trust Tylenol."[5]

Johnson & Johnson also tried to encourage Tylenol capsule users to switch to tablets, which are more difficult to sabotage. In an advertising campaign it offered to exchange tablets for capsules at no charge. In addition it placed 76 million coupons in Sunday newspaper ads good for $2.50 toward the purchase of Tylenol.

Finally, it designed a tamper-resistant package to prevent the kind of tragedy that occurred in Chicago. Extra-strength capsules were now sold only in new triple-sealed packages. The flaps of the box were glued shut and were visibly torn apart when opened. The bottle's cap and neck were covered with a tight plastic seal printed with the company name, and the mouth of the bottle was covered with an inner foil seal.

3. Thomas Moore, "The Fight to Save Tylenol," *Fortune* (November 29, 1982), p. 48.

4. *Ibid.*, p. 49.

5. Judith B. Gardner, "When a Brand Name Gets Hit by Bad News," *U.S. News & World Report* (November 8, 1982), p. 71.

Both the box and the bottle were labeled, "Do Not Use If Safety Seals Are Broken." This triple-seal package cost an additional 2.4 cents per bottle, but Johnson & Johnson hoped it would instill consumer confidence in the safety of the product and spur sales. In addition the company offered retailers higher-than-normal discounts—up to 25 percent on orders.

Consumers who said they had thrown away their Tylenol after the scare were given a toll-free number to call, and they received $2.50 in coupons too—in effect, a free bottle, since bottles of twenty-four capsules or thirty tablets sold for about $2.50.

Over 2,000 salespeople from all Johnson & Johnson domestic subsidiaries were mobilized to persuade doctors and pharmacists to again begin recommending Tylenol tablets to patients and customers. This was similar to the strategy initially used when the product was introduced some twenty-five years before.

The Outcome

Immediately after the crisis, J&J's market share plunged from 35.3 percent of the pain reliever market to below 7 percent. Competitors were quick to take advantage of the situation. Upjohn Company and American Home Products Corporation were seeking Food and Drug Administration permission to sell an over-the-counter version of ibuprofen, a popular prescription pain reliever. Upjohn also granted marketing rights for its brand, Nuprin, to Bristol-Myers Co., maker of Bufferin, Excedrin, and Datril. Upjohn's prescription brand, Motrin—a stronger formulation than Nuprin—was generating some $200 million in 1982, making Motrin the company's biggest-selling drug. And lurking in the wings was mighty Procter & Gamble Company (P&G), the world's heaviest advertiser. P&G was launching national ads for Norwich aspirin and was test-marketing a coated capsule containing aspirin granules.

Yet, there were some encouraging signs for J&J. When *Psychology Today* polled its readers regarding whether Tylenol would survive as a brand name, 92 percent thought Tylenol would survive the incident. This figure corresponded closely with the results of another survey conducted by Leo Shapiro, an independent market researcher, just two weeks after the deaths occurred, in which 91 percent said they would probably buy the product again.

Psychology Today tried to get at the roots of such loyalty and roused comments such as these:

> A twenty-three-year old woman wrote that she would continue to use Tylenol because she felt that it was "tried and true."
>
> A sixty-one-year old woman said that the company had been "honest and sincere."
>
> And a young man thought Tylenol was an easy name to say.[6]

Such survey results presaged an amazing comeback: J&J's conscientious actions paid off. By May 1983, Tylenol had regained almost all the market share lost the previous September; its market share reached 35 percent, which it held until 1986, when another calamity struck.

6. Carin Rubenstein, "The Tylenol Tradition," *Psychology Today* (April 1983), p. 16.

New industry safety standards had been developed by the over-the-counter drug industry in concert with the Food and Drug Administration for tamper-resistant packaging. Marketers under law had to select a package "having an indicator or barrier to entry, which if breached or missing, can reasonably be expected to provide visible evidence to the consumer that the package has been tampered with or opened."[7] Despite toughened package standards, in February 1986, a Westchester, New York, woman died from cyanide-laced Extra-Strength Tylenol capsules. The tragedy of three-and-a-half years before was being replayed. J&J immediately removed all Tylenol capsules from the market and offered refunds for capsules consumers had already bought.

Now the company made a major decision. It decided no longer to manufacture any over-the-counter capsules because it could not guarantee their safety from criminal contamination. Henceforth, the company would market only tablets and so-called caplets, which were coated and elongated tablets that are easy to swallow. This decision was expected to cost $150 million. The president explained: "People think of this company as extraordinarily trustworthy and responsible, and we don't want to do anything to damage that."[8]

By July 1986, Tylenol had regained most of the market share lost in February, and it now stood at 32 percent.

THE INGREDIENTS OF CRISIS MANAGEMENT

Johnson & Johnson was truly a management success in its handling of the Tylenol problem. It overcame the worst kind of adversity, that in which human life was lost in using one of its products, and a major product at that. Yet, in only a few months it recouped most of its lost market share and regained its public image of corporate responsibility and trust. What accounted for the success of J&J in overcoming such adversity?

We can identify five significant factors:

1. Keeping communication channels open
2. Taking quick, corrective action
3. Keeping faith in the product
4. Protecting the public image at all costs
5. Aggressively bringing back the brand

Effective communication has seldom been better done. Rapport must be gained with the media, to enlist their support and even their sympathy. Alas, this is not easily done, for the press is inclined to sensationalize, criticize, and take sides against the big corporation. Johnson & Johnson gained the needed rapport through corporate openness and cooperation. In the disaster's early days it sought good two-way communication, with the media furnishing information from the field while J&J gave full and honest disclosure of its internal investigation and corrective actions.

7. "Package Guides Studied," *Advertising Age* (October 18, 1982), p. 82.

8. Richard W. Stevenson, "Johnson & Johnson's Recovery," *New York Times* (July 5, 1986), pp. 33–34.

Important for good rapport, company officials need to be freely available and open to the press. Unfortunately, this goes against most executives' natural bent so that a spirit of antipathy often is fostered.

When product safety is in jeopardy, quick corrective action must be taken, *regardless* of the cost. This usually means immediate recall of the affected product, and this can involve millions of dollars. Even if the fault lies with only an isolated batch of products, a firm may need to recall them all since public perception of the danger likely will transfer to all units of that brand.

Johnson & Johnson kept faith with its product and brand name, despite the counsel of experts who thought the Tylenol name should be abandoned because public trust could never be regained. Of course, the company was not at fault: There was no culpability, no carelessness. The cause was right. Admittedly, in keeping faith with a product there is a thin line between a positive commitment and recalcitrant stubbornness to face up to any problem and accept any blame. But J&J's faith in Tylenol was justified, and without it the company would have had no chance of resurrecting the product and its market share.

Johnson & Johnson strove to protect its public image of being a socially responsible and caring firm. The following Information Box discusses *social responsibility* and presents the J&J credo regarding this. It was interesting to note that this credo was still prominently positioned in company annual reports ten years later. If there was to be any chance for a fairly quick recovery from adversity, this public image had to be guarded, no matter how beset it was. With the plight of Tylenol well known, with corrective actions prompt and thorough, many people were thus assured that safety was restored. We should note here that for the public image to be regained under adverse circumstances, the corrective actions must be well publicized. Public relations efforts and good communication with the media are essential for this. And, again, it helps when the fault of the catastrophe is clearly not the firm's.

A superb job was done in aggressively bringing back the Tylenol brand. In so doing, coordination was essential. Efforts to safeguard the public image had to be reasonably successful, the cause of the disaster needed to be conclusively established, the likelihood of the event ever happening again had to be seen as virtually impossible. Then aggressive promotional efforts could fuel the recovery.

Johnson & Johnson's efforts to come back necessarily focused on correcting the problem. Initially it designed a tamper-resistant container to prevent the kind of tragedy that had occurred in Chicago. Extra-strength capsules were now to be sold only in new triple-sealed packages. When another death occurred in 1986, the company dropped capsules entirely and offered Tylenol only in tablet form.

With the safety features in place, J&J then used heavy promotion. This included consumer advertising, with the theme of safety assurance and company social responsibility. J&J offered to exchange capsules for tablets at no charge. It offered millions of newspaper coupons good for $2.50 toward the purchase of Tylenol. Retailers were also given incentives to back Tylenol through discounts, advertising allowances, and full refunds for recalled capsules with all handling costs paid. These efforts, directed to consumers and retailers alike, bolstered dealer confidence in the resurgence of the brand.

INFORMATION BOX

SOCIAL RESPONSIBILITY AND THE JOHNSON & JOHNSON'S CREDO REGARDING IT

We can define social responsibility as the sense of responsibility a firm has for the needs of society, over and above its commitment to maximizing profits and stockholders interests. The following credo of J&J illustrates the wide circle of corporate social responsibility that more and more firms are beginning to accept.

Johnson & Johnson's Credo[9]

We believe our first responsibility is to the doctors, nurses, and patients, to mothers and all others who use our products and services. In meeting their needs everything we do must be of high quality. We must constantly strive to reduce our costs in order to maintain reasonable prices. Customers' orders must be serviced promptly and accurately. Our suppliers and distributors must have an opportunity to make a fair profit.

We are responsible to our employees, the men and women who work with us throughout the world. Everyone must be considered as an individual. We must respect their dignity and recognize their merit. They must have a sense of security in their jobs. Compensation must be fair and adequate, and working conditions clean, orderly, and safe. Employees must feel free to make suggestions and complaints. There must be equal opportunity for employment, development, and advancement for those qualified. We must provide competent management, and their actions must be just and ethical.

We are responsible to the communities in which we live and work and to the world community as well. We must be good citizens—support good works and charities and bear our fair share of taxes. We must encourage civic improvements and better health and education. We must maintain in good order the property we are privileged to use, protecting the environment and natural resources.

Our final responsibility is to our stockholders. Business must make a sound profit. We must experiment with new ideas. Research must be carried on, innovative programs developed and mistakes paid for. New equipment must be purchased, new facilities provided, and new products launched. Reserves must be created to provide for adverse times. When we operate according to these principles, the stockholders should realize a fair return.

INVITATION TO DISCUSS

"Such statements are only pious platitudes. Social responsibility requires more than lip service." How would you answer this?

UPDATE

Johnson & Johnson has been an enduring growth company, with sales reaching $36 billion in 2003, and profits $6.6 billion. It ranks as the largest and most diversified health care company in the world. Its products now range from blockbuster prescription

9. From a company recruiting brochure and annual reports.

drugs, to professional products such as sutures, surgical accessories, and catheters, to a wide list of consumer products such as Tylenol, bandages, and toiletries.

With this broad product mix, how important is Tylenol to J&J today? In 1997, $1.3 billion, or almost 6 percent, came from Tylenol. (In 1982, at the time of the contamination, Tylenol contributed 8 percent of the $5.9 billion total company sales.) J&J heavily promoted Tylenol to maintain this prominence. In 1997, for example, the company's domestic ad budget for Tylenol was estimated at $250 million, more than Coca-Cola spent for Coke.[10]

WHAT CAN BE LEARNED?

Any company's nightmare is having its product linked to death or injury. Such a calamity invariably results in fear and loss of public confidence in the product and the firm. At worst, such disaster can kill a company, as happened with some canned-food firms whose products were contaminated with the deadly botulism toxin. The more optimistic projections would have a firm losing years of time and money it had invested in a brand, with the brand never able to regain its former robustness. In the throes of the catastrophe, J&J executives grappled with the major decision of abandoning the brand at the height of its popularity or keeping it. The decision could have gone either way. Now with hindsight, we know that the decision not to abandon was unmistakably correct, but at the time it was recklessly courageous.

Faced with a catastrophe, a brand may still be saved, but cost might be staggering. J&J successfully brought back Tylenol, but it cost hundreds of millions of dollars. The company's size at the time, over $5 billion in sales from a diversified product line, enabled it to handle the costs without jeopardy. A smaller firm would not have been able to weather this, especially without a broad product line.

Whenever product safety is an issue, the danger of lawsuits must be reckoned with. In the absence of corporate neglect, the swift constructive reaction, and the fact that the company could hardly have anticipated a madman, J&J escaped the worst scenario regarding litigation. Still, hundreds of millions of dollars in lawsuits were filed. Such suits accused J&J of failing to package Tylenol in a tamper-proof container, and the legal expenses of defending were high. The threat of litigation must be a major consideration for any firm. Even if the organization is relatively blameless, legal costs can run into the millions, and no one can predict the decisions of juries.

Copycat crimes are a danger. Although other firms in an industry stand to gain an advantage in a competitor's crisis, they and firms in related industries need to be alert for copycat crimes. By November, a month after the deaths, the Food and Drug Administration had received more than 270 reports of chemicals, pills, poisons, needles, pins, and razor blades in everything from food to drinks to medications. Fortunately, no deaths resulted from these incidents. But FDA Commissioner Hayes worried: "My greatest fear is that because of the notoriety of the case and the financial damage to the company, someone else will take out his or her grudges on

---

10. Thomas Easton and Stephen Herrera, "J&J's Dirty Little Secret," *Forbes* (January 12, 1998), p. 44.

a product and do something similar."[11] Actually, the Tylenol case was not the first time products had been deliberately contaminated. Eyedrops, nasal sprays, milk of magnesia, foods, and cosmetics have all been targets of tampering. An Oregon man was sentenced to twenty years in prison for attempting to extort diamonds from grocery chains by putting cyanide in food products on their shelves.

A firm can come back from extreme adversity with good crisis management. Certainly, one of the major things we can learn from this case is that it is possible to come back from extreme adversity. Before the Tylenol episode, most experts did not realize this. The general opinion was that severe negative publicity resulted in such an image destruction that recovery could take years. The most optimistic predictions were that Tylenol might recover to about a 20 to 21 percent market share in a year; the pessimistic predictions were that the brand would never recover and should be abandoned.[12] Actually, in eight months, Tylenol had regained almost all of its market share, to a satisfactory 35 percent. For such a recovery, a firm has to manifest unselfish concern, quick corrective action, and unsparing spending, and it must have a good public image before the catastrophe.

Contingency planning can aid crisis management. Although not all crisis possibilities can be foreseen, or even imagined, many can be identified. For example, contingency plans for worse-case scenarios can be developed for the possibility of food and medicine tampering or the loss of major executives in an accident of some sort. Sometimes in such planning, precautionary moves may become evident for minimizing the potential dangers. For example, with food and medicine tampering, different containers and sealed bottle tops might virtually eliminate the danger. And with executive accidents, many firms have a policy that key executives not fly on the same flight or ride in the same car.

Concern for ethics and social responsibility can pay dividends. On September 21, 1999, the *Wall Street Journal* reported the results of a nationwide survey of 10,830 people conducted on-line the previous month by Harris and the Reputation Institute. It was a public opinion study designed to determine how major U.S. corporations ranked as to reputation and corporate image.[13]

J&J ranked number one. Coca-Cola came in number two. But Exxon, a decade after the huge oil spill in Alaska (described in Chapter 15), had not shaken the negative image. Respondents cited J&J's heritage as the premier maker of baby products, as well as its handling of the Tylenol crises of 1982 and 1986 as influencing their opinions.

Even after seventeen years, the superb handling of the Tylenol crisis was still remembered and appreciated by the general public. Let's hope that J&J does nothing to tarnish that fine reputation.

CONSIDER

Can you think of other learning insights?

---

11. "Lessons That Emerge from Tylenol Disaster," *U.S. News & World Report* (October 18, 1982), p. 68.

12. "J&J Will Pay Dearly to Cure Tylenol," *BusinessWeek* (November 20, 1982), p. 37.

13. Ronald Alsop, "The Best Corporate Reputations in America," *Wall Street Journal* (September 23, 1999), pp. B1 and B6.

QUESTIONS

1. Did J&J move too far in recalling all Extra-Strength Tylenol capsules? Would not a sufficient action have been to recall only those in the Chicago area, thus saving millions of dollars? Discuss.

2. How helpful do you think the marketing research results were in the decision on keeping the Tylenol name?

3. "We must assume that someone had a terrible grudge against J&J to have perpetrated such a crime." Discuss.

4. "J&J's 'recovery' has to be attributed to the fact that some evil person was to blame, and not J&J. The situation would not have worked out so well if J&J had major culpability." Discuss.

5. Assuming that J&J was at least partially to blame in not having adequate security, for example, should it have revised its crisis plan, and if so, how? Support your position.

6. "The Tylenol episode represents great crisis management. Ethics and social responsibility was hardly a factor. The company acted in its own best interest by taking advantage of the situation to cast an aura of great concern for its customers, but the bottom line was still the only concern." Do you agree with the curious statement of company self-interest under the guise of great concern for customers?

HANDS-ON EXERCISES

1. Assume this scenario: It has been established that the fault of the contamination was accidental introduction of cyanide at a company plant. Now, how will you, as CEO of J&J, direct your recovery strategy? Give your rationale.

2. Assume this scenario: It has been established that the fault of the contamination was deliberate introduction of cyanide by a disgruntled employee. This person had a serious grievance about sexual harassment, and such grievances in the past had always been downplayed. The publicity about this has leaked out. Now, as CEO, what would you do?

TEAM DEBATE EXERCISE

Debate both sides of the burning issue at the height of the crisis of keeping the Tylenol name and trying to recoup it, or abandoning it. Do not use the benefit of hindsight for this exercise.

INVITATION TO RESEARCH

Can you find any instances of J&J not always having been a good citizen with superb customer concern? If so, investigate and draw conclusions about J&J's enviable position as a role model. Are there any other learning insights?

CHAPTER TWENTY-THREE

Herman Miller: Role Model in Employee and Environmental Relations

*H*erman Miller, Inc., an office-furniture maker based in Zeeland, Michigan, had long been a celebrated company, extolled by numerous business texts, including Tom Peters' best seller, *A Passion for Excellence,* and *The 100 Best Companies to Work For in America* by Robert Levering and Milton Moskowitz. Its furniture designs have been displayed in New York's Museum of Modern Art. It was a model of superb employee relations, and it stood in the forefront with environmentally sensitive policies. This company had been a paragon for almost seven decades.

But in the 1990s, circumstances began changing, and not for the best from Herman Miller's perspective. While sales had generally been increasing, although far from robustly, profits were seriously diminishing. Herman Miller remained the high-price, high-cost contender in an increasingly competitive market, and a market that itself was only expanding modestly. Amid these difficulties, one could wonder whether the enlightened approach to management might be turning out to be an albatross. Should it be modified or even abandoned?

BACKGROUND

D. J. DePree founded the company in 1923 in a small town in west-central Michigan. He named it Herman Miller after his father-in-law, who provided startup capital. For seven decades it was run by the DePree family, devout members of the Dutch Third Reformed Church, and they maintained a paternalistic relationship with their employees through the decades.

Employee Relations

Early on, the family sought to set a kinder, gentler tone with employees, offering profit-sharing and employee-incentive programs long before they were fashionable. Along with this, participative management almost bordering on democracy was practiced. (See the following Information Box for a discussion of participative management.) This helped create a loyal work force that turned out well-made products that could be sold at premium prices.

Through the 1960s and 1970s the company prospered with the expanding office furniture industry. D. J.'s sons, Hugh and Max, took the enterprise public but continued to nurture employees' commitment to the company. For example:

- In the 1980s, when hostile takeovers threatened many firms, the company instituted "silver parachutes" for all employees so that any who might lose their jobs would receive big checks.

- It may be the only company in the United States to have a *vice president of people.*

INFORMATION BOX

PARTICIPATIVE MANAGEMENT: IS IT THE BEST?

Directing or issuing instructions to subordinates as to what is to be done can take two extremes. In *participative direction,* the manager consults with the people responsible for doing the task about how best to accomplish it; the subordinates participate in the decision. *Authoritative direction* is simply issuing orders unilaterally, with no consultation with or participation by subordinates. Sometimes more extreme positions have been identified: *dictatorial* and *democratic.* The following diagram depicts the range of managerial styles:

dictatorial	authoritative	participative	democratic

←—————— degree of subordinate involvement ——————→
least   in planning and decision making   most

The democratic style is similar to participative except that the subordinates get to vote, with the decision going to the most votes. In participative style, the manager may or may not go along with the ideas of subordinates.

Several advantages come from a greater use of participation. People tend to be more cooperative and enthusiastic when they have some involvement in the planning. Not uncommonly, better decisions also come with the different experiences and points of view. The executive may even become more a coordinator of ideas than a "boss." In such an atmosphere employee development is maximized.

The major drawback is time. Consultation takes time. Many decisions are too minor to be worth such discussion. Other times actions have to be taken quickly and there is little time for participation. And if employees are new and untrained, if they lack interest, or if they are not very competent, no benefit would be likely.

The best managers tend to use participation whenever they can, especially where the decision directly involves employees. But they choose their opportunities carefully. It can be used with just one or two subordinates, or with a whole group.

INVITATION TO DISCUSS

Do you think another objection to a participative management style is that it undermines the manager's authority? Why or why not?

- In a time of escalating top executives' salaries by 1990 to as much as a hundred times the companies' lowest wages, Herman Miller limited the top salary to no more than twenty times the average wage of a line worker in the factory.
- Employees were organized into work teams and every six months both workers and their bosses evaluated each other.
- In the middle 1980s, Max DePree, in the interest of ensuring the fullest career development of promising managers, announced that he would be the last member of the family to head up Herman Miller. Henceforth, the next generation of DePrees would not even be permitted to work at the company.

Of course, there had never been any serious efforts to unionize the workforce.

Product Development

Since 1968, the company had turned its attention to designing products for a so-called Action Office. It introduced components, such as desk consoles, cabinets, chairs, flexible panels, and the like, that could give flexibility, and some degree of privacy, to the workplace. It emphasized innovative designs, and dealt with a number of "enormously gifted but extremely high-strung designers."[1] These vaulted Herman Miller into the top ranks of the industrial design world.

The company regularly budgeted between 2 and 3 percent of sales for design research, double the industry average. Sometimes its commitment to doing what was right (rather than what was best) brought it to a new level of corporate consciousness. For example:

- In the 1970s, an enormously successful desk chair called the Ergon was introduced. Millions of these designed-for-the-body chairs were sold. Then an advanced desk chair called the Equa was proposed. It would cost about the same as the Ergon. At this point many companies would have scrapped it rather than cannibalize (take sales away from) their star. But Herman Miller introduced it nevertheless.
- In March 1990, the Eames chair, the company's signature piece, was given a routine evaluation of the materials used. This was a distinctive office chair with a rosewood exterior finish, priced at $2,277. The research manager, Bill Foley, realized that two species of trees used, rosewood and Honduran mahogany, came from vulnerable rain forests. The decision was made to ban the use of these woods once existing supplies were exhausted, even though the CEO, Richard H. Ruch, predicted that this decision would kill the chair.[2]

Environmental Sensitivity

Few firms have shown the concern for the environment that Herman Miller has. In addition to the rain forest example above, here are several other instances of such concern:

- The firm cut the trash it hauled to landfills by 90 percent since 1982.

1. Kenneth Labich, "Hot Company, Warm Culture," *Fortune* (February 27, 1989), p. 75.
2. D. Woodruff, "Herman Miller: How Green Is My Factory?" *Business Week* (September 16, 1991), pp. 54–55.

- It built an $11 million waste-to-energy heating and cooling plant, thus saving $750,000 per year in fuel and landfill costs.

- Herman Miller employees used 800,000 Styrofoam cups, material anathema to waste disposal. Then it distributed 5,000 mugs and banished Styrofoam. The mugs carried this admonition, "On spaceship earth there are no passengers ... only crew."[3]

- The company spent $800,000 for two incinerators that burned 98 percent of the toxic solvents coming from the staining of woods, thereby exceeding Clean Air Act requirements. CEO Ruch, under questioning from the board of directors for the costly exceeding of standards, stated that having the machines was "ethically correct."[4]

EMERGING SOBERING REALITIES

By 1995, Herman Miller was a $1 billion corporation. But given that its sales in 1989 had been almost $800 million, this was not a significant accomplishment, especially since profits had slid from over $40 million in most of the 1980s to $4.3 million in 1995. And in 1992, it recorded a net loss of $3.5 million, its first loss ever. Table 23.1 shows the trend in revenues for selected years from 1985 to 1995. Table 23.2 shows the net income disappointments during these years. Earnings by 1995 were 90 percent less, on higher sales, than in many years in the 1980s. And net income as a percent of revenues had been declining steadily from 1985, from 8.3 percent to only 0.4 percent in 1995.

Perhaps most indicative of the worsening performance of Herman Miller was in its "competitive battles." A close competitor, one with virtually the same size and aiming at similar markets, was Hon Industries. Table 23.3 shows the sales and net income of Hon during these same years. Unlike Herman Miller, Hon's profits had risen steadily, and net income as a percentage of revenues was two to three times better in the 1990s. Figures 23.1 and 23.2 show these competitive battles graphically.

TABLE 23.1 Herman Miller Revenues, 1985–1995

	Millions	Percent Change
1985	$492	
1987	574	17.6
1989	793	38.2
1991	879	10.8
1993	856	(2.6)
1995	1,083	26.5

Source: Company public records.

Commentary: While somewhat erratic, the increase in sales should hardly in itself be a cause for alarm. But this does not tell the whole story of Herman Miller's problems. See the next table.

3. *Ibid.*

4. *Ibid.*

TABLE 23.2   Herman Miller's Total Net Income, and Percent of Sales, 1985–1995

	Millions	Percent of Sales
1985	$40.9	8.3
1987	33.3	5.8
1989	41.4	5.2
1991	14.1	1.6
1993	22.1	2.6
1995	4.3	0.4

Source: Company public records.

Commentary: Here the trend is far more serious than in Table 23.1. The trend in total profits is steadily downward since the 1980s, despite the increase in sales during most of these years. While the results for 1995 are particularly troubling (and resulted in the chairman's "retirement"), of particular concern is the erosion of profits as a percentage of total sales. And this is not for a single year but for all of the 1990s.

Any top executive has to be concerned with the fortunes of the company's stock price, and the satisfaction of shareholders. While Hon Industries' stock had climbed fourfold in the last decade, Herman Miller's barely moved: In 1985, its over-the-counter shares sold at $24; in 1995 they were about the same—this in the midst of the greatest bull market in stock market history.

J. Kermit Campbell became the company's first outsider CEO in 1992. He had had a thirty-two-year career at Dow Corning. In an annual report, he seemed to

TABLE 23.3   Sales and Profit Performance of Major Competitor, Hon Industries, 1985–1994

	Revenues (millions)	Net Income (millions)	Income as Percent of Sales
1985	$473.3	$26.0	
1987	555.4	24.8	5.5
1989	602.0	27.5	4.5
1991	607.7	32.9	5.4
1993	780.3	44.6	5.7
1994	846.0	54.4	6.4

Source: Company public records.

Commentary: Hon and Herman Miller are surprisingly close in total sales. If anything, Herman has been growing slightly faster than Hon. But looking at profits tells a different story. While Herman's profits have been badly eroding. Hon's have steadily been increasing. And the improvement in profits as a percent of sales for Hon is impressive indeed, while this is the great source of Herman Miller's trepidation.

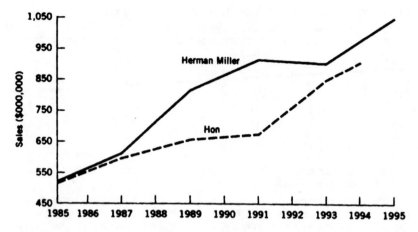

Figure 23.1 *The Competitive War:* sales comparisons, Herman Miller and Hon, 1985–1995.

espouse all the best values of the DePrees: "I truly believe that there is something in human nature that wants to soar."[5]

Campbell was named chairman in May 1995 when Max DePree retired. He acted quickly to cut costs, and, in the process, to discharge several top executives. The head of Herman Miller's biggest division, workplace systems, a twenty-year veteran, was let go. Also, the company's chief financial officer was removed. Campbell's goal was to pare selling and administrative costs to 25 percent from the current 30 percent.

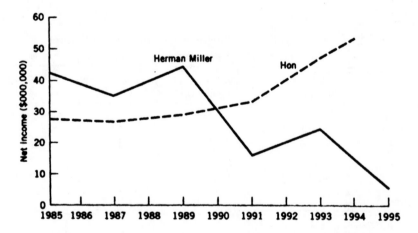

Figure 23.2 *The Competitive War:* net income comparisons, Herman Miller and Hon, 1985–1995.

5. Justin Martin, "Broken Furniture at Herman Miller," *Fortune* (August 7, 1995), p. 32.

He wanted to cut about 200 employees from a workforce of 6,000, doing so through early retirements but also from firings. He closed plants in Texas and New Jersey, as well as several showrooms. At this point, Herman Miller was rapidly losing its reputation as one of the best companies to work for in America. But Campbell could point out that survival was more important than preserving a pristine worker relationship.

Campbell's tenure proved to be short. In mid-July, barely two months into his chairmanship, on the same day the company announced its annual results and the nearly 90 percent drop in profits from the previous year, his departure was also announced. What was not clear was whether the board was dissatisfied with Campbell's cost-cutting as being too little or too much.

In any case, the board named Michael Volkema as new chief executive. Volkema had joined Herman Miller in 1990 when it acquired cabinetmaker Meridian. He had the reputation of being driven and charismatic, and he was young—only thirty-nine. He had come to the board's attention for his cost-cutting efforts in the small Meridian operation ($100 million in sales).

Problems in the Changing Market

The marketplace was hardly the same in the 1990s as it was in the heydays of the 1960s and 1970s. Sales of office furniture were not expected to grow at more than 5 percent, even if corporate profits remained high. A basic shift in demand was blamed for this: Computer technology required fewer layers of management, leading to general downsizing of office space needs.

Not only was total demand growing slowly, but the premium-end of the market, which had long been Herman Miller's niche, was also drying up as businesses in general chose to reduce costs by using lower-priced furniture.

In 1994, Herman Miller introduced the new Aeron chair, made from a mesh material that helped keep the body cooler. Although its design was unique and artistic, it retailed for up to $1,150, hundreds of dollars more than most other office chairs. Sales were disappointing.

Given limitations in the business market, the company turned optimistic for the home office sector. "We'll have 40 million to 50 million people working some part of their day at home," Campbell predicted. He hoped that the firm's quality image would be especially appealing to a significant part of this market.[6] So, the company introduced its first home office line, carrying a price tag of $1,799 for a desk. Early results were not promising; hundreds of OfficeMax and Office Depot stores featured fully acceptable desks for no more than $725.

Herman Miller's problem of arousing demand for its admittedly high-quality, well-designed furniture was further impeded by the company's traditional practice of doing very little product advertising. While such a strategy worked in decades past, was it still appropriate in the 1990s?

---

6. Marcia Berss, "Tarnished Icon," *Forbes* (July 31, 1995), p. 45.

ANALYSIS

A central issue in the Herman Miller shift toward operational mediocrity and deterioration in recent years had to do with its enlightened management style toward both employees and the environment. Long the model for superb employee relations, Herman Miller faced a dilemma: In an age of impersonal cost-cutting and downsizing, can a company be competitive with altruistic policies that protect employees and the environment? Perhaps more to the point, were Herman Miller's problems the result of such policies being unrealistic today, or was something else wrong, something having little to do with employee relations and environmental concerns?

Let us address the crucial question: Do the best in employee relations add unacceptable costs? What employee relations are we talking about? Giving employees participation in many decisions? Giving them profit-sharing incentives? Giving them opportunities for advancement as far as their abilities will take them? Making them feel wanted and appreciated, and part of a team? Giving them a feeling of job security at a time when so many firms were downsizing and forcing many employees out, whether done under the guise of early retirement or outright forced discharges? Involving them with products they can take pride in? Do such things add to unacceptable costs against lean-and-mean competitors?

While these questions or issues could be debated at some length, perhaps the only question that really is a detriment to achieving necessary cost savings is that of job security. Some paring down might need to be done to stay competitive costwise, especially in a computer age when some middle management and staff positions can be consolidated.

Unfortunately, management and workers alike must face the grim realities of today's environment: that their skills and experience may no longer be as needed today. That they must be prepared to shift their jobs and learn new skills, or be prepared for early retirement, no matter how enlightened the firm. To compete, it must be "lean" if not "mean." Such early retirements or terminations can be done meanly or empathetically. Empathetically suggests reasonable early retirement incentives, help with finding alternative employment or with the training needed to develop new skills. Counseling can be important—and time. Time to adjust to the harsh realities and to pursue alternative employment opportunities before being cast out. All these add some costs. But an organization does not have to be mean in seeking to be competitive. Can't a firm be kind to loyal employees, even if it adds a little to its costs temporarily?

Regarding the environment, did Herman Miller lose money by not using for its chairs certain tropical hardwoods found in rain forests? Maybe some; yet substitute woods should have proven acceptable to virtually all customers. Other costs, such as going beyond 1990 Clean Air Act requirements for incinerators and building an $11 million waste-to-energy heating and cooling plant, resulted in some cost savings, although not as much as the investments made. On the other hand, substituting reusable mugs for Styrofoam cups reportedly resulted in cost savings of $1.4 million.[7] So, environmental concern and action does not have to result in major additional expenditures.

It seems, then, that indicting the altruistic policies of Herman Miller for its less-than-laudable recent operating results might be mistaken. Perhaps the blame rather

7. Woodruff, p. 55.

lies in the aged strategy: high-quality, well-designed products, priced at the top of the market, with the major promotional reliance on word-of-mouth rather than advertising. What worked well in the 1980s and before may need to be reevaluated in the 1990s and beyond. This is more an age of austerity, with aggressive competitors and category-killer chains, such as Office Depot, offering good merchandise at prices half or less those of Herman Miller. In particular, perhaps Herman Miller should have tested the waters for medium-priced goods. It would not need—or want to—discard its quality reputation, nor abandon the high end of the market. Rather, it could have expanded its offerings downward from the very-high end.

Herman Miller also seemed to have miscalculated in the receptivity of the home-office market to its high-priced furniture. While undoubtedly a few wealthy individuals would willingly pay the steep price for a desk and other furniture of highest quality at the cutting edge of design, this market might not be very sizable.

UPDATE

Michael Volkema changed things for the better, after the painful downsizing and restructuring of Herman Miller in the industry slump of the mid-1990s. By the end of 2000, five years under Volkema, sales almost doubled to $1.938 billion and operating income went from $1.2 million to $140 million for a net income percent of revenues of 7.2 percent. Comparing with the major competitor, Hon Industries, revenues were almost the same, but Herman Miller's net income was well above Hon's of $106 million and net profit percentage of 5.2 percent.

In January 2000, *Forbes* selected Herman Miller to its "Platinum List," a list of exceptional corporations that "pass a stringent set of hurdles measuring both long- and short-term growth and profitability."[8]

Volkema had expanded the narrow high-end customer base to emerging and mid-size businesses, and homes. In three years he spent more than $200 million on computer systems and other technology, aimed at assuring speedy delivery, and another $100-million-plus on research and development for new products. To attract consumers, a Web site was developed, featuring office furniture specially designed for this market.

Employees are still catered to, with a new plant in Holland, Michigan, that is bright and airy, with workers assembling furniture to music by U2, the Allman Brothers, and Sting. "A sign near the front door boasts that workers there haven't been late in shipping a single order in 75 days."[9]

WHAT CAN BE LEARNED?

A firm has to adapt to changing competitive forces. Not many firms can afford the luxury of decades of undeviating policies and strategies. Most find that some adaptability is essential for the dynamic environment they face.

8. Brian Zajac, "The Best of the Biggest," *Forbes* (January 10, 2000), pp. 84, 85.

9. "Reinventing Herman Miller," *BusinessWeek* (April 3, 2000), p. EB88; and Ashlea Ebeling, "Herman Miller: Furnishing the Future," *Forbes* (January 10, 2000), pp. 94–96.

Such alertness to changing conditions is not difficult. Nor does it require constant research and investigation. Most changes do not occur suddenly and without warning. Indeed, the business press is quick to highlight innovations and changing circumstances. The rise of the super-office-equipment chains, such as OfficeMax, Staples, and Office Depot, were widely heralded and discussed, and their great growth was very visible. Before its changeover, Herman Miller made no attempt to cope with the obvious changes in the office furniture market. The company either did not grasp the significance of change, or else judged its high-end niche to be solid and not contracting.

In adversity altruistic concerns become dulled. It is perhaps only natural that when firms face hard times, their benevolent tendencies toward employees and their proactive treatment of the environment lessens, and sometimes even disappears. Where downsizing is indicated, actions toward employees, even longtime ones, sometimes become ruthless. "Voluntary" early retirement may be mandatory, and severance pay far from generous.

But survival of the company is at stake, management counters critics. In a widely quoted statement, Albert Dunlap, the merciless terminator described in an earlier chapter, said, "I see no point in sacrificing 100 percent of the employees for the 35 percent who ought to leave."[10]

Objectively, one wonders how many companies have grown so fat that more than one-third of the employees should be laid off.

Shareholder discontent is unhealthy for executives. This is as it should be. Stockholders have the right to agitate for drastic shakeups when the company fortunes, as reflected in unsatisfactory stock prices, show little promise of improving, especially when competitive firms are doing much better, as Hon Industries was. Such comparisons indicate that the disappointing performance is not industry-related but reflects the failings of current and past executives.

Executives who wish to keep their jobs should be concerned with shareholder satisfaction. Of course, this is easier said than done. Sometimes a company's problems are too deepseated for easy remedies. But this leaves the current executives vulnerable to hostile takeovers by those who think the parts of the firm are worth more than the whole entity, and that it should be broken up, or that the bloated cost structure requires severe pruning by a new administration willing to wield a mean ax.

On the other hand, a complacent and management-dominated board may perpetuate incompetence far too long,and leave shareholders little recourse but to sell their stock, probably at a sizable loss.

A firm can keep, or regain, the growth mode without abandoning higher ethical standards. As we see with the rebirth of Herman Miller, a firm can still be true to its desired higher ethical standards. Some deadwood products and employees may have to be phased out, and a leaner, more efficient structure imposed, but environmental concerns and employee relations are by no means at odds with running an efficient and highly competitive firm.

---

10. Kenneth Labich, "Why Companies Fail," *Fortune* (November 14, 1994), p. 53.

CONSIDER

Can you think of additional learning insights?

QUESTIONS

1. "A worker-sensitive firm is bound eventually to face a competitive disadvantage. It cannot control its labor costs." Evaluate this statement.

2. Do you see any risks in Herman Miller lowering its quality and its prices? Do you think it should have done so?

3. What do you think of the "enlightened" policy announced by Max DePree as he retired that henceforth no DePree will ever work for the firm again, in order that able people can have unimpeded career paths within the company? Discuss as many facets of this policy change as you can.

4. Evaluate the statement by Dunlap of Scott Paper that "I see no point in sacrificing 100 percent of the employees for the 35 percent who ought to leave."

5. What do you think of the decision to forgo using an attractive wood because it was taken from the rain forest, which needs to be protected?

6. What would be your prescription for a successful change manager? You might want to compare with Al Dunlap, and with Campbell who only lasted two months at Herman Miller.

HANDS-ON EXERCISES

Before

1. Operating results for fiscal year 1987 have just come out. They show that net income dropped 11.9 percent from the preceding year and 19 percent from 1985. What is even more troubling, net income as a percent of sales fell from 8.3 percent in 1985 to 5.8 percent. What do you propose at this time?

After

2. It is July 1995. Chairman Campbell has just "resigned" under pressure from the board. You have been named his successor. What do you do now? (You may have to make some assumptions, but keep them reasonable and state them specifically.) Don't be bound by what actually happened. Maybe a different strategy would have been more successful.

TEAM DEBATE EXERCISE

Debate both sides of the controversy of whether a firm with enlightened and empathetic employee relations can compete in a climate of aggressive competitors and severe downsizing.

INVITATION TO RESEARCH

What is the situation with Herman Miller today? Is Michael Volkema still chief executive? Has Herman Miller continued its turnaround? Can you find any recent information about its employee and environmental relations?

CHAPTER TWENTY-FOUR

Conclusions: Lessons From The Past

As noted in the introduction, we are on the side of business. We want it to do a better job in its interface with society. All kinds of problems assail the firm that does not respond to the pressures of society. These include lawsuits, boycotts, governmental restrictions and regulations, and a besmirched public image. Although we have described a number of corporate misdeeds, we want to be more constructive than critical. We seek to identify how to avoid and how to cope with ethical and public-image dilemmas in the future.

INSIGHTS REGARDING OVERALL CORPORATE BEHAVIOR

Pervasiveness of Top Management Ethics

For better or for worse, the attitudes and actions of top executives—whether they be scrupulously honest and ethical or something far less—permeate an organization. The chief executive is the model. He or she sets the tone, influencing the behavior of the next tier of executives, and down the line to rank-and-file employees, although there might be an occasional exception or whistleblower. A number of cases have shown the contagious influence of a top executive who was more interested in short-term performance than in acting ethically: ITT, Union Carbide (Ohio Valley pollution), General Dynamics, and others.

Related to the top executive's influence over a company is the often-mechanistic mindset of executive committees, which value the firm's immediate best interests over customer and employee safety, integrity, and environmental protection. We saw this in the Corvair case, where top GM executives sacrificed customer safety—sometimes even the safety of their own family members—in order to save a few dollars per car on a part that would have made the car more stable under extreme conditions. Acting alone, none of these executives would likely have made such an uncaring decision; acting as a group, the corporate bottom line was paramount, with its myopia; GM's group-think could not recognize the potential negative long-term impact on the firm.

Dangers in Short-Term Profit Emphasis

Top management may not be directly involved in questionable dealings, but it promotes such behavior by strongly insisting on short-term profit maximization and performance goals. When these goals are difficult to achieve and not achieving them can be met with severe penalties, the climate is set for undesirable conduct: deceptive advertising, overselling, and other illegal practices, such as bribery and price fixing (as in the ADM case). We are not advocating that goals be toned down, that expectations be reduced, or that performance incentives should not be used. But the pressure by top management to reach those goals and accept no excuses can trigger unethical actions. This is especially likely in an organization where high moral standards and the customer's best interests are not the rule. We encountered this in a number of cases, particularly the General Dynamics, MetLife, and the S&L cases.

For one not in the communication network, there are subtle signs of a less-than-desirable ethical climate. See the following Issue Box for such symptoms that can put a newcomer on guard.

Top Management Is Ultimately Responsible

After catastrophes, but also after other corporate misdeeds, top management should not escape culpability, even though we have seen examples where this was done: such as in GM's Ralph Nader discreditation efforts, MetLife's deception, and ITT's Chilean adventures. Blame shifting by top executives is a repudiation of responsibility. No manager can escape accountability for the actions of subordinates. With catastrophes, such as Bhopal and the Alaskan spill, the top executive should be actively and visibly in charge (even though, in the heat of emotion, officials in India were abusive to the CEO of Union Carbide). The presence of top executive Lawrence Rawl at the environmental disaster scene would have helped Exxon's public image and muted some of the criticisms regarding the company's carelessness and callousness.

A top executive's worst abuse of power and his or her mantle of responsibility is to loot the firm for personal enrichment to the detriment of stockholders, creditors, employees, and communities, usually done by "cooking the books" with fraudulent accounting. In recent years, we have seen widely publicized examples of high-flying firms such as Enron, Tyco, Parmalat in Italy, and WorldCom (described in Chapter 9), collapsing from such practices. The falsified accounting has even resulted in profits being overstated by tens of billions of dollars, as in the case of WorldCom. In all these firms top management has tried to escape any responsibility, claiming they knew nothing of such illegal actions by their subordinates. This refusal to accept any responsibility should be unacceptable. As this is written, a number of key executives are under indictment, although Kenneth Lay, CEO of Enron, seemed for many months to have avoided being targeted.

The Gray Area of Ethical/Unethical Practices

A fair number of practices are unethical at the extreme, but opinions may differ about lesser instances. Part III describes three cases of well-known firms whose actions have been questioned.

ISSUE BOX

GUIDES TO DETECTING AN UNETHICAL CLIMATE

A newcomer to a firm or to a different organizational unit of the firm faces a period of adjustment and learning the customary behavior and expectations. The following are subtle clues of a disregard for ethical standards in this organization:

"Well, maybe just this once…"

"No one will ever know…"

"It doesn't matter how it gets done as long as it gets done."

"It sounds too good to be true."

"Everyone does it."

"Shred that document."

"We can hide it."

"No one will get hurt."

"What's in it for me?"

"This will destroy the competition."

"We didn't have this conversation."

INVITATION TO DISCUSS

As a young trainee, how would you react to encountering widespread clues such as these that good ethical standards are lacking in this organization? As a new middle-level executive, what would be your reaction?

Source: Lockheed Martin Corp. "Ethical and Legal Conduct Guidelines," as reported by Jennifer Scott Cimperman, *Cleveland Plain Dealer* (May 28, 2004), pp. C1 and C3.

Wal-Mart, the largest and perhaps most efficient firm in the world is undeniably a godsend to many consumers because of its low prices. But others see it as a big bully to suppliers, competitors, communities, and even employees. Should Wal-Mart back off and be more compassionate?

Nike, with its outsourcing of production to much cheaper labor, even child labor, in Third-World countries to minimize its costs, has been roundly criticized by activists. But Nike is not alone in these practices. Indeed, outsourcing is gathering momentum among all kinds of firms, not only for cheaper production jobs but for cheaper higher-level jobs, as well. The great issue is whether outsourcing is getting out of hand. This will be a major political issue in the 2004 presidential campaign.

The lies of Daimler in the merger with Chrysler that this was to be a "merger of equals," when it was instead an acquisition by German masters, seems hard to condone as ethical, and the courts may decide this. But is this really so unacceptable in the battlefield of negotiations and maneuvering from power?

The Fallacy of a "Follow-the-Leader" Syndrome

We saw several cases in which all (or most) firms followed their competitors in stooping to the lowest level of ethical and legal conduct: many members of the S&L industry, and most of the defense contractors in the 1980s and before, are examples of this.

There are usually reasons for following the herd: (1) since everyone else is doing it, it must be the thing to do, and (2) if we don't do likewise, we will be at a competitive disadvantage and our viability may even be threatened. Reflection shows the fallacy of such thinking. The herd or mob is seldom right and prudent; it more often exercises reckless abandon. Unethical or illegal actions may escape detection or strong opposition in the short run, but such actions invariably get their just deserts.

Attempts to Cover Up Are Invariably Found Out

Such coverups usually result in far worse consequence for the company than a forthright admission of blame. We saw this in the Dalkon Shield case. With the Dalkon Shield, the prolonged denials and coverup compounded personal injuries and even fatalities and led eventually to lawsuits that gutted the company. Even GM was guilty of a coverup when it ignored the safety reports on the Corvair and attempted to discredit its severest critic. Exxon, in the throes of its *Valdez* mishap, also yielded to the temptation to do some finger-pointing. It is human nature to try to blame someone else, or otherwise try to escape blame. But this is difficult to do today, with investigative reporting and a suspicious public.

Risks of Extreme Cost-Cutting

In prosperous times, many organizations succumb to frivolous spending and bloated staffs. In more sober times, cost-cutting prevails. Both extremes have dangers. Too much overhead and infrastructure can drastically affect profits, especially during lean times. But excessive cost-cutting may be even more perilous. We saw in the two major catastrophes, Bhopal and the Alaskan oil spill, that cost-cutting severely affected safety measures and contributed greatly to the gravity of the problem and the consequent handling of it. Al Dunlap's decimating of Sunbeam and Scott Paper is an extreme example of cost-cutting.

Importance of the Public Image

A firm's image—how it is viewed by its various publics—came under attack in many of these cases: General Motors; Union Carbide; Nestlé; A. H. Robins with its Dalkon Shield; United Way; the S&L industry; General Dynamics; Lockheed and the defense industry; Exxon—all their reputations were besmirched by the publicity stemming from their misdeeds. Although we cannot identify the impact on sales and profits of a deteriorating image, we can speculate that there are serious consequences. Yet, many firms ignore their public image, take actions detrimental to such an important asset, or overlook the constraints as well as the opportunities that an image affords. A bad reputation is difficult to overcome. It can affect the customer base, the quality of employees and executives, the cooperation of vendors and creditors, the surveillance of regulatory agencies, and—not the least—the attention of the press. The press is both influenced by a firm's reputation and instrumental in creating it.

Power of the Press

We have seen the power of the media in a number of cases: General Motors, Union Carbide, Nestlé, the Dalkon Shield, United Way, the S&Ls, General Dynamics, Lockheed and the defense industry, the Exxon oil spill, and Johnson & Johnson's Tylenol. The media's power is most often wielded in a critical way: to hurt a firm's public image. The media can fan a problem or exacerbate an embarrassing or imprudent action. Its inclination is to emphasize the negative, since this is usually more sensational. In particular, with well-known firms, the media can trigger the herd instinct, increasing the number of people who are protesting and criticizing, but, it is also possible to use the media in a positive way, as Johnson & Johnson was able to do in its recovery from the Tylenol disaster.

We can make these generalizations regarding image or reputation:

1. A good image can be quickly lost if a firm relaxes its efforts to please customers and protect its caring position with respect to society and the environment.

2. It is usually difficult and time consuming to upgrade an image.

3. Large, well-known firms are particularly vulnerable to critical public scrutiny and must be careful to protect their reputation.

4. Marketing efforts, such as advertising, selling, product quality and safety, and pricing usually have the strongest impact on public image. They tend to be the most visible and the ones most susceptible to abuse and criticism.

5. The power of special interest groups—such as environmentalists and AIDS activist groups—is strengthened by media focus.

6. Public-image problems are seldom corrected by public-relations efforts. For example, public relations could do nothing for Nestlé and Exxon, or for the defense industry. An overall corporate commitment to correcting the problem must be taken—far beyond mere lip service or bought publicity.

INSIGHTS REGARDING SPECIFIC OPERATIONAL ASPECTS

Product Safety

A number of cases involved product or plant safety. In today's litigious environment, firms are particularly vulnerable in this area of their operation. They must be concerned with liability suits. Any hint of problems must be thoroughly investigated. Some notable firms, such as GM, Nestlé, Firestone/Ford, and A. H. Robins, were negligent in this regard. When the worst-case scenario occurs, a firm must go for a salvage strategy: correct the situation, make restitution, admit any faults, and recognize the likelihood that liability suits may damage the company. This course of action may be difficult to pursue, but the key objective should be to salvage the company, to leave its resources and its reputation in a position so that it can climb from the depths. Robins did not do this, nor did many of the S&Ls. The other cases that we examined did.

Any firm faced with heavy liability suits must recognize that its very viability can be in jeopardy. Obviously, a firm should try to avoid this situation in the first place, by minimizing carelessness or lack of concern, by investigating suspicions promptly and thoroughly (it helps here if the company encouraged good communications from its employees) and by being prepared to cooperate fully with the media and other investigators.

Vulnerable Pricing Practices

Collusion on pricing is so obviously illegal and easily prosecuted that one wonders how it ever happens. Price fixing is illegal under the first federal antitrust law, the Sherman Act of 1890. The simple act of conspiring to set prices or bids is all that needs to be proven; it does not matter whether competition was injured. ADM's price fixing with overseas partners was inexcusable, and dumb.

The exorbitant prices charged the government by General Dynamics and a good part of the defense industry in the 1970s and 1980s, attests to the temptation to take full advantage in any looseness in monitoring and other controls, and thereby fleece the taxpayers. Because of a lack of competition and the importance of the projects for national defense, the government was less able to punish these offenders as severely as they should have been, although some top executives were replaced with all their benefits intact.

Environmental Concerns

Several cases featured companies confronted with major environmental problems: Union Carbide, for example, in both the Ohio Valley and the Bhopal catastrophe, and Exxon in Alaska. From these disasters, we see the importance of environmental planning as one part of long-range strategic planning, and also the need for contingency planning for the worst-case scenario, unlikely though this might seem.

Worst-case scenario planning should not overlook product disasters. For example, Johnson & Johnson's Tylenol calamity was beyond what reasonable people would ever have expected, but contingency planning for a worst-case scenario would have made the company's reactions less stressful. Similarly, contingency planning by Robins might have saved the company from its unsuccessful, ill-fated attempts to cover up the Dalkon Shield's defects.

The power and influence of the environmentalists and their ally, a press that is often hostile to business, should not be lost on any business firm today. The remedy is not to assume a combative or adversarial stance, but to join the ranks of those who are concerned about the environment. After all, we live in one world. We have a mutual interest in preserving it for ourselves and our children, even if the bottom line of profits might have to be sacrificed a little.

Cautions in Foreign Operations

Many firms today do business worldwide. Although this presents great opportunities, it also poses some problems, some ethical dilemmas, and some opportunities for abuse. The most obvious abuse was ITT's interference in Chilean politics. ITT used such a heavy hand that the president of Chile, Allende, lost his life. Whether or not ITT can be directly blamed for this, few would accept the idea that corporate self-interest supersedes a foreign government's internal affairs. Such questionable practices have a critical effect on the image of the United States abroad. Bribery of foreign officials, which came to light during the Lockheed and defense industry scandals, motivated the enactment of the Foreign Corrupt Practices Act of 1977, which made such bribery by U.S. firms illegal. Union Carbide's acceptance of lower operating standards in its Third-World operations led to the Bhopal accident—that and the company's laissez faire policy of loose or nonexistent controls over its foreign managers and technicians. The lesson to be learned is that standards and controls must be even more rigidly applied in countries where workers and managers may be less competent than they are in more economically and educationally advanced countries.

The Nestlé case raises the issue of promoting unsafe products in foreign markets. Nestlé became the focus of strong and lasting criticism regarding its heavy promotion of infant formula in developing countries where sanitation was questionable and native mothers were prone to unsafe practices. Was it ethical for Nestlé to seek a marketing advantage in such environments? Although there were compelling social arguments for doing what Nestlé did, the crescendo of criticism forced the company to accede to the militants' demands.

We can also question the ethics of promoting the use of tobacco in foreign countries when the industry was under a health cloud here in the United States—indeed, most mass-media promotion of tobacco was banned. Is heavy promotion of what many consider an unsafe product ethical in light of a more easily influenced foreign user?

THE NOOSE TIGHTENS FOR QUESTIONABLE PRACTICES

A Tobacco Industry on the Ropes

For more than a hundred years the tobacco industry has been subject to criticism. It defended its own self-interest by contesting all claims of health hazards or by blaming smokers or creating any of their health problems. Powerful special-interest groups supported its position in the halls of government for many decades. Only in recent years have the bastions crumbled. Now the industry has been brought to heel with hundreds of billions of dollars in damage suits and restitution. Philip Morris, the industry's greatest defender, now is even running commercials warning against the dangers of tobacco. What a turnaround!

Abusive Business Practices Today Face
Ever-Greater Risks for the Seller

We saw how the misleading selling by MetLife sales reps led to massive legal problems as state attorneys general pounced on such consumer abuses. Today, attorneys general, as well as class-action lawyers eager to attack any semblances of misconduct in order to enrich themselves in the process, are scrutinizing more industries and firms, from finance companies, stock brokers, mutual funds, stock exchanges, to health groups, retailers, and manufacturers. (For example, see Robert Lenzner and

Emily Lambert, "Mr. Class Action," *Forbes* [February 16, 2004], pp. 82–90.) Added to these are the investigative and consumer relations reporters who are quick to listen and publicize consumer allegations of misconduct.

Firms Can Fall Rather Innocently into Denounced Practices

In view of the changed operating environment of today, a firm can innocently find itself in the critical public limelight over practices it had never realized could invoke such violent reactions. R. J. Reynolds with its Joe Camel could hardly have predicted both the success and the hostility its cartoon character would foster. Nor could Nike with its outsourcing for lower-cost production. Even Wal-Mart had to be shocked at the hostile climate it was engendering among some people and communities. But Firestone and Ford should have recognized the dangers they faced in ignoring the life-threatening attributes of Ford Explorers fitted with Firestone tires.

What is a firm to do? Can it possibly anticipate all the negative repercussions resulting from what it thought were legitimate and customary marketing practices?

Prudence would dictate management's approaching possible troublesome actions carefully and with input from experts in the field as to any possible negative reactions. Unilateral actions may result in an initial competitive advantage, but may hurt a firm's overall image and reputation. Management's sensitivities to potential controversial areas should be given a much finer tuning than ever before. It helps if likely problems can be identified before they become serious, so that efforts can be planned to avoid them. Such efforts may involve a different brand name, a different targeting of customer groups, or less aggressive promotions. In some cases, the whole project may better be abandoned than risk confrontational publicity. Even past policies and practices may need to be reevaluated: their susceptibility to investigation and condemnation may be just around the corner.

Is such caution really warranted today? This is for each firm to judge. Do the gains outweigh the risks? Can we get away with this, or are we likely to be targeted? Certainly not all abusive practices will be uncovered by the press and by governmental investigators. But the consequences of being targeted may far outweigh any short-term profit-maximization. Top management may even save their own positions through more caution.

CONTROVERSIES

These are some of the controversies we encountered in the book:

- How far should we go in sacrificing jobs and economic benefits for a cleaner environment? The Union Carbide story about the pollution of the Ohio Valley looked at that issue. There is no simple answer to this, nor one that everyone would agree upon, not even with cost–benefit analysis.

- How much weight should be given to cost–benefit analyses? Cost–benefit analyses lead to a host of disagreements, despite their façade of rationality. For example, are the costs involved in cleaning up factory pollution involving massive investments in pollution control or plant shutdowns with consequent economic hardships worth the benefits of a little better air quality? How do you put a dollar figure on "a little better air quality"? How much better should we demand? We saw a similar cost–benefit controversy with double-hulled tankers. The risk of oil spills would be somewhat reduced, but is the added cost and additional ship traffic a suitable tradeoff?

- Should multinational firms follow U.S. standards and policies abroad? This was an issue with Union Carbide at Bhopal and ITT in Chile. Although many maintain that domestic policies should prevail, others strongly disagree.

- Do white-collar offenders get off too lightly? In most of the cases, the perpetrators received no prison sentences or fines. Even the light sentences that the price-fixing conspirators received were less than a pickpocket might expect. When top management escapes all legal blame in most cases, we're left to wonder.

- Should the ethical standards of the United States be foisted on the rest of the world? Even some laws and regulations are not without their criticism, particularly the Foreign Corrupt Practices Act, which prohibits payoffs to foreign officials by U.S. multinationals hoping to encourage purchases of their products and systems. How can U.S. firms compete equally with foreign competitors who have no such restrictions? When in Rome, should we not do as the Romans do?

- Does the end justify the means? This question was addressed with respect to the ITT case. The end, so ITT believed, was to protect its property from being taken over by a socialist Chilean government. Did this end justify trying to unseat the government of Chile? Some would maintain that the end never justifies the means, for where do we draw the line? Terrorists justify all their crimes against innocent humanity as their means toward the end of certain freedoms. But is this acceptable?

- How tolerant should we be of firms that are vital to national security? Can defense industry's abuses be tolerated because the companies are so important? Should we apply different standards of conduct and retribution to some firms than to others? Are there other options than rigorously punishing for major violations or "wrist slapping"? Closer monitoring and more careful auditing of defense contractors have been proposed, but the execution left something to be desired. But, is this a suitable option?

We confront a sample of socioethical issues without coming up with clear positions. Unanimity of opinion will probably never be obtained. Sometimes positions even fly in the face of majority opinion, such as when environmentalists demand things that will affect jobs in a particular community. The challenge of assessing the relative merit of various conflicting claims is a major one.

FINAL INSIGHTS

One Person Can Make a Difference

Sometimes, one courageous and dedicated person can make a difference in a company's conduct—even a nation's conduct, as with Ralph Nader. Nader was instrumental in ushering in a new social attitude of intolerance for companies that victimize the consumer and the environment. Sometimes private citizens take it upon themselves to protest and organize and use publicity—for example, West Virginia's Mr. and Mrs. Hagedorn, who finally pressured Union Carbide into cleaning up the Ohio Valley air pollution. Sometimes, a new management team or chief executive can foster a changed orientation, much as Elaine Chao at United Way.

One person can certainly make a difference in a negative way—for example, Harold Geneen of ITT, Charles Keating of the Lincoln Savings and Loan, Al Dunlap of Sunbeam and Scott Paper, and William Aramony of United Way.

This Is an Era of *Caveat Vendidor*: Let the Seller Beware

Thanks to Ralph Nader and other consumer activists, a new social attitude has emerged: "Let the seller beware." This replaces the old philosophy of "let the buyer beware" that dominated the marketplace for many decades. The Yankee horse trader characterized that era of "let the buyer beware." In those days, shrewd purchasers might drive a hard bargain; less-sophisticated purchasers were often victimized. At a time when a person's livelihood, and even very life, might depend on a horse, this aspect of business was not a matter to be treated lightly.

Nowadays, most businesses are concerned with fair treatment of their customers, if for no other reason than to maintain their positions in a competitive environment. Government agencies, the press, and the threat of legal action are all deterrents to less-than-desirable practices in the marketplace. Although abuses still creep in, they are seldom tolerated for long.

Adversity Need Not Be Forever

Most firms recover from their problems. Even Bhopal did not destroy Union Carbide, although it weakened it. Nestlé had some years of combating worldwide criticism and boycotts, but this eventually passed. But industry is more conscious of public opinion and governmental scrutiny than it once was. MetLife, ITT, defense contractors—the firms incurred no permanent consequences, although some executives were forced to retire, and perhaps harsher penalties should have been imposed. And Exxon's oil spill was barely a blink, despite the bad press and environmentalists' denunciations.

However, several cases showed more drastic and permanent consequences. Robins handled the Dalkon Shield disaster terribly, and the harmful effects and the consequent flood of personal injury suits destroyed the company. Many of the S&Ls did not survive their rash speculations, and their leaders faced jail terms. So, a firm cannot be assured that negligence or opportunism or simply bad luck will be overcome. But, it usually is.

Adversity can create opportunities. Johnson & Johnson found its public image even stronger as a result of its compassionate handling of the Tylenol problem. Some found that the S&L mess created financial opportunities for stronger and more prudent players.

Desirability of a Trusting Relationship

Perhaps the most important lesson we can learn from these cases is the desirability for businesses to seek a trusting relationship with their customers (as well as with their other publics, especially employees and suppliers). Such a trusting relationship suggests concern for customer satisfaction and fair dealings. The objective is loyalty and repeat business, a durable and mutually beneficial relationship, which is contrary to the philosophy of short-term profit maximization, corporate self-interest, and coercive practices with employees and dependent suppliers.

Such a philosophy and attitude must permeate an organization. It can easily be short-circuited despite pious public-relations statements if a general climate of opportunism and severe performance pressure prevail. Let's face it! Top management sets the tone. In the days before GM's confrontation with Ralph Nader, the tone of all auto manufacturers was not product safety. "Safety doesn't sell," was the traditional cliché of the entire industry. It took an aroused public and, finally, governmental pressure for car safety to assume a higher priority in auto manufacturing boardrooms. This was certainly not a trusting relationship, unlike the Tylenol case.

Here, at this conclusion, is perhaps a fitting place to mention Herman Miller, the maker of quality and innovative office furniture. For over seven decades, it was the paragon of altruism, humanity, and environmental concern to its employees and to the larger community. Then in the 1990s it found itself losing ground to its competitors and disappointing its stockholders.

For the first time, it was forced to lay off some people and abandon its philosophy. But these layoffs were still done with humanity. Critics were quick to lay its problems to being too nice, too altruistic. Its long-held philosophy was discredited, and a harsher climate was proposed—in the interest of stockholders. But its problems were not so simply compartmentalized as being too nice. Rather, they were problems that beset many firms: not keeping abreast of changes in the business environment and customers' needs and wants. By restructuring and changing its business strategy to cope with these changes, in January 2000, Herman Miller made *Forbes* magazine's "platinum list," a list of exceptional corporations that "pass a stringent set of hurdles measuring both long- and short-term growth and profitability."[1] Employees are still catered to, as is the environment.

CONSIDER

Can you think of other lessons from the past that we have neglected to include?

1. Ashlea Ebeling, "Herman Miller: Furnishing the Future," *Forbes* (January 10, 2000), pp. 94–96.

QUESTIONS

1. How would you combat a follow-the-leader attitude in your firm in an industry where questionable practices prevail? Might this change depend on your executive level?

2. Would you expect a trusting relationship to be effective in an industry—such as used cars, home repairs, and recreational land—where no repeat sales are likely? Why or why not?

3. You seek a symbiotic and trusting relationship with all your publics. Is it possible to please them all?

4. Do you think our ethical behavior is better than twenty years ago? Fifty years ago? One hundred?

5. "Being empathetic and compassionate to your suppliers and employees only sets you up to be taken advantage of." Discuss.

6. Do you think the Golden Rule "Do unto others as you would have others do unto you" works in the competitive business environment?

HANDS-ON EXERCISES

1. Your firm has had a strategy of bad rapport with the press. How would you attempt to improve the situation?

2. You are concerned about the air pollution your plant is generating. The lowest-cost estimate to correct the situation is $200 million. In the absence of any industrywide standards, you worry that your unilateral action to clean up will jeopardize your competitive position. How would you handle this dilemma?

TEAM DEBATE EXERCISE

"The United States has no business trying to foist its ethics and values on the rest of the world." Debate.